MORAL APPRAISABILITY

MORAL

APPRAISABILITY

Puzzles,

Proposals,

and Perplexities

ISHTIYAQUE HAJI

New York • Oxford
Oxford University Press
1998

Oxford University Press

Oxford   New York
Athens   Auckland   Bangkok   Bogota   Bombay   Buenos Aires
Calcutta   Cape Town   Dar es Salaam   Delhi   Florence   Hong Kong
Istanbul   Karachi   Kuala Lumpur   Madras   Madrid   Melbourne
Mexico City   Nairobi   Paris   Singapore   Taipei   Tokyo   Toronto   Warsaw

and associated companies in
Berlin   Ibadan

Published by Oxford University Press, Inc.
198 Madison Avenue, New York, New York 10016

Oxford is a registered trademark of Oxford University Press

Library of Congress Cataloging-in-Publication Data
Haji, Ishtiyaque.
Moral appraisability: puzzles, proposals, and perplexities
Ishtiyaque Haji.
p.   cm.
Includes bibliographical references and index.
ISBN 0-19-511474-4
1. Ethics.   2. Free will and determinism.   3. Responsibility.
I. Title.
BJ1461.H26   1997
170—dc21   96-40432

1 3 5 7 9 8 6 4 2

Printed in the United States of America
on acid-free paper

For my mentors

PREFACE

Among the grandest of philosophical puzzles is a riddle about moral responsibility. Almost all of us believe that each one of us is, has been, or will be responsible for at least some of our behavior. But how can this be so if determinism is true and all our thoughts, decisions, choices, and actions are simply droplets in a river of deterministic events that began its flow long, long before we were ever born? The specter of determinism, as it were, devours agents, for if determinism is true, then arguably we never initiate or control our actions; there is no driver in the driver's seat; we are simply one transitional link in an extended deterministic chain originating long before our time. The puzzle is tantalizingly gripping and ever so perplexing—because *even* if determinism is false, responsibility seems impossible: how *can* we be morally accountable for behavior that issues from an "actional pathway" in which there is an *in*deterministic break? Such a break might free us from domination or regulation by the past, but how can it possibly help to ensure that the reins of control are now in *our* hands?

This book is concerned with aspects of this age-old grand puzzle. I distinguish between moral responsibility and moral appraisability, the latter being more restrictive than the former. To say that a person is morally appraisable for an action is to say that the person is deserving of either moral blame or praise for that action. I begin by explaining what moral appraisability is. I propose, roughly, the following analysis: one is morally appraisable for performing some action just in case one performs it freely (that is, one has what I call "volitional control" in performing it), autonomously (that is, it issues from what I call an "authentic evaluative scheme"), and in the belief that one is doing something morally obligatory, right, or wrong. Next, I trace certain implications of the analysis. Specifically, first I suggest that the conditions registered in the analysis, with suitable amendments, capture conditions for nonmoral but other normative varieties of appraisability like etiquettical or prudential appraisability. One result of this exploration into varieties of appraisability that will undoubtedly strike many as controversial is that, even if appraisability is not undermined either by determinism or indeterminism, most of us most of the time are not *morally* appraisable for what we do. Second, I discuss the implications of the analysis for what I dub "intersocietal" attributions of blameworthiness: people who are not part of a particular culture—"outsiders" relative to a culture—often attribute blame to a person within that culture for doing something regarded as morally repulsive by the outsiders. Relying on the epistemic element of my analysis—that blameworthiness requires *belief* in what is wrong (and not "objective" wrongness)—I argue that outsiders' attributions of blame are probably frequently erroneous. Third, I address the concern of whether addicts can be morally appraisable for behavior that is, in some significant fashion, caused by the drug or drugs to which they are addicted. Fourth and finally, falling back partly on conclusions I draw regarding appraisability for unconscious thoughts, I argue that we can be appraisable for some of the thoughts of our dream selves (at least if dreams are experiences involving mental activity). My last objective in this work is to motivate the suggestion that the three conditions laid down in the analysis of appraisability I defend are threatened neither by determinism nor by (certain varieties) of indeterminism.

My chief expository device is the use of a whole slew of cases in which agents act or are acted on in various ways that highlight one of the three aspects of moral appraisability under discussion: the freedom or control aspect, the epistemic aspect, or the autonomy or authenticity aspect. The cases serve to set up various riddles about appraisability. I follow with proposals for resolution, and, finally, I discuss residual (often numerous residual) problems or perplexities.

The book, I think, will be of interest to philosophers and students of philosophy. Those in related disciplines, like law, should, I expect, also unearth something of value in it. But I very much hope, in addition, that people from all walks of life, engaged in practices like praising, blaming, rewarding, and punishing—practices that frequently contribute toward making our lives vibrant, cataclysmic, or comic—will find something engaging in the ensuing pages. In the interest of readability, I have striven to keep the prose simple and devoid of unnecessary technical expressions.

Some of the writing for this book was done in 1995, during my tenure of a Summer Fellowship for College Teachers from the National Endowment for the Humanities (NEH). I am grateful to the NEH. Various chapters were refined and completed in the following summer during which my work was partially supported by a Faculty Summer Research Fellowship and the President's Faculty Minority Research Grant (awarded by the University of Minnesota), and a McKnight Summer Fellowship for the Arts and Humanities. I thank the Office of the Vice President for Research of the University of Minnesota and the McKnight Foundation for their generous support.

Parts of the following previously published articles of mine appear either verbatim or modified in the book: "Liberating Constraints," *The Journal of Philosophical Research* 22 (1997); "Blameworthiness, Character and Cultural Norms," *The Journal of Social Philosophy* 27 (1996); "Moral Responsibility and the Problem of Induced Pro-Attitudes," *Dialogue: Canadian Philosophical Review* 35 (1996); "An Epistemic Dimension of Blameworthiness," *Philosophy and Phenomenological Research* 57 (1997); "Autonomy and Blameworthiness," *Canadian Journal of Philosophy* 24 (1994); and "Doing the Best One Can and the Principle of Alternative Possibilities," *Southwest Philosophy Review* 10 (1994). I am grateful to the editors and publishers for their permission to use material from these essays.

I owe a special debt to Michael Zimmerman, Al Mele, and John Fischer. It was really Michael who rekindled my interest in the grand riddle of responsibility; he provided detailed comments, which were insightful and constructive, on a late draft of the entire manuscript, as well as on a number of exploratory essays on responsibility. I am extremely grateful to him for his supererogatory efforts to help, his support, and his companionship. Al helped considerably with early versions of some chapters, and I thank him for his commentary. I am also deeply indebted to John Fischer and Mark Ravizza, from whose work I have benefited greatly; my special thanks to John for his tremendous support. Fred Feldman has been a constant source of assistance and encouragement; indeed it was on Fred's strong recommendation that I began work on the book. I thank him for all his help and support. I am very grateful to Gary Matthews, who convinced me to take Augustine's views on the moral dream problem seriously. Many other friends and colleagues helped in one way or another with portions of the material in the book. In particular, I thank Ken Akiba, David Copp, Beth Dixon, Peter French, Lory Lemke, Michael McKenna, and Kadri Vihvelin. My sincere thanks, too, to Dwight Purdy for his enormous confidence in me and his friendly reassurance. I give special thanks to Cynthia Read of Oxford University Press, and to Robert Milks and the production staff at Oxford for their invaluable editorial assistance.

I would like to express my deepest gratitude, finally, to Shaheen my wife, for the love she gave me to see the work to completion and for all the "bad-Ish" sorts of things with which she had to put up during the times I worked on the book, and to my mother, Khatoon, who has been a wonderful, wonderful source of inspiration.

CONTENTS

MORAL APPRAISABILITY

ONE

‡━━‡

INTRODUCTION

Our day-to-day behavior serves to confirm the rather unremarkable conviction held by almost all of us that most, if not all, persons are morally responsible agents. So, for instance, we are willing to adopt, and do in fact adopt, a whole cluster of attitudes toward persons—such as moral abhorrence and resentment, moral admiration and forgiveness, *some* of the so-called "reactive attitudes"— which it seems inappropriate to have toward creatures, like koala bears, which we don't take to be morally responsible agents.[1] In addition, we treat persons or react to them in ways appropriate only to creatures that are morally accountable agents. We blame and punish people for some of their transgressions, and honor and praise others for some of their good deeds, but we hardly ever, if at all, react in these ways to our pets, at least when the praise or blame—or more generally— the appraisal in question is *manifestly* moral. I might have good grounds to believe that Kate's kitten, Kitty, was causally responsible—she played a causal role—in the untimely death of Golda the neighbor's pet goldfish, but it would be inappropriate, it appears, to blame Kitty or to punish her for her deed in a way in which we would blame a cruel youth for draining Golda's bowl. I might reward Fido for frightening off the thief by his resonant barking, but it seems it would be wrong to believe that Fido is deserving of moral praise for his behavior.

On the deep-seated presumption that people are morally responsible agents, we frequently *hold* each other morally accountable for some of our actions or omissions or the consequences of our actions or omissions. In turn, when we do,

3

we do so presumably because we believe that we *are* in fact morally responsible for these things; we are, for instance, suitable candidates for moral praise or blame on the basis of having done or having omitted to do specific things. Furthermore, our ordinary dealings with people in everyday life reveal that we have a rudimentary understanding of the conditions that have to be met in order for someone to be blameworthy or praiseworthy for the particular events she brings about.[2] We standardly believe, for instance, that a person's accessibility to praise or blame can be undermined by ignorance or force. While the following cases (some clearly not mundane) bring to light some of this understanding, they also motivate a number of puzzles that expose the issues to be dealt with in this book, and that help to steer, structure, and organize the ensuing discussion.

I. THREE CASES AND A HOST OF PUZZLES

Imagine, to begin, that unbeknownst to Bond, a minute electronic device has been implanted in his brain.[3] Xenia can use the device to induce desires and intentions in Bond without her electronic manipulations being "felt" or detected by Bond. Suppose Xenia implants in Bond a powerful desire to kill Smernof, a distant associate of Bond, together with the beliefs that the desire is irresistible and that Bond will be fulfilling his moral and professional duty by killing Smernof. Though the electronically induced desire is not in fact irresistible, Bond could resist it only with a great deal of difficulty and only at the expense of suffering considerable psychological damage. Bond, true to what he perceives to be his moral and professional calling, acts on this desire and does away with Smernof. Ordinary wisdom dictates that this case (call it "Secret Agent") is one in which Bond, it appears, is not morally deserving of blame for killing Smernof.

According to one strand of thought often traced back to Aristotle, the judgment that Bond is not blameworthy rests squarely on the view that Bond was forced to act as he did; he was simply a marionette of Xenia. Bond did not act voluntarily; he lacked the sort of control over his action of killing Smernof that is required for moral blameworthiness. Secret Agent is relevantly similar to a host of other cases in which a person's accessibility to praise or blame is undermined by lack of appropriate control. So, for instance, suppose Joy, the victim of hypnosis to which she did not consent, acts on an irresistible posthypnotic suggestion and stabs Mel. Or suppose Hera, not in any way culpable for her addiction, is overpowered by her irresistible desire for the drug, and she injects herself with a dose. Here again, we would not want to hold Joy blameworthy for stabbing Mel, or Hera blameworthy for shooting herself up with heroin. And once again, our judgment that they are not to blame is intimately affiliated with the idea that these unfortunate characters lack relevant control over their pertinent actions. These sorts of cases motivate the condition that a person is morally to praise (or to blame) for performing an action only if she is able to exercise control over that action.

Consider, now, another case which is also one in which some party is not morally to blame for a particular action. Suppose, unbeknownst to Sam, Ralph has replaced the sugar in the bowl with a sugar look-alike that is deadly. Sam invites Kate over for some refreshment, and drawing from the bowl, dissolves what he mistakenly takes to be a spoonful of sugar into Kate's coffee. To his horror, Kate rolls over, stone dead after her first sip. Surely Sam is not morally to blame for dissolving the poison in Kate's coffee, nor is he morally to blame for Kate's death. Notice that in this case ("Sweet Deception") our judgment that Sam is not to blame is presumably not anchored in the idea that Sam was unable to exercise control over pouring the look-alike into Kate's beverage. Clearly, Sam was not coerced, he was (we can assume) not compelled to act by the force of an irresistible desire, and he could (again, let's assume) easily have refrained from acting as he did. These considerations suggest that control is not the relevant "responsibility-undermining factor" in "Sweet Deception." Rather, our judgment that Sam is not to blame for poisoning Kate derives, it seems, from another Aristotelian proposal that in order to be praiseworthy or blameworthy for performing an action, one must not be relevantly ignorant of what one is doing.

Finally, reflect on yet another case. Call this one "Psychogen." Imagine that neurology and neurosurgery have so progressed that not only can particular pro-attitudes like desires, volitions, intentions, or goals be induced in an individual (with or without the individual's consent or knowledge), but one individual also can be molded psychologically to be just the kind of person the surgeon, or someone else for that matter, desires. Jenny is an exceptionally talented artist; her passion is painting. She devotes almost every waking moment of her life to her work. Apart from her art, she has exquisitely refined tastes in wine and food. Jim, in contrast—a friend and admirer of Jenny's—is devoid of aesthetic sensibilities or abilities; moreover, he is no connoisseur of food and drink. He is, though, an excellent stockbroker. His knowledge of the markets is truly extraordinary, and his competence at correctly predicting swings and trends of various stocks is something to marvel at. Suppose Max the famous eccentric neurologist, eager to put to test a new technique of psychosurgery, manages to slip a potion into Jenny's wine which ensures that Jenny's slumber is long and deep. During her sleep, Mad Max works on Jenny and turns her into a psychological twin of Jim.[4]

It goes without saying that when Jenny awakens there are profound changes in her, which, from her own inner perspective she cannot but accept. The remarkable psychosurgery has endowed her with a new set of values, goals, preferences, and the like, while "erasing" competing values, goals, preferences, and so on. Suppose that when Jenny recovers from psychosurgery she has no suspicions whatsoever that she has fallen victim to Max. She picks up the morning paper, and after perusing some columns makes a brilliant investment decision to help out a needy friend of hers. She then acts on that decision: she buys, with the funds entrusted to her by her friend, 500 shares of NEUROMED stocks. Is she praiseworthy for this deed? Many of us, I believe, if we were aware that she was an unlucky victim of Max's psychosurgery, would say "No." But what precisely grounds our response? Seemingly, it is not that Jenny lacked the appropriate sort of control over her action that is required for praiseworthiness. To drive home this point, I think we would agree that had Jim made the same sort of decision and acted on it, no one (barring unusual circumstances) would have suspected him of lacking control; but Jenny is a psychological *twin* of Jim. With respect to the relevant action, they would be equal in the amount of control they exercise. So it seems that the control condition—whatever it precisely amounts to—needed for moral praiseworthiness is satisfied. Nor is Jenny relevantly ignorant of what she is doing. She is not being deceived, the facts in the papers are correct, she is reasoning well, and her perception and appreciation of the situation are not in any way distorted or perverse.[5] So it appears that the epistemic requirement—again whatever it precisely amounts to—for praiseworthiness is also satisfied. It seems that Jenny's not being praiseworthy clearly has something to do with her "global manipulation." One suggestion is that Jenny is no longer an autonomous agent—she is no longer self-directing. The idea is that when Jenny buys the stocks, she fails to act autonomously, or she acts on actional elements like desires and decisions with respect to which she is not autonomous; they are not authentic or "truly Jenny's own." If this suggestion is more or less correct, then there appears to be a third ingredient to moral responsibility: autonomy or "authenticity" of the springs of one's actions.

Understandably, some of us, however, may not be so sure about Psychogen. In particular, we might have legitimate concerns over whether *Jenny* survives the psychosurgery. A reasonable alternative that suggests itself is that the "initial" person (the person who exists prior to global manipulation), whom we can call "Jenny1," has simply gone out of existence; thus, she is not praiseworthy for the new behavior. A new person—"Jenny2"—has come into existence, and if she is indeed a psychological twin of Jim, she may well be responsible for her actions.

In light of this preliminary concern, consider this modified version of Psychogen. Suppose Jenny1 and Jim do share certain goals, values, and preferences. Assume that these "shared elements" are left intact (in Jenny1) by the psychosurgery. Suppose, in addition, that some of Jenny1's goals, preferences, values, etc. that compete or "clash" with those of Jim's are also left intact, together with some of Jenny1's memories. Call the set of Jenny1's competing psychological elements that are left intact the "minimum competing set." Assume, in addition, that the members of the minimum competing set, in conjunction with the shared elements, are the bare minimum of psychological elements required to preserve personal identity so that we can be assured that Jenny1 *is* identical to Jenny2. Finally, assume that the memories of Jenny1's that are left intact and all her competing psychological elements that are members of her minimum competing set are "repressed"; although Jenny2 does have them, she cannot, unlike Jenny1 "access" them. It would seem that Jenny1 is still identical to Jenny2. Now suppose Jenny2 (who is just Jenny1) awakens from psychosurgery (to which she did not consent and of which she has no knowledge) and performs the good deed of investment. Is she praiseworthy for this deed? I would think not, even though she exhibits, relative to this action, the same sort of control that Jim would have exhibited over this sort of action had he performed it. Again, her not being praiseworthy has something essential to do with her global manipulation.

Now if we agree that Jenny2 in modified Psychogen is not praiseworthy for the pertinent deed, then I would think that Jenny2 in (original) Psychogen, even on the assumption that in this (original) case Jenny2 is not identical to Jenny1, should also not be praiseworthy for the germane deed. And this is because the two Jenny2s in each version of Psychogen are on equal terms relative to the ascription of responsibility for the deed of investment. After all, although Jenny2 in modified Psychogen, unlike her counterpart in the original case, possesses competing psychological elements and some original memories, these are "repressed"; they play no role whatsoever in the actual sequence of events culminating in her deed of investment. And it is, as I will argue, what occurs in the actual progression of events that results in action that is crucial to responsibility. I shall, however, not press my case here. Rather, should the reader still have doubts about whether Jenny2 in original Pychogen is not praiseworthy for her behavior, I invite him or her to substitute (where appropriate) modified Psychogen for original Psychogen in subsequent discussions involving Psychogen.[6]

It might be thought that cases like Secret Agent and especially Psychogen are too bizarre to be of any help in framing puzzles about responsibility or in acquiring insight into responsibility. But I think this conclusion is a mistake. It goes without saying that some of these cases (and some of the ones soon to be introduced) *are* quixotic and divorced from everyday life. Still, this fact should not diminish their philosophical significance. The cases, however unusual, may help us uncover perfectly general principles about responsibility, principles, for example, pertaining to conditions that are to be satisfied if persons are to be blameworthy for their actions. Indeed, as we shall see, it is frequently some of the more bizarre aspects of the cases that point us in the right direction.

Now to frame some puzzles. Secret Agent both registers a conventional bit of wisdom and prompts an obvious query: it lends credibility to the widely accepted idea that responsibility for an action requires control over that action. We are at home with this idea, for instance, in adjudicating criminal cases in which the defendant pleads insanity. But precisely what sort of control is needed for responsibility? Is Bond morally blameless for squeezing the trigger, for example, by virtue of the fact that he had no real alternatives? Remember, his action issued from a near *irresistible* desire. Secret Agent motivates another sort of riddle. Suppose a mother has a literally irresistible urge to rush into the blazing room to rescue her child. Some might plausibly suppose that the mother *is* responsible for saving the child even though she acted on an irresistible urge. But then how does Bond differ relevantly from the mother? Why think that Bond is not morally responsible for squeezing the trigger while the mother is morally accountable for the rescue when the actions of both stem from irresistible or near irresistible springs?

Sweet Deception, just like Secret Agent, both highlights an accepted moral and solicits a natural question: it enforces our view that ignorance (of some sort) is an excusing condition, but at the same time it raises the taxing question of exactly what the epistemic requirements for moral responsibility amount to. Limiting ourselves to blameworthiness and praiseworthiness, is it, for instance, the strong condition that a person is blameworthy (or praiseworthy) for performing an action only if that person knows that that action is wrong (or right or obligatory)? As knowledge entails truth, such a condition implies that a person is to blame (or praise) for performing an action only if that action is in fact wrong (or right or obligatory). Is this condition correct? Isn't it possible for a person to be blameworthy for performing an action she believes is wrong but is in fact obligatory?

Among the whole cluster of puzzles raised by Psychogen are these: in order for an agent to be morally responsible for an action, must that agent perform that action autonomously, or must she be autonomous with respect to some of the elements, like desires or intentions, that give rise to the action? Does responsibility, that is, presuppose autonomy? If so, precisely what notion of autonomy? Or does Psychogen merely tell us something about control? Is it simply a case in which all of Jenny's actions subsequent to her psychosurgery are ones she is compelled in some sense of 'compel' to perform?

2. AIMS

I have three broad aims. First, I want to develop more fully and carefully some of the puzzles mentioned above and some additional ones. All of these, in one way or another, focus on praiseworthiness or blameworthiness. To introduce a convenient bit of terminology, let's say that a person is *morally appraisable* for performing an action if and only if she is either morally blameworthy or praiseworthy for performing that action. In the end, the cluster of puzzles with which I commenced direct our attention to this central issue: What conditions must be satisfied in order for an agent to be morally appraisable for some action? Now I think a person can be morally *responsible* on account of some action, but not deserving of praise or blame for that action; the concept of moral responsibility is broader than that of moral appraisability. If one is praiseworthy or blameworthy for something, then one is morally responsible for that thing, but one can be morally responsible for, say, performing an action, even though one is not deserving of praise or blame on account of that action. Suppose, for example, that Moneypenny—a teller at the bank—is held up by Shotgun Sam. "The money or your life!" barks Sam. Suppose the threat is very real. Sizing up the situation, Moneypenny, promptly and with precision, follows the orders of the bank and complies with Sam's demands: he hands over the money. This case ("Holdup") is one in which, arguably, though Moneypenny is morally responsible for forking over the dough to Sam, he is not deserving of praise or blame for doing so. I believe he is responsible, roughly, because he is an appropriate candidate for *some* reactive attitude, or because he has done something for which there is *some sort* of "credit"—a credit that doesn't amount to praise—in his "ledger of life."[7] Throughout this book my emphasis will be on uncovering conditions required for moral appraisability, that is, for moral praiseworthiness or blameworthiness, and not directly for moral responsibility. Second, I address various proposed solutions to these puzzles and reveal some of their inadequacies. Finally, I propose some of my own solutions, discuss them critically, and point out leftover problems or "perplexities" as I shall call them. What will unfold in the ensuing chapters, then, is a set of puzzles, proposals, and remaining perplexities concerning moral appraisability. My hope is to work toward a set of conditions necessary and sufficient for a restricted range of ascriptions of appraisability: I will focus primarily on appraisability for intentional actions. Although most of the discussion will address appraisability, much of what I have to say, I believe, will apply equally, with adjustments, to responsibility in general. And though most of the discussion will focus strictly on appraisability for *actions*, the discussion, I believe, will at least point the way toward uncovering conditions of appraisability for intentional failures to act, and for the outcomes of actions.

I stress that even if one is convinced, perhaps on the basis of considerations having to do with the supposed incompatibility of causal determinism, or the existence of God, with the sort of freedom required for appraisability, that no one is in fact or ever could be appraisable for anything, it is still worthwhile to understand the concepts of blameworthiness and praiseworthiness; and gaining insight into these concepts is one of my key aims.[8]

To help bring into relief one target concept—moral blameworthiness—I call attention to the following preliminaries. Moral blameworthiness is concerned primarily with a type of normative appraisal of a person and only derivatively with the appraisal of the person's behavior; fundamentally at issue in such appraisals is the moral worth of the person with respect to a particular bit of behavior of hers. When a person is morally blameworthy for performing an action, the blame in consideration is manifestly inward and not overt. It is the sort of blame registered when we say things like "she is deserving of blame for pilfering the pie"; or "she is to blame for letting the candle go out." The fact that a person can be deserving of moral blame even in the absence of anyone else's being aware that she is so deserving underscores the inward nature of such blame. In contrast, outward blame amounts to the outward expression of blame by words, gestures, or actions. It often comprises things like overt rebukes or reprimands, and it can be expressed by nonverbal behavior as when one deliberately turns a cold shoulder to a person, or one deliberately snubs a person. Overt blame, of course, may be misplaced. We may *hold* a person to blame, and blame her overtly, for doing something for which she is not in any way inwardly blameworthy.

Moral blameworthiness is frequently (but not always) closely associated with the moral beliefs a person thinks important in guiding her behavior. When an agent is deserving of moral blame for doing something, often (but again not always) the agent does something she takes to be in violation of the moral standards she endorses and on which she typically relies to arrive at practical judgments or decisions about what to do. It is in virtue of the agent's having done something she believes is below par that it is frequently fitting in instances of moral blameworthiness for the agent to have negative feelings or attitudes (like regret, or remorse) toward herself, and for other parties to adopt appropriate negative attitudes toward her. But I stress that these feelings or attitudes are *not* necessary elements of blameworthiness; a person can be deserving of blame on account of doing something even though she feels nothing like remorse or guilt for doing that thing, and even though nobody else is aware that she is to blame for doing that thing, and so even though nobody else vents or expresses negative feelings in reaction to her doing of that thing. In addition, it is possible for a person to be aware of moral constraints or standards, and yet deliberately shun these in favor of, say, prudential ones in guiding her life. Imagine such an agent willfully doing something that she takes to be morally wrong but in her long-term pruden-tial self-interest. Such an agent would have acted in accordance with the norma-tive standards—prudential ones—to which she bears allegiance and which she takes to be authoritative in guiding her conduct. Yet, in this case, she could well be deserving of moral blame for her action. So one can do something for which one is *morally* to blame even if one does not take oneself to have done something in violation of the normative standards to which one would like one's behavior to conform. Moral blameworthiness, then, is *not* connected *essentially* with nega-tive feelings on the part of the agent or third parties, or with outward censure including practices like punishment, or with the violation of normative standards one endorses. Rather, I believe that the crux of the concept of blameworthiness is this: an agent is morally to blame on account of performing some action, A, if that agent has a belief (even a dispositional one) that A is wrong, she has this belief irrespective of whether or not she cares about morality (she may, for in-stance "identify" with prudential norms), she performs A despite the belief that it is morally wrong, and she believes (at least dispositionally) that she is performing A. (Of course, augmenting this core are other conditions like the agent's being in appropriate control of the action she takes to be morally untoward.)

Preliminaries about our second target concept—moral praiseworthiness—can be understood in a similar fashion. Moral praiseworthiness amounts to inward praise. This sort of praise has nothing essential to do with "positive" feelings or attitudes on the part of the agent or others, or with outward practices like the bestowing of rewards, or with acting in conformity with the normative standards with which one "identifies." Rather, moral praiseworthiness primarily gauges the moral worth of an agent on the basis of whether the agent has done something he believes is morally obligatory or permissible.

3. SYNOPSIS

Appraisability requires control: there has been a long-standing view that one can-not be blameworthy or praiseworthy—or "appraisable" as I shall say—for per-forming an action unless one controls the action in an appropriate way. In chapter 2 I begin by examining the view of control captured by the principle of alterna-tive possibilities, one version of which says that one is appraisable for an action only if one could have done otherwise. On this view, the requisite sort of control for appraisability entails the existence of real options. One motivation for the principle of alternative possibilities is given eloquent expression by Joel Feinberg (1980, pp. 30–44). Feinberg invites us to think of life as a kind of maze of railroad tracks. Chugging along a trunk line, one may come to a point where one has no choice at all but to continue moving straight ahead; all other possibilities of movement along side tracks have been closed off. As, at this point, one can only move directly ahead with no freedom to change tracks, one lacks real choice; one is *forced* to move straight ahead. Feinberg's thought, then, seems to be that if one performs an action under conditions where one could not have done otherwise, one performed the action under compulsion, and hence one could not be deserv-ing of praise or blame for that action.

If the principle of alternative possibilities is true, and Feinberg is right about the view that lack of alternative options implies compulsion, then the prospects of appraisability seem dim indeed if causal determinism is true. Causal determinism is, roughly, the view that for any given time, a complete statement about the facts of the world at that time, together with a statement of the laws of nature, entails all truths regarding what happens after that time. So if determinism is true, the facts of the past with the laws of nature entail one unique future; the future, if determinism is true, is not a maze of forking tracks—it is simply a closed trunk line leading straight ahead. But then it seems to follow (on pain of being committed to the dubious view that a person is able to alter the past or the laws of nature) that if determinism rules the world, no person can do other than what she in fact does. Hence, if determinism is true, and a person is appraisable for an action only if she could have done otherwise, we quickly reach the unsettling conclusion that no one is appraisable for any of one's actions.

However, I argue in chapter 2 that "Frankfurt-type" examples undermine Feinberg's rationale for the principle of alternate possibilities—that lack of alternatives implies compulsion. These examples forcefully suggest that an agent can "freely" perform an action even if he could not have done otherwise.[9]

A second rationale for the principle of alternative possibilities relies on considerations of "ultimate control." Again, suppose causal determinism is true. Then our choices and actions are simply elements in a lengthy sequence of deterministic events that started long before we were born. One might, hence, argue that if determinism is true, we never really *initiate* our choices or actions; we are simply one insignificant link in a long deterministic chain. But if we fail to be real initiators, and so fail to make any genuine contribution to our choices or actions, how can we possibly exercise the relevant sort of control over them required for appraisability? The idea here, then, is that we *must* be able to do otherwise in order to be real initiators of our choices and actions; we must be able to initiate causal sequences culminating in behavior by making some causally *undetermined* decisions or choices (see, e.g., Kane 1995).

A virtue of this important rationale for the principle of alternative possibilities (as suggested, for example, by Robert Kane) is that it forces us to confront issues of agency. For it is sensible to interpret Kane as proposing that one is an appropriate subject of appraisability only if one is an undetermined initiator of at least some of one's choices or actions.

One of my aims in chapter 2 is to argue that Kane may well be mistaken: undetermined initiation of action is not *required* for the requisite sort of control for appraisability, nor must one be an undetermined initiator of one's choices or actions to be an appropriate candidate for appraisability. I suggest that while undetermined initiation does not add anything to control, it need not diminish control either. My strategy is to develop an account of control—the sort required for appraisability—that does not require that we be undetermined initiators but that is compatible with persons' being such initiators. Prior to developing such an account, I raise a perplexity.

I argue in chapter 3 that whether a fully general principle of alternative possibilities is true, a principle that extends across all actions regardless of their normative statuses, depends centrally on whether certain precepts of moral obligation are true. For example, I argue that if some varieties of utilitarianism (a normative moral theory that tells us what makes obligatory acts obligatory and wrong acts wrong) are true, then no agent can perform an action to which there are no alternatives that is wrong; and hence that no agent can be morally to blame or praise for performing a *wrong* action to which there are no alternatives (as there are, if utilitarianism is true, no such actions). I argue, in addition, that if the 'ought' implies 'can' principle—that is, the principle that one ought (morally) to perform an action only if one can perform that action—is true, and if the principle that one has a moral obligation to perform an action only if it is morally wrong for one not to perform that action is also true, then, once again, no action to which there are no alternatives can be wrong. One may well be appraisable for performing such an action, but even if one is so, one will not thereby be appraisable for performing a *wrong* action. If, speaking loosely, there is a requirement of alternative possibilities for wrongness, and causal determinism rules out genuine alternatives, then though causal determinism may not subvert the sort of control required for appraisability, it may threaten the very foundations of morality.

In chapter 4, I revert to the issue of control. I begin by arguing against Susan Wolf's "normative" account of control (1990) according to which the type of control needed for moral appraisability is freedom to act in accordance with the True and the Good. I then discuss problems that plague a "hierarchical" view of control which, pared down to its fundamental core, says that a person has control over an action—again, the kind required for appraisability—if there is an appropriate "fit" or "mesh" between the (first-) order desire from which the action issues and other higher-order desires (or other higher-order propositional attitudes) of the person.[10] Finally, I develop a view of control that is a variant of the ancient idea that one has the right type of control over an action needed for appraisability only if the action is responsive to one's practical reasoning. I adopt the view defended by Alfred Mele (and others) that deliberative intentional action involves (1) some psychological basis for evaluative reasoning (like desires and beliefs); (2) a judgment recommending a course of action made on the basis of such reasoning; (3) an intention or decision formed or acquired on the basis of such a judgment; and (4) an action executing that intention or decision (Mele 1995). I develop 1 by suggesting that an agent's reasoning that leads to first-person practical judgments about what to do involves an assessment of reasons for or against action by appeal to an *evaluative scheme* of the agent's. Such a scheme comprises doxastic constituents, specifically, beliefs about normative standards to be invoked in evaluating reasons for action, and beliefs about deliberative principles the agent thinks appropriate to arrive at practical judgments about what to do. It also comprises motivational elements like long-term ends or goals constitutive of the agent's values, and pro-attitudes to utilize the normative standards and deliberative principles which the agent endorses, to secure her goals, and to make decisions about what to do or how to act in particular circumstances. I then introduce the notion of volitional control, which, in outline, says that an action performed by an agent is under her volitional control if and only if, holding constant the proximal desire that gives rise to that action and the agent's evaluative scheme, there is a scenario with the same natural laws as the actual world in which, relying on her evaluative scheme, the agent forms an intention or arrives at a decision to do something other than that action, and he successfully executes that intention or decision. An action over which an agent exercises volitional control is responsive to the agent's practical reasoning.[11]

In chapter 5 I take up some objections to my account of volitional control. One appeals to cases like Secret Agent. On my view, Bond (in Secret Agent) is not appraisable for killing Smernof as he does not exercise volitional control over his action of killing Smernof. An objector might claim that Bond is not appraisable as he did not act on a desire that was "truly his own" or "authentic"; he was not autonomous relative to this desire of his. (Remember, the relevant desire was implanted in Bond by Xenia.) Appraisability for an action, the objector might propose, presupposes autonomy with respect to that action or its causal springs like (its proximal desire).[12] A second objection directly challenges my view that a person cannot be appraisable for an action unless that action is under her volitional control. Consider, for instance, a mother who has a literally irresistible desire to run into a burning house to save her child; assume that the mother is unable to acquire (at the germane time) motivation to refrain from saving the child. The objector might insist that the mother *is* appraisable for saving the child. Presumably, on the objector's view, she is deserving of praise for saving the child; and she is so deserving even though saving the child is *not* under her volitional control: as she acts on a desire that is irresistible, there is no scenario in which, holding constant that desire, her evaluative scheme, and the laws of nature, she forms an intention to do otherwise and successfully executes that intention. In this sort of case, typically the agent takes herself to have acted autonomously or freely; she takes herself to have acted in conformity with her character or in conformity with her "deep self."[13]

To meet these objections, I propose that a person who acts from weakness of will may not be autonomous with respect to her akratic action, although she could be appraisable for it. When, for instance, weak-willed Fred eats the pie contrary to his consciously held decisive best judgment, there is a sense in which he fails to conduct himself autonomously, though he may well be blameworthy for eating the pie. So appraisability, it seems, does not (in one sense) presuppose autonomy. To develop this view, I distinguish between autonomy with respect to one's decisions or intentions—"decisional autonomy"—and autonomy with respect to one's actions—"actional autonomy." I argue that actional autonomy presupposes decisional autonomy; one cannot be autonomous relative to an action unless one is autonomous with respect to the decision (or intention) from which that action issues. My view has the implication that akratic Fred is not autonomous with respect to his decision to eat the pie; he has, after all, a "higher ranked" decision, namely, the decision to refrain; consequently, as actional autonomy presupposes decisional autonomy, he is not actionally autonomous with respect to eating the pie. Nevertheless, he *is* blameworthy for eating the pie. My view also implies that the devoted mother *is* decisionally autonomous with respect to her decision (or intention) to save the child, but she is not actionally autonomous relative to her action of saving the child. Her being decisionally autonomous provides the basis for an explanation of why she takes herself to have acted autonomously or freely. The mother is not actionally autonomous relative to her action of saving the child as she does not exercise volitional control over saving the child. Her failing to exercise volitional control over saving the child accounts for her not being appraisable for saving the child.

In chapter 6, I propose that there is a kernel of truth in the view that appraisability presupposes autonomy. Reflect on Psychogen. When Jenny awakens from psychosurgery (to which she did not consent) and executes an astute investment decision, we don't think she is appraisable for her action. But why not? Because she is, after surgery, a psychological twin of Jim, the sort of control that Jim would have exercised had he made the investment decision and acted on it is the same sort of control that Jenny should now exercise (other things remaining equal) over *her* making the decision and acting on it. Indeed, we may simply assume that Jenny *does* have volitional control over her investment action. So if Jenny is not appraisable for this action, the reason cannot be that it is an action over which Jenny fails to exercise the type of control required for appraisability. Rather, I suggest that Jenny is not appraisable for this action as it ultimately issues from an engineered-in evaluative scheme with respect to which Jenny is not autonomous; in the terminology I shall adopt, Jenny's action issues from an unauthentic evaluative scheme. The issue I then confront is this: Under what conditions is an agent's evaluative scheme authentic? I approach this issue indirectly by addressing (in chapter 6) the following problem concerning appraisability and induced pro-attitudes: Why is action which ultimately arises from pro-attitudes like desires or values, induced (in the absence of consent) by techniques such as direct manipulation of the brain, hypnosis, or value engineering, frequently taken to be action for which its agent is not morally appraisable? The solution that I offer to this problem paves the way for formulating and defending sufficient conditions for an agent's evaluative scheme's being authentic, a task I undertake in chapter 7.

Aristotle argues that to be appraisable for an action, one must perform that action voluntarily *and* one must not act in ignorance. In addition to control and autonomy (or authenticity), there is an epistemic dimension of moral appraisability. This dimension is the topic of chapters 8 and 9. In the former, I argue against any epistemic component which entails that a person is blameworthy (or praiseworthy) for performing an action only if that action is in fact (objectively) wrong (or objectively obligatory or right).[14] In the next chapter I propose that appraisability is affiliated with one's perceptions about what is wrong or obligatory. Specifically, I defend the view that an agent is morally blameworthy (or praiseworthy) for performing an action only under the condition that she has the belief (perhaps a dispositional one) that it is wrong (or obligatory) for her to perform that action and this belief plays an appropriate role in the performance of that action. I explicate the role an agent's belief that a prospective action of hers is wrong (or obligatory) must play in the production of her action if she is to be appraisable for that action. Toward this end, I make use of cases involving akrasia and self-deception.

Finally, in chapter 10, I collect the results of the preceding chapters and offer a principle (I dub "Appraisability") that outlines, roughly, the following analysis of appraisability: one is morally appraisable for performing an action just in case one performs it freely (one has volitional control in performing it), autonomously (it issues from authentic springs of action), and in the belief that one is doing something morally obligatory, right, wrong, or amiss (an agent may believe, for instance, that her action is permissible but still morally indecent).

In the next four chapters, I trace some implications of Appraisability for a number of issues. In chapter 11 I argue that apart from moral appraisability, we can make conceptual sense of other varieties of appraisability like, for example, etiquettical or prudential appraisability; and I show that the conditions recorded in principle Appraisability, with minor amendments, also serve to capture conditions for these other varieties of appraisability; they serve, that is, to capture conditions under which persons are nonmorally but normatively (and not merely causally) appraisable for their behavior. In chapter 12 I discuss the implications of principle Appraisability for what I call "intersocietal" attributions of blameworthiness. The concern here is this: people who are not part of a particular culture—"outsiders" relative to a culture—often attribute blame to a person within that culture for performing what the outsiders regard as a morally abhorrent action. Appealing to the epistemic condition that is a constituent of principle Appraisability, I argue that the outsider's attribution of blame is probably frequently mistaken. In chapter 13, I address the following concern about addicts. Can they be morally appraisable for behavior that is, in some notable fashion, caused by their use of the drug or drugs to which they are addicted? I answer that while many can, many others may lack "appraisability-grounding control" over their pertinent actions. In chapter 14, I take up the intriguing problem examined by, among others, Plato and Augustine, of whether we can be blameworthy or praiseworthy for the thoughts of our dream selves. I argue, relying partly on conclusions I draw regarding appraisability for unconscious thoughts, that we can indeed be appraisable for some of the thoughts of our dream selves. Finally, I conclude, in chapter 15, by framing what may be a grand perplexity. I argue that though causal determinism does not undermine moral appraisability by undermining freedom to do otherwise, causal determinism will undermine such appraisability if one of conditions required for moral appraisability, contrary to what principle Appraisability implies, is a condition that entails or appeals to morality. That is, if in order for a person to be morally blameworthy or praiseworthy for an action of hers, some condition that entails that some action is either wrong or obligatory must be satisfied, then causal determinism will undermine moral appraisability, as nothing can be wrong or obligatory in a fully determined world. I end, on a somewhat more cheery note, by suggesting that some varieties of nonmoral but normative responsibility may remain unscathed by determinism even if appraisability requires objective wrongness or obligatoriness.

APPRAISABILITY, ALTERNATIVE POSSIBILITIES, AND ULTIMATE CONTROL

I. ALTERNATIVE POSSIBILITIES AND CONTROL

Historically, there has been a venerable association of moral appraisability with control. Aristotle, for example, gives powerful expression to the idea that a person is morally appraisable for performing an action only if that action is in his control. He says that whatever "is done in ignorance, or though not done in ignorance is not in the agent's power, or is done under compulsion, is involuntary"; and "[s]ince virtue is concerned with passions and actions, and on voluntary passions and actions praise and blame are bestowed, on those that are involuntary pardon, and sometimes also pity, to distinguish the voluntary from the involuntary is presumably necessary for those who are studying the nature of virtue, and useful also for legislators with a view to the assigning both of honours and of punishments" (*Nicomachean Ethics* 1109b30–35).[1]

Furthermore, there has been a long tradition in which the sort of control required for moral appraisability entails the existence of genuine alternative possibilities. Again, Aristotle sets the stage when he says:

> The end, then, being what we wish for, the means what we deliberate about and choose, actions concerning means must be according to choice and voluntary. Now the exercise of the virtues is concerned with means. Therefore virtue also is in our power, and so too vice. For where it is in our power to act, it is also in our power not to act, and *vice versa*; so that, if to act, where this is noble, is in our power, not

to act, which will be base, will also be in our power, and if not to act, where this is noble, is in our power, to act, which will be base, will also be in our power. (*Nicomachean Ethics* 1113b1–14)

The picture of control affiliated with this tradition is intuitively attractive and very natural. We think of ourselves as having, on numerous occasions in life, real alternative options or pathways. Although we follow one, we tend to believe that we could have taken a different path that was genuinely accessible to us. Also, we very naturally and typically think that we have *control* over our behavior insofar as we were able to do otherwise. We frequently assume that a lack of alternative pathways undermines control, and that if all our options but one are closed, and we venture down the one open pathway, we don't do so voluntarily. The "alternative option" paradigm of control is eloquently articulated by Joel Feinberg in his essay "The Interest in Liberty on the Scales." Feinberg says:

> We can think of life as a kind of maze of railroad tracks connected and disjoined, here and there, by switches. Wherever there is an unlocked switch which can be pulled one way or the other, there is an 'open option;' wherever the switch is locked in one position the option is 'closed.' As we chug along our various tracks in the maze, other persons are busily locking and unlocking, opening and closing switches, thereby enlarging and restricting our various possibilities of movement. . . . Suppose that Martin Chuzzlewit finds himself on a trunk line with all of its switches closed and locked, and with other 'trains' moving in the same direction on the same track at his rear, so that he has no choice at all but to continue moving straight ahead to destination D. On the 'open option' theory of liberty, this is the clearest example of a total lack of liberty: all of his options are closed, there are not alternative possibilities, he is forced to move to D. But now let us suppose that getting to D is Chuzzlewit's highest ambition in life and his most intensely felt desire. In that case, he is sure to get the thing in life he wants most. Does that affect the way the situation should be described in respect to liberty? According to the theory that one is at liberty to the extent that one can do what one wants, a theory held by the ancient Stoics and Epicureans and many modern writers too, Chuzzlewit enjoys perfect liberty in this situation because he can do what he wants, even though he can do nothing else. But since this theory blurs the distinction between liberty and compulsion, and in this one extreme hypothetical case actually identifies the two, it does not recommend itself to common sense. . . . If Chuzzlewit is allowed no alternative to D, it follows that he is forced willy-nilly to go to D. (1980, pp. 36–39)

Feinberg's hypothetical case lends support to what many take to be a powerful and attractive principle of control—the principle of alternative possibilities (PAP)—which says that moral appraisability requires the existence (at some appropriate juncture in the path leading to action) of genuine alternative possibilities; one must have the freedom to will, choose, or do otherwise.[2] Some clarification of what "alternative possibilities" amount to here is in order. The relevant conception is one according to which A and B are alternative possibilities for agent, S, at a possible world, w, at a time, t, only if the obtaining of each of them (that is, of A and B) is consistent with the conjunction of all the facts of the past (in w) relative to t and the laws of nature of w. In this sense of 'alternative possibilities', if S did A at t, then even if all the facts of the past relative to t were held constant—even if, for instance, among the facts held constant are S's reasons and motives for doing A at t—S could have done B instead.[3]

2. CAUSAL DETERMINISM AND FREEDOM TO DO OTHERWISE

Among other things, the principle of alternative possibilities has been the cynosure of a great deal of philosophical attention, for the reason that, if true, then considerations as intuitively reasonable as the principle itself quickly lead to a startling and exceedingly disturbing conclusion: nobody has been, is, or ever will be appraisable for his behavior. One version of one influential skeptical argument that generates this conclusion relies on three plausible views. The first, which John Martin Fischer has dubbed the "Principle of the Fixity of the Past," is meant to capture the idea that the past is over and done with; it is "fixed" and "out of our control" (1994, p. 9). We may think that the future is a garden of forking paths, but the past is not like that; we have no control over certain facts about the past. The principle says that if a person's performing a certain action would require some actual fact about the past *not* to have been a fact, then the person *cannot* perform that act.

The second view central to the skeptical argument is another eminently sensible commonsense view that natural laws, just like the past, are also "fixed" and out of our control. This idea is encapsulated in the Principle of the Fixity of the Laws, which says that if a person's performing a certain action would require that some actual natural law *not* be a law, then the person *cannot* perform that act.

Finally, the third element is the thesis of causal determinism. It says that for any given time, a complete statement of the facts about the world at that time, in conjunction with a complete statement of the laws of nature, entails all truths as to what happens after that time.

Now the skeptical argument, as Fischer explains, can be summarized succinctly in this fashion. Suppose some person, S, performs some ordinary act, X, like eating a strawberry, at some time, t2.

> [I]f determinism is true, and s1 is the total state of the world at t1, one of the following conditionals must be true:
>
> (1) If S were to refrain from doing X at t2, s1 would not have been the total state of the world at t1.
>
> (2) If S were to refrain from doing X at t2, then some natural law which actually obtains would not obtain.
>
> (3) If X were to refrain from doing X at t2, then either s1 would not have been the total state of the world at t1, or some natural law which actually obtains would not obtain.
>
> But if (1) is true, then . . . [via the Principle of the Fixity of the Past] S cannot refrain from doing X at t2. Similarly, if (2) is true, then . . . [via the Principle of the Fixity of the Laws] S cannot refrain from doing X at t2. Finally, if (1)'s truth implies that S cannot refrain from doing X at t2, and (2)'s truth implies that S cannot refrain from doing X at t2, then it follows that if (3) is true, S cannot refrain

from doing X at t2. The conclusion of this argument is that if determinism is true, then S cannot do anything other than what he actually does at t2. Generalizing this result, . . . if determinism is true, none of us is free to do other than what he actually does. (1994, pp. 62–63)[4]

The conclusion of this argument, together with the principle that moral appraisability requires alternative possibilities, would then generate the incredible result that no one has been, is, or ever will be appraisable for what she actually does.

Not everyone accepts the skeptical argument. Some people have disputed the Fixity of the Past principle, others have questioned the claim that natural laws are "fixed" and beyond our control, and yet others are dubious about causal determinism. But arguably, the skeptic's challenge is sound. At least I am willing to grant that the version of the skeptical argument we have canvassed, or an appropriately restructured one, establishes the conclusion that no one is free to do other than what one actually does. I am unwilling, nevertheless, to concede that this conclusion undermines moral appraisability by undermining control. And I am so unwilling because I don't believe that the kind of control required for moral appraisability is one that entails the existence of alternative options. However naturally inclined we may be to accept the principle of alternative possibilities, I believe that "Frankfurt-type" examples forcefully recommend reassessing our ideas about control.

3. FRANKFURT-TYPE EXAMPLES

Following John Locke, Harry Frankfurt has generated a series of examples challenging the view that moral appraisability requires alternative possibilities.[5] In broad strokes, a Frankfurt-type example is one where an agent successfully acts on her intention to perform an action, not knowing that had she chosen, or had she been about to choose, or had she shown any inclination to choose otherwise, something or some agent—a "counterfactual intervener"—would have forced her to act as she in fact did. Since the intervener does not interfere at all in the ordinary sequence of events that culminates in the agent's performing the action, the agent can be held, and is indeed morally appraisable, for what she did. As an illustration, imagine that, despite harboring the belief that squeezing the trigger (for the purpose of killing Max) is wrong, Jones, on her own, arrives at a decision to kill Max, and when the moment is right successfully executes her vile decision. Unbeknownst to her, had she revealed even the *slightest* sign of not intending or deciding to murder Max, Dark Demon, who had scrupulously been monitoring the situation all along, would have, via direct manipulation of Jones's brain, caused her to form an intention to squeeze the trigger and to act on that intention. As the demon does not show her hand in the straightforward sequence of events that culminates in Jones's squeezing the trigger, it appears that Jones is morally blameworthy (and so morally appraisable) for squeezing the trigger even though she could not have done otherwise. She is blameworthy, roughly, because her action of squeezing the trigger is under the control of her practical reasoning, it issues from autonomous actional elements (like beliefs and desires), and she performs it in spite of her belief that squeezing the trigger is wrong.

The alternative possibilities theorist might concede that Jones could not have refrained from squeezing the trigger, but still insist that *somewhere* along the pathway of events that ended in Jones's squeezing the trigger, Jones *did* have relevant alternatives. She did have the freedom, for instance, to begin to choose otherwise. Indeed, an essential ingredient of a Frankfurt-type example is that there be *some* event in the "alternative sequence" that plays the role of a trigger which sets into motion, or signals, intervention on behalf of the intervener. And where there is such an event, as there must be in a Frankfurt-type case, one will find what Fischer has called a "flicker of freedom" (1994, p. 10).

Fischer argues that this sort of strategy will not in the end help the alternative possibilities theorist:

> The problem . . . is that it seems . . . we can systematically reconstruct the Frankfurt-type examples . . . so that there is some sign or indication which would *precede* the initiating action and which could be read by the "counterfactual intervener". . . . Further, and this is the important point here, the evincing of such a sign . . . [need] not even . . . [be] an action, and . . . [would] certainly not plausibly [be] thought to be robust enough to ground responsibility ascriptions. . . . [For example, suppose the triggering event were] some involuntary sign, such as a blush or twitch or even a complex neurophysiological pattern. . . . [I]t is reasonable to ask how the addition of an alternative possibility of *this sort*—a triggering event which is not even an *initiating action*—could possibly transform a case of no control (of the relevant kind) into a case of control. How exactly does the addition of an alternative possibility which is (say) an involuntary blush or twitch transform a case of lack of control into a case of control? The thought that the presence of this sort of etiolated alternative possibility can make *this sort of difference* is puzzling. (1994, pp. 144–45)

As I understand him, Fischer urges that, setting aside *robust alternative possibilities*—alternative possibilities that are intentional choosings or doings—all other "alternative possibilities" left over in Frankfurt-type cases, such as not being inclined to do something, or hesitating, or blushing are not robust enough to ground ascriptions of moral appraisability; they are mere flickers of freedom. Hence, Fischer concludes, moral appraisability does not require the kind of control that entails alternative possibilities. I shall return to the issue of whether Fischer has had the last say on control and alternative possibilities below in the section on "ultimate control."

Provisionally, the following summary seems apt. Aristotle was right to insist that moral appraisability requires control. But Frankfurt-type examples developed by Locke and Frankfurt, and refined by Fischer, exert commanding pressure to renounce the view that the relevant sort of control is freedom to do otherwise. In addition, Frankfurt-type examples strongly suggest that an incompatibilist—a person who believes that causal determinism is incompatible with moral appraisability—who endorses incompatibilism because he believes that the control required for moral appraisability is freedom to do otherwise, and that causal determinism is incompatible with this sort of control, might well want to reassess her incompatibilism.

Not all incompatibilists, however, believe that causal determinism threatens appraisability in virtue of ruling out alternative possibilities. Derk Pereboom is an incompatibilist of this sort (see Pereboom 1995). I examine his interesting views below.

4. CONTROL AND DETERMINISTIC CAUSAL PROCESSES — PEREBOOM'S VIEWS

Pereboom concedes that Frankfurt-type examples undermine the notion that responsibility requires alternative possibilities. However, he also believes that these examples do nothing to dislodge the "incompatibilist's most fundamental claim" (1995, p. 27), which, he insists, is *not* to be conflated with the view that "moral responsibility requires that, given all of the factors that precede one's choice, one could have done otherwise than what one actually did" (1995, p. 26). Rather, it is the claim that "moral responsibility precludes being determined in virtue of a causal process that traces back to factors beyond the agent's control" (1995, p. 23). To elaborate, Pereboom's explains that if causal determinism is true, then even the relevant agent like Jones in a Frankfurt-type example, just like any other agent for that matter, is not morally responsible for her actions. And she is not because as "we wind our way back along the deterministic chain of causes that results in . . . [her] reasoning and desires, . . . we eventually reach causal factors that are beyond . . . [her] control-causal factors that . . . [she] could not have produced, altered, or prevented. The incompatibilist intuition is that if an action results from a deterministic causal process that traces back to factors beyond the control of the agent, he is not morally responsible for the action" (p. 23).

Pereboom advances a set of interesting cases in an attempt to defend the "fundamental incompatibilist claim," beginning with a fanciful one of creation.

> CASE 1: Mr. Green is like an ordinary human being, except that he was created by neuroscientists, who can manipulate him directly through the use of radio-like technology. Suppose these neuroscientists directly manipulate Mr. Green to undertake the process of reasoning by which his desires are modified and produced, and his effective first-order desire to kill Ms. Peacock conforms to his second-order desires. The neuroscientists manipulate him by, among other things, pushing a series of buttons just before he begins to reason about his situation, thereby causing his reasoning process to be rationally egoistic. His reasoning process is reasons-responsive, because it would have resulted in different choices in some situations in which the egoistic reasons were otherwise. Mr. Green does not think and act contrary to character, since the neuroscientists typically manipulate him to be rationally egoistic. (p. 23)

Pereboom's verdict is that, intuitively, in this case Green is not morally responsible for the murder "because he is determined by the neuroscientists' actions, which are beyond his control" (p. 24). Next, Pereboom adopts the following strategy. He advances three additional cases that he believes are not relevantly different, at least in respect of Green's lack of responsibility, from case 1. These cases, in conjunction with the verdict that Green is not morally responsible for the murder in case 1, are designed with a view to convincing us that Green is not responsible for the murder in *any* of the cases. And he is not responsible *because* his action results from a deterministic causal process tracing back to factors beyond his control. The cases, in the order presented by Pereboom, are these:

CASE 2: Mr. Green is like an ordinary human being, except that he was created by neuroscientists, who, although they cannot control him directly, have programmed him to be a rational egoist, so that, in any circumstances like those in which he now finds himself, he is causally determined to undertake the reasons-responsive process and to possess the set of first and second-order desires that results in his killing Ms. Peacock. (p. 24)

CASE 3: Mr. Green is an ordinary human being, except that he was determined by the rigorous training practices of his home and community to be a rational egoist. His training took place at too early an age for him to have had the ability to prevent or alter the practices that determined his character. Mr. Green is thereby caused to undertake the reasons-responsive process and to possess the organization of first and second-order desires that result in his killing Ms. Peacock. (p. 24)

CASE 4: Physicalist determinism is true. Mr. Green is a rationally egoistic but (otherwise) ordinary human being, raised in normal circumstances. Mr. Green's killing of Ms. Peacock comes about as a result of his undertaking the reasons-responsive process of deliberation, and he has the specified organization of first and second-order desires. (p. 25)

Pereboom claims that we are "constrained to deny moral responsibility to Mr. Green in the first three cases" (p. 25). He grants, however, that one may have a predilection to believe, especially if one has no prior commitment to incompatibilism, that Green *is* morally responsible for the murder in case 4. To resolve this quandary, Pereboom suggests that the best explanation for the intuition (if one has it) that Green is not responsible for killing Peacock in the first three cases is that Green's action "results from a deterministic causal process that traces back to factors beyond his control" (p. 25). But then as "Mr. Green is also causally determined in this way in case 4, we must, despite our initial predilections, conclude that here too Mr. Green is not morally responsible. And more generally, if every action results from a deterministic causal process that traces back to factors beyond the agent's control, then no agents are ever morally responsible for their actions" (p. 25).

5. CRITICISM OF PEREBOOM

Despite the appeal of Pereboom's strategy, I believe that ultimately it is not convincing. A number of considerations lead me to reject it. I shall offer a detailed account of the relevant sorts of considerations in chapters 4 and 5. For our immediate concerns, the ensuing preliminary reflections should suffice. At the heart of Pereboom's approach is the claim that we are "constrained to deny moral responsibility to Mr. Green in the first three cases." I want to suggest that cases 1 and 2 at least can be developed in two distinct ways. In the first way, Green *is* (intuitively) morally responsible for killing Peacock; whereas in the second, although Green can plausibly be taken not to be morally responsible, the best explanation for his lack of responsibility is *not* conclusively the explanation that his action traces back to causal factors beyond his control. Rather, there is an alternative explanation that, if not better, is just as compelling as Pereboom's.

Let's first record an important distinction introduced by Ferdinand Schoeman. It is standardly believed that action which ultimately issues from pro-attitudes like desires, volitions, goals, and intentions, induced by techniques such as direct manipulation of the brain or hypnosis, under conditions in which the agent has not consented to being so manipulated, is action for which its agent is not morally responsible. In discussing this issue, Schoeman distinguishes different sorts of possible cases. One sort involves what Schoeman calls "global manipulation" (1978, p. 295) in which all of an agent's pro-attitudes have been induced by some other agent. Psychogen, in which Jenny is transformed into a psychological twin of Jim is a case of this sort. Another type of case involves "local manipulation" in which only certain desires, or values, or other pro-attitudes are instilled in a person who is left otherwise psychologically intact (Schoeman 1978, p. 297). As Pereboom describes them, cases 1 and 2 exhibit local manipulation. Green is first created by neurophysiologists who endow him with a certain character, personality, and psychological profile. He is then "locally manipulated" by them. (Think of case 2 as a case in which the local manipulation is "pre-programmed": in circumstances like those in which Green now finds himself, the "local" effects of the neuroscientists come into play; in other circumstances, Green is left on his own.) Consider now, two different ways in which the first two cases can be developed. For brevity, I limit attention to case 1.

Imagine, in what we dub the "first scenario," that Green is indeed the creation of neurophysiologists. It is worth mentioning that this unusual feature of Green's life is not essential to the moral of this scenario. Green could equally well have been the product of Merlin the Magician or of an omnipotent being. Suppose the neurophysiologists can, when they want, cause Green to form certain intentions, arrive at certain decisions, or make certain choices, and to act accordingly, by directly stimulating Green's brain; they have, that is, the ability to "locally manipulate" Green. And suppose they can do all this without the manipulations being "felt" or detected by Green. Suppose that on a certain occasion, the neuroscientists electronically manipulate Green, instilling in him various pro-attitudes, which contribute centrally to Green's killing Peacock. Assume that the instilled pro-attitudes, like the desire to kill Peacock, have strong motivational force but are *not* irresistible. Had he wanted to, Green could have resisted them by relying on his own reasoning processes. This last assumption is legitimate as, presumably, Pereboom's set of cases is meant to provide support for the "fundamental incompatibilist claim" that actions originating from factors over which one has no control are not ones for which one can be morally responsible, in a *non*-question-begging way.

If one has no prior commitment to incompatibilism, this scenario may well elicit the intuition that Green *is* morally responsible for killing Peacock. It would not be uncommon to react to the first scenario in some such way as this: "True, Green did come into existence in a rather weird way. But why should this matter? After all, Green could have been snapped into existence by God. Green *was* locally manipulated, and that's not nice at all. But though he acted on the instilled pro-attitudes, these didn't compel him to do anything. He could have resisted them, but he didn't. And that's why he bears responsibility."

One might, nevertheless, resist this sort of reaction by calling attention to this modification of the first scenario: assume that Green's very capacity or inclination to resist acting on the induced desire to kill Peacock is itself the product of local manipulation. Suppose this time around, exercising the "locally induced" capacity to resist, Green thwarts the induced desire to kill Peacock. Surely, one might urge, Green is not morally responsible for failing to kill Peacock, even though he now, as in the unmodified version of the first scenario, has the ability to resist killing Peacock. And again, the explanation of why he is not responsible, one might claim, is that the causal factors that issue in his omission lie beyond his control.

This response, however, is inadequate. To see that it is so, consider the *entire* cluster of Green's induced pro-attitudes and capacities. Suppose, on the one hand, that given this cluster, it is still possible for Green to "fall back" to his *non*induced pro-attitudes and capacities, and thwart the influence of the instilled cluster. Then, it seems, Green may well be responsible for killing Peacock. And if he were, it is very plausible that he would be because, despite the instilled cluster, he still has the ability to exercise his own deliberative capacities, to decide in the light of his own reflection whether or not to kill Peacock, and to execute his decision. On the other hand, suppose that the local manipulation renders Green unable to exercise his "own deliberative capacities"—those with which he was endowed when created. Then the case is analogous to what I call the "second scenario" discussed below. In this scenario, Green is not morally responsible for killing Peacock, but arguably *not* for the reason that his action is generated by causal factors that lie beyond his control.

In this second scenario, which contrasts relevantly with the unmodified (but not the modified) version of the first, the instilled pro-attitudes that move Green to action are irresistible. So, for example, supposing that the desire to kill Peacock is "implanted" in Green, Green cannot, in this scenario, resist acting on this desire. The second scenario may well elicit the intuition that Green is not morally responsible for the killing. However, what might ground this intuition is an explanation to the effect that Green was not autonomous or self-governing with respect to his action (or some of its instilled causal springs) of killing Peacock. He was simply a puppet of the neuroscientists. Further, it is not in the least obvious that this explanation is tantamount to the explanation that Green is not responsible in virtue of his action's resulting from causal factors beyond his control. We can appreciate that these two explanations are different by noting that our explanation, but not Pereboom's, relies on the (rough) idea that the local manipulation to which Green falls victim in the second scenario (and in the modified first) is manipulation that temporarily disrupts agency. In the grips of the instilled irresistible pro-attitudes, Green's "actional agency" is subverted, and is temporarily "replaced" by some "foreign agency." (Interestingly, in his insightful discussion of the effect on our reactive attitudes like forgiveness and resentment of the [supposed] justified belief that incompatibilism is true, Pereboom does *not* take causal determinism itself to subvert agency [1995, pp. 37–41].) I suggest that even in a fully determined world, we could distinguish between cases in which an agent performs an action on "his own," and those in which he is forced to act on irresistible engineered in pro-attitudes. Compatibilists have insisted, with considerable plausibility, on distinguishing between compulsion and causation. All actions may well be caused, but that does not entail that all such actions are compelled.[6] It is, then, subversion of autonomy or agency, one might urge, and not lack of control over the relevant string of causal factors, that explains why Green is not responsible for the killing in the second scenario.[7]

6. ULTIMATE CONTROL

The incompatibilist may remain unmoved. Indeed, some incompatibilists might well *agree* that it is ultimately considerations of agency that motivate their view about the incompatibility of determinism with the kind of control required for moral appraisability. This brand of incompatibilist might remind us that if causal determinism is true, then our thoughts, decisions, choices, and actions are simply elements in a sequence of deterministic events that began long before we were born. Hence, the incompatibilist might urge, if determinism is true, we never really ultimately *initiate* our choices or actions; we are simply one intermediate coupling in a protracted deterministic chain extending a long, long way back in time. Determinism, the incompatibilist's worry continues, is incompatible with persons making any genuine contribution to their choices, decisions, actions, etc. that they are not causally determined to make. Moral appraisability presupposes control, but the relevant sort of control, from the incompatibilist's perspective (or at least from the perspective of incompatibilists of a certain sort) requires some indeterministic break in the causal sequence culminating in action; the agent must be able to initiate causal sequences leading to behavior by making some causally undetermined decisions or choices (see Kane 1995). As an illustration of undetermined choice, assume that an agent's choice or decision to do something is preceded by an effort of the agent's will; such efforts of the will give rise to choice or decision. These efforts are "tryings or strivings . . . they are mental efforts directed at getting one's ends (purposes, intentions) sorted out, rather than efforts to move one's body" (Kane 1995, p. 127) Assume, further, that the effort of will that terminates in choice is indeterminate: it is causally open whether an effort of the sort to choose A will issue in a choice of A. Then the choice in which an effort of will terminates will be undetermined (Kane 1995, pp. 127–28). As another illustration, suppose one's decisions or choices are deterministically caused by one's "best judgments" about what to do, and these judgments, in turn, are caused (partly) by one's belief states or events that "come to mind" and play a role in one's deliberations. Assume that such doxastic states are indeterminate: it is causally open which will come to mind and play a role in one's reasoning. Then, at the onset of deliberation, one's best judgment and one's decision or choice about what to do will be undetermined.[8] In this, and only in this fashion, by being an undetermined initiator, the incompatibilist might insist, can one exercise the requisite control for moral appraisability. For this sort of incompatibilist, indeterministic breaks—perhaps in the processes leading to best judgments about what to do—guarantee that an agent's freely performed acts are really "up to the agent." Further, such breaks allow for an agent's having more than one physically possible future and the future's truly being a garden of forking paths: they provide room for its being true that the agent could have judged, intended, and acted otherwise than she did.

Advocating this sort of agential view, Robert Kane proposes that what motivates incompatibilism generally is "the idea that agents can be 'ultimately responsible' for at least some of their actions," (1995, p. 120) and the conditions for ultimate responsibility amount to:

> (i) (The Explanation Condition) A free action for which the agent is ultimately responsible is the product of the agent, i.e., is caused by the agent, in such a way that we can satisfactorily answer the question "Why did this act occur here and now rather than some other?" (whichever occurs) by saying that the agent caused it to occur rather than not, or vice versa, here and now.
>
> (ii) (The Ultimacy Condition) The free action for which the agent is ultimately responsible is such that its occurring rather than not here and now, or vice versa, *has as its ultimate or final explanation the fact that it is caused by the agent here and now.* The explanation is "ultimate" or "final" in the sense that no other explanation of the outcome that goes beyond the explanation in (i) is possible. . . . [C]onditions (i) and (ii) imply that free choices or actions *cannot be determined.* In short, incompatibilism—with its requirement of indeterminism of free choices or actions—is a consequence of ultimate responsibility in the sense of (i) and (ii). More specifically, it is condition (ii), the Ultimacy Condition, which . . . [entails indeterminism]. . . . If a free action were determined by past circumstances, given the laws of nature, there would be an explanation for why the agent acted as he or she did that was other than, or went beyond, saying that the agent caused the doing or the doing otherwise here and now. (Kane 1995, pp. 120–21)[9]

Fischer, as we have seen, concludes that the right sort of control needed for moral responsibility does not require alternative possibilities: Frankfurt-type examples show that robust alternative possibilities are not essential for responsibility; and nonrobust alternative possibilities—flickers of freedom like involuntary blushes, or not being strongly inclined to do something, or hesitating, or efforts of will—he thinks are too weak to ground ascriptions of responsibility. Recently, Alfred Mele has suggested that contrary to Fischer's views, incompatibilists may contend that

> non-robust alternative possibilities, rather than grounding correct ascriptions of moral responsibility, are only part of the grounding mix. . . . They [that is, incompatibilists] may claim that the possession of at least non-robust alternative possibilities is necessary for moral responsibility because it is necessary for indeterministic initiation, and that the latter is required for moral responsibility. (Mele 1996, sec. 3)

The incompatibilist, Mele proposes, may insist that being an indeterministic initiator does require that one have at least nonrobust alternative possibilities, as possession of such possibilities is necessary for one's not being a mere link in a deterministic causal chain.

We have, then, two diametrically opposed views of control: some incompatibilists urge that it is necessary that we be undetermined initiators of our actions if we are to be morally appraisable for performing them; and they may add that possession of nonrobust alternative possibilities is necessary for moral appraisability as it is necessary for indeterministic initiation of action. Compatibilists only require that we be "intermediate initiators," with no commitment whatsoever to alternative possibilities of any variety. Which view is correct? There is, of course, no easy answer here.

As Kane notes, a traditional worry with the sort of incompatibilism he advocates is that the ultimacy condition, with its entailment of indeterminism, threatens control: if action issues from *indeterminate* events, how *can* the action be thought to be "the product of the agent," and caused by the agent in such a way that we can satisfactorily answer the question "Why did he perform this act here and now rather than some other?" by saying that "the agent caused it to occur rather than not, or vice versa, here and now"? Addressing this worry, Mele has persuasively proposed that it is possible to make room for incompatibilist

"ultimate control" while preserving a considerable measure of nonultimate agential control by treating the process from proximal decisive better judgment through overt action in a compatibilist way and finding a theoretically useful place for indeterminacy in processes leading to proximal decisive better judgments. (Mele 1995, p. 212)

Mele's idea is straightforward and elegant. Assume that there is some compatibilist account of control (CC) that does not entail nor preclude the existence of indeterministic breaks in the causal sequence of events that culminates in full-blown intentional action. The sequence may involve the following constituents: some psychological basis for evaluative reasoning including the agent's beliefs, values, and desires; an evaluative judgment made on the basis of such reasoning which recommends a particular course of action; an intention formed on the basis of that judgment; and an action executing that intention. Suppose Jones intentionally does A, and the conditions specified by the compatibilist account of control, CC, are satisfied. Assume that these conditions ensure that Jones has considerable *deterministic* proximal agential control over the events leading from decisive better judgment through overt action. Now introduce, for instance, doxastic indeterminacy of the sort to which we adverted above. Assume that it is causally undetermined whether certain of Jones's nonoccurrent beliefs will enter into Jones's deliberations about whether to A. So it is causally open, when Jones begins to deliberate, whether Jones will form a decisive best judgment to A, and in fact A. The introduction of such indeterminacy appears to satisfy the incompatibilist's requirement for ultimate control. Still, such indeterminacy need not erode control. It needn't as once the relevant beliefs have entered into his deliberations, Jones exercises significant deterministic agential control (of the type specified by CC) over the events leading from the formation of a decisive better judgment to action. As Mele explains:

> if it is causally undetermined whether a certain belief will enter into Jones's delibera-
> tion, then Jones lacks deterministic proximal control over whether the belief enters
> his deliberation. But this need not be an impediment to Jones's proximal control
> over how he deliberates in light of the beliefs that *do* enter his deliberation. He may
> have considerable proximal control over how carefully he deliberates in light of
> these beliefs, over whether he deliberates in ways that violate his deliberative princi-
> ples, and so on. (Mele 1995, p. 215)

Suppose Jones does A in a fully deterministic world and he satisfies the conditions of control laid down by the compatibilist account CC. Then I take it that Mele's idea is that the sole introduction of doxastic indeterminacy-holding unchanged Jones's deterministic proximal control (as specified by CC) in the pathway from decisive best judgment to overt action-should not erode control, but should suffice for incompatibilist "ultimate agency." In sum, Mele contends that, in principle, an agent-internal indeterminism may provide for indeterministic agency while impeding or restricting our control over what happens only in domains in which we have no greater control on the hypothesis that our world is deterministic. He adds that, even if determinism is true, it is false that, with respect to each consideration—each belief, desire, and so on—that comes to mind during our deliberation, we are in control of its coming to mind; and some considerations that come to mind without our being in control of their so doing may influence the outcome of our deliberation (see Mele 1995, ch. 12).

The "Meleian" strategy is promising, but it does raise a fundamental concern. What precisely is to be gained, in the way of control, by the introduction of indeterministic breaks of the sort envisaged? The breaks do permit for an agent's having more than one physically possible future and for its being true that the agent could have judged, intended, and acted otherwise than she did. But surely, the presence of such breaks do little to persuade us that *the agent* ensures that he has more than one physically possible future, etc. Which beliefs enter the agent's deliberations is indeterminate, and as a result of *such* indeterminacy the forking paths future is guaranteed. But the compatibilist might urge that *the agent* contributes no more to control in this scenario, the scenario with indeterminacy, than he does in a fully determined world. Look at the matter in this way: on the Meleian strategy, the threat of indeterminacy to control decreases as the model of control more closely approximates the model of control specified by CC, a model that stresses *deterministic* proximal control. But then the compatibilist like Fischer who advocates CC can rightfully urge that the value of indeterministic initiation of action for control is illusory. What *more* do we get, by way of agential control, by introducing indeterministic initiation of action? (Of course, the compatibilist need not endorse the view that indeterminism, strategically located within the process of deliberation, *erodes* or *diminishes* control.)[10]

In *Free Will and Values*, Kane remarks that

> what determinism takes away is a certain sense of the importance of oneself as an
> individual. If I am ultimately responsible for certain occurrences in the universe [by

being an undetermined initiato
importance that is missing if I d

The compatibilist might take Kaɪ
cited are construed as providing sup_k
we discovered that our world is fully ↲
as a result of this discovery, our choices
importance. Still, this deprivation certaɪɪ
ist's view of control. After all, we freque
obtain, or states of affairs we know we ca
find unappealing many things that are true
what many of us find thoroughly unappealinɢ
the discovery, see our lives in a new guise, bɪ
the Hobbesian view that we are egoists. Assuɪ
supposition that we discovered our world to be
our lives or choices would not be robbed of any
difficult to see how any of this would undermine the

Finally, yet on the issue of what is to be gained, in the
indeterministic break, an incompatibilist might respond: if the break doɪ
at the right juncture in the pathway leading to action, nothing is gained; but if
occurs at the right juncture (possibly, at the point of decision-making), then what
is gained is freedom from control by the past, in what one does. (I take this to be
the most forceful incompatibilist or libertarian tug. Of course, many libertarians
(Kane is one exception) would want to supplement this with some account of
agent-causation; they would say that, while freedom from control by the past is
necessary for freedom of action, it is not sufficient.) This idea is powerfully attractive, but I believe its appeal attenuates if we take seriously the suggestion that
appraisability (or responsibility, or control) depends on what occurs in the actual
sequence of events. To see this, assume that the right juncture for an indeterministic break is at the point of decision, and Michael, in an indeterministic world,
enjoys freedom to decide otherwise. However, assume that on a certain occasion
Michael forms an intention to A straightaway, and A-s straightaway, giving no
thought at all to intending otherwise. It seems to me that if the pathway leading
to Michael's A-ing is otherwise "clean"—free of responsibility undermining factors—then Michael has control over A-ing and is responsible for A-ing. Now
consider Michael's counterpart, Jackson, in a deterministic world in which he
lacks freedom to intend (or decide) otherwise; no relevant indeterministic breaks
occur in this world. Imagine that on a specific occasion Jackson forms an intention to B straightaway, and B-s straightaway. (Of course, his intending to B is
causally determined.) Indeed, perhaps Jackson falsely believes that he can intend
otherwise, but on this occasion gives no thought at all to intending otherwise.
Assume that the pathway leading to Jackson's B-ing is responsibility-wise "clean."
Finally, compare the pathway leading to Michael's A-ing to the one leading to
Jackson's B-ing. Aren't they relevantly on equal footing when it comes to ascriptions of responsibility, even though Michael has freedom from control by the past,
but Jackson does not? We can go even further. Suppose omnipotent Creator could

ndeterministic or a deterministic
es that Jackson should live out his
B-s straightaway in this world, the
nat Jackson is not responsible for B-ing
nad he done B straightaway in Michael's inde-
y should turn on such matters of cosmic luck
reciate the intuitive force of the incompati-
unding control requires freedom from con-
ns 7 and 8 below should further illuminate

natory route. I sketch an account of control
etermined initiators. The account will then,
to the compatibilist. However, the account
g undetermined initiators. So some incompati-
alue in the account as well. Before adumbrating
ve some final remarks to make regarding the sig-
lists might attach to Frankfurt-type cases.

FRANKFURT-TYPE CASES AND INCOMPATIBILISM

As I have suggested above, it is open to an advocate of the principle of alternative possibilities to insist that underlying the view of control this principle is meant to capture is the idea that *we* are the ultimate sources of our actions: to have the right sort of control for appraisability, it must be up to *us* to have the intentions and wills that we do have, and it must be up to *us* to initiate our choices or deliberations; we must, if we are to be appraisable for our actions, have the power to form our intentions or have the will that we want to have. Reflect, once again, on the restructured Frankfurt-type cases in which the triggering event is not an intentional doing of the agent, but something like a blush or a neuron firing. Perhaps, the advocate of alternative possibilities (or an incompatibilist) might concede, such Frankfurt-type cases may show that the agent does not have access to nonrobust alternative possibilities, but maintain, consistently with this conces-sion, that the cases do nothing whatsoever to undermine the view that the agent (in the actual sequence leading to action) fails to have the *power* to form a differ-ent intention, or have a different will than the intention she does form or the will she does have. And as such examples fail to undermine this view, they are really irrelevant to calling into question the underlying view of control expressed by the principle of alternative possibilities. To sharpen this incompatibilist's as-sessment of the relevance of Frankfurt-type cases to "incompatibilist control," dis-tinguish as Michael McKenna has proposed, between the having of a power and the exercising of that power.[11] McKenna claims that "What [Fischer's] amended [or restructured] counter-examples . . . show is that in the alternative sequence an agent might be precluded from exercising this kind of power [the power to have a different will or form a different intention], but it does not mean that, in the actual sequence, this kind of power was not possessed by her" (sec. 5). So maybe the incompatibilist will urge that it is possession of the pertinent power—

the power to form an intention or to have a will other the intention or will that gives rise to one's action, and not the exercising of that power that is fundamental to the incompatibilist's conception of control.

I believe, however, that Fischer's restructured Frankfurt examples do indeed show that the agent (in the actual sequence) fails even to have the power to form a different intention or have a different will. For consider the following principle about power possession:

> Power: If agent S has the power in circumstances A to C (or to not-C), then S can C (or not-C) in A.

Principle Power really says that there is no power whose manifestation is impossible; if one has the power to do something in certain circumstances, then one can in those circumstances do that thing. Suppose, in a restructured Frankfurt-type case, Jones C-s on her own, executing her intention to C. Since she did in fact C, she must have had the power to C, and as she formed an intention to C, she must have had the power to form that intention. But did Jones, in the restructured Frankfurt-type case, with the counterfactual intervener—Max—waiting in the wings, have the power to form the intention to not-C? It seems not, at least if Power is true: there are no circumstances in which Max is waiting in the wings, Max has the steadfast intention to intervene and cause Jones to C should the relevant triggering event (like a blush) come to pass, and Jones forms an intention to not-C. It is Max's ability to intervene, together with his unshakable conditional intention to do so, that renders Jones unable (in her circumstances) to form an intention to not-C.

McKenna proposes a response on behalf of the advocate of the principle of alternative possibilities (a libertarian in his case):

> How might the libertarian respond? She might demand clarification of what is involved in the circumstances mentioned in . . . [Power]. If circumstances A are fixed by the *actual scenario*, including any kinds of counter-factual factors, or overdetermining circumstances, then perhaps in . . . [Frankfurt-type cases, Power] shows that S does not exercise a power to intend to C or not-C. But if circumstances A in . . . [Power] are fixed, not by the actual scenario, but by the *actual sequence* which brought about S's . . . [C-ing], then in capturing the relevant kind of libertarian control to intend to C or not-C, the libertarian can reasonably argue that the counter-factual intervention would have to be factored out of the circumstances A relevant to . . . [Power]. . . . The libertarian insists at t-1 upon a power characterized as the power to intend to C or not-C. Now, *what* are the circumstances *at t-1*? The counter-factual mechanism is set up to reliably predict what will transpire at t without the aid of intervention. Should the mechanism predict that S will not-C at t, *then*, at t-2 the mechanism preempts the formation of the intention at t-1. But according to the libertarian, in the *actual* sequence, at t-1, S exercises a genuine power to intend to C or not-C. In the *actual* sequence, the counter-factual mechanism at t-1 is *not* operative. The fact that the only available outcome in the actual *scenario* is that S intend to C, does not mean that at t-1 in the *actual sequence* S did not have the power to C or not-C. For in the actual sequence, the fact that S chose to exercise that power at t-1 by intending to C at t, does not mean that at t-1, S could not have instead intended to not-C. If S does not *exercise* her power in a

certain way at t-1 this does not mean that she *lacks* the ability to do so. Thus, if the libertarian carefully specifies the circumstances in . . . [a Frankfurt-type case] in the actual sequence at t-1, she can argue that S does retain the power to intend to C or not-C. (sec. 6)

McKenna's point that, from the fact that a person fails to exercise her power to, let's say, not-C at a certain time, it does not follow that she does not then have the power, is trivially true; if I have a certain power, but fail to exercise it, I do have the power. We can grant the more substantial point that possibly, if S fails to C in circumstances A, it does follow from S's failure to C that S lacks the power to C in A. For example, I am now, in the circumstances in which I now find myself, not eating a banana, but I believe that I now (absent a "Banana Vener" waiting in the wings!) do have the power to eat a banana. But reconsider McKenna's claims that (1) the fact that the only available outcome in the actual *scenario* is that S intend to C, does not mean that at t-1 in the *actual sequence* S did not have the power to C or not-C; and (2) for in the actual sequence, the fact that S chose to exercise that power at t-1 by intending to C at t, does not mean that at t-1, S could not have instead intended to not-C. Claim 2 is puzzling as it *appears* merely to assume what is at issue, namely, that S at t-1 has the power to form an intention to not-C. So let's turn to 1. In 1, McKenna grants that the only available outcome in the actual *scenario* is that S intends to C. Now consider the actual *sequence* at time t-1, and ask whether at this time in the actual sequence—that is, whether at this time as things actually progressed— S (in the restructured Frankfurt-type case) had the power to form the intention to not-C, given principle Power and the presence of Max. Assume that the trigger mechanism is ultrasensitive keyed to something like a blush that predates the formation of intentions. Either S blushes or fails to at t-1. If S then blushes, then Max guarantees that S cannot then form the intention to not-C. Suppose S fails then to blush. Note, firstly, that it does not follow from S's failure to blush at t-1 that S then has the power to form an intention to not-C. Note, secondly, that given the presence of Max, and assuming that Max is an irresistible, infallible, and steadfast intender, there is no time *in the actual sequence* at which S can form the intention to not-C; and, furthermore, there is no time *in the actual sequence* at any possible world at which S can form the intention to not-C *if* Max (in those worlds) is waiting in the wings.

McKenna might object that in attempting to show that S does not, in the actual sequence, have the power to form the intention to not-C, counterfactual intervention has not been "factored out of the circumstances"; I have still appealed to Max's conditional intention to prevent S from forming the intention to not-C, and any such appeal is illegitimate. My response to this sort of objection is forthright: we require some cogent independent justification of why appeal to a counterfactual intervener is somehow nonproprietary in attempting to ascertain whether S has a certain power *in the actual sequence*. McKenna seems to recognize the need for such independent justification. He says:

> It is worth noting that there are many garden variety statements of power the analysis of which requires the elimination of extraneous variables. Take a case of overde-

termination. Suppose that my car quits running altogether and that my (trustworthy) auto mechanic learns that two factors simultaneously but independently caused the car's failure. One was that the fuel pump broke and the engine received no fuel. Another was that the electrical system burned out of the vehicle and it could not carry any charge to create a spark. Consider now the first causal explanation, that the fuel pump broke. For that explanation to show that the fuel pump was an independently sufficient cause of my car's failure, certain counterfactuals have to be true. Most notably, it has to be true that if the fuel pump had not failed, and *if there were no other conditions independently sufficient for my car's failure*, then the car would not have quit running. To show here that the failure of the fuel pump was causally sufficient in bringing about my car's failure, other causal conditions must be factored out of the counter-factuals relevant to ascertaining the truth of the causal claim under consideration. The libertarian can insist upon a similar treatment of the power relevant for ascriptions of responsibility. To understand this kind of power one must focus upon what transpires in the actual sequence of events, *not* in the actual scenario. For there are other causal variables in the actual scenario which might pollute a proper characterization of the power actually at work in the actual sequence. (sec. 6)

McKenna's principal point is this: just as, to determine whether failure of the fuel pump was causally sufficient in bringing about my car's failure, other causal conditions must be factored out of the counterfactuals relevant to ascertaining the truth of the causal claim under consideration, so the incompatibilist can insist that to determine whether S, in the actual sequence, has the power to form the intention to not-C, certain "causal conditions"—like the presence of Max—must be factored out of the counterfactuals relevant to ascertaining the truth of the "power-possession" claim under consideration. But this view of McKenna's is problematic for the following reasons. Assume that in order to determine whether the fuel pump was an independently sufficient cause of my car's failure, this counterfactual would have to be true:

CF1: If the fuel pump had not failed, and there were no other conditions independently sufficient for my car's failure, then the car would not have quit running.

What analogous counterfactual would have to be true to determine whether S in the actual sequence (in the restructured Frankfurt-type example) had the power (at t-1) to form the intention to not-C? McKenna, it appears, suggests the ensuing:

CF2: If S had preferred to not-C at t-1, and had no external conditions prevented S from doing so, then S would have formed the intention to not-C at t (where t is later than t-1).

But whereas the truth of CF1-type counterfactuals may well be relevant to ascertaining whether some event is an independently sufficient *cause* of another, CF2-type counterfactuals are *not* relevant to ascertaining whether some individual possesses some sort of power at or during a period of time. That this is so is easily confirmed by pondering such examples as these: Suppose I am chained to a post (at time t); as I am shackled I don't then have the power to flee. But a germane CF2-type counterfactual:

CF2*: If I had preferred to flee at t-1, and had no external conditions (such as the condition of being shackled to the post) prevented me from doing so, then I would have formed the intention to flee at t,

is true, thereby implying falsely that I have the power to flee when shackled!

It seems to me, then, that we have not been given sufficient reason to believe that an agent like Jones, in a restructured Frankfurt-type case, who successfully executes an intention to C (on her "own") has the power (in the actual sequence) to form an intention to not-C and to act on that intention.

8. ONE LAST ASSAULT ON FRANKFURT-TYPE CASES

Finally, let's examine David Widerker's "fresh look at Frankfurt's attack on PAP [the principle of alternative possibilities] from a libertarian viewpoint" (1995, p. 247). Widerker attempts to show that Frankfurt's attack "does not succeed when applied to mental acts such as deciding, choosing, undertaking, forming an intention, that is, mental acts that for the libertarian constitute the basic *loci* of moral responsibility" (1995, 247). Widerker begins by exposing a number of assumptions he employs in his assault on Frankfurt-type cases:

First, the version of libertarianism I intend to defend is the view that an agent's decision (choice) is free in the sense of freedom required for moral responsibility only if (i) it is not causally determined, and (ii) in the circumstances in which the agent made that decision (choice), he could have avoided making it. Second, I take 'a given act A' in PAP [a person is morally responsible for performing a given act A only if he could have acted otherwise] to refer to an action such that the agent was aware, at the time, that he was performing it (or was trying to perform it) and with regard to which he believed that he could have done otherwise. Third, I shall adopt a fine-grained account of action individuation, and shall thus treat 'A' in PAP as a variable for actions themselves, rather than actions under A-descriptions. (1995, pp. 247–48)

Next, Widerker summarizes a standard Frankfurt-type case and argues that it does not impugn PAP. The essentials of the case are these:

(1) If Jones is blushing at t1, then, provided no one intervenes, Jones will decide at t2 to kill Smith.

(2) If Jones is not blushing at t1, then, provided no one intervenes, he will not decide at t2 to kill Smith.

(3) If Black sees that Jones shows signs that he will not decide at t2 to kill Smith, that is, sees that Jones is *not* blushing at t1, then Black forces Jones to decide at t2 to kill Smith; but if he sees that he is blushing at t1, then he does nothing.

Finally, suppose that Black does not have to show his hand, because

(4) Jones is blushing at t1, and decides at t2 to kill Smith for reasons of his own. (1995, pp. 249–50)

The case is, of course, meant to show that Jones is responsible for making the decision to kill Black even though he could not (in his circumstances) have avoided making it. Widerker questions whether the case shows any such thing by scrutinizing 1. He says:

> Note that the truth of (1) cannot be grounded in the fact that Jones's blushing at t1 is, in the circumstances, causally sufficient for his decision to kill Smith, or in the fact that it is indicative of a state that is causally sufficient for that decision, since such an assumption would . . . [not be] accepted by the libertarian. On the other hand, if (1) is not thus grounded, then the following two options are available to the libertarian to resist the contention that Jones's decision to kill Smith is un-avoidable. He may either reject (1), claiming that the most that he would be pre-pared to allow is
>
> (1a) If Jones is blushing at t1, then Jones will *probably* decide at t2 to kill Smith. . . .
>
> But (1a) is compatible with Jones's having the power to decide not to kill Smith, since there is the possibility of Jones's acting out of character. Or the libertarian may construe (1) as a conditional of freedom in Plantinga's sense . . . that is, as
>
> (1b) If Jones is blushing at t1, then Jones will *freely* decide at t2 to kill Smith,
>
> in which case the libertarian may again claim that in the actual situation when Jones is blushing at t1, it is within his power to refrain from deciding to kill Smith at t2. (1995, p. 250)

As, barring its being causally determined, it is hard to see how Jones's decision is unavoidable, Widerker concludes that Frankfurt's attack on the principle of alternative possibilities as applied to decisions fails.

I believe, however, that Widerker's assault, though challenging, is not conclu-sive. To see this, it appears that the gist of Widerker's qualms regarding Frankfurt-type cases distills to this: consider the actual sequence of events in which Jones decides at t2 to kill Smith. Either Jones's blush is (infallibly) indicative of a state, JB, which is such that if it obtains, then Jones cannot refrain at t2 from deciding to kill Smith, or the blush is indicative of some state, JB*, which, if it obtains, leaves it open that Jones can decide at t2 to kill Smith. Unlike JB, JB* does not close off the possibility of Jones's reaching the decision not to kill Smith. Suppose, on the one hand, that Jones blushes, JB obtains, no one intervenes, and Jones decides at t2 to kill Smith. Then even apart from the counterfactual intervener, Black, Jones could not avoid deciding at t2 to kill Smith, and so Frankfurt's strategy is undermined: it is no longer the case that Jones could, in the absence of Black, have decided otherwise, and, hence, it is no longer the case that the libertarian need concede that were Black not on the scene, Jones would have been morally responsible for deciding at t2 to kill Smith. Suppose, on the other hand, that Jones blushes, JB* obtains, no one intervenes, and Jones decides at t2 to kill Smith. Then once again Frankfurt's strategy is undermined, for if Jones *is*, on this option, responsible for deciding to kill Smith, it is (assuming other condi-tions of responsibility are met) *because* he could have refrained at t2 from deciding to kill Smith. We can reasonably take Widerker to be issuing the following challenge. For a Frankfurt-type case to prove its point, that freedom to do otherwise is not the sort of control required for responsibility, design a case with these ingredients: (1) start with a scenario in which the counterfactual intervener of Frankfurt's variety is absent, Jones is responsible for the decision to kill Smith, and the actual pathway of events leading to Jones's reaching this decision allows for "libertarian freedom"; the pathway is so specified that the libertarian herself would concur that Jones freely decided at t2 to kill Smith. (2) Now add a counterfactual intervener like Black to this scenario so that it is in virtue of *this* addition, and *not* in virtue of any alteration in the "libertarian pathway" of events culminating with Jones's decision to kill Smith, that it is no longer the case that Jones could have refrained from arriving at this decision.

I'll accept the gauntlet. Drawing on Mele's suggestions (1995, p. 216), suppose Jones is at an indeterministic world at which he decides on his own at t2 to kill Smith. He arrives at this decision, in part, on the basis of a decisive best judgment he makes. Assume that, at the onset of his musings, it is causally undetermined whether various considerations will come to his mind and enter into his deliberations about his decision to kill Smith. It is, then, at the inception of his deliberation, causally open whether Jones will make the pertinent best judgment and, subsequently, the decision to kill Smith. With this specification of the actual sequence pathway, a libertarian (or more cautiously, a libertarian of a certain sort) should find the judgment that Jones *is* responsible for his decision at t2 to kill Smith congenial, as the indeterminism in the pathway leading to this decision allows for its being the case that Jones could have decided otherwise. Ingredient 1 is, therefore, in the dish. Now for the cream. Add a Frankfurt-type counterfactual intervener, Black, to the scenario, and assume that Black intervenes if and only if he believes that Jones will not make the decisive best judgment that favors the decision to kill Smith which he, Black, wants Jones to make. Specifically, should Jones make the judgment that he ought not to kill Smith, *then* (and only then) will Black intervene and cause Jones to alter the judgment. The presence of Black ensures that Jones could not have decided otherwise. This is because there is no scenario in which Black (who is an infallible predictor of Jones's decisions and whose intentions cannot be thwarted, and who is steadfast in his intentions to ensure that Jones decides to kill Smith) is all the while waiting in the wings and Jones decides otherwise than he actually does. Assume, finally, that there is no need for Black to intervene as Jones decides appropriately on his own. Now if Jones is an indeterministic initiator in the initial scenario in which Black is absent, he should also be one in the second scenario with Black on the scene, and consequently, if he is responsible for his decision in the first, he should also be responsible for his decision in the second.

A libertarian might rejoin that even in the initial scenario with Black not on the scene, at best Jones is responsible for his decisive best judgment, as this is something he could have avoided making, but he is not responsible for the decision to kill Smith if, having made the decisive best judgment, it was unavoidable for him to decide as he did. It is, however, unclear on what grounds we should believe this is correct, unless covert appeal is being made to a principle of this sort: an agent freely decides on something at a time only if, at the time, the agent could have made some alternative decision. But this principle is implausibly strong: I may freely swallow the magical potion, knowing fully that, having done so, I won't be able to refrain from deciding to kill Smith; and yet if I do take the potion, I will be appraisable for the decision.

A libertarian may still not capitulate and may insist that the very intuition (if one has it) that Jones is morally responsible for making the decision to kill Smith, in the Frankfurt-type case in which Jones is an indeterministic initiator, overtly or surreptitiously relies on, or is overtly or surreptitiously grounded in the view that Jones's decision (in the case) is *not* causally determined; the indeterminism at the right juncture in the causal pathway leading to Jones's decision allows for Jones's having more than one physically possible future in a way that depends crucially on *Jones's* mental doings. Hence, the indeterminism guarantees that agency is back in the picture, as with such indeterminism, it appears that there is an explanation of why the agent decided (or acted) as she did that *cannot* be fully captured merely by appealing to past conditions of the world and the laws of nature. And, further, this is why, it might be urged, the case begs the question against the libertarian. The charge would be that the Frankfurtian is attempting to refute a version of libertarianism by critical reliance on an intuition (that Jones is responsible for his decision) which is itself "grounded on" libertarian considerations. *This*, it might be claimed, is nonproprietary.

I believe, though, that the relevant intuition *need* not be so grounded. First, as I explained above, it is not transparent how indeterministic gaps, at theoretically strategic junctures, help put agents back in the driver's seat. Second, the crucial factor that "informs" our intuition regarding Jones's being responsible for his decision may well be that the *relevant causal sequence is free of what we would intuitively take to be responsibility-undermining factors*: Jones is a good deliberator, he acts for reasons in the absence of ignorance, he is not being manipulated or coerced, his actional springs are "his own," etc. It is true that in the indeterministic world Jones's decision is not causally determined, and Jones does, in this world, have the power to decide otherwise. But this power appears to play no role at all in the actual pathway of events that ends with Jones's decision; the power is simply not "acted upon" or executed. One wonders how mere possession of such a power, even when it fails to "come into play" in the actual pathway of events could explain why Jones (in this world) is *in control*, but why Jones, were he at a determined world at which he lacked this power, would not be. Notice the following. In the indeterministic world, assume that at the time of deciding to kill Smith, Jones also has the power to celebrate the impending murder by going to the movies in the evening. It would be an error (to say the least) to appeal to this power to explain why Jones is morally responsible for his decision to kill Smith, as the power plays no role in the etiology of that decision. Similarly, although Jones in the indeterministic world has the power to decide not to kill Smith, this power, like the power of deciding to go to the movies, seems irrelevant to an explanation of why he is morally responsible for his deadly decision. Jones acts for reasons, and there is a reasons-explanation of why he decided as he did that need not invoke the power, for instance, to form a different decisive best judgment than the one formed.

The *deep* moral of Frankfurt-type cases, I suggest, is simply that appraisability depends on what occurs in the actual sequence of events. There are a plethora of mundane cases in which some agent performs some action, A, is appraisable for doing A, has (let's simply assume) the ability to do other than A, but in which this ability plays no role in the actual pathway of events that generates A. The ability to do otherwise, then, seems superfluous to an account of why the agent is appraisable for A-ing. Similarly, one might add that being an indeterministic initiator may not contribute significantly to an account of appraisability, unless it can be shown that indeterministic initiators have an element of control pivotal to appraisability that "deterministic agents" lack.

Should one still insist that the intuition that Jones is responsible for his deadly decision in the Frankfurt-type case does rest on one feature of the relevant actual sequence in the indeterministic world, namely, that in that sequence, Jones did have the power to avoid making the deadly decision, the Frankfurtian might counter with this suggestion: Why couldn't the intuition equally rest on the view that Jones *believes* that he has the power to avoid making the decision that he does make?

"Look," the libertarian might say trying yet again, "on the former description of the Frankfurt case, it appears that it is causally open which best judgment Jones will make. Whichever he makes, assume that intervening between this judgment and the final decision is some actional element like Kane's effort of will. Black (in the former description of the story), unable to predict which judgment Jones will make, monitors the judgment actually made, and then, should the need arise, intervenes and alters this judgment. Consider, though, this redescription of the case. Suppose Jones's final decision is *immediately* preceded by, perhaps, an *indeterminate* effort of will (or some indeterminate actional element) so that it is undetermined which decision—either the one to kill Smith or to forbear—Jones will make until one or the other of them actually has been made. As the indeterminate element immediately precedes the decision, counterfactual intervener Black *cannot* predetermine which decision Jones will make; Black will just have to wait and see, not having any cue for 'Frankfurt-type intervention.' But then if Jones, exerting the appropriate effort, does decide to kill Smith, he would have done so on 'his own': he would have been able to decide otherwise, and hence *he* would have been appraisable for killing Smith. If Black could somehow disrupt the indeterminacy or its effects prior to Jones's deciding one way or the other, Black could ensure that Jones decides to kill Smith, but in this case, Black and not Jones would be responsible for the decision. Either way, Frankfurt's case is undermined."

This rendition of the "no cue for intervention" objection is surmountable. If the indeterminate effort of will leads to the undetermined decision, there can, in principle, be intermediaries (such as, for instance, neurophysiological changes) that can serve as appropriate signals for intervention on the part of Black. Nevertheless, the crux of Widerker's problem now crystallizes. Suppose the *making of the decision itself*, Widerker might stress, is indeterminate. Given identical (or near identical) pasts and identical laws, Jones could have decided one way or the other. Correct prediction is in principle, under these circumstances, not possible. How then, it might be challenged, can a Frankfurt-type case be constructed to show that Jones is responsible for making the decision to kill Smith even though he could not have decided otherwise?

This is indeed a formidable challenge and in the end, *perhaps,* it cannot be met. Still, the Frankfurtian need not admit defeat. For one thing, we have already seen that if indeterminacy occurs far enough back in the causal pathway terminating in an action, like Jones's killing Smith, then Frankfurt examples do show that Jones can be to blame for killing Smith, or for making the decision to kill Smith, even though Jones could not have refrained from killing Smith or making a decision other than the one he in fact made. (If there are indeterministic breaks, *where* they actually occur is a contingent matter. For creatures like us, they may well occur at the juncture of decision-making; in some other possible world populated with humanoids capable of intentional action, the breaks may occur at the point of decisive best judgment.) This already gives us significant reason to believe that freedom to do (or decide) otherwise is not *required* for responsibility (though, having such freedom need not undermine responsibility). For another thing, indeterminists like Kane theorize that when agents are morally responsible for what they do, they have freedom to do otherwise since at least some of their actional elements like decisions, being the outcomes of indeterminate events, are undetermined. Other indeterminists, though, like Randolph Clarke (1993) and Timothy O'Connor (1993), believe that *agent-causation* is required to explain the control agents have over their free actions: they alone produce the undetermined outcome that occurs. Consider, now, this thought experiment. Suppose free actions (in the sense of 'free' required for responsibility), though not determined by antecedent circumstances (i.e, though not event-determined), are *agent-*determined or agent-caused. Suppose that in cases in which an agent faces an inner conflict between duty and temptation, there is a systematic correlation between agent-causing the decision to act on duty and certain changes in the brain, and likewise between the decision to thwart duty and neuron firings, which can be detected *prior* to the actual decision's being made. (Another possibility is that when a person agent-causes a decision to do something, that decision *is* also event-caused by other events. This sort of two-fold causation is not manifestly incoherent. If it did occur, of course, an agent would not be free to decide otherwise.) So although such decisions would be agent-caused, one would be able to arrive at highly reliable predictions about which decision the agent would actually make. Then Frankfurt-type examples could, it seems, be constructed to show that though an individual agent-causes a decision of hers, and hence is responsible for it, she could not, for all rhyme and reason, have decided otherwise. Imagine that if the counterfactual intervener detects brain activity correlated with the agent's making the decision not congenial to the intervener, the intervener intervenes in the brain thereby determining the outcome he wants. The moral of this thought experiment is simple: possibly, if agents on occasion have freedom to do otherwise, they have such freedom for reasons *other than* indeterminacy of Kane's variety. John Earman (1986) has argued that even the laws of classical Newtonian worlds in which all physical properties are determinate allow for the possibility of different (determinate) futures given the same (determinate) pasts. This opens the door for "counterfactual intervention" as "real" freedom to do otherwise would not, it appears, be a barrier against the existence of suitable cues for counterfactual intervention in the actual sequence of events leading to action, and the making of correct predictions. If this is true, then appropriately constructed Frankfurt-type cases would suggest that freedom to do otherwise is not required for responsibility. Finally, suppose the incompatibilist differentiates various sorts of freedom or control, one type—"indeterminist freedom"—involving indeterminist breaks at strategic junctures in the pathway to action, and others—"compatibilist" ones—not involving such breaks, and then claims that (i) indeterminist freedom is a sort of freedom many of us believe is both well worth wanting and better than compatibilist varieties; and (ii) *hence,* that indeterminist freedom is the kind of freedom required for responsibility. The Frankfurtian can accept i but not ii as ii simply fails to follow from i. The Frankfurtian can go further and even concede i*: indeterminist freedom is not just believed to be better than all compatibilist varieties but is in fact "objectively" better; it is more valued by some *and* it is more *valuable.* Still, ii is not entailed by i*, as is strongly evidenced by pairs of cases, like those considered above, that are analogous save that in one the agent does A in a determined world, and in the other does A in a world in which A issues from a decision or intention that is not causally determined. In either, it seems, the agent is appraisable for doing A. In general, one can concede that it may well be true that it is "objectively" better to have two-way control over A-ing in the sense that given the same or near same past and identical laws of nature, one can A and one can refrain from A-ing, without conceding that in the absence of such two-way control, one cannot be appraisable for A-ing. Perhaps what in the end deeply divide compatibilists and incompatibilists are value judgments about which sort of control—compatibilist or incompatibilist—is better or more worth having. But this is an issue distinct from the metaphysical one of which type of control is required for moral appraisability.

In sum, it appears that Widerker's fresh attack need not foreshadow calamity for the Frankfurtian.

9. CONCLUSION

Appraisability requires control, but as Frankfurt-type examples powerfully suggest, the right type of control does not necessitate the availability of genuine alternative possibilities. Hence, even if causal determinism is incompatible with freedom to do otherwise, it cannot in virtue of *this* incompatibility, subvert moral appraisability. Incompatibilists like Pereboom propose that causal determinism undermines appraisability because it entails that one's actions are the result of causal factors operative even long before one's birth, and that if an action results from a deterministic causal process that traces back to factors beyond one's control, one is not morally appraisable for that action. I have argued, however, that Pereboom's efforts to sustain his account of why causal determinism subverts responsibility is, to say the least, controversial. The discussion on Pereboom lends credibility to the following. Imagine an agent like Green, otherwise very much like ordinary persons, who is the creation of an incredibly bright and ambitious set of neuroscientists. Green is endowed with a personality and character, and a rich psychological, cognitive, and emotional life. Despite his unusual origin, we can easily distinguish cases in which, at least intuitively, Green bears moral appraisability for his behavior and those in which he does not. For example, if local manipulation resulted in equipping Green with an irresistible desire to kill Peacock, Green would not be morally appraisable for the killing. But if Green were to have arrived "on his own" at a decision to kill Peacock, and were to have acted on this decision, we would intuitively believe that he shouldered moral appraisability for the killing. Speaking somewhat metaphorically, Green's case suggests that it is a mistake to suppose that only a self that lies outside the causal nexus of physically determined events—a noumenal self—can be an appropriate candidate for moral appraisability. Moreover, it is a mistake to suppose that only actions not produced by processes beyond our causal control are ones for which we can be appraisable.

We are confronted, then, with the task of giving an account of the right sort of control required for moral appraisability. I shall produce an outline of such an account shortly. Prior to doing that, I want to generate a perplexity. Suppose causal determinism is indeed incompatible with freedom to do otherwise. Then though determinism will not, in virtue of this supposition, subvert appraisability, it may paradoxically subvert the very foundations of morality. This perplexity is the topic of the next chapter.

T H R E E

MORAL OBLIGATION AND
ALTERNATIVE POSSIBILITIES

Possibly, causal determinism rules out alternative possibilities; if determinism is true, then perhaps no person can do anything other than what he actually does. This implication of determinism, however, need not threaten appraisability *insofar* as the implication is meant to undermine *control*—the sort constituted by freedom to do otherwise. As we saw in the last chapter, Frankfurt-type examples help alleviate the worry that causal determinism subverts moral appraisability *by* ruling out alternative possibilities. These fascinating examples go a long way toward suggesting that the control required for moral appraisability does not entail the existence of genuine options. There is, nevertheless, an intriguing view in the literature according to which appraisability for a certain class of actions does re-quire alternative possibilities. Susan Wolf has recently argued that right and wrong actions are asymmetric with respect to the requirement of alternative possi-bilities for moral responsibility: whereas one can be responsible for a right action that one could not have avoided performing, one cannot be morally responsible (or appraisable) for a wrong action that one could not have avoided performing (Wolf 1990).

In this chapter, I argue that one-half of Wolf's asymmetry thesis—the half that says that one cannot be morally responsible for a wrong action that one could not have avoided—may well be correct but *not* for the reasons advanced by Wolf. I show that if certain principles of moral obligation are true, then wrong actions require alternative possibilities. That is, these principles of moral obligation entail that no person can perform an action at a time which is *wrong* unless she could have done something other than that action at that time. Hence, no person can be *morally responsible* for performing an action at a time which is wrong, unless she could have done otherwise. It follows that if these principles of moral obligation are true, and they imply that there is a requirement of alternative possibilities for wrong actions, then causal determinism, in virtue of ruling out alternative possibilities, may well threaten the foundations of morality.

1. WOLF'S ASYMMETRY THESIS

Wolf motivates the asymmetry thesis, partly, by contrasting examples of seemingly right and wrong (or good and bad) actions that are unavoidable. Regarding the first half of the thesis, in one of the examples, a woman on an uncrowded beach sees a young boy struggling in the water in obvious need of aid. Thinking that the boy requires her help, she immediately swims to his rescue. Wolf assumes that it is literally impossible for the woman to refrain from saving the child "because her understanding of the situation is so good and her moral commitment so strong" (1990, p. 82). For a woman with her moral character, leaving the child to drown is either "unthinkable" or simply not a thought that can be taken seriously (1990, p. 59).[1] Wolf concludes that even though the woman is not free to do otherwise, she is praiseworthy (and so appraisable and responsible) for saving the child. Wolf defends the second half of the asymmetry thesis by adducing a range of cases involving kleptomania, drug addiction, hypnosis, and deprived childhoods in which agents are apparently not appraisable for performing seemingly wrong (or bad) actions even though they could not have done otherwise. Wolf claims that the judgment that they are not appraisable derives from the fact that the agents could not do the right thing for the right reasons. Consider, for instance, a kleptomaniac who recognizes reasons not to steal but cannot act in accord with these reasons because of her irresistible urges to shoplift. According to Wolf, it would be inappropriate to hold such a person blameworthy for her acts of shoplifting.[2]

These types of examples lead Wolf to the conclusion that the freedom requirement for moral responsibility is asymmetrical. She summarizes her "Reason View" of moral responsibility in this way:

> According to the Reason View, . . . responsibility depends on the ability to act in accordance with the True and the Good. If one is psychologically determined to do the right thing for the right reasons, this is compatible with having the requisite ability. . . . But if one is psychologically determined to do the wrong thing, for whatever reason, this seems to constitute a denial of that ability. For if one *has* to do the wrong thing, then one *cannot* do the right thing, and so one lacks the ability to act in accordance with the True and the Good. The Reason View is thus committed to the curious claim that being psychologically determined to perform good actions is compatible with deserving praise for them, but being psychologically determined to perform bad actions is not compatible with deserving blame. (1990, p. 79)

2. EVALUATION OF THE ASYMMETRY THESIS

Wolf's discussion of the asymmetry thesis conflates the distinction between good acts and right acts, and bad (or evil) acts and wrong acts. Let's say that an act is *overall bad* if and only if, were it performed, it would produce more intrinsic evil than intrinsic goodness. Similarly, an act is *overall good* just in case its performance would produce more intrinsic goodness than intrinsic evil. It seems perfectly possible for an agent to be in a situation in which all her options are overall bad. Still, allowing for even modest consequentialist considerations, it is not unreasonable to assume that of these options, the one that is least overall evil, is the one the agent ought morally to do. So let's distinguish two versions of the asymmetry thesis:

> AST1: To be morally responsible for overall bad (or evil) actions, one must be able to do otherwise, but this ability is not required to be responsible for overall good actions.

> AST2: To be morally responsible for wrong actions, one must be able to do otherwise, but this ability is not required to be responsible for right actions.

Addressing AST1 first, John Fischer and Mark Ravizza have effectively argued against the first half of this thesis. They develop a Frankfurt-type case ("Villain") in which a vile character, Joe, is appraisable for performing a bad action although he could not have done otherwise. Joe decides (for his own perverse reasons) to push a child off a pier for the purpose of causing her to drown in the violent surf. Had Joe shown any sign of not acting on his decision to kill the child, a device in his brain would have caused him to acquire the decision and to act on it. But Joe acts on his own, independently of any interference from the device. In this sort of case, it is sensible to suppose that Joe is deserving of blame, and hence is morally responsible, for performing an overall bad action even though Joe could not have done otherwise. Fischer and Ravizza conclude that Wolf's asymmetry thesis (assuming that that thesis is AST1) is false; good and bad actions are symmetric with regard to the lack of a requirement of alternative possibilities for moral responsibility (Fischer and Ravizza 1992a; see also Fischer and Ravizza, 1992c).

What about AST2? It might reasonably be supposed that Villain also calls into question the first half of AST2. After all, Joe's gruesome deed seems to be paradigmatically wrong, and it appears evident that he is deserving of blame for performing it. Despite these initial considerations, it is not so obvious that AST2 is false. In fact, one type of utilitarian would agree that Joe's act of pushing the child off the pier is overall bad, but deny that his act is wrong *if* he could not have done otherwise. Indeed, according to this type of utilitarian, there is a requirement of alternative possibilities for wrong actions. The ensuing discussion will motivate the important point that whether there is a fully general requirement of alternative possibilities for moral appraisability for actions, no matter what the normative status of an act—no matter, for instance, whether it is wrong or obligatory—turns crucially upon what sort of normative ethical theory is true.

3. A UTILITARIAN'S ASSESSMENT OF ASYMMETRY THESIS 2

The cases Wolf advances in support of the first half of AST2, like Villain, are supposed to be ones in which some agent performs (what is meant to be a wrong action) that the agent could not have avoided performing. Can there be such an action? If a case is a correctly described *Frankfurt-type* case, then it appears that the relevant agent in the case cannot intentionally avoid performing the action that he in fact performs. But can such an action be wrong? Let's consider a utilitarian reply.

Act utilitarianism is an ethical theory that purports to tell us what makes right acts right, wrong acts wrong, and obligatory acts obligatory; it attempts to specify necessary and sufficient conditions for the rightness, wrongness, and obligatoriness of acts. To state the theory succinctly, we introduce the notion of the utility of an act. An act's utility is the difference between the total amount of intrinsic good it would produce (if performed) and the total amount of intrinsic evil it would produce (if performed). Traditionally, utilitarianism has been associated with the axiological view that the sole intrinsic good is pleasure and the sole intrinsic evil is pain.[3] The argument to be developed below is neutral among axiologies. Consider, now, as a typical act utilitarian theory, the following:

> AU: Of all the alternatives open to an agent, S, at a time, t, as of t, it is morally obligatory for S to do A if and only if, as of t, the utility of S's doing A is higher than the utility of S's doing any other alternative.

Associated with AU are the standard principles about right and wrong: an act is wrong if and only if it is not right; and an act is right if and only if its utility is at least as high as that of any alternative. The underlying idea of the theory is simple and compelling: obligatory acts, roughly, are those that bring about the greatest balance of intrinsic goodness over intrinsic badness; they are acts that make the world best off.

AU appeals to the notion of an act's alternatives. It turns out that the concept of alternatives is notoriously difficult to explicate. In what is to come, I presuppose the following which I take to be unproblematic: acts are alternatives for an agent at a time only if each is performable by that agent at that time.[4]

It is now fairly straightforward to see that if AU is true, then an action to which there are no alternative possibilities is not wrong. Suppose agent S does act A of necessity; that is, suppose S does A as a result of S's own intention to do A, but S cannot intentionally avoid doing A. In Villain, for instance, Joe pushes the child into the water of necessity. Since A is the only alternative open to S, by default the utility of S's doing A is higher than that of any of S's "alternatives," and AU consequently implies that it is obligatory for S to do A.[5] Hence, if AU is true, it is impossible for an action to which there are no alternatives to be wrong; it is thus, if AU is true, impossible for an agent to be morally appraisable (or responsible) for performing a wrong action to which there are no alternative possibilities. It then follows that if AU is true, the first half of asymmetry thesis AST2 is correct.

Versions of consequentialism more sophisticated than AU yield similar results. Consider, for example, Fred Feldman's theory.[6] The theory builds on the idea that at each moment or time of moral choice, there are several possible worlds accessible to a person as of that time: there are, at the time, various ways in which a person might live out her life; for each of these complete "life histories," there is a possible world—the one that would exist if she were to live out her life in that way. Roughly, a possible world is accessible to a person at a time if and only if it is still possible, at that time, for the person to see to the occurrence of that world. A world may be accessible to a person at a time, but once the person behaves in some way other than the way in which he behaves in that world, it is no longer accessible; it has been "bypassed." Once bypassed, a world never again becomes accessible. As a person moves through life, she inexorably pares down the stock of worlds accessible to her.

Making use of the notion of accessibility, one can say that a state of affairs is possible for a person as of a time if and only if it occurs in some world still accessible to the person at that time. Let 'Ks,t,p' abbreviate 'there is a world accessible to s as of t in which state of affairs p occurs.' 'Ks,t,p' is equivalent to 'as of t, s can still see to the occurrence of p'. 'Ks,t,p', it should be cautioned, does not mean 'as of t, s can still *make* p occur'. If p happened in the past, or is a necessary truth, or is otherwise out of my control, then it occurs in every world now accessible to me, but I cannot now "make p happen." No matter what I do, p will occur (or has occurred).

Corresponding to the 'K' operator, which is a sort of possibility operator, is a 'U' operator, which is a sort of necessity (or "unalterability") operator. 'Us,t,p' abbreviates 'p occurs in every world accessible to s at t'. Thus, if p is a "hard fact" about the past, or if p will occur no matter what I do, or if p is a metaphysical or physical necessity, p is unalterable for me now.

On Feldman's theory, actions are morally judged not by appeal to the value of their outcomes, but by appeal to the values of the accessible possible worlds in which they are performed. Worlds may be ranked in accordance to a value-relation; each world is as good as, or better than, or worse than, each other world. A world is best if no world is better than it is. Again, for purposes of "value-wise" ranking worlds, one can supply one's favorite axiology. The theory can now be stated in this way:

> MO: A person, s, ought, as of t, to see to the occurrence of a state of affairs, p, if and only if p occurs in all the intrinsically best worlds accessible to s as of t.[7]

Let 'Os,t,p' abbreviate 'p occurs in all the intrinsically best worlds accessible to s at t'. MO validates a version of the Kantian principle that 'ought' implies 'can' as Os,t,p entails Ks,t,p. Strikingly, it also turns out that unalterability implies obligation. That is, this is also true if MO is true:

> UO: Us,t,p entails O,s,t,p. (Feldman 1986, p. 43)

UO says, roughly, that if something is unavoidable for an agent as of a time, then it is obligatory for that agent as of that time. In a Frankfurt-type case like Villain, it is unavoidable for Joe that he push the child off the pier. So UO entails that it is obligatory for Joe that he push the child off the pier. Hence, if MO is true, we can once again derive the result that it is not possible for an action which an agent could not avoid performing to be wrong; so it is not possible for an agent to be morally appraisable (or responsible) for performing a *wrong* action to which there are no alternatives. If true, then, MO secures the first half of asymmetry thesis AST2.

To assess better the implications of AU or MO for a requirement of alternative possibilities for moral responsibility for wrong actions, I now turn to possible objections to the utilitarian's affirmation of the first half of asymmetry thesis AST2, and possible replies to these objections. In discussing these objections and replies, the utilitarian's position will be more fully appreciated.

4. OBJECTIONS TO THE UTILITARIAN'S STANCE AND POSSIBLE REPLIES

Objection 1

If AU is true, then it is obligatory for Joe to push the child off the pier. But surely any theory with this sort of consequence must be false. After all, Joe acts just as he would have had he been able to avoid pushing the child off the pier. How can the *mere* lack of alternatives "transform" a wrong act into an obligatory one?

At least two possible replies are available to the defender of AU. First, the utilitarian might insist that there is a morally relevant difference between a case in which Joe pushes the child off the pier of necessity, and one in which Joe could have avoided pushing the child off the pier. There are no alternative possibilities in the first case, but there are some in the second. As there are no alternatives open to Joe in the first case, one should accept the consequence of AU that Joe's performing the unavoidable action of pushing the child off the pier is obligatory.

Second, the defender of AU might modify AU so that it does not have the result that Joe's pushing the child off the pier is obligatory. The theory can be amended in this way:

> AU*: As of t, it is morally obligatory for S to do A if and only if, as of t, S can do A, and, as of t, S can do other than A, and, as of t, the utility of S's doing A is higher than the utility of S's doing other than A.

If we include the second conjunct in the standard principles of right and wrong associated with AU*, then AU*, in conjunction with its associated principles, has the consequence that when S does A of necessity, S's doing A is neither right nor wrong nor obligatory. We can say, in this sort of case, that it is gratuitous for S to do A. Two features of AU* merit particular attention. First, AU* is diverse from AU: the two theories imply different things about the normative status of any act performed of necessity. Second, even if AU* and not AU is true, there can be no *wrong* act that an agent performs of necessity for which that agent is morally appraisable (or responsible); at best, there can be a gratuitous act that an agent performs of necessity for which the agent is appraisable (or responsible). Indeed, Joe's devious act in Villain is just an act of this sort.

Suppose, because of possible problems with the traditional variety of utilitarianism, one moves from an act utilitarian theory to a "world utilitarian" one of Feldman's variety. Feldman indicates that should one find UO unacceptable, one could introduce a new obligation operator, 'O*,' defined in this way: 'O*s,t,p' is true if and only if p does not occur in all the worlds accessible to s as of t, but p does occur in all the best of these worlds (Feldman 1986, p. 43). 'O*s,t,p', then, means the same as 'O,s,t,p and Ks,t,not-p'. This sort of moral obligation entails 'can avoid'.

Objection 2

A second objection is suggested by Peter van Inwagen's defense of the following principle, which he calls "the principle of possible prevention,"

> PPP1: A person is morally responsible for a particular event only if he could have prevented it.

The principle of possible prevention has obvious similarities to the principle of alternative possibilities (see van Inwagen 1983, 1978), and I believe, it expresses the view that a person is morally responsible for a particular event only if he could have brought about a different particular event. Van Inwagen accepts this principle of event individuation:

> E: x is the same particular event as y if and only if x and y have the same causes.

If one accepts E, then one might well deny that Frankfurt-type examples undermine PPP1, for in cases such as Villain it might be argued, there *are* alternative possibilities open to the agent. The objector might insist that Joe is responsible for the particular act of pushing the child off the pier because it *is* an act to which there were alternatives: had he shown signs of doing otherwise, Joe would still have pushed the child off the pier, but his pushing the child off the pier would have been a *different* act (or event) from the one actually performed, because it would have had different causes. The objector may concede that the "event universal" that is Joe's pushing the child off the pier is one to which there are no alternative possibilities and so one for which Joe is *not* morally responsible: had Joe pushed the child off the pier on his own, or had he pushed the child off the pier as a result of electronic stimulation of his brain, one and the same event universal—Joe's pushing the child off the pier—would have obtained. Think of event universals as kinds of states of affairs that can be "realized" in various different ways; these sorts of states of affairs can be correctly described and can be "brought about" by different persons, or by the same person, on different occasions in different ways. If I take the high road to Rome and you take the low road, each one of us brings about the same event universal that is some person's taking some road to Rome. But I bring about an event *particular* that is different from the one that you bring about. So the advocate of the principle of possible prevention might say that Joe could have brought about a different event than the event particular of Joe's pushing the child off the pier on his own. Since there are genuine alternative possibilities in Villain, if we assume that actions are events,

(AU) does not imply that the act of Joe's pushing the child off the pier is obligatory. Nor is it the case that AU* implies that Joe's act is gratuitous.[8]

The act utilitarian, however, has a reply to the objector's charge that it is false both that if AU is true, then Joe's pushing the child off the pier is obligatory, and that if AU* is true, Joe's pushing the child off the pier is gratuitous. Even if we accept van Inwagen's controversial principle of event individuation, the utilitarian can deny that when Max intervenes and directly manipulates Joe's brain, Joe's resulting action constitutes an alternative in the relevant right sense of 'alternative'.[9] For an action, A, a utilitarian might insist, is an alternative for some agent, S, only if were S to do A, A would issue from S's own volition (an intention or decision) to do A, and not from a volition that would in a clear sense *not* be S's own. When Joe kills the child as a result of activation by Max of the device in his brain, Joe acts (if he acts at all) on an "external" volition that is not his.

But this response may not satisfy the objector, for she might simply insist that Max's device can be used to instill a volition in Joe which Joe then executes. Such a volition *would* be Joe's *own*. This rejoinder, in turn, though, should not satisfy the utilitarian. The utilitarian can, it seems, plausibly suggest that such an implanted volition would *not* qualify as Joe's own since, roughly, Joe did not *autonomously* acquire this volition. The sense of 'autonomy' here is left unspecified, but at least intuitively, Joe is not autonomous with respect to the acquisition of the implanted volition. In addition, the utilitarian might insist on the following. Taking Fischer's cue, reconstruct Villain so that the "trigger mechanism" is not any intentional doing of Joe—it isn't a volition or action. It might simply be the firing of a neuron that predates the germane intentional doing, or perhaps even a blush systematically correlated with Joe's possible inclination not to push the child off the pier. If this sort of trigger mechanism were to set off Max's device, as a result of which Joe would push the child off the pier, Joe's pushing the child off the pier would clearly be a different event particular than would be the event particular that is Joe's pushing the child off the pier on his own. But now, the utilitarian might query, how could *this* sort of "alternative," the one that would result from the activation of the ultra sensitive trigger, possibly qualify as a *genuine alternative*—as an event particular that *Joe could have brought about*, and for which he would have been appraisable had he in fact brought it about? This sort of alternative *is* a different event particular than the one that obtains in the actual sequence; still, it is hard to believe that it is an event particular over which Joe would have exercised the right sort of control, whatever it precisely amounts to, for moral appraisability. Furthermore, the utilitarian might insist, the advocate of PPP1 who associates appraisability (or responsibility) with alternative possibilities presumably construes PPP1 as stating that a person is morally appraisable (or responsible) for a certain event particular only if he could have brought about an event particular of a different type which is such that in bringing about that event particular, he would exercise the right sort of control needed for moral appraisability or responsibility (again, whatever it precisely amounts to) over that event particular (see Fischer 1982, p. 32; 1986, p. 54). After all, PPP1 is meant to be a principle that captures some insight about *control*. It would be remarkable to suppose that it captures any such insight on the interpretation that a person is appraisable (or responsible) for an event particular only if he could have brought about an alternative—an event particular of a different type—even if this alternative were of the sort that resulted from activation of an ultra sensitive trigger, or an alternative that the person is compelled to bring about, or more generally, an alternative which is such that there are clear responsibility-undermining factors in its etiology.

Finally, the advocate of AU or AU* has one more card to play. Suppose one were to grant that there are two distinct event particulars that Joe could bring about, the event particular that is Joe's pushing the child off the pier on his own (call it "E1") and the event particular that is Joe's pushing the child off the pier as a result of electronic stimulation of his brain (call it "E2"). Still, it is not at all clear whether the utility of E2 exceeds that of E1, and so it is not at all clear whether Joe's bringing about E1 is wrong. Hence, Villain and the cases used by Wolf to support the first half of asymmetry thesis AST2 are not transparently ones in which some agent performs an action that is wrong.

Available to the world utilitarian is a different sort of reply. MO validates the following principle about doing the causal or logical consequences of what one ought to do. If an agent, s, cannot see to the occurrence of p without seeing to the occurrence of q, then q will be obligatory for s if p is. That is, letting $p \to q$ to be the material conditional, this principle is true if MO is true:

MO/MO: $(Os,t,p$ and $Us,t,(p \to q))$ entails Os,t,q. (Feldman 1986, pp. 41–42)

Suppose it is obligatory that Joe pushes the child off the pier on his own. Then, given MO/MO, the state of affairs *Joe pushes the child off the pier* is obligatory as this state of affairs is entailed by the state of affairs *Joe pushes the child off the pier on his own*. For similar reasons, if it is obligatory that Joe pushes the child off the pier as a result of electronic stimulation, then according to MO it is also obligatory that Joe pushes the child off the pier. Hence, if MO is true, the event particular/event universal distinction won't have any bearing on the judgment that Joe ought to see to the occurrence of pushing the child off the pier in Villain.

Objection 3

The Kantian thesis,

> K: S has a moral obligation to perform [not to perform] A only if it is within S's power to perform [not to perform] A,

is true.[10] But so is the following principle, which connects wrongness with ability:

> W: It is morally wrong for S to perform [not to perform] A only if it is within S's power to perform [not to perform] A.

When we note that

> OW: S has a moral obligation to perform [not to perform] A if and only if it is morally wrong for S not to perform [to perform] A,

we can derive (from OW and W) the following principle of alternative possibilities concerning moral obligation:

OAP: S has a moral obligation to perform [not to perform] A only if it is within S's power not to perform [to perform] A.

But now revert to Villain. If AU is true, then Joe's pushing the child off the pier is obligatory. However, Villain is supposed to be a Frankfurt-type case in which it is not within Joe's power to refrain from pushing the child off the pier; so given OAP, it cannot be the case that Joe's pushing the child off the pier is obligatory. Hence AU must be false.

Once again, the utilitarian has a reply. If the utilitarian accepts OW and W, and hence OAP, the utilitarian can insist that AU* and not AU represents her official theory. But as we have seen, AU* does not imply that it is obligatory for Joe to push the child off the pier; AU* implies that it is gratuitous for Joe to push the child off the pier. Similarly, if the world utilitarian accepts analogs of OW and W, she can insist that the obligation operator, O*, and not plain O is definitive of her theory.

Objection 4

Reflect on the sort of moral appraisal one would be inclined to make about Joe in Villain. Clearly, Joe is morally blameworthy for pushing the child off the pier. But one is blameworthy for performing an action only if one has a moral obligation not to perform that action. But then, given (OW), one is blameworthy for performing an action only if it is wrong for one to perform that action. Since it is incontestable that Joe is blameworthy for pushing the child off the pier, Joe's pushing the child off the pier must, contrary to what AU, or AU*, or MO, or MO* implies, be wrong.

The utilitarian should agree that Joe is deserving of blame for pushing the child off the pier. But he should insist that it is a mistake to associate blameworthiness with (objective) moral obligation in the way in which the objector does, as the following case (call it "Cure") strongly suggests. Suppose doctor Deadly is responsible for the treatment of some patient, Victim. Suppose all the available evidence indicates that Victim is suffering from a dangerous disease that we will call "Malady." Suppose Malady can easily be cured by administering one dose of medicine A, but exacerbated to the point where it proves fatal if a patient suffering from it is given a single dose of medicine B. Suppose wicked Deadly gives Victim medicine B with the express intention of killing Victim. But luckily, suppose the diagnosis is incorrect. Victim is in fact suffering from Malaise, a disease that gives rise to symptoms almost indistinguishable from the ones to which Malady gives rise. Suppose, finally, that a dose of B given to a patient suffering from Malaise safely cures the patient, but a dose of A given to a patient stricken with Malaise instantly kills the patient. It appears pretty evident that Cure is a case in which Deadly ought to give B, it is false that Deadly ought not to give B, and Deadly is blameworthy for giving B.

There is a distinction between what can be called "subjective moral obligation" and what can be called "objective moral obligation." The idea is that the concept of objective moral obligation concerns itself with what one's moral obligations really are, whereas that of subjective moral obligation concerns itself with what one believes one's moral obligations really are. The concept of subjective moral obligation can be explicated in terms of the concept of objective moral obligation in this way: an agent, S, has a subjective moral obligation as of a certain time, T, to do an action, A, if and only if S believes that, as of T, S (objectively) ought to do A.

It is open to the utilitarian to associate blameworthiness with subjective moral obligation in the following manner: an agent, S, is blameworthy for performing a given act A only if S has a subjective moral obligation not to perform A. Very sketchily, this principle amounts to the view that a person is blameworthy for performing an action only if she performs the action in light of the belief that she is doing wrong. This principle is an attractive and plausible competitor to the one that associates blameworthiness with objective moral obligation. Indeed, this sort of principle will be developed and defended in chapter 9, where the epistemic requirements of moral appraisability will be discussed.[11]

To collect results, so far I have attempted to show that whether there is a fully general requirement of alternative possibilities for moral appraisability for actions, a requirement that holds no matter what the (objective) normative status of an act—whether, for example, it is right, wrong, or obligatory—depends partly upon what sort of moral theory is true. I have argued that if AU (or AU*), or MO (or MO*) is true, no one can be appraisable for performing a wrong action to which there are no alternative possibilities. And this is because these theories entail that no one can perform an action that is wrong unless he could have performed some alternative instead. So, for example, in Villain which is a Frankfurt-type case, Joe is blameworthy for pushing the child off the pier, but this act of his is not wrong. In addition, I have also argued that if OW and W are true, then no one can be appraisable for performing an obligatory action to which there are no alternative possibilities.[12]

Notice that one can derive this very same conclusion—that no one can be appraisable for performing a wrong action to which there are no alternative possibilities—even if one endorses the following theory that is expressly deontological. Assume that each act is a prima facie duty of some stringency. The relevant theory can be stated in this way:

> D: It is obligatory for S to perform A if and only if S can do A, and A is a *prima facie* duty that is more stringent than any other of S's alternatives.[13]

Clearly, if D is true, there cannot be a wrong action to which there are no alternative possibilities. Assume, for instance, that in Villain, Joe has promised to push the child off the pier. Since he has promised, we can assume that Joe has a prima facie duty of fidelity to push the child off the pier. As Joe cannot refrain from pushing the child off the pier D, just like AU*, implies that Joe does no wrong when he pushes the child off the pier.

Other moral theories, however, yield interestingly different results in cases like Villain. For example, one might defend some pluralist moral theory according to which an intentional killing of Joe's variety is wrong. Perhaps this sort of theory places great weight on intentions (or motives), insisting that the moral status of an act turn, significantly, on the sorts of motives that generate action; "bad" motives, generally resulting in wrong actions and "good" motives in permissible actions. Such a strongly intentionalist theory would, presumably, yield the result that Joe's pushing the child off the pier is wrong.[14]

I want, finally, to discuss another route, a relatively "theory neutral" route, to the conclusion that no action to which there are no alternative possibilities can be wrong. Reconsider these principles that we introduced earlier on:

K: S has a moral obligation to perform [not to perform] A only if it is within S's power to perform [not to perform] A, and

OW: S has a moral obligation to perform [not to perform] A if and only if it is morally wrong for S not to perform [to perform] A.

K is the 'ought' implies 'can' principle, and OW is simply a standard principle of moral obligation. It is hard to contest these principles. In fact, it is reasonable to suppose that the mark of *any* adequate theory of moral obligation—any theory that specifies necessary and sufficient conditions for the obligatoriness of actions (like AU)—should "validate" these principles. We might think of K and OW as deontic axioms. But now notice that K and OW entail that there is a requirement of alternative possibilities for wrong actions:

WAP: It is morally wrong for S to perform [not to perform] A only if it is within S's power not to perform [to perform] A.

In the derivation of WAP from K and OW, I have assumed that the sense in which, according to K, one must "be able" to do something to have a moral obligation to do it, is the same sense in which, according to WAP, one must "be able" to do otherwise for what one does to be wrong. If WAP is true, then there can be no Frankfurt-type case in which an agent performs an action of necessity that is wrong. For suppose S is in a Frankfurt-type case. In any such case, S does A of necessity. Hence, in any such case, it is false that it is within S's power not to perform A. It follows, given WAP, that in any such case, it is false that it is wrong for S to do A. So, for instance, when Joe in Villain pushes the child off the pier, WAP allows us to conclude that Joe's pushing the child off the pier is not wrong, as Villain is a Frankfurt-type case in which Joe could not have refrained from pushing the child off the pier.

It's now easy to see (via a different set of considerations from those adduced above) that if no person can do anything other than what he or she does in a world—perhaps because causal determinism is true, and such determinism is incompatible with freedom to do otherwise—then no action of this person in such a world is obligatory. For were some action, A, in such a world obligatory for some person, then failing to do A would be wrong for that person in that world. But it is not true that any action in such a world would be wrong for any person, and hence it is not true that failing to do A would be wrong for that person. It is, then, false that A would be obligatory for that person.

5. A NEW INCOMPATIBILIST WORRY

The considerations in the last section—specifically, the result that there is a requirement of alternative possibilities for wrongness—provides the incompatibilist with a spring board to launch a new attack against Frankfurt-type examples. These sorts of examples are meant to show (among other things) that the ability to do otherwise is not a necessary condition of moral appraisability. However, exploiting the result that wrongness requires alternative possibilities, an incompatibilist, as David Copp argues, may insist that Frankfurt-type examples show no such thing, or at least that such examples fail to show that the ability to do otherwise is not a necessary condition for *moral blameworthiness*.[15] Let's introduce the notion of a Frankfurt-pair. Start with a standard Frankfurt-type example, FT1, in which a counterfactual intervener ensures that some agent, S, cannot refrain from A-ing and in which S A-s on "S's own" and is intuitively morally responsible for doing so. Now consider an example, FT2, which is just like FT1 but without the counterfactual intervener in which S can A on S's own, S can refrain from A-ing on S's own, S A-s on S's own, and S is intuitively morally responsible for A-ing. FT1 and FT2 constitute a Frankfurt-pair. Using a fine-grained view of event or act individuation, Copp advances the following:

> [One version of PAP, the principle of alternate possibilities, is] that a person is *blameworthy* for an action only if he could have done otherwise. Let us call this principle, PAP "with respect to blameworthiness". . . . [It] appears that Frankfurt-pairs do not undermine this principle. . . . PAP with respect to blameworthiness follows from the maxim that "ought" implies "can" together with the specific finely-nuanced assumption that a person is blameworthy for an action only if the action was wrong. A person's action was wrong only if the person was required to refrain from it. And given the maxim, a person was required to refrain from an action only if she could have refrained from it. Given the finely-nuanced view, it follows that a person is blameworthy for her action only if she could have done otherwise. Therefore, given the finely-nuanced assumption, PAP with respect to blameworthiness is a corollary of the Maxim. We cannot reject PAP with respect to blameworthiness unless we reject either the Maxim or the finely-nuanced view about blame.

Reconsider Villain. Assume that according to K, the sense of "being able" to do something to be morally obligated to do it is the same sense of "being able" to do something operative in the Frankfurt-type twin of a Frankfurt-pair in which an agent is unable to do something other than what she in fact did. Copp's moral appears to be that in this case, Jones is *not* morally blameworthy for pushing the child off the pier, and he is not as his act of pushing the child off the pier is not (objectively) wrong. It isn't wrong, as Jones could not (in his circumstances) have done otherwise, and there is a requirement of alternative possibilities for wrongness. Jones may be blameworthy for being willing to act wrongly, or for forming the intention to push the child, or perhaps even for the state of affairs that is

Jones's executing his intention to push the child off the pier, but he is *not* blameworthy for the state of affairs that is *Jones's pushing the child off the pier*. Copp concedes that there is a "broad" sense of 'responsible' "such that, even if coercion excuses a person from blame for his action, it does not follow that he lacked moral responsibility for his action." Elaborating this broad notion of moral responsibility (of which appraisability is a species), Copp says:

> [L]et me propose . . . that, in the broad sense, moral responsibility for an action is a matter of *deserving a moral response* on the basis of the action. In cases where we are blameworthy for an action, we deserve blame. In some other cases, we may deserve praise on account of an action. In the neutral cases, however, we deserve neither praise nor blame. . . . I will say that in such cases we deserve a "morally neutral reaction" for our actions. . . . I will reserve the term "response-worthiness" for this broad notion of responsibility. . . . We can interpret PAP in light of this [broad] notion of responsibility. I will speak of PAP "with respect to response-worthiness."

Copp argues that given his account of the broad notion of responsibility, what Frankfurt needs is the intuition that an agent's (like Jones's) act in a Frankfurt-type case such as Villain is one for which he is broadly morally responsible in that it would be legitimate to assess his performance with respect to whether he deserves a moral response on account of his action. His view is that an agent like Jones *would* deserve to be responded to for his action "in the way that is appropriate given that . . . [his] action was not wrong"; in Copp's terminology, this means Jones deserves a "morally neutral response" for pushing the child off the pier (as his action, according to Copp) is not wrong but permissible. So, interestingly, Copp believes that Frankfurt-type examples *do* show that the ability to do otherwise is not a necessary condition of the performance of an action for the performance of which the agent deserves a moral response; such examples defeat PAP with respect to response-worthiness, but leave intact PAP with respect to blameworthiness.

Copp concludes that the incompatibilist's intuition that no one is appraisable on account of their actions in a fully determined world, and the standard explanation of the intuition, that determinism rules out alternative possibilities, are partially vindicated:

> I have argued that Frankfurt-pairs do not undermine PAP with respect to blameworthiness. Because of this, the incompatibilist's position is partially vindicated. For suppose that the truth of determinism would mean that no-one could ever do otherwise than he does. It would then follow from the conjunction of determinism and PAP with respect to blameworthiness that no-one is ever blameworthy for his action. And given the maxim that "ought" implies "can", it would follow that no-one's action is ever wrong.

I'll begin assessment with a promissory note. Copp believes that PAP with respect to blameworthiness is a corollary of the maxim that 'ought' implies 'can': he thinks we cannot reject PAP unless we reject either the maxim or the finely nuanced view about blame (that a person is morally blameworthy for an action only if the action was wrong). I believe, though, that PAP is *not* a corollary of the maxim. In chapter 8, I shall argue against the finely-nuanced view about blame, and show why the maxim is left unblemished even if PAP with respect to blameworthiness is rejected (see chap. 8, sec. 2). Let's now address other aspects of Copp's instructive views.

Notice that the incompatibilist's case against Frankfurt, as advanced by Copp, is cogent only if one associates appraisability for an action with the actual "deontic" or normative status of that action. This association specifies that there is an essential connection between blameworthiness and objective wrongness, and praiseworthiness and objective obligatoriness or rightness. As suggested above, though, a Frankfurtian can resist this move by dissociating appraisability with actual deontic wrongness or obligatoriness, and affiliating it with belief in what is objectively wrong or obligatory. Indeed, the Frankfurtian might urge that Frankfurt-type examples like Villain provide convincing grounds for *renouncing* the "objective associationist view" in favor of the "subjective (or doxastic) associationist view."

The incompatibilist, however, might well remain unmoved: she might pull in her reins, and remain faithful to her position that Jones cannot be blameworthy for an action if that action is not in fact wrong. In response to associating blameworthiness with belief in what is objectively wrong, Copp considers a Frankfurt-type example ("Alberta-2") in which some person (Alberta) forms an intention to lie and lies, in the absence of knowing that she could not have refrained from forming the intention to lie and to lie (given Count Venor the counterfactual intervener):

I have argued that Alberta is not blameworthy for lying in Alberta-2 because she was not wrong to lie. . . . [Haji's] objection is that she *is* blameworthy for lying because she *believed* she was acting wrongly in lying. She was *willing* to do what she believed to be wrong, and so she is liable to blame or censure. Hence, . . . [Haji's] objection continues, despite the moral difference between Alberta-1 [a non-Frankfurt-type case just like Alberta-2 with no counterfactual intervener] and Alberta-2, Alberta-2 still defeats PAP. Alberta is blameworthy for lying in Alberta-2 despite the fact that she could not have done otherwise.

The objection depends on inferring that Alberta is blameworthy *for lying* from the claim that she is blameworthy because she lied in the belief that she was doing something wrong. I agree that we are inclined to feel that Alberta is blameworthy in Alberta-2, and the most obvious thing to blame her for is the fact that she lied. But in light of the fact that Alberta was not wrong to lie, I think it would be a mistake to think she is blameworthy for lying. She may still be blameworthy for being willing to act wrongly, for example, or for permitting herself to be the kind of person who would act wrongly to save herself embarrassment. Our inclination to blame her can be indulged without blaming her for lying. We presumably think that she was wrong to be willing to act wrongly—or we may think she was wrong to permit herself to be this kind of person—and if so, we can hold that this is what she is blameworthy for.

My position reflects a finely-nuanced view of what it is *for which* a person deserves blame or censure: A person is morally blameworthy for something only if the thing is a moral offense. Given this finely-nuanced view, Alberta is *not* blameworthy *for lying* in Alberta-2. She has the definitive reply to anyone who would censure her for lying, for she was not wrong to lie; her lying was not a moral offense. But her being willing to act wrongly, or her permitting herself to be the kind of person who would act wrongly to save herself embarrassment, arguably was a moral offense.

Copp's response deserves careful attention. First, it merits mentioning that an advocate of the view that blameworthiness is to be associated with belief in what is wrong may well adopt (as I do) a fine-grained view about event individuation and still insist that Alberta (in Alberta-2) is blameworthy for lying. "Objectivists" about blameworthiness, those who affiliate blameworthiness with objective wrongness, and Subjectivists, those who affiliate blameworthiness with belief in what is wrong, can, it seems to me, be agreed on a fine-grained view of event individuation.

Second, as Fischer persuasively shows, we can systematically reconstruct the Frankfurt-type examples so that the triggering mechanism is not even an intentional action—it may be a blush or some neurophysiological event. Suppose Alberta-2 is reconstructed in this fashion. Then, given the 'ought' implies 'can' principle, the principle that there is a requirement of alternative possibilities for wrongness, and the objectivist's view about blameworthiness, Alberta in reconstructed Alberta-2 is *not* to blame for lying, for trying to lie, for being willing to lie, or for forming the intention to lie. Replace Alberta's action of lying with the action of her intentionally, deliberately, and nonwaywardly killing her innocent child (as her malevolent spouse-to-be refuses to marry her unless she "gets rid of the nuisance"). Then in the reconstructed Frankfurt-type case, Alberta is not blameworthy for killing her child, attempting to kill her child, being willing to kill her child, forming an intention to kill her child, judging that she should (to secure a potential marriage) kill her child, etc. But this result, I submit, is incredible! Surely, there are powerful *intuitive* grounds to suppose that Alberta is to blame for various of these things as (we can stipulate) she acts just as she would have in the absence of the intervener.

Anticipating this sort of objection, Copp says:

My reply to this objection is two-fold. First, despite our initial intuitions about Alberta-2, we may have to concede that Alberta is *not* blameworthy, properly speaking, for she may not *deserve* any blame if she had no control in the end over her actions, intentions, and character. Despite this, Alberta clearly does have a moral flaw . . . for she is the kind of person who would be willing to act wrongly to save herself embarrassment. It may be that this thought is all that should survive of our initial intuitions about the case. . . . Second, . . . it does seem to me that a person can be blameworthy for permitting herself to be a certain kind of person. Alberta clearly is the kind of person who is willing to lie to save herself embarrassment. My description of the case left it open how she came to be this way, but if she had control over the kind of person she is, she then must at least have permitted herself to be this kind of person. . . . [I]f we view Alberta as *blameworthy* rather than simply as morally flawed, the best candidate for an offense for which she might deserve blame is her permitting herself to be morally flawed, if indeed this is how she came to be morally flawed.

Of the two replies in the twofold response, the first advocates renouncing our intuitions that Alberta is to blame for various things, like lying, or forming an intention to lie, or being willing to lie, in favor of the alternative that she is not blameworthy, properly speaking, for any of these things. On Copp's view, Alberta did not deserve blame for these things if she had no control over them, and this for the reason that they *could* not be wrong without her having control over them. The sort of control Copp has in mind is, of course, freedom to do otherwise. But it is not in the least obvious (as I will argue at length in the next chapter and as others have argued) whether it is this sort of control that anchors ascriptions of moral appraisability. Indeed, Copp concedes that Frankfurt-pairs are designed (at least partially) to challenge this view of control. Consequently, it seems improper to appeal to this very view of control in an attempt to provide an advocate of Frankfurt-pairs with an explanation of why Alberta in (restructured Alberta-2) is not (supposedly) to blame for her actions, intentions, character, and so on. In addition, both replies once again assume that one cannot be morally to blame for something if it is not a moral offense, that is, if it is not objectively wrong. Copp, then, seems to assume that not being wrong is itself an appraisability-subverting factor. But again, Frankfurt-pairs can be used to challenge this assumption. We need, in the way of a response to such a challenge, something more than staunch insistence on the correctness of the view that one can't be deserving of blame for something unless it is a moral offense. Copp's rich paper is generously accommodating. Consider the following three candidates for "something more."

1. First Candidate

Given his notion of broad responsibility, response-worthiness responsibility, Copp might contend that in the reconstructed Frankfurt-type case, Alberta is broadly responsible for things like killing the child, attempting to kill the child, being willing to kill her child, etc. She is broadly responsible in that "Alberta deserves to be responded to for her action[s] given that [these actions were] not wrong." So, Copp might suggest, even in the reconstructed Frankfurt-type case, our intuitions that Alberta is blameworthy for various things like being willing to kill her child are once again confused. We should reject these intuitions in favor of the view that Alberta is broadly responsible for being willing to kill her child, forming an intention to kill her child, etc.

Grant, to make headway in discussion, Copp's broad notion of responsibility. One potential worry for this sort of response hinges on Copp's suggestion that in a Frankfurt-type case like reconstructed Alberta-2, the agent's action is morally permissible. One might plausibly insist that just as 'ought' implies 'can', so 'right' implies 'can'. If 'right' *does* imply 'can', then Alberta's action of killing the child would not, in the reconstructed Frankfurt-type example, be permissible. I argued above, that in a world in which one cannot do otherwise than one does, one's actions cannot be wrong or obligatory. Why suppose that in such a world one's actions could be permissible as opposed to gratuitous? Copp, might, however reject the 'right' implies 'can' principle, or simply accept this principle and opt for the alternative that Alberta's action *is* morally gratuitous. Further, Copp might say, in virtue of being morally gratuitous, Alberta deserves the apposite moral response for killing her child, to wit, a *morally neutral one*. There would, however, still be burdensome problems with this stance. Firstly, it seems to be at odds with some of the things Copp has to say about morally neutral reactions. Copp explains that on the broad usage of 'moral responsibility',

> we are [broadly] morally responsible for our actions where we are blameworthy for them. But in some cases where we are [broadly] morally responsible for our actions, we are not blameworthy for them. In some cases, we are praiseworthy, but in most cases our actions are morally trivial or morally neutral, and although we are responsible for them, we are neither blameworthy nor praiseworthy. We deserve to be viewed "neutrally" for them, for they are permissible actions performed for permissible reasons and acceptable motives. . . . In the neutral cases . . . we deserve neither praise nor blame. . . . I will say that in such cases we deserve a "morally neutral reaction" for our actions.

This passage strongly suggests that a person is deserving of a morally neutral reaction or response on account of performing an action only if that action is morally trivial or neutral—it is a permissible or perhaps gratuitous action performed for permissible reasons and acceptable motives. But Alberta's action of killing the child in reconstructed Alberta-2 is definitely *not* a morally *trivial* action performed for permissible reasons and acceptable motives. Alberta kills in a cruel, cold, and calculating manner; her motives are positively vile.

Secondly, think of Alberta (in the reconstructed Frankfurt-type case), first being willing to kill her child, then forming an intention to kill her child, and finally executing her despicable intention. If Alberta is deserving of a moral response for these things, the response clearly seems *not* to be a morally *neutral* one; rather, the appropriate response, if anything, should be a strongly "negative" one. In the event that Copp insist that a "morally neutral reaction for our actions" *may* be a strongly negative one, then I think we are owed an explanation of how this reaction would differ substantially from the moral reaction that would be appropriate were Alberta blameworthy for killing her child.

2. Second Candidate

Copp attempts to marshal additional support for his view that a person is blameworthy for something only if the thing is a moral offense—only if the thing is morally wrong—by directing our attention to examples of moral luck:

> Consider Alberta-3, which is like Alberta-1 except that Alberta inadvertently tells the truth in Alberta-3. She intends to say, falsely, "This is not my daughter." But instead, because of a slip of the tongue, she says truly, "This is Dot, my daughter." The person she refers to is her daughter, Dot. As a result of her slip of the tongue, therefore, Alberta does not act wrongly in saying what she says. So far, then, Alberta-2 and Alberta-3 are morally on a par. In neither case does Alberta do anything wrong in saying what she says. In both cases, according to the finely-nuanced view, we should view her as not being blameworthy for saying what she says, but we may view her as blameworthy for being willing to act wrongly.
>
> According to the alternative view . . . however, Alberta is blameworthy for her action in all three of the Alberta cases because in each case she spoke in the belief that

she was acting wrongly. I will call this view the "coarse-grained view." It blurs the fact that Alberta-2 and Alberta-3 are morally similar to each other and different from Alberta-1. In Alberta-1, the basis on which Alberta deserves blame includes the fact that her action is wrong. In Alberta-2 and Alberta-3, however, Alberta does not act wrongly and the basis on which she deserves blame is her willingness to act wrongly. The coarse-grained view blurs this fact because it says that Alberta is blameworthy of her action in all three cases. . . . [T]he coarse-grained view gives us the odd result that a person may be to blame *for* X even though she deserves blame on the basis of *something else*, and she does not deserve blame *on the basis of* X. In such a case, the proponent of the coarse-grained view owes us an explanation of what connects deserving blame for X with deserving blame on the basis of this something else. More generally, the proponent owes us an explanation of what is meant by "for X" in the expression, "is to blame for X." The finely-nuanced view takes the simple line that a person is to blame for X just in case she deserves blame on the basis of X.

Several comments are in order. Notice that Alberta-3 is simply relevantly like Cure, in which Deadly clearly seems blameworthy for injecting the patient with medicine B. Deadly takes himself to be doing wrong by injecting the drug; by sheer luck, it turns out that injecting the patient with B cures the patient (instead of killing him). Similarly, if Alberta in Alberta-3 takes herself to be doing wrong when she says "This is dot my daughter," and as a result of sheer luck—a slip of the tongue—she does what is right or at least not wrong, why should she be excused from being to blame for what she says?

In addition, the Subjectivist who associates blameworthiness with belief in what is wrong can accommodate the view, if it is correct, that Alberta in some of the versions of the Alberta cases, may be blameworthy for being willing to do wrong, or for forming an intention to do wrong: she would be blameworthy for the latter, for instance, if she believed she was doing wrong in forming an intention to do wrong (other conditions of moral appraisability being satisfied). We can now see that the label "coarse-grained" is a misnomer. The Objectivist (like Copp) and the Subjectivist differ over the appropriate *desert base* for blame, given a somewhat liberal construal of these bases. On the Objectivist view, a person is to blame for X just in case she deserves blame on the basis of X under the condition that it is wrong for her to do (or bring about) X. On the Subjectivist view, a person is to blame for X just in case she deserves blame on the basis of X under the condition (roughly) that she does (or brings about) X in light of the belief that she is doing wrong in X-ing. Hence, by 'for X' in the expression, 'is to blame for X', the Subjectivist means precisely what the Objectivist means. It is an error to suppose that the Subjectivist's view blurs moral distinctions, and fails to discriminate finely among various states of affairs or actions for which a person may be deserving of blame. Indeed, the Subjectivist view is as finely discriminatory here as is the finely-nuanced view. Copp and I reach different verdicts over whether Alberta is to blame for various things in the different Alberta cases since we rely on different desert bases (as broadly construed above), and *not* because one view is more finely nuanced, relative to discriminating among various states of affairs for which a person deserves blame, than the other.

There are, I believe, further difficulties with Copp's position that Alberta in Alberta-2 or in reconstructed Alberta-2, or Jones in Villain, or any agent in a relevantly analogous Frankfurt-type case, is not to blame for her germane actions. I propose that appraisability for an action—that is, being to praise or blame for an action—turns essentially on what occurs in the actual sequence of events culminating in action. Assuming that there are no appraisability-undermining factors (such as coercion, or direct manipulation of one's will) in the actual sequence, the crucial question is this: How did the agent conduct herself in the actual sequence? Imagine a case just like Villain save that in this case (Villain*) there is no counterfactual intervener, and that Jones* (Jones's counterpart) could have refrained from pushing the child to its death. Villian* is a case in which it would appear that the incompatibilist would grant that Jones* is blameworthy for pushing the child. Now compare the actual sequence of events that ends with Jones*'s pushing the child off the pier in Villain*, with the actual sequence of events terminating in Jones's pushing the child off the pier in Villain. They are not relevantly different; there is *nothing* about them that suggests asymmetric attributions of appraisability, *at least if we approach them in the absence of assuming either the Subjectivist's or Objectivist's view about appraisability.* In addition, I reiterate the position that appraisability is concerned first and foremost with a type of normative appraisal of a *person.* Of course, persons can be appraised, and are, on account of what they do, but one should distinguish between the moral worth of a person (with which appraisability is fundamentally concerned) and the normative evaluation of an act. As appraisability is concerned primarily with the former, in appraising persons for what they do, the focus should center on how persons perceive what they are doing. Jones (in Villain) is unaware of the counterfactual intervener; why should the mere presence of the intervener influence our judgments regarding the moral worth of Jones insofar as the appropriate bit of this worth is "expressed" or constituted by the event in question, Jones's pushing the child? The intervener renders it true, by ensuring that Jones cannot do otherwise than what he in fact does, that Jones's pushing the child is not wrong. But it goes without saying that the presence of the intervener, by virtue of rendering it true that Jones's pushing the child off the pier is not wrong, cannot in any way influence the moral worth of Jones vis-à-vis his action of pushing the child; Jones conducts himself in exactly the same sort of fashion as does his counterpart who is free to do otherwise. The fact that Jones's act of pushing the child is not wrong in Villain is simply incidental to the manner in which Jones behaves. For these reasons, I believe that the normative status of acts is also incidental to appraisability. Of course, I do not deny that there may well be nontrivial connections between the appraisability of persons and the normative evaluation of acts. One possible connection is this: an agent who performs an act in light of realizing that it is wrong for her to perform that act may be blameworthy to a higher degree than an agent who performs an act in the mere belief that she is doing wrong by performing the act. But it seems to me that both agents would be blameworthy, in the first instance, roughly on account of performing the act in light of the belief that they were doing wrong.

The issue here can be approached in this light: when we appraise people in our day-to-day dealings with them, purely fortuitous happenings of the sort that occur in Cure (in which by mere luck Deadly saves the patient instead of killing her as he intended) in no way dislodge our moral evaluation of the *agent*. We don't think any the better of Deadly on account of the happy turn of events. We are pleased, relieved, or perhaps even grateful that things turned out well for the patient. Still, we would persist in regarding Deadly vis-à-vis the episode of injecting the patient with B in the same light; presumably, we would hold him blameworthy for forming the intention to kill, for executing that intention, *and* for injecting the drug (should the execution of the intention amount to something different from the injection of the drug). Hence, the mere fact that it turns out that Deadly's injecting the drug is not wrong, it appears, is inconsequential to our appraisal of Deadly with respect to that action.

3. Third Candidate

There is one final bit of interesting argumentation in Copp's piece for the "finely-nuanced view" that blameworthiness should be associated with objective wrongness:

> [M]y account of response-worthiness can be used to defend both the finely-nuanced view about blameworthiness, and a more general finely-nuanced view about response-worthiness. If a person deserves some response, there must be a *basis* for her desert of it. A person who deserves gratitude, for example, deserves it on the basis of something that makes gratitude distinctively appropriate, and this is that *for which* she deserves gratitude. Similarly, if someone deserves blame, there must be a basis for her desert. The basis for her desert of blame is what she deserves blame *for*, and this must be some kind of moral offense, since it must be something in light of which blaming her would be distinctively appropriate. Hence, a person is morally blameworthy for something only if the thing is a moral offense.

Desert *does* require a base: whenever a person deserves something, there is some fact to which we can appeal—some desert base—in order to explain why she deserves what she deserves. Suppose someone deserves blame on account of doing something. It isn't at all clear to me why the desert base *must* be a moral *offense*, something that is objectively wrong. Why can't the desert base be something the agent takes to be a moral offense? Why wouldn't *this* sort of desert base be "something in light of which blaming . . . would be distinctively appropriate"? Just as Objectivists and Subjectivists about blameworthiness can agree on a fine-grained view of event individuation, and they can agree on what each means by 'for X' in the expression, 'is to blame for X', so they can agree on desert's requiring a base, and that if one is deserving of blame for something, there must be an appropriate desert base that explains why one is deserving of blame for doing that thing. It seems to me, then, that appeal to the undeniable view that desert requires a base does not favor the Objectivist's view over the Subjectivist's (or vice versa of course).

6. CONCLUSIONS

I shall end by framing a perplexity. Asymmetry thesis AST2 says that to be morally responsible for wrong actions, one must be able to do otherwise, but this ability is not required to be responsible for right actions. It may initially seem that Frankfurt-type cases, like Villain, in which some agent performs an evil act that he could not avoid performing, straightforwardly undermine the first half of this asymmetry thesis. But it turns out that the evil act in Villain may not be wrong. Indeed, I have argued that if certain theories of moral obligation (like AU) are true, then the evil act *cannot* be wrong, as these theories entail that there is a requirement of alternative possibilities for wrongness. Further, we have also seen that if the 'ought' implies 'can' principle (K), and the principle that obligatory acts are acts it is wrong for one not to perform (OW) are true, then once again no act to which there are no alternative possibilities can be wrong. Hence, the first half of asymmetry thesis AST2 may well be true. Joe in Villain is blameworthy for his act of pushing the child off the pier, but that act, if AU, or K and OW are true, is not wrong.

We saw in the last chapter that causal determinism threatens freedom to do otherwise; arguably, if determinism is true, then no person can do other than what he in fact does. Frankfurt-type examples suggest that even if determinism is incompatible with freedom to do otherwise, it is not incompatible with moral appraisability—at least if we limit ourselves to the control condition—as the type of control needed for moral appraisability is not freedom to do otherwise. The explorations in this chapter, however, raise a new concern. If certain theories of moral obligation (like MO), or a set of deontic principles like the set whose elements are the 'ought' implies 'can' principle, the principle that an obligatory act is one it is not wrong to perform, and the principle that it is wrong to perform an act only if one can perform that act, are true, then—speaking somewhat loosely—wrongness and obligatoriness require alternative possibilities; one's action cannot be wrong or obligatory unless one could have done otherwise. So while causal determinism, by way of ruling out alternative possibilities, will not threaten "appraisability-grounding" control, it may threaten *morality*. No action that an agent performs will be wrong or obligatory if causal determinism is true. This result is, to say the very least, perplexing.

Suppose causal determinism does undermine morality in the way explained. Then it might be thought that determinism also undermines praiseworthiness and blameworthiness. For, it might be urged, one can be blameworthy for performing an act only if that act is in fact wrong, and one can be praiseworthy for performing an act only if the act is in fact obligatory. On the supposition that causal determinism "rules out" wrongness and obligatoriness (by way of ruling out alternative possibilities), it would follow that no person is deserving of blame or praise for anything she does.

This second threat to appraisability, however, as I have already suggested, can also be evaded. I shall argue in chapter 9 that blameworthiness and praiseworthiness are not associated with (objective) wrongness and obligatoriness, respectively. Rather, I will suggest that they are much more closely affiliated with the agent's own beliefs or perceptions about what is wrong or obligatory.

Our immediate concerns, however, have to do with control. In the next chapter, I outline the type of control that I believe is required for moral appraisability.

FOUR

APPRAISABILITY
AND CONTROL

An individual can properly be morally appraisable for performing an action only if he controls that action in an appropriate way; this much is clear. But if the sort of control is not freedom to do otherwise, what *does* it consist in? I will begin by examining Wolf's "Reason View," which does not eschew the traditional approach—an approach that always requires alternative possibilities—altogether. The view is intriguing, because, if correct, what is required for appraisability is not a purely metaphysical ability but a "distinctive intellectual power [having both metaphysical and normative elements], the power to exercise right Reason and to govern one's actions accordingly" (1990, p. 71). Though arresting, I will argue that Wolf's Reason View of control is unacceptable. I will then critically examine an "Hierarchical" account of control which, roughly, conceptualizes the relevant sort of control as consisting in a "mesh" or appropriate "fit" between different sorts of desires of an agent. Finally, I will develop an outline of "volitional control" which, I believe, is indicative of the right sort of control for appraisability.

1. WOLF'S REASON VIEW

In a nutshell, what Wolf calls the "Reason View" amounts to the view that "the freedom necessary for responsibility consists in the ability (or freedom) to do the

65

right thing for the right reasons . . . to choose and to act in accordance with the True and the Good" (1990, p. 94). Elaborating, Wolf says:

> what we need to know if we are to find out whether we are free and responsible beings is whether we possess the ability to act in accordance with Reason. Since Reason is here understood to refer to the highest faculty or set of faculties there is, the faculty or set of faculties that, in most circumstances, will help us form true beliefs and good values, this amounts to the suggestion that we need to know whether we have the ability to think—and on the basis of our thought, to act—well rather than badly. That is, we need to know whether we have the ability to choose and to act on the basis of the right reasons for choosing and acting. And since we can assume that if one acts according to the right reasons one will perform the right action, the ability we are concerned with might be described as the ability to do the right thing for the right reasons. The question of whether we have this ability is not so much a metaphysical as a metaethical, and perhaps also an ethical, one. For we cannot answer it unless we know what counts as doing the right thing and having the right reasons. (1990, pp. 70–71)

These claims of Wolf, as we noted in the last chapter, imply an interesting asymmetry thesis: whereas one cannot be morally appraisable for a bad action that one could not have avoided, one can be morally appraisable for a good action that was unavoidable. So the Reason View does not discard alternative possibilities altogether. In sum, on the Reason view, the type of control required for moral appraisability is the freedom to act in accord with the True and the Good.

2. CRITICISM OF THE REASON VIEW

We have already discussed one serious shortcoming of this view: as Fischer and Ravizza have adeptly argued, Frankfurt-type examples can be constructed to show that good and bad actions are symmetrical with respect to not requiring alternative possibilities for moral appraisability.

There is a second serious fault with the Reason View. Wolf underscores the point that "According to the Reason View, . . . it is only the ability to do the right thing for the right reasons . . . that is required for responsibility" (1990, p. 81). It appears, however, that a person could deliberately harden his heart to the supplications of morality, and so not be able to act in accord with the True and the Good and *still* be fully appraisable for his actions. Consider the following case. Suppose, well aware of moral restrictions, Glaucon has decided to develop his character in such a way that his true guiding principle is one of self-interest. It is then only in cases in which the requirements of morality and those of self-interest fortuitously coincide that Glaucon does what is right or good, but even in such cases, it is self-interest that impels Glaucon to action. Imagine, now, that having "freely" and willfully developed his character in this direction, Glaucon is literally unable to refrain from pocketing a gold coin that he spies on the otherwise deserted stretch of road. When he pockets the coin Glaucon acts in conformity with his character. His options are constrained by his earlier deliberate efforts to thwart requirements of the True and the Good in favor of maximizing self-interest. Indeed, it would have been foreign to Glaucon's constructed nature to do the moral thing if he could have done better for himself by doing something immoral instead. But although Glaucon cannot now act in accord with the True and the Good, it seems evident, or it is at least clearly possible, that he is blameworthy for pocketing the coin. His manner of conduct is relevantly analogous to what it would be were he to consent to being hypnotized for the purpose of ensuring that he pockets the coin. In the latter case, there would be little doubt about his culpability, even though he could not thwart the (let's suppose) powerful posthypnotic suggestion.

Wolf might respond to this case by saying that Glaucon is indirectly responsible for pocketing the coin because he was indirectly capable of acting according to reason. She might say, Glaucon freely decided, when he *did* have the capacity to act in accordance with the True and the Good, to shape his character in a certain way; consequently, he must be appraisable for at least some actions that "issue from" his acquired character.

This reply, however, isn't fully satisfactory. Wolf's view does support the reasonable verdict that Glaucon is appraisable for acquiring his "self-interested character." But it fails to support the further plausible verdict that he is also appraisable for pocketing the coin, a deed of his that issues from this character, *if* "it is *only* the ability to do the right thing for the right reasons . . . that is required for moral responsibility."

Lastly, Wolf's Reason View, I believe, suggests something very sensible about control: it suggests that in order for a person to be morally responsible for an action of hers, that action must, in some fashion, be responsive to her practical deliberations. But now consider Polus, a saintly character who cannot but act in accordance with the True and the Good on each occasion of choice. Unlike Glaucon, Polus has freely, and for the "right reasons," intentionally set out to make himself a saintly person, and he has succeeded. Is he appraisable—specifically, is he praiseworthy—for his subsequent saintly deeds? The answer, I recommend, is that he isn't, at least not if his saintly actions are no longer responsive to his practical reasoning. Needless to say, assessment of this recommendation awaits clarification of the sort of reasons-responsiveness at issue. I simply note that should this answer be correct, we have one more reason to doubt the Reason View.

Glaucon has decided that he wants to be a certain sort of person. Among other things, he wants to be the type of person who always acts on his "self-interested" desires, the desires, which if translated into action, would most further *his* own ends. He would prefer to act on his self-interested desires even if he had conflicting "moral desires" to do the right thing for the right reasons; it is his self-interested desires that he wants to be motivated by. Contrast Glaucon's "mental economy" with Meno's. Meno is doing his very best to stop smoking. He has rid himself and his home of all cigarettes, he avoids the company of smokers, he has stopped frequenting bars and restaurants that permit smoking, he has asked his friends to help him kick the habit, and so on. He succeeds in not smoking for five days. But on the evening of the sixth, just after having received news of a close friend's demise, he loses the battle to refrain from entering the smoke shop. In he hops, purchases a packet of Sportsman and, not liking himself at all for what he does next, quickly lights up and inhales deeply.

Meno, unlike Glaucon, acts on a desire that he wants not to be motivated by; he acts on a sort of desire that he would rather *not* have at all. This brings us to the hierarchical account of control.

3. HIERARCHICAL CONTROL

In a seminal paper, Harry Frankfurt asserts that one essential difference between persons and other creatures is to be found in the structure of persons' wills (Frankfurt 1971). *Persons,* unlike simpler animals and young children, are able to form *second-order* desires, and "have the capacity for reflective self-evaluation that is manifested in the formation of second-order desires" (1971, p. 7). On Frankfurt's view, an agent has "a desire of the second order either when he wants simply to have a certain desire or when he wants a certain desire to be his will [that is, his motivating desire]" (1971, p. 10). So, unlike a first-order desire, which is a desire for a course of action or perhaps a state of affairs, a second-order desire is one whose object is another actual or possible desire of the agent whose desire it is. For instance, Meno's desire that he not have the desire to smoke is a desire of the second order. A desire to have a desire that one does not yet have, or a desire to be motivated more often by one sort of desire than another, are second-order desires. Frankfurt distinguishes between mere second-order desires and second-order volitions. A mere second-order desire is a desire to have a particular first-order desire but not to act on this first-order desire. Conducting research on addiction, I may want to have a first-order desire for a drug without acting on that desire. In contrast, a second-order volition is a second-order desire that a first-order desire be one's motivating desire, or as Frankfurt says, "one's will" (1971, pp. 9–11).

Relying (partly) on the difference between first- and second-order desires, and on the distinction between different sorts of second-order desires, Frankfurt differentiates various kinds of freedom. One is supposed to exemplify the type of control required for moral appraisability. On Frankfurt's theory, one has freedom of action when one is able to do what one wants, and when one has freedom of action, one is free do otherwise (1971, p. 14). Frankfurt believes that even little children and many nonhuman animals have this sort of freedom. As freedom of action entails having genuine alternative options, Frankfurt-type examples show that it is not the kind of freedom (or control) required for moral appraisability.

Just as freedom of action is being able to do what we want, freedom of will, Frankfurt says, is being able to will as we want. More precisely, one has freedom of the will when one has the power to make, as a result of a second-order volition, at least one of one's first-order desires, other than the one that actually motivates one to act when one does, the one that motivates one to act when one does (1971, p. 15). So again, as with freedom of action, one has freedom of the will only if one could have "willed otherwise." And once again, as freedom of the will entails having genuine options, this time the option to have willed otherwise (that is, the option to have made some other first-order desire one's motivating desire), appropriately constructed Frankfurt-type examples show that freedom of the will is not the right sort of freedom (or control) required for moral appraisability.

Finally, Frankfurt suggests that one *acts freely* when one secures conformity of one's second-order volition and one's will (where one's will is constituted by one's motivating desire) (1971, p. 15). Apparently, Frankfurt's view amounts to the view that when one's act is caused (in a suitable way) by one's second-order volition, this is sufficient for having exercised the appropriate control over that action required for moral appraisability.[1]

Departing somewhat from Frankfurt's view, let's now construct a "generic" account of hierarchical control.[2] Let's say that an agent, S, hierarchically endorses a first-order desire, D, to perform some action, A, if and only if S has a second-order volition, V, (relative to D) that D be S's motivating desire, and S has no second-order desires that conflict with V. Thus, when an agent hierarchically endorses a first-order desire of hers, she wants that desire to move her all the way to action; she wants to be motivated by that desire. Also, let's say that an agent, S, exercises hierarchical control over an action A if and only if S does A, and A is caused (in a nondeviant appropriate way) by a desire which S hierarchically endorses. Finally, the proponent of hierarchical control can be taken to be committed to this principle:

> HC: A person is morally appraisable for performing an action only if she exercises hierarchical control over that action.

HC yields intuitively correct results in a host of cases including Glaucon's and Meno's. Glaucon and Meno, we noticed, differ in an interesting way in their motivational constitution. Glaucon, it appears, *is* morally appraisable for pocketing the gold coin. When he pockets the coin, he wants to be motivated by the self-interested desire to keep the coin; hence, he hierarchically endorses the desire to keep the coin, and exercises hierarchical control over keeping the coin. Meno, however, struggles against his first-order desire to smoke the cigarette. Despite his wanting not to act on this desire, the desire gets the better of him; he fails (hierarchically) to endorse it. Hence, when he succumbs to this desire, he lacks hierarchical control over his action. HC proclaims, rather plausibly, that Meno is not morally appraisable for lighting up.

The account of hierarchical control enjoys some other advantages. For instance, it appears that a person can exercise hierarchical control over an action even if the person could not have done otherwise. Causal determinism, then, does not undermine this sort of control. More along the same lines, the account implies that, insofar as the control condition of moral appraisability is concerned, the factors that explain control (and so ascriptions of appraisability) need not appeal to anything other than the agent's here-and-now (or current-time slice) psychological constitution. In particular, no appeal need be made to historical factors—factors concerning *how* the agent came to acquire her desires, or intentions, or other springs of action. An account of control, not pegged to such "historical factors," may be thought to enjoy a significant advantage over one which does appeal to such factors. For one might believe, as some incompatibilists like

Pereboom do, that if one fails to have causal control over the historical factors that give rise to the springs of one's action, one cannot be appraisable for performing the action.

4. PROBLEMS WITH HIERARCHICAL CONTROL

Despite its advantages, the account of hierarchical control is also plagued with its share of pressing problems. While several of these have been catalogued in the literature, I want to call attention to two.[3]

First, Frankfurt describes an addict (call her "Hera") who:

> hates . . . [her] addiction and always struggles desperately, although to no avail, against its thrust. . . . [She] tries everything that . . . [she] thinks might enable . . . [her] to overcome . . . [her] desire for the drug. But these desires are too powerful for . . . [her] to withstand, and, invariably, in the end, they conquer . . . [her]. . . . [She] is an unwilling addict, helplessly violated by . . . [her] own desires. (1971, p. 12)

Assume that Hera acts on an irresistible desire for heroin. It's pretty clear that Hera lacks hierarchical control over taking the drug. In addition, Hera also lacks free will because her "will is outside [her] control"; her desire for the drug will cause her to act "regardless of whether or not [she] wants this desire to constitute her will" (Frankfurt 1971, p. 19). So far, so good; Hera, it would seem, is not morally appraisable for taking the drug when her motivating desire is irresistible.

Compare Hera's plight with the plight of the willing addict (call her "Coco"):

> Suppose that . . . [her] addiction has the same physiological basis and the same irresistible thrust as the [addiction of the unwilling addict] . . . but . . . [she] is altogether delighted with . . . [her] condition. . . . [She] is a willing addict, who would not have things any other way. If the grip of . . . [her] addiction should somehow weaken, . . . [she] would do whatever . . . [she] could to reinstate it; if . . . [her] desire for the drug should begin to fade, . . . [she] would take steps to renew its intensity.
>
> The willing addict's will is not free, for . . . [her] desire to take the drug will be effective regardless of whether or not . . . [she] wants this desire to constitute . . . [her] will. But when . . . [she] takes the drug, . . . [she] takes it freely and of . . . [her] own free will. I am inclined to understand . . . [her] situation as involving the overdetermination of . . . [her] first-order desire to take the drug. This desire is . . . [her] effective desire because . . . [she] is physiologically addicted. But it is . . . [her] effective desire also because . . . [she] wants it to be. . . . [Her] will is outside . . . [her] control, but, by . . . [her] second-order desire that . . . [her] desire for the drug should be effective, . . . [she] has made this will . . . [her] own. Given that it is therefore not only because of . . . [her] addiction that . . . [her] desire for the drug is effective, . . . [she] may be morally responsible for taking the drug. (Frankfurt 1971, pp. 19–20)

Frankfurt's discussion of the willing addict is intriguing but puzzling. It unearths difficulties for the account of hierarchical control. Frankfurt believes that his willing addict is morally appraisable for taking the drug. But why exactly? As a first stab, one might compare Coco's situation with Glaucon's. Just as Glaucon has taken purposive steps to develop and act on self-interested desires, so we can suppose Coco has taken purposive steps to cultivate desires—even irresistible ones—for taking the drug. Both Coco and Glaucon are appraisable for their (relevant) actions, it might be claimed, roughly because of the manner in which they acquired their desires. They are appraisable, both causally and morally, for acquiring certain desires and perhaps also for maintaining those desires, and so are appraisable for acting on them.

However, this sort of explanation, with its reliance on how one acquires the springs of one's actions, would not be congenial to a "current time-slicer" like Frankfurt. Frankfurt insists that "to the extent that a person identifies himself with the springs of his actions, he takes responsibility for those actions and acquires moral responsibility for them; moreover, the questions of how the actions and his identifications with their springs are caused are irrelevant to the questions of whether he performs the actions *freely* or is morally responsible for performing them" (1988c, p. 54).[4]

Another explanation of why Frankfurt supposes the willing addict like Coco to be morally appraisable for taking the drug, even when she acts on an irresistible desire, is simply that she has secured conformity between her second-order volition concerning her first-order desire to take the drug, and this first-order desire. In other words, Coco exercises hierarchical control over taking the drug, even though her taking of the drug is caused by a literally irresistible desire. This explanation is unburdened by any appeal to how Coco comes to acquire the springs of her action.

But this sort of explanation (call it the "strictly hierarchical explanation"), free from associations with historical considerations, has serious difficulties, as is highlighted by the following cases. First, reflect on Poppy's Plight. Suppose Poppy has (nonculpably) acquired a desire to take a particular drug. Unlike Glaucon, she has not decided to mold her character in a certain fashion; she hasn't decided, for instance, to become an addict. Rather, like so many of our mundane wants, she has simply acquired a desire to take a certain drug. Assume that when she first acquires this desire, it is resistible. Assume, in addition, that when she acquires this desire, she hierarchically endorses it: she has a second-order volition, which does not conflict with any of her other second-order desires, that the first-order desire to take the drug be her motivating desire. Suppose Poppy has happily been acting on this sort of desire for some time but, unbeknownst to her, the relevant desire has now become irresistible (or has been replaced by an irresistible one). Even if she wanted to, she could no longer refrain from taking the drug. It is at least reasonable to suppose that, although she doesn't know it, Poppy has now lost appraisability-grounding control over her taking of the drug; she is no longer in the driver's seat. She no longer seems morally appraisable for taking the drug even though she exercises hierarchical control over taking it. What this scenario suggests is that second-order volitions, which are after all, just desires, do not really have any unique and substantial role to play in the explication of control.

To develop this last thought, reflect on this variation of Poppy's predicament: suppose that, once again, Poppy finds herself with a first-order desire to take the drug, a desire which she *can* resist. Suppose that initially, she has no second-order volitions concerning this desire. She reflects for a while. She is aware that taking the drug isn't good for her, but decides that she should indulge anyway. Pretty clearly, none of Poppy's simple reflections over whether she should take the drug *need* be "second-order;" they *could* be, but they needn't be. Assume, then, that none of her reflections *are* second-order, and assume, finally, that she acts on her decision. It seems that Poppy could, under these circumstances, be morally appraisable for taking the drug: there are no "appraisability-undermining factors" in the actual sequence of events that culminate in Poppy's taking the drug. Now let's amend these initial circumstances by imagining that in addition to the first-order desire for the drug, Poppy acquires a second-order volition concerning the (resistible) first-order desire; she now wants this first-order desire to be her motivating desire. Perhaps she believes that, given some of the reasons she has for not taking the drug, she will augment the force of the motivation to take the drug by wanting the desire to take the drug to be the desire that moves her all the way to action. If she was appraisable for taking the drug under circumstances in which she didn't have the relevant second-order volition, surely she should now, having acquired the second-order volition, still be appraisable (other things being equal). Nothing of significance, at least as far as appraisability for Poppy's taking the drug goes, seems to have changed. But then acquisition of the second-order volition seems to have contributed nothing to control.

There is a second sort of case which suggests that the strictly hierarchical explanation of why Frankfurt's willing addict is appraisable for taking the drug is not right. Suppose a bunch of evil neurosurgeons can, without Sara's being aware of it, directly stimulate her brain, thereby causing her to have desires and losing others. Suppose the neurosurgeons, using their technique of brain stimulation, succeed in implanting in Sara a desire to take a drug and a second-order volition concerning that desire. Suppose they also succeed in eradicating all second-order desires that conflict with the implanted second-order volition. In order words, they engineer in endorsement; they manipulate Sara in such a way that she not only finds herself with a desire for the drug, but she also hierarchically endorses it. Since the implanted first-order desire for the drug is irresistible, Sara acts on it. In this case, it seems that Sara is not morally appraisable for taking the drug *because* she lacks appraisability-grounding control; she is simply a marionette of her manipulators. According to the strictly hierarchical explanation, however, Sara *would* be morally appraisable for taking the drug (assuming other conditions of moral appraisability like epistemic ones are satisfied), as she exercised hierarchical control over taking the drug.

Recently, Eleonore Stump has proposed a revision of Frankfurt's account of freedom of the will which, she believes, enables the (revised) account to escape the objection that endorsement can be engineered (see Stump 1993a,b). She says that an agent's intellect is the computing faculty of the agent. She then proposes that:

> An agent has a second-order volition V_2 to bring about some first-order volition [or desire] V_1 in himself only if the agent's intellect at the time of the willing represents

V₁, under some description, as the good to be pursued. A second-order volition, then, is a volition formed as a result of some reasoning (even when the reasoning is neither rational nor conscious) about one's first-order desires. (1993b, p. 216)

With regard to the "wayward source problem" of engineered-in, second-order volitions, Stump's promising solution is this:

On the revised account, an agent forms a second-order desire by reasoning (rationally or otherwise, consciously or not) about his first-order desires; and a second-order desire is a direct result of an agent's intellect representing a certain first-order desire as the good to be pursued. Given this connection between intellect and second-order desires, an agent cannot be a passive bystander to his second-order volitions. To be a second-order volition, a volition must be the result of reasoning on the agent's part. Even if it were coherent to suppose that one agent, say, Verkhovensky, could directly produce some reasoning in the mind of another, such as Stavrogin, that reasoning would not be Stavrogin's but rather Verkhovensky's. . . . If Verkhovensky continuously produced thoughts in Stavrogin, then Stavrogin would have ceased to be a person and would instead be something like Verkhovensky's puppet. On the other hand, suppose Verkhovensky produced thoughts in Stavrogin's mind only occasionally, so that Stavrogin remained a person. In the computations leading to an action, Stavrogin's own intellect would take cognizance of the thought Verkhovensky had produced in Stavrogin's mind, and Stavrogin would then either accept or reject Verkhovensky's thought as a result of Stavrogin's own reasoning. . . . As Stavrogin acts, then, the first-order volition stemming from his reasoning and the accompanying second-order desire will be Stavrogin's and not Verkhovensky's. Either way, Stavrogin would not have any second-order volitions produced by Verkhovensky. So, on the revised Frankfurt account, an agent's second-order volitions cannot be produced by someone else. (1993b, pp. 219–20)

In light of these suggestions of Stump, a revised hierarchical account of control can be formulated in this way: First, Stump disambiguates the term 'second-order desire.' She says that an effective (or alternatively, a motivating) desire is a desire to move an agent all the way to action if unimpeded. Stump explains that "when an agent wants to make a certain first-order desire his . . . [effective desire], then he has a second-order desire [or what, following Frankfurt's usage, we have been calling a "second-order volition"]; and when this second-order desire is effective, that is, when . . . [the agent] succeeds in making that first-order desire his . . . [effective desire], then he has a second-order volition" (1993a, p. 242). So Stump's use of 'volition' is more restrictive than Frankfurt's. Second, we reemphasize that according to Stump, a second-order volition is a volition formed as a result of some reasoning (even when the reasoning is neither rational nor conscious) about one's first-order desires. Third, agent S S-hierarchically endorses a first-order desire D, to perform some action, A, if and only if S has a second-order volition, V, (relative to D) that D be S's motivating desire, and S has no second-order desires that conflict with V. Fourth, S exercises hierarchical control over A if and only if S does A, and A is caused (in a nondeviant suitable way) by a desire that S S-hierarchically endorses. Finally, revised hierarchical theory says that a person is morally appraisable for performing an action only if she exercises hierarchical control over that action.

Stump's suggestive attempt to deal with the wayward source problem merits a number of comments. Notice, first, that her revision forces a retreat from the "current-time slice" view: on her view, whether an agent is morally appraisable for performing an action at a time is not determined solely by the configuration of his psychological elements that generated his action at that time. Rather, the *genesis* of those elements is pivotal. Stump stresses that a second-order volition *must* be the result of reasoning on the agent's part.

One problem with Stump's revised account is this: I have argued, in discussing Poppy's plight, that it is possible for an agent to be morally appraisable for performing an action even if the action is the product of actional elements like beliefs, desires, intentions, and so forth, none of which have been formed or acquired on the basis of second-order reasoning. Poppy, in forming an intention to take the drug, need not have reasoned about the sorts of desires or beliefs she wants to have, or the desires by which she wants to be motivated. If such cases are possible, the revised view fares no better than the original in explaining how Poppy can be morally appraisable for an action that does not issue from a desire she S-hierarchically endorses.

Here is another problem. Suppose Sam comes across a wallet chock full of money lying on the desk of an otherwise deserted office. He finds himself pulled in both directions—he wants to pocket the money and he wants to return it to its owner. Sam values being the sort of person who always does what is morally right. His values, and reflection on his first-order desires concerning the money, cause him to form the all-things-considered judgment that he ought to return the money. The judgment, in turn, causes him to acquire the second-order volition that his desire to return the money be the one on which he acts. This second-order volition, then, is a result of Sam's "intellect representing a certain first-order desire as the good to be pursued." Assume that Sam has no second-order desire that conflicts with this second-order volition. So Sam S-hierarchically endorses his first-order desire to return the money. But now suppose Sam succumbs to weakness and *akratically* pockets the cash. Since he acts on a desire that he does not S-hierarchically endorse (he has no second-order volition that he be motivated by the desire to keep the money), the hierarchical account yields the result that Sam is not morally appraisable for pocketing the cash. This result, however, is pretty controversial. Surely one can be morally appraisable for performing an action even if it is an akratic one.

Finally, there is a third problem with the revised account. The account is not neutral about the basis of second-order volitions. These volitions are volitions formed as a result of some reasoning about one's first-order desires. It is this constraint that provides hope for an answer to the wayward source problem. On the revised view, Sara is not morally appraisable for taking the drug as her taking of the drug is not an action that issues from an appropriately formed second-order volition. The volition concerning the desire on which Sara acts is not the product of reflection on Sara's part on her first-order desires; rather, it is an engineered-in, second-order desire. But now reconsider Psychogen in which Max, the mad neurologist, transforms Jenny (in the absence of her knowing anything about the transformation psychosurgery), into a psychological twin of Jim. Suppose Jenny has awakened from surgery. She performs what would normally be a praiseworthy deed, which is caused (in part) by a second-order volition concerning the relevant first-order desire. And suppose this volition is the result of *Jenny's* reasoning about her first-order desires. Such a case of global manipulation is not intuitively one in which some agent continuously produces thoughts in another. I'm still inclined to judge that, contrary to the implication of the revised hierarchical view, globally manipulated Jenny is *not* in fact praiseworthy for the deed.

In light of these difficulties with the hierarchical view, it is worth seeking a different account of control.

5. VOLITIONAL CONTROL

Reconsider Hera's plight. Assume that Hera is not in any way to blame for her addiction, and that on a certain occasion she finds herself in the grips of an irresistible desire to inject herself. Although she forms an intention not to take the drug, which is generated partly on the basis of a desire to refrain from taking the drug, she eventually loses the battle and shoots up. In this sort of case, I am inclined to believe, with Frankfurt, that Hera lacks the type of control over her action needed for moral appraisability.

I want to develop an account of control sensitive to the idea that an agent exercises the relevant sort of control over an action (or its causal springs) only if the action is responsive to the agent's practical reasoning. The action must be guided in a suitable fashion by the agent's own reasons if the agent is to be appraisable for performing it. So I need to provide at least an outline of an account of the role of reason in ascriptions of appraisability.

I assume, taking the lead of Alfred Mele and others, that full-blown deliberative action involves (1) some psychological basis for evaluative reasoning (e.g, pro-attitudes like values and desires, and beliefs); (2) a first-person practical judgment made on the basis of such reasoning that recommends a particular course of action; (3) an intention or decision formed or acquired on the basis of that judgment; and (4) an action executing that intention or decision (see Mele 1995, pp. 13, 177). I propose that an agent's deliberations that generate first-person practical judgments about what to do involve an assessment of reasons for or against action, by appeal to an *evaluative scheme* of the agent's. An agent's evaluative scheme comprises, roughly, these constituents: (a) normative standards the agent believes (though not necessarily consciously believes) ought to be invoked in an assessment of reasons for action, or beliefs about how the agent should go about making choices. The standards offer guidance within and across specific "domains." So, for instance, Jenny might believe that financial decisions should be made on the counsel of her stockbroker even though the recommendations of the latter pay little heed to morality, culinary choices should be made in accordance with Julia Child's recommendations, and moral choices should be based on the teachings of her religion. I make no presumptions about norms being shared by agents. Unlike Jenny, James might believe that all decisions across economic, culinary, etiquettical, or aesthetic domains should be made on the basis of some utilitarian moral principle. (b) The agent's long-term ends or goals he deems worthwhile or valuable. James, for example, may underscore his commitment to attempting to maximize overall happiness whenever he acts. (c) Deliberative principles the agent utilizes to arrive at practical judgments about what to do or how to act. For instance, James may believe that the best way to maximize utility is to rely on rules of thumb like "keep your promises," "don't cheat," "don't steal," etc. (d) Lastly, motivation to act on the basis of the normative standards in a and goals in b using the deliberative principles in c.

Evaluative schemes enable agents to assess (among other things) their desires, objects of their desires, feelings, thoughts, and reasons for action. The reasoning involved in such assessment need not, of course, be consciously undertaken. Nor need it be immaculate; it could be ill-informed, hasty, careless, or irrational in some other way. Given this sort of assessment, one can (somehow) arrive at first-person *all-things-considered judgments* about what to do or how to act in particular circumstances. It is true that some first-person practical judgments can be overridden by others. Sam, for instance, may have judged that it is prudentially best for him to take the money, but this judgment need not have committed him to action as he did not (we can assume) take such judgments to be overriding. Rather, we can suppose that he takes moral judgments to trump prudential ones in cases of conflict. So every thing considered, we can assume that Sam judged it best not to take the money. All things considered judgments to perform an action *commit* an agent to action in the sense that the agent *settles* on, or holds herself ready to perform, the action. It is possible for one to fail to perform an action on which one has settled because of external impediments, or preponderant motivation to do something else. Hera, overcome by an irresistible desire for the drug, does something she is not settled upon doing.[5] But in the absence of such internal and external impediments, an agent will normally carry out the action on which she is settled.

Using 'desire' broadly to refer to any pro-attitude having inherent motivational force, I assume each intentional action is caused (in part) by some proximal desire. Let's call such a proximal desire the "motivational precursor" of the action. Now we can introduce the crux of the notion of volitional control:

> Volitional control: Action, A, performed by agent, S, is under her volitional control if and only if, holding constant the motivational precursor of A and S's evaluative scheme, there is a scenario with the same natural laws as the actual world in which, relying on her evaluative scheme, S arrives at a decision or forms an intention to do something other than A, and she successfully executes that decision or intention.[6]

For a desire in one scenario to be the same desire as a desire in another scenario, the two should have the same relative strength—they must have the same strength relative to competing desires. I provisionally propose that an agent is morally appraisable for performing an action only if she has volitional control over that action.

As I said above, what motivates this picture of control is the ancient idea that an agent exercises the right sort of control (required for moral appraisability) over an action only if the action is responsive to the agent's practical reasoning. An action that is under an agent's volitional control is responsive to the first-person practical judgments to do something made by the agent, and to the decision or intention to do things formed on the basis of such judgments. Such an action is, then, responsive to the agent's practical reasoning.

Preliminary clarifications regarding my *account* of the notion of volitional control will, hopefully, shed some light on the notion. First, suppose S actually does A. How, one might query, can the motivational precursor of A be held constant, in a counter-to-fact scenario in which S decides, instead, to do B and B-s? Wouldn't a decision to do B (rather than A) be based on a proximal desire to do B? In response, the requirement that the motivational precursor of A be held constant does *not* amount to a requirement which entails that if S B-s in the counterfactual scenario, the motivational precursor of A, say DA, will *also* be the motivational precursor of B. Rather, the correct understanding is that in the alternative scenario in which S B-s, S in that scenario also have DA (in addition to other pro-attitudes S might already have or could acquire).

Second, I have claimed that for a desire in one scenario to be the same desire as a desire in another, the two should have the same strength relative to competing desires. But then, one might believe, I am encumbered with another worry: How can it be that, in the alternative scenario, all desires retain their same relative strengths? Wouldn't this mean that, if in the one scenario the desire to do A is stronger than the desire to do B, this would also hold for the alternative scenario? What then would explain S's doing B?

The concern just raised appears to rest on this sort of actional principle: If an agent wants more to do A than she wants to do anything else she takes to compete with A, and if she believes she can A, then she will intentionally A, or at least try to A, if she intentionally does anything.[7] I shall here simply indicate that this principle is controversial as Randolph Clarke has recently argued. Clarke proposes that even if *total* motivational strengths of competing desires are held fixed, factors like habit may be sufficient to move the agent to act on a weaker desire:

> Suppose that certain neural pathways in the brain are associated with voluntary behavior of certain sorts. Suppose that when such a pathway is frequently activated, neurological changes occur such that less stimulation is then required to activate the pathway. (There might, for example, be an increase in the amount of neurotransmitter released with each action potential (firing) of initiating neurons and an increase in the number of receptor sites available at the adjacent postsynaptic membranes.) Now suppose that habitually performing a certain type of action in certain circumstances thus alters the neural pathways involved in the performance of actions of that type. Then, it may be that a relatively weak desire is sufficient to move the agent to perform an action of the sort that she has made habitual, while a stronger desire is required to move her to perform an alternative. Thus it may be that on some occasion, the agent desires more strongly to perform an alternative action but instead does what she habitually does. She is, as it were, resting on an incline, and the weaker force, in that context, is sufficient to move her in its direction. (1994a, p. 6)

Even if one disagrees with Clarke, there is another way to respond to the worry that, holding constant the relative strengths of desires across scenarios, there wouldn't be a suitable "desire-belief" explanation regarding why S B-s in the counterfactual scenario if S A-s in the actual. The key lies in clarifying the notion of sameness of relative strength of desires. Several factors (as Mele has noted) can contribute to the motivational strength of a given desire (Mele 1987a, chap. 5). Mele proposes that the positive motivational base of a desire is the collection of all occurrent motivations of the agent that make a positive contribution to the motivational strength of that desire; similarly, the negative motivational base of a desire is the collection of all occurrent motivations that make a negative contribution to its motivational strength. The positive and negative motivational bases of a desire constitute its total motivational base. Mele argues that the total motivational base of a desire need not determine its (total) motivational strength. The strength of a desire can also be affected by attentional factors, such as focusing on the desired aspects of the object of the desire, or by cognitive matters such as vividness of representation, or by habit (Mele 1987a, pp. 67–72). Reverting, now, to the account of volitional control, we can offer this elucidation: for a desire in one scenario to be the same desire as a desire in another, the two should have the same total motivational bases. Suppose S (in the actual world) desires more strongly a strawberry sundae than a hot fudge sundae (where relative strength, is determined exclusively by the desire's total motivational base). Suppose, in a counterfactual scenario, S still retains the desires for the two sundaes, these desires have the same motivational bases as they had in the actual world, but S in this scenario sees a delectable hot fudge sundae being prepared. S may, in this world, be more motivated overall to order a hot fudge sundae than to order a strawberry sundae. Holding constant the relative strengths of desires, then, is perfectly compatible with there being an appropriate explanation of why S B-s rather than A-s in the counterfactual scenario. In addition, holding fixed relative strengths of desires is also, of course, compatible with the agent's acquiring new desires in the alternative scenario—ones she did not have in the actual world.

The centrality of volitional control to moral appraisability—volitional control as the factor that appears to ground our ascriptions of moral appraisability-paves the way to accommodate the intuition that agents in Frankfurt-type cases *are* (or *can* be) morally appraisable for what they do. Consider this Frankfurt-type scenario. Suppose Jones decides (on his own) to kill Max and on the opportune occasion successfully (and nondeviantly) executes her nefarious decision. Unbeknownst to her, had she shown any sign or inclination not to will or decide to murder Max, Dark Demon, who had carefully been monitoring the situation all along, would have, via direct manipulation of Jones's brain, caused her to will to kill Max and to act on the volition to kill Max. As the demon does not interfere with the unproblematic sequence of events that culminates in Jones's killing Max, it appears that Jones is morally appraisable for the killing even though she could not have done otherwise. I submit that Jones is morally appraisable for, say, squeezing the trigger, as she exercised volitional control over that action. Jones's lethal action is *responsive* to Jones's evaluative judgment to kill Max, a judgment made on the basis of her evaluative scheme, and to Jones's decision to kill Max, which itself presumably derives from the appropriate evaluative judgment. That it is so responsive is confirmed by noting that there is an alternative scenario (one in which, for example, Dark Demon is not waiting in the wings) in which Jones has the motivational precursor to kill Max, decides against acting on this proximal desire, and victoriously exercises restraint.

In contrast, as Hera acts on an irresistible desire to take the drug, there is no scenario with the same natural laws as the actual world in which Hera has the motivational precursor of her taking the drug, forms an intention partly on the basis of her evaluative scheme to refrain from taking the drug, and successfully executes this intention. Hera thus acts without the relevant sort of control—volitional control—required for moral appraisability over her taking of the drug.

One might wonder why an agent, like Jones, who squeezes the trigger (and thereby kills Max) and who has volitional control over squeezing the trigger, has appraisability-relevant control over squeezing the trigger *just* because of the existence of the sort of alternative scenario in question. There seems, after all is said and done, no guarantee that Jones has *access* to this scenario; the alternative world, in other words, need not be accessible to Jones. My reply is that as I don't hold that moral appraisability requires alternative possibilities, I don't need to commit myself to the view that some alternative is *accessible* to the agent. Alternative scenarios are relevant to ascertaining whether what the agent does *is sensitive to her practical deliberations* in the manner explained above: suppose Jones nondeviantly squeezes the trigger, acting "on" the motivational precursor, DST; her squeezing of the trigger is sensitive to her practical deliberations if there is an alternative scenario in which she has DST, she intends or decides to do something other than squeeze the trigger, and she executes the relevant intention or decision.

It should, I hope, now be evident that the notion of volitional control is not meant to capture the idea that an agent has appraisability-grounding control over an action just in case he could do otherwise than he does were it not for the presence of a counterfactual intervener. Rather, lack of volitional control over one's germane action indicates that the action is inappropriately sensitive to one's practical deliberations. To emphasize a point already made, in my view, appraisability-grounding control does not require alternative possibilities even when no counterfactual intervener is in the wings.

Lastly, it might be charged that I seem not to appreciate that the sort of control manifested in intentional action (action that issues from one's practical reasoning) may not be the sort of control that is either necessary or sufficient for *free* action. I am, however (echoing Frankfurt) willing to grant that there are various kinds of freedom, and that volitional control may not be the sort of control required or sufficient for some varieties of free action. So, for instance, perhaps little children and dogs (and "normal" adult human beings as well) sometimes perform actions that are not intentional but free in some sense of 'free'. I will then be committed to the view that these agents cannot be *appraisable* for such actions. If there are varieties of freedom, some may not go hand-in-hand with the type of *control* required for appraisability.

6. REFINEMENTS

The contours of the notion of volitional control are in place. Pressure from the ensuing preliminary objection motivates refinements. In "Alcoholic" Alvin is a long-term drinker. His drinking problems are not attributable to anyone else, but his life has been fraught with challenging adversities and personal tragedies. He has had to face more than his fair share of these taxing trials and tribulations, and he has had to do so more or less on his own. It is no wonder that his drinking is uncontrolled.[8] Suppose, alone in his home, Alvin finds himself with a powerful desire to drink the glass of vodka in front of him. Assume that Alvin *can* on this occasion resist acting on the desire but only at the expense of suffering considerable psychological damage. With little hesitation, Alvin quaffs the drink. It certainly seems that Alvin is not morally appraisable for taking the drink—he lacks appropriate control over his action. However, there are clearly scenarios in which, holding constant the natural laws, Alvin's evaluative scheme, and the motivational precursor of his taking the vodka, Alvin forms an intention to refrain and successfully executes that intention. There are scenarios, for instance, in which Alvin has different habits and a different character (he can muster much more self-control), and there are ones in which he has a supportive family, a far less demanding job, and ample financial means to combat his problem. Cases like Alcoholic force us to confront the taxing problem of *delimiting* the counter to fact scenarios operative in the notion of volitional control. Are there any guidelines governing scenario eligibility? Although drawing principles that segregate the eligible scenarios promises to be daunting, I recommend, as a start, the following.

First, hold constant across scenarios the agent's character and psychological constitution. If Alvin is a person with moderate strength of will, scenarios in which he exhibits immense will power are ineligible. Indeed, I recommend that the (relevant) agents across scenarios be psychologically continuous.[9] The notion of psychological continuity is to be understood in this way: person x is psychologically connected to person y if and only if there are a significant number of psychological connections between x and y, where these connections are relations of similarity, or identity, or causal dependence among psychological states. For instance, x may have the same desires, beliefs, and aims that y has; x may have memories of a certain experience as y had that experience; or x may perform a certain act because y decided to perform it. Person x at time t is psychologically continuous with person y at t* if and only if there is a series of persons at times such that x is the first and y the last member of the series, and each person at a time in the series is psychologically connected to the preceding person in the series. This condition of psychological continuity is sensitive to the plausible idea that questions about moral appraisability are questions about an agent who endures through time. Second, it is undeniable that our own past histories exert a good deal of influence in molding our characters and psychologies. In Alcoholic, it may not be unreasonable to suppose that Alvin cannot muster sufficient self-control partly as a result of factors like his upbringing, his native endowments, interaction with peers, and the various challenges he has had to face. I propose that eligible alternative scenarios be ones in which Alvin has the same psychological and motivational history as he has in the actual scenario up to (or at least very close to) the time of the relevant action (which, in Alcoholic, is Alvin's taking the vodka): we hold constant, in the alternative scenarios, the historical factors that contribute to the formation of the agent's character and his psychological constitution, and those that give rise to the conative elements (like desires) on which the agent acts in the actual scenario. Other elements, like doxastic ones that enter into the agent's deliberations, or attentional factors (like selective focusing) can, of course, vary across scenarios. Third, we can grant that even in a (counter to fact) scenario in which Alvin's character, psychological constitution, and history are held constant, should certain "external" factors obtain in the scenario, Alvin would be able to form an intention to refrain from the drink and act on it. Alvin, for example, might in this scenario *now* find himself with a supportive spouse, a life ridded of much stress, and ample financial means to combat his drinking problem. Were such a scenario an eligible one, we would once again derive the unacceptable result that Alvin does (in the actual scenario) possess volitional control over his guzzling the vodka. To cope with this sort of worry, notice that factors like having a supportive family, freedom from much stress, and plentiful financial means are ones that Alvin, in his *actual* circumstances, needs to restructure or reshape significantly his life; such factors are, moreover, *not* realistically within his reach. (It would seem that if Alvin *did*, in his actual circumstances, have avenue to these factors, but did not access or make use of them, we would [other things equal] hold him appraisable for taking the drink.) Such "external" factors appear to be pertinently similar to various "internal ones" like irresistible cravings that are intuitively "appraisability-undermining." I suggest that relevant alternative scenarios be free of resources or factors of the type not realistically accessible to the agent in the actual scenario, and required by the agent (in the actual scenario) for serious restructuring of his life.

Further complications with specifying the appropriate alternative scenarios are exposed by cases of this sort. Suppose Crack is addicted to some narcotic. He is aware that if he refrains from taking a dose at a particular time he will either die or suffer radical psychological damage. Assume, as well, that by a sheer act of will, one that would cause him to experience considerable psychic imbalance, he would refrain from taking the dose at that time if refraining would preserve enough of the drug to save the life of a friend. So Crack could refrain under an exceptional-for-him circumstance from acting on the desire to take the drug. Yet it seems that just like Hera, Crack is not appraisable for taking the drug. Similarly, we can imagine an agent who, under unexceptional-for-her circumstances, finds it singularly difficult to resist her desire not to enter the sea, given her great fear of the oceans. Yet in the exceptional-for-her circumstance in which her baby were drowning, she would, with great difficulty, act against her desire and attempt a rescue. My intuitions are that in an unexceptional-for-her circumstance in which she is aware that some adult is drowning, and in which she fails to enter the waters to help, she is not appraisable for failing to enter the waters, again because she lacks relevant control over her desire. As Alfred Mele has commented, it is possible that a person who in ordinary circumstances cannot resist his desire to do something can do so in exceptional ones; it is also possible that an agent who can resist his desire to do something in ordinary circumstances cannot do so in exceptional ones (Mele 1992a, pp. 87–88). Sid, for example, may in ordinary circumstances be able to resist his desire to smoke, but cannot do so when he is under great stress. I doubt whether there is any easy way of distinguishing ordinary from exceptional circumstances, and this is another perplexity. I suggest, tentatively though, that the alternative scenarios to which the concept of volitional control appeals be ones in which the agent not do otherwise (if she does indeed do otherwise) because what moves her to do otherwise are things like *extreme* fear, panic, anxiety, stress, depression, or nervousness; the alternative scenarios must be unexceptional for the agent.

To sum up results, the account of volitional control says this: S has volitional control over her action A if and only if there is a world satisfying certain conditions at which S intends or decides to do something other than A and succeeds in (nondeviantly) doing so. These conditions include: the world's having the same laws as our (the actual) world, S's having the same evaluative scheme and the same character and psychological constitution, S's having the same "conative history" until (or very close to) the time of action (S would, then, in this world have the proximal desire that gives rise to A in the actual world), and the world's not including conditions that would be exceptional for the agent, for example, extreme fear, panic, etc. Roughly, part of the idea I am attempting to capture is that someone has volitional control just in case his intentions, decisions, or actions are sensitive to at least some beliefs about what the world is like. So if there is a world at which Fred is psychologically just the same except that he believes that if he eats a second piece of mud pie his significant other will think he is a fat slob and leave him, and at this world Fred refrains from eating the piece of pie, then Fred has volitional control over his eating of the pie.

Some might protest that if the eligible worlds include the same history as well as the same laws as the actual world, then if determinism is true, there are *no* eligible worlds where any agent does other than what she actually does. This view is plainly correct, but the eligible worlds in the account of volitional control are not "law-wise" *and* "past-wise" identical to the actual world. To bring this out, reflect on Mele's important observation that even on the hypothesis that our world is deterministic, it is false that, with respect to each belief that comes to mind during our deliberation, we are in control of its coming to mind (Mele 1995, pp. 215–16). (Of course, if determinism is true, everything on this doxastic front *is* causally determined.) This opens up the possibility that in alternative eligible worlds, given certain antecedent conditions that do not obtain in the actual world, different beliefs (from the ones in the actual world) come to an agent's consciousness during that agent's reasoning about what to do. As an illustration, suppose that in our world certain nonoccurrent beliefs come to Fred's mind during his deliberations about whether to eat the pie (and it is causally determined which of these beliefs come to his mind). These beliefs, together with various other factors like selective focusing, failing to take into account the long-term effects of eating the pie, etc., result in Fred's eating the pie. Now consider an alternative world with identical laws to ours and that does not include conditions that are exceptional for Fred in which Fred has the same desires, values, character, and psychological constitution as he has in the actual world and the same *conative* history up to the time of action (remember, we hold constant across worlds the historical factors that lead to the conative elements like desires that Fred has in the actual scenario). Suppose that in this world, a *different* batch of nonoccurrent beliefs enters into Fred's deliberations about whether to eat the pie (and it is causally determined that this batch enters into Fred's deliberations in this world). Nothing in the description of volitional control precludes this possibility. A big sign on the door of Fred's refrigerator (together with other appropriate antecedent conditions) absent in the actual world may be sufficient to ensure that the beliefs that enter into Fred's deliberations in this world are different from those that enter into his deliberations in the actual world. But then it is perfectly possible that, given this different set of beliefs, Fred decides differently in this world and refrains from eating the pie. Fred simply treats *these* beliefs as he treats other doxastic input to deliberation; using these beliefs in an attempt to decide whether he ought to eat the pie, he decides against indulging and executes his relevant decision.

Despite the four conditions constraining world eligibility summarized above, some might still press the following sort of objection, first advanced (I believe) by Ferdinand Schoeman.[10] Imagine a person, Kassim, who kills a number of passengers on the Staten Island Ferry with a saber. Suppose he would have killed the passengers under all possible circumstances save one: he would have refrained if he believed it was Friday and thus a religious holiday. Intuitively, this highly irrational individual should not be considered morally appraisable for the killings although he exercises volitional control over his pertinent actions. After all, Kassim's actions are responsive to utterly bizarre reasons.

I believe the objection's verdict that Kassim is not morally appraisable for the killings may well be correct. But I disagree with the objection's implicit rationale—that Kassim failed to exercise the right kind of control required for moral appraisability—for this verdict. As I understand the notion of volitional control, a person's actions may be responsive to reasons he takes to be reasonable, but which may be "objectively" bizarre or bizarre from somebody else's point of view. Suppose it's a deeply entrenched belief of Kassim's that Friday is a holy day and that this day should be given up to meditation. Imagine that this belief, together with others deriving from his religion, play a central role in Kassim's conducting the daily chores of living. Why should the mere fact that Kassim's killings are not responsive to a whole array of "reasonable" reasons but *are* responsive to a "bizarre" reason call into question Kassim's control over his actions? Should we say of Kassim's occidental counterpart, Kass, who would have killed under all conditions except one—he would have refrained if he believed that by refraining God would see to it that he ended up in heaven—that Kass fails to exercise relevant control? The reasons to which Kass's and Kassim's barbarous actions are responsive may be "objectively" bizarre but not so deemed by the agents themselves. Indeed, they may play the sort of role in the practical deliberations of these agents that "objectively" mundane reasons play in the deliberations of others. Why should we be willing to attribute control to these others but not to Kassim or Kass?

Consider, now, a variation of Kassim's case which is just like the former save that Kassim this time around is totally deranged. Suppose demented Kassim kills a number of passengers on the Ferry, and he would have killed them under all conditions with the exception of one: he would have refrained if he believed it was Friday. One might object that in this case ("Krazy Kassim"), Kassim *does* have volitional control over his killing the passengers, but since he is totally demented, it is clear that he does not exercise the right sort of control required for moral appraisability over any of his actions.

In response, recall that the underlying idea of volitional control is this: an agent exercises the right type of control for moral appraisability over an action only if the action is responsive to the agent's *practical reasoning*. The notion of volitional control, then, presupposes that agents who have the capacity to exercise volitional control over their intentional actions have the ability to engage in genuine practical deliberation. One should distinguish bad reasoning or deliberation from an activity that does not really amount to reasoning at all. So, for instance, a deranged person who attempts to engage in reflection but who manages only to string together random thoughts or beliefs on the basis of which he acts has not engaged in any reasoning. Analogously, a person who hopelessly misunderstands all the inputs to deliberation-like motivational attitudes such as desires and beliefs will not succeed in engaging in practical deliberation. In addition, there may be problems in processing the inputs to deliberation—problems pertaining to what the agent is capable of doing with that information—that undermine reasoning. For instance, if a person cannot engage in reasonably reliable means/end reasoning (given informational input), then that person lacks the capacity to engage in practical reasoning. There is, I believe, a minimal threshold level of rationality in deliberation; should this level not be met, the agent's so-called "deliberative activities or processes" would simply fail to qualify as genuine deliberation. Once the threshold has been met, it is possible to make gradations with respect to the quality of reasoning; it is then possible, for example, to distinguish good reasoning from bad reasoning given deliberative inputs. There are, of course, problems with identifying precisely where the threshold lies. But the problems on this score are not unique to the account of volitional control being defended; *any* notion of control that appeals to an agent's deliberations will have to presuppose a distinction between genuine deliberation and "deliberative activities" that do not count as deliberation.

Kassim in Krazy Kassim is totally demented. I assume, then, that his "deliberative activities" fall below the threshold level of rationality required for legitimate practical reasoning. In consequence, he fails to qualify as an appropriate subject of moral appraisability. Should it be assumed that Kassim's deliberative activities *do* (in this case) meet the threshold, then I see little reason to deny that Kassim exercises volitional control over his killing the passengers. (This does not, as I remarked above, commit me to the view that Kassim is to blame for the killings.)

Admittedly, the four guidelines governing scenario eligibility that have been proposed are sketchy, need refinement, and are probably not sufficient to overcome all potential worries regarding scenario eligibility. (The last condition, for instance, suffers from the unhappily vague distinction between exceptional and unexceptional circumstances, a pressing perplexity.) But I believe that they do go some way toward illuminating the concept of volitional control.

Finally, I address one more preliminary worry with the condition that a person is morally appraisable for performing an action only if that action is under her volitional control. The objection appeals to cases in which a person freely and intentionally sees to it that a subsequent action of hers is not under her volitional control. As a representative case, suppose Poppy agrees to swallow a magical potion, fully knowing that having done so, she will be unable to refrain from killing an enemy. Presumably Poppy is morally appraisable for the killing, although having imbibed the potion, she lacks volitional control over the killing. The objection points up the need for a "tracing principle." Poppy's being appraisable traces, roughly, to an earlier action of hers—her taking the potion—over which she did enjoy volitional control. Suppose an agent lacks volitional control over an action, A, of hers, roughly, in virtue of the fact that she has intentionally taken deliberate steps, over which she has volitional control, to see to it that she lacks volitional control over A, or to bring about A with the realization that either she will lack volitional control over A, or that she will not be able to refrain from A-ing. If we call A-type actions "appraisably nonvolitional responsive actions," then the condition for moral appraisability corrects to the following: one is morally appraisable for performing an action only if one has volitional control over that action or that action is an appraisably nonvolitional responsive action.

7. CONCLUSION

It should be evident that a person could exercise volitional control over an action even if she had no other genuine alternatives; having this sort of control over an action is compatible with unfreedom to do otherwise. Causal determinism does not, then, threaten this kind of control by virtue of ruling out alternative possibilities. This is an attractive feature of volitional control. However, it might also be thought that this account of control is infected with severe defects. In the next chapter, I turn to a set of examples which appear to show that volitional control is not even required for appraisability: the examples seem to show that a person can be appraisable for an action even though he fails to exercise volitional control over the action. Developing a response to this problem will help illuminate and further refine the notion of volitional control.

FIVE

✛▸━◂✛

APPRAISABILITY, AUTONOMY,
AND CONTROL

I. IS VOLITIONAL CONTROL REQUIRED
FOR MORAL APPRAISABILITY?

Ancient wisdom counsels that appraisability requires control. I have proposed that the relevant type of control is volitional control; an agent's action must be under the control of her practical reasoning if she is to be morally appraisable for it. If this is so, then there is a forthright explanation of why Bond is not blameworthy for killing Smernof in Secret Agent, one of the cases with which we began. Recall, in Secret Agent, Bond is the puppet of Xenia. By electronically controlling his brain, Xenia implants in Bond a powerful near-irresistible desire to kill Smernof, together with the beliefs that the desire is irresistible and that it is Bond's moral (and professional) duty to kill Smernof. When Bond acts on this desire, he does not exercise volitional control over his squeezing the trigger. So he is not blameworthy for his lethal action.

However, not everyone will accept this explanation of Bond's not being to blame. Some will urge that there is an alternative better rationale: Bond is not blameworthy because he did not act on a desire that was "truly his own"; he was not autonomous with respect to this desire of his. On this alternative, moral appraisability presupposes autonomy.

The advocate of the autonomy view might, further, directly challenge the condition that appraisability requires volitional control. She might ask us to focus on the following sorts of cases in which, it is claimed, the relevant agents are autonomous with respect to certain actions, lack volitional control over them, but are still morally appraisable on account of performing them. A devoted lover might find that he cannot bring himself to betray the person whom he loves even for all the riches of the world or for all the fame he ever desired. Indeed, he finds himself unable (at the pertinent time) to acquire the motivation for betrayal. A mother may have a literally irresistible urge to run into a burning house to save her child who is at risk; failing to attempt a rescue would be unthinkable for her. Again, the mother is unable to have (at the relevant time) the motivation to refrain from undertaking a rescue. A nurse might find that she cannot abandon care of the sick and orphaned infant to whom she has grown attached even when the allotted funds for the infant's care have been exhausted. Relevantly like the other two, the compassionate nurse is unable at the time to possess motivation to give up care. To these agents certain courses of action are not real alternatives; they are simply not options among which they can choose as they please. The unavailability of the relevant range of alternatives (in the mother's case, for instance, the alternative to remain outside the blazing home) makes it plausible to claim that their freedom of choice is circumscribed. A salient sort of constraint operative in these cases is, in an intelligible fashion, one that is internal to the agents: their commitment to what they in fact undertake to do is so strong that they cannot will to perform any alternative. If we entertain the controversial but not unreasonable assumption that it is not possible for an agent to perform an action without having and being able to acquire (at the germane time) some sort of pro-attitude, like a volition or a desire, to perform the action in question,[1] or that it is not possible for an agent to perform an action in the presence of sufficiently strong contra-attitudes toward that action, then it seems that our agents literally could not have avoided doing what they did.[2] Indeed, given their natures, it is questionable whether there are any circumstances in which parts of their nature responsible for their restraint are still constitutive of our agents, the agents will or decide to do otherwise than what they did in fact do, and the agents do otherwise. In the terminology that we have introduced, it is questionable whether there are alternative scenarios in which, holding constant the natural laws, the agents' evaluative schemes, and the motivational precursors of their actions, the agents can form an intention to do otherwise than what they in fact do, and execute their intentions. So the mother's running into the flaming house, the lover's remaining faithful, and the nurse's devotion are not under the agents' volitional control. Yet, in conducting themselves as they do, our agents act in conformity with their deepest nature or, speaking somewhat figuratively, their "deepest self." They are, it seems, manifestly not passive or helpless bystanders to their own behavior. As Harry Frankfurt has suggested, our agents may well regard their own behavior as enhancing both their autonomy and their strength of will (1988b, p. 87). Enhancement aside, at least this much is true: typically, such agents *take* themselves to have acted autonomously or freely. Their constrained behavior is liberating; they act so to speak "under liberating constraints." In broad strokes, when an agent performs some action under liberating constraints, the agent could not avoid performing that action, his inability to do otherwise stems from his not being able to will to do otherwise, he could not bring himself to do otherwise or acquire motivation to do otherwise, yet in performing the action, the agent may well regard himself as having acted freely or autonomously, or "in character" (as opposed to "out of character"), or in conformity with his "deep self." Since action under liberating constraints issues from one's "deep self," it seems reasonable to suppose, as some (like Susan Wolf) have recommended, that the person who acts under such constraints is morally appraisable for her action (see, for example, Wolf 1990, pp. 58–59). So it may seem evident that the mother is deserving of praise for saving the child. Likewise, it may appear that the lover is morally praiseworthy for being faithful, and the nurse morally praiseworthy for remaining with the infant. Volitional control, it would consequently appear, falls by the way; it is not even required for moral appraisability.

2. THE AGENDA

Our objector claims that Secret Agent is a case in which Bond is not morally blameworthy for squeezing the trigger, and he is not morally to blame *not* because he lacks volitional control over shooting Smernof, but because he is not autonomous with respect to the shooting. In addition, our objector insists that cases involving liberating constraints—like the case of the devoted mother—are ones in which a person can be morally appraisable for an action even though she does not exercise volitional control over the action. So if the objector is right about these cases, it seems that volitional control has no role to play in an account of appraisability. Three claims of the objector merit serious consideration: (1) volitional control is not required for moral appraisability; (2) persons acting under liberating constraints, like the caring nurse or the devoted mother, are autonomous—roughly in the sense of being self-governing—with respect to their relevant actions, and are morally appraisable for them; and (3) moral appraisability presupposes autonomy: one cannot be appraisable for an action unless one is autonomous with respect to that action.

I shall begin with a case that casts doubt on 3. A weak-willed person who akratically performs an action may not be autonomous with respect to her akratic action, but may well be appraisable for performing that action. So we will be saddled with another puzzle: some cases like Secret Agent appear to show that personal autonomy—autonomy as self-government—is required for moral appraisability, whereas other cases pull in the opposed direction. Where does the truth lie? My response is "somewhere in between." I suggest that any adequate solution to this puzzle must explain why Bond is not blameworthy for the shooting, and why the akrates is nonautonomous—*at least in some compelling sense of 'nonautonomy'*—with respect to his akratic action. To help with this puzzle, I first discuss John Christman's and Richard Double's accounts of autonomy. I argue that these influential accounts do not adequately solve the puzzle; in particular, they run afoul of the strong presumption that akratic action undermines autonomy in *some* nontrivial sense of 'autonomy'. I then distinguish between autonomy with respect to decisions or intentions—"decisional autonomy"—and autonomy with respect to actions or "actional autonomy." Actional autonomy presupposes decisional autonomy: a person cannot be (actionally) autonomous with respect to an action of hers unless that action is caused by a decision (or intention) with respect to which she is (decisionally) autonomous. This distinction between actional and decisional autonomy enables us to assess claims 1, 2, and 3 of the objector. I argue that 3, the claim that one cannot be appraisable for an action unless one is autonomous relative to that action, on a particular reading of 3, is false. The akrates lacks decisional autonomy with respect to his akratic action. As actional autonomy presupposes decisional autonomy, he also lacks actional autonomy with respect to this action. Still, he exercises volitional control over his akratic action, and so (other conditions of moral appraisability being accounted for) he is morally appraisable for his akratic action. I also argue that claim 2, that people who act under liberating constraints *are* appraisable for their relevant actions, is also false. I propose that though such agents may well enjoy decisional autonomy with respect to their relevant actions, they lack volitional control over those actions and are thus not morally appraisable for them. In addition, as I reject 2, and as it is 2 that is offered in support of 1—the objector claims that although persons acting under liberating constraints don't have volitional control over their relevant actions, they are appraisable for those actions—I reject 1. Finally, I shall suggest that despite rejecting 3 (at least on one construal of 3), there *is*, nevertheless, something suggestive about 3; the claim that appraisability presupposes autonomy does signal a kernel of truth, but it is probably not what the advocate of this claim had in mind.

3. SETTING UP A PUZZLE: DOES APPRAISABILITY PRESUPPOSE AUTONOMY?

Secret Agent seems to show that appraisability does indeed require autonomy; one can't be appraisable for performing an action unless one is "self-governing" with respect to that action. Reflect, however, on "Mud Pie," which is a case that lures in the opposite direction. Growls from his belly prompt Fred to pop his head into the refrigerator. His mouth waters at the sight of the pie on the top shelf; its aroma dominates his attention. Fred is perfectly aware that, given his medical condition and certain other subsidiary factors, all things considered, he ought not to eat the pie. Assume that the first-person practical judgment of Fred's, that he ought not to eat the pie, is a judgment that *commits* Fred to action in the sense that were he to fail to act on the judgment, he would do something that is irrational from his own point of view. It turns out, however, that Fred's evaluative assessment of the object of his desire not to eat the pie (his not eating the pie) is misaligned with the motivational strength of this desire; and a little later, still thinking it best not to eat it, Fred carefully embellishes the pie with dollops of cream and then proceeds (intentionally) to feast on it. Imagine that Fred could on this occasion have exercised self-control and refrained from indulging. Pretty clearly, his uncompelled intentional action of eating the pie is an akratic one.[3]

As Mele and others have very plausibly proposed, in a case like Mud Pie, Fred's desire to eat the pie—his "akratic desire"—which is out of line with his all things considered preference, has motivational influence disproportionate to Fred's evaluative assessment of the object of that desire.[4] Fred harbors both the desire to eat the pie and the desire to refrain. Whereas his better judgment assigns diminished ranking to the former, he is much more motivated to act on the former than he is to act on the latter. An explanation of how he comes to have this balance of motivation, given his better judgment, seems adequate to explaining his akratic action. Various explanations of the balance have been proposed, explanations that make use of such things as selective focusing—directing attention to the immediate rewards of eating the pie and avoiding or downplaying the detrimental effects, and failure on the part of the agent to make an effective attempt at self-control.[5]

Fred's intentional action of eating the pie, though free, runs in the face of his better judgment. Personal autonomy seems incompatible with such action; after all, Fred has thwarted his *all things considered* judgment and acted from weakness. Nonetheless, it appears that Fred is certainly deserving of blame for eating the pie.

Secret Agent and Mud Pie set the stage for exploring the challenging issue of whether there is a conceptual connection between autonomy and appraisability. Should one (at least initially) find the alleged moral of Secret Agent more compelling than that of Mud Pie, one might attempt to secure the intuition that appraisability presupposes autonomy by exploiting John Christman's suggestion that "to be free (in a given context) means there is an absence of restraints (positive or negative, internal or external) standing between a person and the carrying out of that person's *autonomously formed* desires" (see Christman 1988, p. 112; 1989, 13). Christman's suggestion appears to be that if an agent, S, acts on a desire, D, to do action, A, then:

FA: S does A freely only if S is autonomous with respect to D.

For if FA is correct and it is a conceptual truth that an agent is appraisable for performing an action only if that agent freely performs that action (where 'free' captures the right sense of control), it follows that an agent cannot be appraisable for performing an action unless the agent is autonomous with respect to the motivational underpinnings of that action.

FA cannot sensibly be assessed without sound appreciation of what it is for an agent to be autonomous with respect to his or her desires. So let's start by considering Christman's "historical" theory of desire autonomy (see Christman 1991, 1993). The discussion will unfold in this direction: I show that FA is implausible. In addition, I argue that Christman's theory is suspect as it relies on a notion of minimal rationality that is questionable. The larger point at issue here is that autonomy of desires, as I propose, is inadequate as a condition of appraisability.

4. FA AND CHRISTMAN'S HISTORICAL ACCOUNT

After revising "the conditions for autonomy . . . originally put forward" in response to "Professor Mele's provocative comments" (1993, p. 281), Christman summarizes his account in this way:

An agent P is autonomous relative to some desire (value, etc.) D at time t if and only if:

(i) P did not resist the development of D (prior to t) when attending to this process of development, or P would not have resisted that development had P attended to the process;

(ii) The lack of resistance to the development of D (prior to t) did not take place (or would not have) under the influence of factors that inhibit self-reflection;

(iii) The self-reflection involved in condition (i) is (minimally) rational and involves no self-deception; and

(iv) The agent is minimally rational with respect to D at t (where minimal rationality demands that an agent experience no manifest conflicts of desires or beliefs which significantly affect the agent's behavior and which are not subsumed under some otherwise rational plan of action.) (1993, p. 288)

Christman explains that the underlying idea of his account is that autonomy is attained when "an agent is in a position to be aware of the changes and development of her character and of why these changes come about" (1991, p. 11). He proposes that self-awareness enables the agent to resist or foster such changes, and recommends that while resisting or fostering such changes, the agent should not be self-deceived, irrational, or under the influence of factors that disrupt self-reflection (1991, p. 11). Christman insists that only "minimal 'internal' conditions for rationality (like consistency of beliefs and desires) would be plausible as conditions for autonomy" (1991, p. 14); and that factors that inhibit self-reflection and so undermine an agent's rationality and self-awareness are things like "hypnosis, some drugs, certain educational techniques, and the like" (1991, p. 19).

Reverting now to FA, the condition that S does action A freely only if S is autonomous relative to the desire (or underlying proximal motivational element) D, that is part of the actual causal sequence of S's doing A, together with this principle (call it "BF") that S is blameworthy for doing A only if S does A freely, entails BA: S is blameworthy for doing A only if S is autonomous relative to D. But this implicate BA is problematic, and the following case illustrates why this is so. Imagine that Jill—a first-rate mechanic—just like Bond, is an implant victim. To amass "spare change" Jill sometimes overcharges some of her customers. Suppose Rex drives in his Ferrari for a service. At the moment Jill sets eyes on the Italian beauty, the implant device is activated and as a result of electronic stimulation Jill finds herself with a desire to amass spare change at Rex's expense. Suppose this desire (Dj) is strong but not irresistible. After careful reflection, Jill acts on Dj. Imagine, further, that had she attended, under conditions of minimal rationality and self-awareness, to the process which generated Dj, Jill would have strongly resisted (or at least attempted to resist) the "development" of Dj. (Assume that Jill has a powerful aversion to being a victim of electronic manipulation.) In this case (Foul Play 1) Jill is not "historically autonomous" relative to Dj (clearly, the first condition of the analysis is not satisfied), but it appears that Jill *is* blameworthy for acting on Dj; she could easily have refrained from playing foul, but she intentionally succumbed to greed. Although she is not historically autonomous relative to Dj, there is still a sense in which Jill governs her actions. Specifically, she is free to exercise responsible choice. Not only can Jill *decide* (and so acquire decisions) to act on a number of relevant desires, she is free to translate any one of these decisions into action.[6] Since BA, the implicate of FA and BF, is false, and BF is a conceptual truth, (FA) must be rejected.[7]

There is another sort of case (Foul Play 2) that, at least preliminarily, appears to highlight the same moral. Suppose Jill acquires the desire to overcharge Rex "on her own," free of any intervention from the implant device. But suppose Jill also has a "conflicting" desire to be fair to her loyal customer. Suppose, after careful deliberation, Jill acts on the former desire (Djj) and overcharges Rex while still retaining the desire to be fair. Once again it appears that Jill is blameworthy for overcharging Rex. But since Jill experiences "'manifest conflicts' in the set of desires and beliefs" (Christman 1993, p. 282) relative to Djj, she is not historically autonomous relative to Djj. In Foul Play 2 it seems that Jill does not satisfy the condition of minimal rationality laid down by Christman for autonomy.

It is open to Christman to rejoin that not every conflict of desires or beliefs undermines autonomy. He is well aware that "there are many internal conflicts of desires and beliefs . . . so mild that they have little effect on behavior. Certainly we would not want to count all individuals who feel the slightest twinge of a counter-desire as lacking autonomy. . . . [Consider] the sprinter who hears a shout that evokes a mild desire to stop running which the sprinter easily ignores. Such a person is moderately conflicted but is clearly autonomous" (1993, pp. 286–87).[8] Christman goes on to propose that:

> a conflict of desires or beliefs indicates a loss of autonomy when that conflict exhibits a noticeable effect on behavior. If the incompatibility of desires is so easily ignored that no significant alteration in one's behavior pattern occurs, then autonomy remains secured. . . . [A] person P is minimally rational at t when P experiences no manifest conflicts of desires or beliefs which significantly effect actions by P at or subsequent to t. (1993, p. 287)

I find this proposal engaging but elusive. Reconsider the sprinter. Christman's idea appears to be that since the sprinter can easily ignore the desire to stop running, this desire will not interfere with the sprinter's strong resolve to run. Hence, as this conflicting desire has no effect on the action the sprinter is bent on performing, the sprinter remains autonomous relative to her desire to run. Well, suppose that Jill in Foul Play 2 is "highly conflicted"; although she has a strong desire to cheat, she also has a strong desire to play fair. Suppose, as well, that after deliberation the former desire carries the moment (the latter desire, of course, need not "extinguish"); Jill *decides* to cheat and cheats. Although Jill was highly conflicted and found it difficult to ignore her desire not to cheat, she resolved to cheat and acted on her resolve. Why should we believe that Jill is not autonomous relative to her desire to cheat? Notice, in addition, that had the desire not to cheat had an effect on Jill's action—had Jill decided to act on the desire not to cheat and then not cheated—we would still retain the intuition that Jill is autonomous relative both to her desire to cheat and her desire not to cheat.

As we have seen, a typical sort of case in which a conflict of beliefs or desires *does*, it appears, undermine autonomy is a sort of case in which the agent acts akratically. Perhaps reflection on this sort of case may help illuminate Christman's proposal. Roughly, akratic action is free, intentional action that is contrary to the agent's better judgment.[9] Suppose what is best all things considered coincides with what is best morally in Mud Pie. In this case, although Fred judges it best (all things considered) not to eat the pie, he freely and intentionally eats the pie, thus acting akratically. We can suppose that Fred has a desire to eat the pie that "conflicts" either with a desire not to eat the pie, or with a desire not to do what is wrong, or with a judgment that it is wrong to eat the pie. Now one might propose that a conflict of desires or beliefs indicates a loss of autonomy when having acted on one of the desires (for brevity, I drop reference to beliefs or judgments); the agent feels she has done something wrong in virtue of not having acted on the conflicting desire, or at least experiences regret or remorse for not having acted on the conflicting desire. But this won't do either. Suppose that in Hard Choice Jones is on lifeguard duty. He spots two children in the otherwise deserted stretch of water who, it is obvious, are in trouble. Jones realizes that he can save only one. He is aware that one of the children has a month to live whereas the other has several years. After some quick but sound deliberation, he saves the one who has several years. Subsequently, he feels remorse for not having acted on the desire to save the other child. Still, at least intuitively, Jones is autonomous relative to his desire to save the child who has several years to live. One can rationally feel remorse (or regret) for not having acted on a conflicting desire, even when one did the best (all things considered or morally) one could, in acting as one did, without compromising autonomy.

Reflection on akratic action prompts yet another interpretation of Christman's proposal that certain conflicts of desires undermine autonomy: a conflict of desires indicates a loss of autonomy when, having acted on one of the desires, the agent feels that she has violated a principle, or ideal, or standard in virtue of not having acted on the conflicting desire. The trouble with this suggestion, however, surfaces fairly easily. A person can, after careful consideration, act on a desire to do what is wrong or what she takes to be wrong (for instance, she could act on a desire to hurt a friend), and then feel that she has acted contrary to an ideal or principle of hers. But the person may well have been autonomous relative to her desire to do wrong.

There is something else amiss with Christman's condition of minimal rationality. The condition specifies that the autonomous individual must not be "guided by *manifestly inconsistent* desires or beliefs" (1991, p. 15). Christman elaborates:

> What this requirement for consistency entails . . . is that the autonomous agent does not act on the basis of mistaken inferences or violation of logical laws. If I believe that 'p' and I believe that 'if p then q,' but I desire something X which is based on the belief that 'not-q,' then the desire for X is not autonomous. (1991, p. 15)

But now consider Bad Reasoner. For reasons over which we need not concern ourselves, Francine Fool desires that Franco not leave the hospital alive. She overhears a remark (R) of Franco's physician that if Franco is not injected with the experimental drug, Franco won't die but will suffer terribly for a long while and then slowly recover. Since she is a bad reasoner, Francine believes R to entail (S) that if Franco is injected with the experimental drug, he will die. Suppose that the belief that S is partly instrumental in causing Francine to desire to inject Franco with the experimental drug. She weighs her options and then acts on this desire (Di). On Christman's account, Francine is not autonomous relative to Di as Di is based on S and Francine believes S on the basis of a mistaken inference. Suppose, now, that freedom presupposes autonomy, and blameworthiness presupposes freedom. Then Francine is not blameworthy for injecting Franco (given Christman's condition of minimal rationality). But once again this result seems unacceptable. Intuitively, Francine is blameworthy for injecting Franco as she exercises control that is indicative of the sort of freedom that is required for moral appraisability. Francine is able to reflect on her options (her reflections need not be, and in fact turn out not to be, logically immaculate), freely make a choice or decision in the wake of this reflection, and freely translate her decision into action.

I have been exploring the view that there is a robust connection between autonomy and blameworthiness. The connection is forged in this way: one can be free only if one is autonomous (FA), and one can be blameworthy only if one is free (BF); so one can be blameworthy only if one is autonomous (BA). I have argued that if Christman's historical account of autonomy is correct, then there is good reason to reject BA, and so good reason to reject FA, on the assumption that BF is a conceptual truth. I have also attempted to show that the historical account rests on a notion of minimal rationality that is problematic. At various junctures, the discussion has raised the possibility that perhaps it is decisions that should be the psychological states to which the predicate *autonomous* primarily applies. It seems, for instance, that Francine acted autonomously in injecting Franco, and Jill (in Foul Play 1) acted autonomously in overcharging Rex, despite the fact that these agents acted on desires that were arguably not "truly their own." Furthermore, the discussion so far, bolstered by the intuition (if one has it) elicited by Mud Pie that Fred is not autonomous relative to his eating of the pie, raises the possibility that there is no essential connection between blameworthiness and autonomy. It is to these possibilities that I now direct attention. I shall assume that in typical cases in which agents act akratically, they fail to act autonomously (at least in some sense of 'autonomous'), and I shall use this assumption as a benchmark to appraise Richard Double's account of autonomy which focuses on agents' choices (see Double 1992).

5. DOUBLE'S ACCOUNT AND AKRATIC ACTION

A central notion in Double's account of autonomy is the notion of one's individual management style:

> Our individual management style [IMS] is that part of our valuational system that (1) expresses how we believe that we should go about making choices; and (2) is part of the causal etiology of our actual choices. Some examples of IMSs would include the following 'management' principles: our 'style' of giving great importance

(or little importance) to the wishes of others or the dictates of morality; the value we place on careful deliberation vs. spontaneity; and the value we see in our ability to concoct justifications for our actions. One's IMS is revealed by one's characteristic way of making decisions, or, more precisely, decisions of certain sorts, since we may think that different approaches are better for different types of choices. (Double 1992, pp. 68–69)

Double advances the following account of autonomy. S's choice C is autonomous just in case (1) C conforms to S's individual management style (the value condition), and (2) C is causally produced by S's individual management style (the efficacy condition) (1992, pp. 68–69).

How does the IMS account fare in relation to akratic action? Suppose Black Jack has a penchant for gambling. Suppose that he characteristically makes gambling decisions on the basis of counsel given him by Lucky Strike; with respect to decisions pertaining to his gambling activities, that is, Black acts on the "management style" principle of giving importance to the counsel of Lucky. Imagine that Black is at the races and, after serious cogitation, correctly judges that it is best for him not to bet on any horse, although he is highly motivated to try his luck. We can suppose that with concerns of life having little to do with gambling, Black makes decisions on the basis of the "Best-for-Black" management style principle. However, true to his relevant domain-specific management principle, Black seeks the counsel of Lucky; the advice given is to put all his remaining money on Slow Boat. I think we can intelligibly suppose that Black (evaluatively) ranks reasons deriving from the Best-for-Black principle higher than he ranks reasons deriving from other domain-specific management style principles. So assume that Black finds himself in a situation in which his best-for-him judgment is out of line with what he is most motivated to do and with what his domain-specific management style principle recommends. Assume, further, that Black acts on the domain-specific principle and places everything down to his last penny on Slow Boat. Having done so, and prior to the race being run, Black feels regret, and he does so *for not having acted in conformity with what he judges best for himself*; although he faithfully follows the germane domain-specific management style principle, Black feels that he has thwarted the standards of "higher reason." Some observations are now in order. First, it is reasonable to suppose that Black acts akratically; though he freely and intentionally acts on a management style principle, Black acts against his better judgment. He freely and intentionally does something that is contrary to what he takes to be good and sufficient reasons not to gamble at the races. Second, in acting against his better judgment, it appears that Black has compromised his autonomy. Neither his decision to bet nor his action of betting is autonomous: though Black has acted on what he accepts as a guiding principle, he has acted against reasons that he takes to be superior to those deriving from the domain-specific principle. Third, it seems that the IMS account dictates that Black has acted autonomously: Black's choice conforms to Black's domain-specific IMS principle, and it is causally produced by this principle.

In a variation of the case, suppose Black judges that *all things considered* he ought not then to bet at all. Suppose, nonetheless, he acts on the domain-specific principle and places all his money on Slow Boat. Once again we can suppose that his all things considered judgment is misaligned with what he is most motivated to do (at the races) and with the prescriptions of the domain-specific principle. Suppose, once more, that prior to the race being run, Black feels that he has done something wrong. In this variation, it appears that Black acts in a manner that is subjectively irrational; his action is irrational from his own point of view. Since he has freely and intentionally acted contrary to an all things considered best judgment, we can safely assume that Black has acted akratically; and if Black ranks reasons deriving from all things considered judgments higher than those deriving from his domain-specific principle, we can assume that neither Black's decision to bet nor the action that issues from that decision is autonomous. Yet, the pronouncement of the IMS account is that Black's choice to place all his money on Slow Boat is autonomous.

If there is a plurality of management style principles, one such principle may exert influence over more than one "domain," and when this happens, it is possible for akratic failure of the kind illustrated to occur. Maybe some sort of ranking of management style principles may help circumvent this problem. But I will not pursue this option here. Rather, I prefer to develop an account that specifically ranks *reasons* for deciding one way or another, and that incorporates what I take to be Double's insight that autonomy requires assessment of choices against standards that agents themselves accept as appropriate for governing behavior.

6. DECISIONAL AUTONOMY

One item on our agenda is this: it has been proposed that people like the devoted mother or the caring nurse who act under liberating constraints are morally appraisable for their germane actions. For example, some will claim that the mother is deserving of praise for rushing into the blazing home to save her child and, similarly, the nurse is praiseworthy for caring for the infant. In addition, it is characteristic of agents who act under liberating constraints that they take themselves to have acted freely or autonomously, and "in character" or in conformity with their "deep self." Action under liberating constraints poses a problem for the account of (volitional) control as agents who act under such constraints lack volitional control over their pertinent actions. So, it has been objected, volitional control is *not* required for moral appraisability.

To meet this objection, I want to distinguish between decisional autonomy and actional autonomy. I propose that agents who act under liberating constraints are *decisionally* autonomous with respect to their relevant actions, but not actionally autonomous relative to those actions. Having decisional autonomy (with respect to the germane actions) explains why such agents take themselves to have acted freely or autonomously. Further, as the account of actional autonomy I develop implies that being actionally autonomous relative to an action requires having volitional control over that action, an agent like the devoted mother who performs an action under liberating constraints lacks volitional control over her action; so she is not morally appraisable for that action.

To construct the concept of decisional autonomy, I shall appeal to the following plausible ideas that have traditionally been associated with autonomy. Autonomy is concerned with principled self-control.[10] When direction is lacking and when an agent fails to act on the basis of any principle, standard, value, or ideal, and acts, for instance, on whim or perhaps purely spontaneously, then even if free and intentional, there is nothing to recommend the behavior as *autonomous*. Whether such behavior is nonautonomous depends essentially on whether the agent has failed to live up to her own values or principles; the agent, to act nonautonomously, must do something in violation of standards that she takes as a basis for appraising her own actions, or her behavior must evidence clear failure of being under his self-direction.

If self-government is pivotal to the notion of autonomy, then it seems that the fundamental bearers of the property of autonomy must be psychological states over which an agent can exercise substantial control. Though we have some influence over the sorts of desires that we have, and over their motivational strength, the degree of control that we wield over them is limited, at least in comparison to the degree of control that we enjoy over the appraisal of the objects of our wants or, more generally, over the appraisal of our reasons for action that figure in the causal genesis of our decisions or intentions. I want to suggest that, to the extent to which our decisions and intentions are more subject to our control than our desires, it is these psychological entities that should take center stage in an account of autonomy. Cases like Foul Play 1 augment the intuition that as subjects of autonomy desires may not be as "basic" as intentions or decisions. Such cases also suggest that historical constraints having to do with the process of desire formation or acquisition may well be pertinent to the issue of what makes a person's desire "truly that person's own." There is a transparent sense in which when Jill acts on an electronically implanted desire, she acts on a "foreign desire"; she does, however, display the sort of mastery that seems relevant to exercising the kind of authority that is required for autonomy (and moral appraisability). (For brevity of exposition, in what follows on decisional autonomy, with the exception of where it matters, I drop reference to intentions.)

Focusing, then, on decisions as the primary instantiators of the property of *being autonomous, deciding* unlike mere choice, at least in a vast array of cases, involves the resolution of uncertainty. In standard cases, that is, if an agent decides to do something, prior to deciding, she is uncertain about whether she will do that thing. The purpose of engaging in deliberation, at least partly, is to settle the uncertainty.[11] When one decides whether or not to act on a desire, one considers one's options and canvasses reasons for or against action on that desire. A decision is made on the basis of *some* evaluative assessment of the relevant reasons. I believe that the evaluative assessment, as far as autonomy is concerned, is person-relative in this sense: each agent relies on an evaluative scheme that she utilizes in a ranking of wanted items or reasons that may differ from that of some "objectively" correct scheme or from the scheme of some other agent. According to this person-relative account, no special status is given to reasons deriving from, for example, moral, religious, prudential, or legal considerations. Rather, the manner in which agents assess reasons is left pretty much to them. Some, but not all agents, for instance, may regard reasons deriving from what they take to be moral considerations to trump those deriving from prudential ones. What matters fundamentally is that the uncertainty which, in standard cases, precedes any event of deciding be resolved on the basis of reasons ranked in some manner by the agent. The person-relative conceptualization of evaluative schemes is incompatible with an agent's fully "embracing" a decision to perform some action, B, if that agent evaluatively ranks the reasons for doing some alternative to B higher than she ranks the reasons for doing B; in a case of this sort, fully "embracing" the decision to B is not possible as the reasons to perform the alternative are *held by the agent* to be decisive or overriding.[12] We said in the last chapter that an agent's evaluative scheme comprises these elements: (a) normative standards the agent believes ought to be invoked in an assessment of reasons for action; (b) the agent's long-term goals or values; (c) deliberative principles the agent utilizes to arrive at judgments about what to do or how to act: and (d) motivation to act on the normative standards in (a) and goals in (b) using the principles in (c). Evaluative schemes enable agents to assess reasons for action, and to *settle* upon courses of action. In settling upon actions, agents hold themselves ready to execute decisions or intentions to perform those actions. Recalling Mele's lesson, settling upon A-ing moves one much closer to actual action—to A-ing—than having a desire, even a preponderant one, to A (Mele 1992a, chap. 9). Smokey, trying her best to quit, may have a preponderant desire to light a cigarette first thing after awakening but may well be settled in resisting the temptation to smoke; she views the question of whether or not to take the early morning cigarette as closed.

Suppose, relying on his evaluative scheme, Fred (in Mud Pie) judges it best not to eat the pie and in light of this judgment decides to exercise restraint. Of course, by the time Fred acts akratically, he abandons his decision not to eat the pie (though he still retains the judgment that it is best to refrain). When he acts akratically, Fred fails to exhibit the control that he would have exhibited had he acted on reasons he deemed best. Fred's weakness betrays his failure to live up to his own values; he acts against the dictates of guiding standards that Fred takes as authoritative for his own conduct. The example suggests this preliminary account of decisional autonomy:

> DA1: S's decision, D, to do A is autonomous if and only if (i) D is caused by S's reasons to do A, and (ii) given S's evaluative scheme, there is no alternative to A which is such that S ranks S's reasons for performing that alternative higher than S ranks S's reasons for performing A.

The working idea of DA1 is that one's decisions are autonomous just in case one has "decisional control" over them. Having decisional control involves having the capacity to assess, in light of one's (person-relative) evaluative scheme, one's own reasons for or against courses of action among which one is undecided, and to shape decisions on the basis of such assessments.

7. PRELIMINARY OBJECTIONS AND REPLIES

One preliminary objection comes from the direction of incompatibilism. Incompatibilists deny that moral appraisability or autonomy is compatible with causal determinism. One sort of incompatibilist claims that if our actions or decisions are the result of a long sequence of causes over which we have no control, then we cannot be morally appraisable for, or autonomous relative to, those actions or decisions. Some advocates of this sort of incompatibilism, like Kane, insist that there must be an indeterministic "break" or "gap" in the sequence of causes at some appropriate place in the process issuing in deliberative intentional action, to make room for "ultimate" control and, hence, for appraisability or autonomy. The account of decisional autonomy (DA1) developed above, however, not only is compatible with, but requires the decision's being caused and thus, it might be objected, rules out incompatibilism by fiat.

This objection, though, is not convincing. On the view of deliberative intentional action adopted here, an agent's intention or decision to do something is formed on the basis of an evaluative judgment, which in turn, is made on the basis of practical evaluative reasoning. Such reasoning, appealing to an agent's evaluative scheme, will "engage" such things as the agent's values, desires, beliefs, and deliberative skills and capacities. As explained in chapter 2, an incompatibilist can consistently maintain that (1) one's decisions are deterministically caused by one's best judgments about what to do, and (2) it is causally open what one will judge it best to do (and so what one will decide to do) when one starts deliberating, as some of one's belief states or events are causally undetermined. For instance, it may not be causally determined which of these doxastic states will "come to mind" and play a role in deliberation. Hence, the account of decisional autonomy proposed does *not* rule out incompatibilist freedom or control by virtue of requiring that our decisions be caused.

Still, the incompatibilist might rejoin that the claim that DA1 is consistent with incompatibilism is correct only if such incompatibilism doesn't place the causal break at the agent's decision. But what if the correct juncture at which the indeterministic break occurs *is* at the point of the agent's decisions? Well, if some decision of an agent's is *not* caused, not even "agent-caused," then I cannot see how such a decision can qualify as autonomous. What would it mean to say that an agent is autonomous relative to some uncaused decision of hers? Suppose the decision is agent-caused. Then decisional autonomy, I propose, would secure a foothold only if the agent did, in some appropriate fashion, rank that decision.

Here is a second preliminary worry. Presumably an agent's reasons for (intentionally) doing some action A will have a conative element—perhaps a desire to do A—and a representational one. Suppose the conative element in some instance involving the agent's decision to do A is not "truly the agent's own"; it may, like Jill's desire in Foul Play 1, be an electronic implant. Still, DA1 may routinely dictate that the agent's decision to do A is autonomous. But then, one may rejoin, one has sown the seeds for an easy rebuttal of DA1. Suppose, due to her depraved upbringing, it was inescapable that Rogue would end up making the sorts of best-from-her-point-of-view decisions that directed her criminal activities, perhaps because it was inescapable that she would end up with the sort of evaluative scheme that she has. How could Rogue possibly be autonomous with respect to her criminal activity?

My response to this sort of worry commonly voiced in the literature [13] is, firstly, to insist that despite being decisionally autonomous with respect to (at least some) of her criminal activity, Rogue may not be *actionally* autonomous with respect to such activity. I shall further develop this point in the next section when I discuss actional autonomy. Secondly, I acknowledge the leverage that historical or developmental factors exert on the shaping of one's decisions. Still, what matters is control. If one's decisions are not really *inevitable* given one's upbringing, then one can still exercise one's authority in making decisions, and one can frequently do so in a way in which one cannot exercise one's authority in shaping the desires that one has. It might be "inevitable," given the social position in which one finds oneself, that one has the desire to amass material wealth, but one may form a decision, and execute that decision, to live a life unencumbered by such wealth. Notice, in addition, that unlike desires that are implantable, it seems false that a decision in the mental action sense of "decision" can be implanted even by omnipotent demons; unlike desires, mental actions are *doings* of agents.[14]

However, it should be conceded that even "decisional doings" can be tainted by autonomy-undermining factors. Imagine the development of a Disrupter Drug that selectively blocks an agent's "access" to certain of that agent's reasons for action. Suppose that had Fred, unbeknownst to him, ingested the Disrupter Drug, he would not have entertained certain reasons for not eating the pie that he otherwise would have, and as a result, he would not have judged it best to refrain. Intuitively, in this counter-to-fact situation, Fred's decision not to refrain from eating the pie would not be autonomous. Analogously, if Fred's decision were made on the basis of an assessment of reasons influenced by hypnosis or something like it, we would not regard the decision as autonomous. Clause ii of DA1 should be amended to accommodate anxieties of this sort. I propose:

> DA2: S's decision to do A is autonomous only if given S's evaluative scheme, there is no alternative to A which is such that in the absence of autonomy-undermining factors, S ranks S's reasons for performing that alternative higher than S ranks S's reasons for performing A.

An obvious perplexity with this condition is that it requires elucidation of what count as autonomy-undermining factors. Roughly, the sorts of factors I have in mind are those that adversely affect the inputs to deliberation, and those that undermine or taint an agent's reflective capacities which are exercised by the agent in making decisions. So, for instance, even if a person's deliberations are immaculate, the decision he makes on the basis of such deliberation will not be autonomous if, unbeknownst to him, he were deliberately fed information crucial to him arriving at his decision that is false. Or decisional autonomy will be compromised if the person acts on engineered-in pro-attitudes, in cases in which the engineering is covert, and the effects of the engineering on her deliberation cannot be thwarted. Similarly, decisional autonomy will be compromised if the person's deliberations are influenced by clandestine conditioning whose effects cannot be foiled. Again, it appears that some (but not all) decisions made under threats or, more generally, under coercion, may well not be autonomous. I would also add to this list that decisions involving akratic deliberation would not be autonomous. So although it would be unrealistic to require of an autonomous agent that the deliberations in which she engages to arrive at a decision be perfectly rational, it is not unreasonable to require that her reflective capacities, or inputs to deliberation, not be undermined or tainted by factors of the sort on our list that usurp autonomy.

I propose that decisional autonomy may well account for the sense or feeling of having acted autonomously or freely in cases in which an agent acts under liberating constraints, provided the agent's autonomous decision to do something successfully (and nondeviantly) issues in action. For example, the devoted mother might offer, in the explanation of her action, a chain of reasoning according to which, given her evaluative scheme, saving the child is the best option to be pursued. That part of her nature constituted by her evaluative scheme could not, in the circumstances, sanction any other alternative. It should be stressed that her actual reasoning need be neither conscious, nor perfectly rational, nor elaborate.

8. ACTIONAL AUTONOMY

Suppose that on the basis of her own evaluative scheme, an agent judges it best to perform some action, and her judgment issues in a DA2-autonomous decision to perform that action, which in turn (nondeviantly) leads to that action's being performed. Then it might plausibly be thought that the agent is autonomous with respect to the action performed. However, it appears that fully autonomous deliberation issuing in a DA2-autonomous effective decision may well culminate in action that is nonautonomous. Let's reconsider and elaborate the case of Poppy the willing addict. Assume that Poppy's addiction to what is now her favorite narcotic begins in this way: a reliable deliberator, Poppy acquires initial motivation to take the drug in a fashion that is clearly autonomous. Poppy is aware that if she acts on this motivation, she may develop irresistible desires for the drug. After due deliberation, Poppy freely takes the drug. Her taking of the drug is, on this inauguratory occasion, undoubtedly autonomous. Reflect, now, on the second occasion on which Poppy is drawn to the narcotic. Suppose, unbeknownst to her, her desire has become irresistible. Poppy again indulges, but she acts just as she would have had the desire not been irresistible. Poppy, of course, regards her drug-taking action as autonomous. But the reality of the situation is that Poppy has lost deliberative control over the desire: there is no scenario (with the same natural laws as the actual world) in which Poppy has that desire, decides to resist it, and effectively does so. In performing an action with respect to which one takes oneself to be autonomous, one need not be aware that control has slipped away and that one is no longer in the driver's seat. We can reasonably suppose that whereas the irresistibility of the desire controls neither Poppy's evaluative judgment to take the drug, nor her proximal decision to do so—Poppy, despite having the desire could have judged and decided otherwise—it does (although Poppy is unaware of this) control her action.[15] Similarly, it appears that although the decision to refrain from taking the drug of Hera (the unwilling addict) is DA2–autonomous, her action of taking the drug cannot tenably be supposed to be under her authority.

Just as autonomous decisions are ones that are under the control of their agent, so autonomous actions should be ones over which their agent exercises control. I propose that the sort of control required by autonomous action is simply volitional control. Hera's taking of the drug is not under her volitional control: as the desire for the drug is irresistible, there is no scenario in which Hera has that desire, decides in light of her evaluative scheme to refrain from taking the drug, and successfully translates her decision into action. Poppy's plight is similar to Hera's. Though Poppy, unlike Hera, is a willing addict, Poppy *lacks* volitional control over taking the drug. Two conditions for actional autonomy can now be summarized thusly:

> AA: S's action A is autonomous only if (i) A is caused (in part) by a DA2-autonomous decision of S's, and (ii) A is under S's volitional control.

Reconsider Poppy's plight. Grant that Poppy's decision to take the drug is DA2-autonomous. Yet Poppy's action of taking the drug is not AA-autonomous: there is no scenario in which Poppy has the (irresistible) desire to take the drug, decides against taking the drug, and successfully translates that decision into action. Contrast Poppy's plight with Della's delight: suppose Della has a strong but not irresistible desire to drink the shake. After some consideration, Della decides to guzzle the strawberry delight. Unbeknownst to her, had she decided or intended otherwise, the berry angel would have implanted in Della an intention to drink the shake and would have seen to it that Della acted on that intention. Della freely gulps down the shake on her own. Arguably, in this scenario the counterfactual intervener guarantees that Della cannot do other than drink the shake. However, it appears that Della is autonomous with respect to drinking the shake. Although Della cannot (in the circumstances) resist the desire to drink the shake, she has volitional control over her drinking the shake: there is a scenario in which Della has this desire (one, for example, in which the berry angel is too engrossed in her own shake-imbibing activities to pay any attention to Della), forms a decision to act against this desire, and successfully executes this decision.[16]

It is controversial whether AA's two conditions suffice for actional autonomy, at least if action under coercion undermines autonomy. In Holdup, Moneypenny must decide between handing over the money or dying. Recognizing the threat to be real, he decides partly as a result of his judgment that it is best to turn over the money, and he acts on this decision. Moneypenny's decision to turn over the money *may* be DA2-autonomous and he has volitional control over turning over the money (there is a scenario, let's suppose, in which he turns hero; though he has the desire to hand over the money, he decides to defy the threat and he acts on the decision). Yet if it is the threat that partly moves Moneypenny to action, and if we believe that threat-prompted actions undermine or at least attenuate actional autonomy, then the conditions in AA are not sufficient for actional autonomy.

Finally, let me stress that while there may well be an overlap between our ordinary or pretheoretic conception (or conceptions) of autonomy and the accounts of decisional and actional autonomy given, it has not been my intention, in developing these accounts, to capture every facet of what we might mean when we say things like "so and so performed the action autonomously." Probably no one account can do justice to all the nuances of autonomy; perhaps there are several different concepts of autonomy. My suggestion, rather, is that the concepts of decisional and actional autonomy are explanatorily useful. With their help, we can steer our way through puzzles that arise when we reflect on things like moral appraisability.

9. AUTONOMY AND APPRAISABILITY

Let's revert, then, to some of the puzzles with which we started in this chapter. If Bond is not morally blameworthy in Secret Agent for shooting Smernof, why is this so? Does Fred in Mud Pie act autonomously when he akratically relishes the pie, and is he blameworthy for eating the pie? Does the devoted mother who acts under liberating constraints act autonomously when she saves her child, and is she morally appraisable for doing so?

Starting with Secret Agent, the intuition that Bond is not blameworthy for killing Smernof is compelling; so is the intuition that Bond is not AA-autonomous relative to his killing Smernof. But I suggest that it is a mistake to suppose that Bond is not blameworthy *because* he is not AA-autonomous. Rather, Bond is not blameworthy for killing Smernof as he had no volitional control over his killing Smernof. Next, in Mud Pie Fred is blameworthy for eating the pie. He didn't act in ignorance, and he did exercise volitional control over eating the pie. But since Fred's decision to eat the pie is not DA2-autonomous (as Fred ranks his reasons for refraining higher than he ranks his reasons for indulging), his act of eating the pie is not AA-autonomous. Finally, the devoted mother is decisionally autonomous relative to her action of saving the child. But she is not actionally autonomous relative to that action, and nor is she morally appraisable for that action as she did not exercise volitional control over it.

These initial results suggest that there is no interesting connection between autonomy—at least decisional or actional autonomy—and moral appraisability.[17] Unfortunately, matters are not so straightforward. There is a deep objection, it might be charged, to the account of decisional (and actional) autonomy so far defended; and this objection brings into plain view a possible association between appraisability and autonomy.

10. A NEW OBJECTION

In the last chapter, we explored an important hierarchical account of control. Just as there is a hierarchical approach to control, so there is a hierarchical approach to autonomy. On the hierarchical approach, an agent is autonomous relative to an action if, broadly, there is conformity between his second-order volition (his desire as to which first-order desire should move him to action) and the first-order desire that does in fact move him to action. On this account, what is required for autonomy is some sort of fit between higher-order volitions and first-order desires. The precise nature of the fit need not detain us here. Various critics have charged that the relevant fit—whatever it is—between these elements can be produced directly by someone or something else via, for example, hypnosis or electronic stimulation of the brain, so that the agent would simply be a marionette of her manipulator.[18] In fact, with the help of Psychogen, we raised this very sort of concern in the preceding chapter when evaluating hierarchical control. The worry, then, is that the hierarchical approach would rule that such a manipulated agent would be autonomous, as the relevant psychological elements stand in the appropriate "autonomy-inducing" relation, even though it is clear that the agent would be nonautonomous. It might be charged, though, that what can be called this "wayward source problem" is easily generalizable. It would, for instance affect Wolf's view on the reasonable supposition that an agent's ability to do the right thing for the right reasons could be electronically induced. It would equally be a problem for the decisional account of autonomy sketched above. For according to that account, a person's decision to perform some action is autonomous if the decision is produced by the person's reasons as assessed by the person against the person's evaluative scheme. The worry is that a person's basic parameters of reasoning, or his values themselves, just as easily as his mere desires, could be the product of direct surreptitious electronic stimulation.

Can this challenge be met solely by appealing to what goes on within an agent's mental life, or must a defensible view of autonomy also be sensitive to *how* agents come to possess the values (and other "inputs" like pertinent information) that figure centrally in the etiology of decision-making? It should be granted that a person's evaluative scheme, a scheme that roughly comprises the very standards the person believes ought to be invoked in an assessment of reasons for action, may itself be waywardly produced. For it appears that ordinary causal processes that *can* be simulated are responsible for the sort of evaluative scheme that an agent endorses. One's heavy reliance on religious tenets, for example, in evaluating reasons for action could be a function of one's religious upbringing. Or a criminal's thwarting of moral principles, and her approbation of, say prudential principles, in assessing her reasons for action may well be a reflection of the ordinary norms of behavior accepted by many in the community in which she finds herself. So being in the state in which one believes that certain principles should inform one's reasons for action, or being in the state in which one desires that one's reasons are assessed against certain guiding principles, are states that should be inducible by processes like clandestine electronic stimulation of the brain. Moreover, it seems possible that the immediate issue of decision—the product of deciding—may also be electronically induced. But an act of deciding, a mental deed, does not appear to be something that is implantable; it is plainly something that an agent *does* (see Mele 1992a, p. 141). Decisional autonomy requires deliberation; it requires *assessing* one's reasons. Of course, the reasons will be assessed against some evaluative scheme that may be waywardly produced, but the assessment itself, a mental action or a string of such actions, cannot be so produced. Consequently, it seems that one can assess even an electronically induced evaluative scheme, just as we assess our ordinary schemes, and decide to accept or reject the scheme, or more reasonably, to alter the scheme if one so desires, as a result of such assessment. The alteration may consist, for example, in repudiating or acquiring certain desires, or in modifying beliefs about normative principles invoked to make evaluative judgments regarding which course of action to pursue.

On the basis of the foregoing sorts of considerations, it might be urged that decisional autonomy would not be compromised, even when an agent appraises reasons for action against an evaluative scheme waywardly produced, on the condition that the agent has reflected on the scheme and has accepted it. One might, moreover, insist that if the account of autonomous decisions is to escape charges of being quixotic, the notion of acceptance should be understood in a rather weak sense. So, for example, it might be proposed that one needn't have reasoned consciously, or at great depth, or rationally about, for instance, principles that express how one believes one should go about making decisions. Nor, it could be added, need one have reflected on, and approved of, the process that generated one's evaluative scheme, as it seems possible for one to accept a set of values despite disapproving of its genesis (for an opposing view, see Christman 1991). An adequate characterization of acceptance might simply, it could be recommended, amount to this: an agent accepts her evaluative scheme if it is the scheme that she characteristically uses in making decisions, and it is a scheme to which she has given, either consciously or otherwise, an evaluative "mental nod" of approval or acceptance. Indeed, an agent's habitual reliance on a certain evaluative scheme, it could be suggested, is indicative of some evidence that the agent accepts the scheme. On this account of decisional autonomy, such autonomy would be a function exclusively of the mental goings-on within a person's head.

However, there is still an irksome complication that plagues this all-in-the-head view of autonomy. Imagine a case like Psychogen. In this case, manipulators operating on an ambitious scale—global manipulators—implant in our devoted mother a set of values fundamentally different from the one with which she is "naturally" endowed. Assume that the mother comes to acquire her new values in ways that bypass her capacity for control over her mental life, and that she is unaware of having been so manipulated.[19] Fully cut off from the cause of the change, the mother is totally passive in the bringing about of her new values. Upon awakening following the night of value engineering, the mother finds that she is indifferent about the welfare of her child, and she cares not a wit for the other things, like playing the violin and reading literature, which formerly gave her life meaning. Assume, in addition, that when she reflects on her engineered values, she wholeheartedly approves of them (see Frankfurt 1987). This result (anticipated by the manipulators) is not surprising as her deliberative judgments are now largely generated by her newly acquired evaluative scheme. Consider, finally, an occasion when her child is in a burning house, the mother decides it is not worth saving him, and her engineered values ensure that she is unable to decide otherwise. Wouldn't the mother's decision, it might challengingly be queried, be nonautonomous even though it is the result of a deliberative process that is informed by an evaluative scheme accepted by her?[20]

It is worth noting that the "bypass" engineering of the sort carried out by the manipulators will undermine autonomy only if it leaves the mother in a condition in which she cannot discard, modify, or "act against" (as it were) her engineered evaluative standards. A collection of values (or a segment thereof) might be engineered-in, but if they permit sufficient latitude to enable the agent to arrive at decisions analogous to the ones at which she would have arrived in the absence of engineering, the engineering would not be autonomy-subversive. Focusing, then, on cases in which bypass engineering yields unsheddable values in an agent, precisely *why* would one think (if one does) that the agent is nonautonomous with respect to possession of those values? Certainly not because the engineering was commissioned by other *agents*. Nonintentional bypass engineering is pretty evidently possible, as in a case in which the mother, without appreciating her predicament, walks across a bypass engineering chamber whose devious workings are automatically activated by passers through. One might focus on the lack of consent by the affected party, or lay emphasis on the fact that the engineering *bypasses* the agent's capacity for control over her mental life and leads to the production of intransigent values.[21] This "Bypass View" has considerable allure, but it also forces the following consequence: reconsider the nonengineered devoted mother. Suppose, simply as a result of emulating her parents and carrying on with the normal business of life, she acquires some of her deep-seated values by means that bypass her powers of control over her mental life. Her acquisition of a large constellation of her parental values, we might say, is *nonrational*. Maybe in this respect we are just like the mother; it seems that at least some, if not many, of our deeply entrenched values are acquired nonrationally. Intuitively, however, there seems to be a difference between this case in which the mother's values are acquired nonrationally and the one in which her values are engineered-in; it seems that in this case, but not in the other, autonomy is intact. The Bypass View implies that such asymmetry is illusory. Perhaps it is, and I shall leave this avenue open.

I want to develop a different view that focuses on agency, and I shall begin to do so in the next chapter. But before turning to that difficult task, we need to tie some ends together. The discussion on engineered evaluative schemes suggests that the autonomy of an agent's decisions (and so actions, as actional autonomy presupposes decisional autonomy) depends, in some crucial fashion, on *how* she comes to acquire certain psychological features that play a central role in the causal generation of those decisions. The account of decisional (and actional) autonomy defended in this chapter must, in consequence, be construed as being conditional upon the agent's evaluative scheme being "truly the agent's own," or, borrowing some terminology from the literature, the evaluative scheme must be "authentic." Return to cases involving action under liberating constraints. Assume that the lover's, the devoted mother's, and the nurse's decisions are all guided by authentic evaluative schemes. Then, as these agents effectively translated the relevant decisions into action, they acted in accord with their "authentic selves," and so, we can plausibly imagine, regarded their behavior as being autonomous. Interestingly enough, a mother all of whose values have been engineered in, may also regard her actions that flow smoothly from decisions evaluated against her engineered values as being autonomous. Her engineered values, from her inner perspective, constitute part of her deep self. There would, however, be something clearly delusive about her feeling of autonomy, even though, from her inner perspective, the globally manipulated mother would be unable to discern her delusion. The authenticity requirement for evaluative schemes uncovers the kernel of truth in the objector's third claim that moral appraisability presupposes autonomy: appraisability presupposes authenticity of evaluative schemes.

Finally, cases of global manipulation like the case of the globally manipulated mother or Psychogen reveal that apart from a freedom-relevant or control condition, and an epistemic condition, there is an autonomy condition of moral appraisability. Actions for which we are morally appraisable must issue from desires, values, deliberative capacities, and so forth that are elements of authentic evaluative schemes. The autonomy (or authenticity) condition is the topic of the next two chapters.

APPRAISABILITY AND
INDUCED PRO-ATTITUDES

In Psychogen, Jenny (in the absence of her consent or knowledge) is molded, via transformation psychosurgery, into a psychological twin of Jim the adept financial investor. When, just after awakening from her surgery, Jenny makes a brilliant investment decision and acts on it, we don't think she is morally praiseworthy for her action. In a sense, we can say that her action is not "truly her own" as it issues from an evaluative scheme that is not "truly her own"; her engineered-in scheme is unauthentic. Psychogen, then, strongly suggests that moral appraisability presupposes action generated on the basis of an authentic evaluative scheme.

What conditions must an agent's evaluative scheme satisfy if it is to qualify as authentic? I shall approach this question somewhat indirectly by first addressing the problem of moral appraisability and induced pro-attitudes. This problem, capsulized, amounts to the following. Why is action that ultimately issues from pro-attitudes like desires, volitions, and goals, induced by techniques such as direct manipulation of the brain, hypnosis, or value engineering, frequently regarded as action for which its agent cannot be morally appraisable? The solution I propose will pave the way for uncovering sufficient conditions for an evaluative scheme's being authentic.

I. THE PROBLEM OF INDUCED PRO-ATTITUDES

Apart from its intrinsic attraction to many, the problem of induced pro-attitudes is of interest for several different reasons. Ferdinand Schoeman, for instance, believes that the problem poses (what he regards as a resolvable but challenging) predicament for compatibilists: if agents can be held morally appraisable for actions that are causally determined, then why should actions that result from induced pro-attitudes be regarded as paradigmatically unfree and for which agents cannot be held appraisable? (1978, p. 293) Robert Kane exploits the problem to launch a libertarian attack against compatibilists (1985, p. 37). He says that a covert nonconstraining controller controls the will of another agent by arranging "circumstances beforehand so that the agent wants and desires, and hence chooses and tries, only what the controller intends." Kane claims that compatibilist accounts of freedom cannot distinguish between cases in which an agent behaves freely and those in which an agent falls prey to the covert nonconstraining control of some other party. I am drawn to the problem for yet other reasons. First, I believe its resolution sheds light on the following hotly debated issue. On one view, an adequate account of free action and moral appraisability is history-sensitive insofar as moral appraisability for an action depends crucially on *how* its agent comes to acquire the various elements (like the motivational springs, deliberative inputs such as beliefs, and intentions or decisions) in its etiology.[1] On a competing view, history-sensitive considerations are irrelevant to explaining and grounding ascriptions of moral appraisability. As we have seen, Harry Frankfurt highlights the relevant gist of such "all-in-the-head" views of moral responsibility when he claims that

> to the extent that a person identifies himself with the springs of his actions, he takes responsibility for those actions and acquires moral responsibility for them; moreover, the questions of how the actions and his identifications with their springs are caused are irrelevant to the questions of whether he performs the actions *freely* or is morally responsible for performing them.[2] (1988a, p. 54)

Suppose the problem of induced pro-attitudes is of no real threat to moral appraisability so that an agent can, for example, be morally appraisable for performing an action even if that action is caused by a pro-attitude acquired via brainwashing to which she did not consent. Then, it appears, we would have pretty compelling prima facie grounds to believe that history-sensitive conditions are *not* pivotal to a correct account of free action and moral appraisability. On the other hand, if induced pro-attitudes do imperil moral appraisability, and do so at least partly in virtue of how the agent came to acquire them, then we will have prima facie reason to believe that an adequate account of moral appraisability must satisfy some historical constraint.

Second, I am drawn to the problem as I believe that coming to grips with it can help with another taxing problem: When is an agent's evaluative scheme authentic?

In this chapter, I begin by examining some recently proposed solutions to the problem of induced pro-attitudes and indicate their inadequacies. I then advance a solution of my own and indicate how it tells against purely all-in-the-head views of moral appraisability. This will prepare the way for tackling the problem of authentic evaluative schemes.

2. SCHOEMAN ON INDUCED PRO-ATTITUDES

In an insightful discussion of the problem, Schoeman distinguishes three sorts of cases in which the desires of agents have been instilled by others (see Shoeman 1978). The first involves global manipulation in which all of a subject's pro-attitudes have been induced by some other agent. Schoeman invites us to fanta-size that neurology and neurosurgery have progressed to the point where not only can particular pro-attitudes be manipulatively induced, "but also where one indi-vidual can be molded psychologically to be just the kind of person the surgeon desires" (1978, p. 295). He imagines a case similar to Psychogen, in which Billy Graham is altered by transformation surgery into a person who is a psychological twin of Woody Allen.[3] Interestingly, Schoeman's verdict is that remolded Billy *is* morally appraisable for his actions, and his position appears to be that Billy is so appraisable even if he did not consent to the remolding:

> I have been maintaining that even in the event of global manipulation, the person altered is every bit as responsible for his subsequent behaviour as is the model on which he is molded. (For those to whom this seems counterintuitive, I suggest read-ing the *Rolling Stone* articles about Patty Hearst and seeing whether you too are not strongly tempted to say *however* Patty was put into the condition described there [for instance, by remolding surgery to which she did not consent], she was acting as a responsible agent-that is to say acting on the basis of reasons which were her own.) So long as a person has the capacity to think and act on the basis of relevant reasons, he is responsible for his subsequent behavior. (1978, p. 296, my emphasis)

The second sort of case advanced by Schoeman features what he calls "local manipulation." Such manipulation results "when certain desires, beliefs, or values are attached to a person left otherwise psychologically intact" (1978, p. 297). Also fundamental to this type of case is the requirement that the induced pro-attitude (or cluster of attitudes) is one on which the agent can avoid acting, or *not* one on which the agent can suppress behaving "only at the risk of experienc-ing considerable psychic unbalance" (1978, p. 297). With respect to cases of this sort, Schoeman says, "Since many of us seem to spontaneously generate desires that we have then to cope with, and since this is just part of what we are ex-pected to deal with in acting responsibly, I do not see how the fact that the desire was induced manipulatively rather than being the result possibly of some random neuron firing can make a difference with respect to responsibility" (1978, p. 297).

The third sort of case also includes local manipulation—only some pro-attitudes are induced leaving the rest of the agent's psychology unchanged—but the ones induced, unlike in the former class of cases, *are* ones which "either the agent finds himself unable to avoid acting on, or are such that the agent can suppress behaving on only at the risk of experiencing considerable psychic unbal-ance" (1978, p. 297). Schoeman claims that:

> In the case of such desires, we shouldn't hold the agent responsible for his behaviour. But the reason for this has decidedly nothing to do with the fact that the desire was induced manipulatively. For if this induced, compulsive, desire were with our agent from adolescence, and not the product of manipulation, or if it just randomly

emerged, still it would be uncontrollable. And it is this factor of uncontrollability, not the issue of etiology, which directly relates to attributions or denials of responsibility. (1978, p. 297)

As I understand Schoeman, an action arising from *any* pro-attitude that is uncontrollable in the sense that the agent either cannot avoid acting on it, or can suppress acting on it only at the expense of suffering considerable psychic unbalance, is one its agent is not morally appraisable for performing.

While there is much in Schoeman's careful discussion with which I agree, I find problematic both Schoeman's assessment of global manipulation cases, and his control condition. Reconsider the example in which psychosurgery to which he has not consented transforms Billy into a psychological twin of Woody. Assume that the surgery preserves personal identity; *Billy* survives the change. Intuitively, globally manipulated Billy is *not* morally appraisable for his actions, and he is not roughly because the entire constellation of pro-attitudes that now underlie his deliberations were not acquired under his own steam; they were forced upon him. Billy's plight seems pertinently comparable to the plight of a person like Bond in Secret Agent who kills as a result of clandestine direct electronic stimulation of his brain; presumably such a person would not be morally appraisable for the killing.

To parry this line of thought, Schoeman might underscore the point that any psychological ability Woody has is an ability both Woody and transformed Billy have, given that the two are psychologically identical (296). If it is open to Woody, then, to alter his values, it is also open to transformed Billy to do so. Furthermore, if transformed Billy has the ability to change his new pro-attitudes and revert to the way he was prior to psychosurgery, then we would not regard the psychosurgery as undermining Billy's moral appraisability for actions he performs subsequent to his transformation. This sort of response, however, can be handled by the stipulation that Woody, like so many adult individuals, is unable to alter his deeply entrenched values. It would then follow that manipulated Billy would also be unable to revert to his former self, given that Billy is a psychological twin of Woody.[4]

Schoeman might insist that the intuition that transformed Billy's engineered pro-attitudes are not "truly his own" can only be validated if there is a "criterion that distinguishes induced from natural desires that is relevant to the responsibility/non-responsibility issue"; Schoeman's view, moreover, is that there can be no such criterion (1978, p. 295). Leaving aside the issue of just why Schoeman believes there can be no such criterion, I think the intuition Schoeman disputes can be supported without adducing any such criterion. Indeed, reflection on Schoeman's own control condition suggests a way to provide the needed support.

The control condition says that an agent is not morally appraisable for actions that result from pro-attitudes (like desires) on which the agent is unable to avoid acting, or on which the agent can suppress behaving only at the risk of experiencing considerable psychic unbalance.[5] A standard "Frankfurt-type" case calls into question the first disjunct. Suppose (in an example which we call "Stooge1") Curly freely decides (partly on the basis of some autonomous desire of his) to slap

Moe, and when the right opportunity presents itself, successfully (and nondevi-antly) acts on his decision. Unbeknownst to him, had he shown any inclination not to will or decide to slap Moe, a powerful being, via direct stimulation of his neurons, would have caused Curly to will to slap Moe and to act on the volition to slap Moe. As the being does not show her hand in the sequence of events that results in Curly's slapping Moe, it seems that Curly is morally appraisable for slapping Moe even though, arguably, his action issued from a desire on which he was unable to avoid acting.

Now consider a "Global Frankfurt-type" example in which (unbeknownst to Moe) an omnipotent being watches over every single action performed by this stooge, and will intervene and compel Moe to perform an action of a certain sort if Moe shows any signs of not performing (on his own) an action of that sort.[6] Suppose, amazingly, Moe always and without hesitation performs the right type of action, thereby obviating any need for the omnipotent being to intervene. Again, in this example (call it "Stooge2") it seems that although Moe could never have done otherwise, Moe is morally appraisable for performing all those actions for which he would have been morally appraisable for performing had there been no omnipotent being waiting in the wings.

Imagine, now, a third case (Stooge3) that is just like Stooge2 but in which Moe is caused to perform every action each one of which he would *not* have done in the absence of intervention by the omnipotent being. (Assume that at each appropriate time the omnipotent being induces in Moe a relevant irresistible pro-attitude on which Moe subsequently acts.) Presumably, in this case Moe is not morally appraisable for performing any of his actions, and he is not roughly be-cause he is compelled to perform each one of them; he fails to execute any of them on his own.

Stooge3, I contend, is relevantly similar to Billy's case. Ponder the first few actions that Billy performs after psychosurgery. Each one of them is ultimately based on engineered pro-attitudes that (we are assuming) Billy cannot thwart. If we are inclined to believe that the omnipotent being compels Moe to act in Stooge3 by inducing irresistible desires in Moe, then equally we should be in-clined to believe that the surgeon compels Billy to act by engendering in Billy types of desires Woody has that turn out to be irresistible. Hence, if there is compulsion in Stooge3, then there should be compulsion in Billy's case, and this provides the support required to validate the intuition that transformed Billy is not morally appraisable for performing his actions, *without* adducing a "criterion which distinguishes induced from natural desires" (1978, p. 295).

I conclude that Schoeman's attempt to deal with the problem of induced pro-attitudes is instructive but unsuccessful. Let us examine another attempt.

3. ANOTHER UNSUCCESSFUL SOLUTION

In "Puppeteers, Hypnotists, and Neurosurgeons" Richard Double, among other things, seeks to show that whatever other problems it encounters, a "Reason-Sensitive" (R-S) account of free will can be defended against "counter-examples involving hypothesized external agents who cause us to have our reflective attitudes" (1989, p. 163). Double's rich discussion is directly relevant to the problem of induced pro-attitudes.

Double starts with this extraction of a "generic" (1989, p. 163) R-S account from Frankfurt's work:

> *Original R-S account:* S's decision d is free if and only if S is able to bring d into accord with S's reflective judgments about the desirability of d. (1989, p. 163)

The proposed counterexamples against this generic account advanced, for example, by Michael Slote (Slote 1980), Gary Watson (Watson 1986), and Robert Kane (Kane 1985, p. 37) all share the common element that a controller like a hypnotist or brain-manipulator can surreptitiously instill in some unfortunate agent the relevant reason-sensitivity condition purported to be necessary and sufficient for moral appraisability, while leaving that agent unfree. Double first attempts to defuse the force of these counterexamples by amending the original R-S account so that it no longer implies that the victimized agents act with free will (and are morally appraisable for their actions):

> *Metaphilosophically Amended Account:* S's decision d is free to the extent that: (1) S is able to bring d into accord with S's reflective judgments about the desirability of d (2) There is no other agent who causes S to have those reflective judgments about d. (1989, p. 165)

It seems that what underlies 2 is Double's view that "One is controlled only if an agent controls you" (1989, p. 165). With regard, then, to the problem of induced pro-attitudes, the metaphilosophically amended account suggests the following:

> Solution D1: (i) An agent, S, is morally appraisable for performing some action, A, only if it is false that A issues from a pro-attitude of S's induced in S by some other agent T. For (ii) S is morally appraisable for doing A only if S does A freely; (iii) S does A freely only if in doing A it is false that S is controlled; (iv) S is controlled with respect to doing A only if some other intentional agent controls S's doing A; and (v) if S does A, and A is caused (at least in part) by a pro-attitude of S's artificially induced in S by some other agent, T, then, in doing A, S is controlled by T, and in virtue of being so controlled, does not freely do A.

There are a number of problems with D1, some of which can be remedied.[7] First, against i and v, if S arranges to be manipulated by hypnotist, T, freely consenting to T's instilling in S a desire to A on the basis of which S does A, then possibly S is not controlled by T with respect to A-ing, and is morally appraisable for A-ing. Points i and v can be amended by requiring something to the effect that T induces the pertinent pro-attitude in S in the absence of S's consent or knowledge. Second, again against i and v, suppose in the absence of S's knowledge, T induces in S a desire to A, but S can easily avoid acting on this desire. Suppose, further, that after due reflection on S's options, S acts on the induced desire and A-s. Here (other conditions being satisfied), S would be morally appraisable for A-ing. Finally, against iv, an agent's freedom can be undermined even in the absence of control by intentional *agents*. For instance, it is possible that a disease affecting the brain causes in S an irresistible desire to A (on the basis of which S A-s); in this case S would fail to exercise control over A-ing and would not be morally appraisable for A-ing.

This last difficulty with solution D1 is also a difficulty (as Double appreciates) for the Metaphilosophically Amended R-S Account. Partly in light of this difficulty, Double proposes further revision of the R-S account which, in turn, suggests an alternative solution to the problem of induced pro-attitudes. To adumbrate the revision, Double begins by introducing a dilemma: either what is induced by a controller like a brain manipulator in some other agent, S, is not amenable to rational consideration and revision, or it is. In the former case, Double suggests, whatever is induced is not reason-sensitive, and if S performs some action, A, on the basis of what is induced, then S does not perform A freely and is not appraisable for A-ing. In the latter case, whatever is induced is reason-sensitive; S can reflect on whatever is induced and act or refrain from acting on that basis. Hence, if S does A on the basis of induced reason-sensitive pro-attitudes, S does A freely and can be morally appraisable for A-ing (1989, p. 167). Taking his cue, apparently, from the second horn of the dilemma, Double's strategy to meet the challenges of controllers like brainwashers (and causal determinism) to an R-S account is to build a strong rationality (or normative) component into that account. Toward this end, he advances the

Irrelevancy Amended Autonomy Variable [R-S] Account: S's decision is free to the extent that S is able to bring d into accord with S's reflective judgments about the desirability of d, that is,

(1) S knows the nature of the beliefs, desires, and other mental states that bring about d; if they were caused by the purposive intervention of an external agent, S knows this also. (self-knowledge)

(2) S goes through critical and nondogmatic consideration of d and the mental states that bring about d in cases where such consideration is appropriate. (reasonability)

(3) S's reasoning concerning d and those other states meet normative standards of intellectual skill. (intelligence)

(4) S possesses the power, at each step in the reflective and decision-making processes, to bring about subsequent mental states according to the normative standards of (2) and (3). (efficacy)

(5) There is a single agent to whom variables (1)–(4) apply. (unity) (1989, p. 169)[8]

How does this autonomy variable account bear on the problem of induced pro-attitudes? We have adopted the following view on full-blown deliberative intentional action. Such action involves (1) some psychological basis for evaluative reasoning (e.g., pro-attitudes like values and desires, and beliefs); (2) a practical judgment made on the basis of such reasoning that recommends a particular course of action; (3) an intention or decision formed or acquired on the basis of that judgment; and (4) an action executing that intention or decision. Suppose pro-attitudes, like certain values, have been induced in an agent, S; these pro-attitudes give rise to a practical judgment to do A; this judgment issues in a decision to A; and there is a smooth transition from S's decision to A to S's A-ing.

> Solution D2: (i) If S or S's decision to A satisfies autonomy variables 1–4, then other conditions of moral appraisability (like epistemic conditions) for S's A-ing being satisfied, S is morally appraisable for A-ing; (ii) If the induced pro-attitudes are causally responsible for, or otherwise prevent, S or S's decision to A from satisfying autonomy variables 1–4, then even if all other conditions of moral appraisability for S's A-ing are satisfied, S is not morally appraisable for A-ing.

Schoeman's global manipulation case, however, casts serious doubt on solution D2. Recall that in Schoeman's case Billy is transformed by psychosurgery into a psychological twin of Woody. Suppose, on the basis of his engineered values, Billy forms a decision to donate a large sum of money to charity and acts on this decision. Assume there is a smooth transition from Billy's decision to Billy's action and other conditions of moral appraisability (whatever these are) for Billy's donating the sum are satisfied. We would not want to hold Billy morally appraisable for donating the sum as Billy is a marionette of his manipulator. Solution D2, though, implies otherwise. Billy or Billy's decision (call it "bd"), to donate the sum, it is plausible to assume, satisfy autonomy variables 1–4: first, Billy knows the nature of the mental states relevant to bd, and he knows, we can stipulate, that bd was formed on the basis of engineered values. Second, the engineering need not prevent critical reflection of bd—indeed, with the instilled evaluative perspective in place, it may enhance such reflection. Included as a feature of the case is the provision that Billy cannot alter his engineered pro-attitudes, but this need not, of course, prevent Billy from revising bd, nor from "revising" other desires on the basis of his deeply entrenched engineered in values. Third, Billy's reasoning concerning bd meets normative standards of intellectual skill. Fourth and finally, Billy possesses the power to bring about subsequent mental states according to the normative standards of the autonomy variables of reasonability and intelligence. An easy way to free D2 of this problem is simply to require that the relevant decision (like Billy's decision to donate money), as well as the pertinent deliberations (like Billy's deliberations that give rise to the decision to donate money), be "truly the agent's own." But then solution D2 will have to be augmented with some condition that specifies when an agent's decisions or deliberations are truly that agent's own. Consequently, D2 as it now stands, unsupplemented by such a condition, is fundamentally incomplete. In summary, I strongly disagree with Double's comment that if "you knew that your decisions satisfied the autonomy variable account, then you should regard yourself free whether determinism or a puppeteer resides at the front of the causal sequence that ends in your decisions. You have everything you should want by way of rational control" (1989, p. 170).

4. A NEW APPROACH

It's time to sketch another solution. Adopting Schoeman's approach, it will be helpful to differentiate a number of cases. Let's start with a case of local manipulation in which a single pro-attitude (like a single desire), or if this is not possible, a small cluster of pro-attitudes, is induced in some agent with the rest of the agent's psychology left unaltered. Suppose, for example, that while strolling by a market in Istanbul, Shaheen falls victim to the manipulation of Ali. The seasoned merchant induces in Shaheen a resistible desire to purchase a rug. Shaheen feels the tug of the desire and, after carefully reflecting on her financial position and other factors, decides to make the purchase; she reasons (placing heavy emphasis on moral considerations) that all things considered she should buy the rug. Presumably Shaheen is morally appraisable for the purchase. Although she acted on a desire that was induced, she exercised the sort of control over this desire and the ensuing action that is typical of the sort of control agents exhibit when they perform actions for which they are morally appraisable: her action was under her volitional control. Further, she did not act in ignorance, and her action did not arise from an unauthentic evaluative scheme.

Relying on the notion of volitional control, we can now advance the following principle germane to the problem of induced pro-attitudes. Suppose agent S's intentional action, A, issues ultimately from some (perhaps induced) pro-attitude PA; PA is one element in the causal sequence leading to A, and it may well be the motivational precursor—the proximal motivational element (like a desire)—of A:

IPA1: If A issues from PA and it is false that S exercises volitional control over A, S is not morally appraisable for performing A. (I assume that S has not taken deliberate steps to see to it that PA is induced in S for the purpose of ensuring that S lacks volitional control over the behavior that issues from PA.)

It is initially tempting to suppose that this principle is also true:

IPA0: If A issues from PA and S exercises volitional control over A, then other conditions of moral appraisability for S's A-ing being satisfied, S is morally appraisable for performing A.

Cases of global manipulation, however, directly challenge IPA0. Let's revert to Billy's case. Having outlined what evaluative schemes are, the case can better be described in this way: Billy undergoes psychosurgery to which he does not consent. The surgery transforms Billy into a psychological twin of Woody. Part of what is involved in such a transformation is that Billy's evaluative scheme is "replaced" by one that is type-identical to Woody's. Suppose after some deliberation (conducted on the basis of his acquired evaluative scheme) Billy arrives at a decision to donate a large sum to charity on which he then acts. Assume that transformed Billy exercises volitional control over his donating the money to charity. Assume, also, that other conditions of moral appraisability, like epistemic ones such as Billy's not being relevantly ignorant of what he is doing, are satisfied. Then IPA0 implies untenably that transformed Billy is morally appraisable for donating the money.

To meet the taxing difficulty posed by global manipulation cases, I want to start by motivating the view that when it comes to ascriptions of moral appraisability, psychological continuity or something very much like it is of paramount importance. The notion of psychological continuity, as I have explained, can be understood thusly.[9] Person x is psychologically connected to person y if and only if there are a significant number of psychological connections between x and y,[10] where these connections are relations of similarity, or identity, or causal dependence among psychological states. For example, x may have the same sorts of desires, beliefs, and goals that y has; x may have memories of experiences as y had those experiences; or x may perform a certain action as y intended to perform it. Person x at time t is psychologically continuous with person y at time t* if and only if there is a series of persons at times such that x is the first and y the last member of the series, and each person at a time in the series is psychologically connected to the preceding person in the series.

Now ponder these considerations which help support the view that psychological continuity (or something similar) matters in ascriptions of moral appraisability. Suppose (unbeknownst to Curly) a powerful being (Omni) induces in Curly an irresistible desire to punch Moe, and Curly, controlled by this desire punches Moe. Clearly, we would not want to hold Curly morally blameworthy for punching the other stooge. If anyone is to blame for the punching, it is Omni; Curly, at least with respect to punching Moe, is simply a pawn of Omni. This unremarkable example serves to highlight a simple point: when an action A of some agent X is controlled, in the absence of X's consenting to being so controlled, by some other agent Y, then if any agent is to be praiseworthy or blameworthy for A (which X performs under the influence of being controlled by Y), it is Y. A similar point surfaces if we modify the case by supposing that Omni controls Curly by globally manipulating the stooge. Imagine that Omni temporarily transforms Curly into a psychological twin of herself for the purpose of achieving a devious end. When transformed Curly ruthlessly kills Black (by squeezing the trigger) upon awakening from transformation surgery to which he did not consent, we hold Omni and not Curly morally to blame for squeezing the trigger. Although Curly squeezes the trigger, it would not be farfetched to describe the case as one in which one agent temporarily "resides" in another for the purpose of securing some end. Such a description would be especially apt if we assume, as we indeed are, that transformation surgery preserves personal identity. Although it is one person, Curly, who undergoes transformation surgery and who squeezes the trigger, it is two different agents in the sense of 'agency' pertinent to moral appraisability who undergo surgery and squeeze the trigger, respectively.

Well, what is this notion of agency? As a first approximation, it appears that for purposes of attributing moral appraisability, we focus on psychological agents—entities that instantiate an interesting or sufficiently rich psychological profile. It is such entities, we believe, that are rationally appropriate candidates for praise or blame and for the reactive attitudes or feelings like gratitude, love, respect, and resentment with which we frequently react to a person when we regard the person as a morally appraisable agent.[11] The person that is Curly prior to surgery is a different psychological agent than the person that is Curly after transformation surgery—the two differ psychologically and may even be psychologically discontinuous. I suggest that it this sort of consideration that partly accounts for our inclination to say that Curly is not appraisable for squeezing the trigger (but some other *psychological* agent is).

I now want somewhat to refine the notion of agency that is presupposed by our attributions of moral appraisability. I shall then explain how of all of this is germane to the problem of globally induced pro-attitudes. *Normative agency*, the sort pertinent to normative appraisals, is traditionally conceived at least partly as the capacity to appraise and exercise motives; it is deliberative processes that have traditionally been associated with agency. I want to capture this idea in the proposal that the appropriate subjects of attributions of moral appraisability are normative agents. To be a normative agent, an individual must have an evaluative scheme. Recall that one element of an individual's evaluative scheme comprises beliefs regarding which normative standards or principles the agent thinks ought to be invoked in (the agent's) assessment of reasons for action, or normative principles the agent believes ought to be invoked in (that agent's) making choices. In order to be *morally* appraisable, that is, morally to blame or praise for an action, these normative principles must include a set of moral principles or moral norms. To elaborate, the agent must be morally competent in a minimal sense: she must understand the concepts of rightness or obligatoriness and wrongness, and she must be able to appraise—morally—various choices, courses of action, consequences of action, thoughts, etc., in light of the moral norms that are partly constitutive of her evaluative scheme. (There is no requirement, of course, that appraisals, when made either consciously or not, be perfectly rational.) The agent, we can say, must be minimally morally competent in order to be a suitable subject of praise or blame.

I propose that it is a *sufficient* condition of an individual's being the sort of normative agent that is an appropriate candidate of praise or blame at a time, t, if that individual has at t (i) an evaluative scheme with the requisite moral elements—the agent is minimally morally competent; (ii) deliberative skills and capacities; for example, the agent has the capacity to apply the normative standards that are elements of its evaluative scheme to evaluating reasons; and (iii) executive capacities—the agent is able to act on (at least *some* of) its intentions, decisions, or choices. An individual (like a toddler) who fails to have deliberative or executive capacities will be able to exert much less control, if any, over its actions than an individual who does have such capacities. I take condition ii to entail that the agent is (at t) able to engage in genuine deliberation; his deliberative activities must meet the threshold of rationality below which such activities fail to count as bona fide deliberation.

Reverting to the problem of globally induced pro-attitudes, an individual like Curly will probably not be a normative agent at some time in his life (that is, he will probably lack the property of being a normative agent at some time in his life); then, lacking the deliberative (or executive) capacities characteristic of normative agency, he would not have been a normative agent when he was a newly born baby, nor would he be one if he were lobotomized. In addition, global manipulation cases make it pretty evident that an individual may instantiate the properties definitive of one normative agent at one time but of a different normative agent at a different time. When Omni, for example, performs transformation surgery on Curly, the surgery endows Curly with a set of properties definitive of normative agency then already instantiated by Omni, and "eradicates" the set of properties definitive of normative agency instantiated by Curly prior to undergoing surgery. Speaking loosely, we can say that the surgery destroys one normative agent and replaces it with another. Again, speaking loosely, it does so for the reason that normative agents have their evaluative schemes essentially: if E is the evaluative scheme of normative agent, N, then *having* E is an essential property of N.[12]

In light of the discussion of normative agency, I propose the following principle. Let's say that an agent S *broadly consents* to pro-attitude PA's being induced in S if and only if either S gives ordinary consent to PA's being induced in S; or S would not object to PA's being induced in S if, given S's normal deliberative capacities, S were to reflect on PA's being induced in S, under conditions S takes to be favorable or unobjectionable, to making decisions relevant to restructuring or reshaping S's life. For example, suppose S freely consents to Max's request to implant in S a cluster of pro-attitudes; then S has given broad consent. In another example, knowing that she is trying to reduce her intake of caffeine, suppose that by various persistent suggestions, Jake tactfully induces in Jasmine a desire to cut down on the number of cokes she drinks in a day. Jasmine never gives overt free consent to the desire's being thus induced in her. But assume that if she were thinking about modifying her long-standing habit of consuming large quantities of caffeine, under conditions she considered unobjectionable for making decisions about such things, she would not object to the desire's being induced in her in the manner in which Jake induces it in her. Again, Jasmine has given broad consent. Suppose S's action A is caused in part by a set of induced pro-attitudes, PA, members of which may well be the motivational precursor of A. The relevant principle is this:

> IPA2*: If at time, t, S has the property of being normative agent, N, and at t PA is induced in S without S's broad consent *via* a process destructive of N (but not of personal identity), then if S does A and A is caused in part by some member of PA, S is not morally appraisable for performing A.[13]

The psychosurgery to which he did not (broadly) consent transforms Billy into a psychological twin of Woody, eradicating the property of being normative agent, BillyN, and "replacing" that property with the property of being normative agent WoodyN. Hence, IPA2* implies that transformed Billy is not morally appraisable for any of his actions that derive from his engineered values.

Reconsider *modified* Psychogen. It calls for a slight modification in IPA2. In this case Mad Max transforms Jenny into a psychological twin of Jim. "Jenny1" refers to Jenny prior to psychosurgery, and "Jenny2" denotes Jenny after the surgery. Unlike original Psychogen, the transformation surgery does not destroy all the goals, values, preferences, and the like of Jenny1's that compete with those of Jim's. Indeed, enough of Jenny1's competing psychological elements are retained by Jenny2 (so that it is pretty clear that Jenny1 is identical to Jenny2), but these competing elements are repressed; Jenny2 cannot "access" them. In this unusual case, arguably Max's surgery does not *destroy* Jenny1's property of being normative agent, say, NJenny1. Still, Jenny2 is not praiseworthy for her deed of investment, a deed she performs after recovering from surgery. To handle this sort of worry, IPA2* can be modified in this way:

> IPA2: If at time, t, S has the property of being normative agent, N, and at t PA is induced in S without S's broad consent via a process that either destroys N (leaving intact personal identity) or completely "represses" N (as in modified Psychogen), then if S does A and A is caused in part by some member of PA, S is not morally appraisable for performing A.

5. OBJECTIONS, RESPONSES, AND A TANTALIZING PROPOSAL

So far I have dealt with cases of local manipulation in which the induced pro-attitudes generate actions over which the agents lack volitional control, and with cases of global manipulation in which normative agency is destroyed. It might be objected that there are hard cases involving local manipulation not destructive of normative agency, the induced pro-attitudes give rise to actions over which the agent has volitional control, but—and here's the rub—in which the agent is *not* morally appraisable for performing such actions. IPA1 cannot handle such cases as this principle rules out moral appraisability only in cases involving pro-attitudes that generate actions over which agents do not exercise volitional control. IPA2 is of no help either as in these cases normative agency is left intact and not disrupted in any way. Here is an illustrative example of a hard case: [14] A leader habitually recruits orphaned children and subjects them to this sort of conditioning: they are rewarded with praise and treats when, during daily exercises in reasoning aloud about what to do, they take what they believe are the leader's interests into account; otherwise, rewards are withheld. The children are never told that the leader's interests should be taken into account, and some of the successfully conditioned ones never come explicitly to believe this; they acquire their engineered deliberative habits, which significantly shape their psychological constitution, via techniques that bypass their capacities for cognitive control over their own mental lives. By engendering in the successfully conditioned children deliberative habits that suit his own ends, the leader exerts a good deal of control over some of their deliberative reasoning. Suppose Ernie is one of the successfully conditioned children. Suppose, further, that on a certain occasion Ernie's deliberation, governed by the instilled habits, culminates in Ernie's performing A. It might now be urged that Ernie is not morally appraisable for A-ing despite its being the case that the engineering leaves Ernie free to exercise volitional control over A and is not of the global manipulation variety.

Grant that Ernie is not a victim of global manipulation. But should it be granted that he is not morally appraisable for A-ing? [15] Assume, on the one hand, that the leader's engineering leaves untouched Ernie's capacities to become aware of his new deliberative habit, to reflect critically on it, and to counter its influence; the engineering leaves Ernie free to endorse or thwart the instilled habit. Then there is little reason to believe that Ernie is not morally appraisable for A-ing (other conditions of moral appraisability being satisfied). For Ernie's position would be no different from the position in which people from all walks of life frequently find themselves. A person might be influenced in her deliberations by a charismatic political leader, her parents, or her lover and do various things in light of these deliberations. Still, if the influence leaves her free to bring her critical capacities untainted by the influence to bear on her pertinent deliberations, and to act in accordance with their recommendations, she would (other conditions being satisfied) be morally appraisable for the actions that issue from such deliberations. Assume, on the other hand, that the engineering that bypasses Ernie's relevant capacities for control over his mental life *prevents* Ernie from becoming aware of his instilled deliberative habit *and* from countering its influence. Then it seems that Ernie would not be morally appraisable for A-ing. But then too IPA1 would yield this very result as it appears that A would not be under Ernie's volitional control: there is no scenario (with the same natural laws as the actual world) in which, given the motivational precursor of A, Ernie forms a decision to do other than A and successfully translates that decision into action.[16]

There is another objection that needs addressing. I have assumed that global manipulation preserves personal identity (even though it can destroy normative agency). But this assumption may well be questioned, perhaps partly on the basis that, for instance, transformed Billy is *radically* psychologically disparate from original Billy; indeed, I have admitted that original Billy has the property of being one normative agent while transformed Billy has the property of being another. Suppose global manipulation does destroy personal identity so that transformed Billy is not identical to original Billy. Global manipulation, then, would induce not just radical qualitative change but substantial change. Still, transformed Billy *would* be a morally responsible agent (or so it might be submitted); he would be appraisable for at least some of his actions, just as an adult with full deliberative capacities created at an instant by God would be a morally appraisable agent. But then, the objection continues, we have a deep puzzle. Consider two global transformation cases that are otherwise alike except that in one Billy survives the transformation but in the other he does not; in the latter, transformed "Billy" is not identical to Billy. IPA2 yields the unpalatable result that in the former case the transformed individual is not morally appraisable for his subsequent actions, whereas in the latter the transformed individual is. How can this be so? How can the mere fact that Billy survives transformation surgery make such a drastic difference to ascriptions of moral appraisability when all other relevant facts remain the same?

I have a twofold response to this objection. First, my inclination is to deny that transformation surgery destroys personal identity. Granted, pre- and post-surgery Billy *are* considerably different, psychologically; nevertheless, they may be psychologically continuous. Billy's case would then be relevantly analogous to cases of religious or ideological conversions in which the pre- and postconversion persons have significantly different personalities, characters, ambitions, and goals, but are still psychologically continuous. In these cases, there is enough continuity, it seems, to "validate" ascriptions of sameness. My intuitions are that even in an incident in which the individual who was, say, James, prior to the onset of the sickness that ultimately resulted in this individual's being in an irreversible coma, the individual who now finds himself in an irreversible coma is identical to James, although this comatose individual is not psychologically continuous with "pre-sick" James. So *perhaps* there is more to personal identity than psychological continuity, but I admit that this view is controversial. Second, I will argue in the next chapter that even magical agents, those created at an instant with evaluative schemes fully intact and deliberative capacities already in place, may not be appraisable for their actions *if* their evaluative schemes are not properly acquired.

Lastly, assume that Billy survives the extensive psychosurgery—identity is preserved. There is temptation not to hold Billy appraisable for his postsurgery actions. But Michael Zimmerman has suggested to me (in personal correspondence) that this can be acknowledged *without* invoking an autonomy/authenticity condition; think of IPA1 and IPA2 as precursors of such a condition. We could refine our ascriptions of appraisability by invoking "facets" or "slices" of the agent (as I have done when I talk about normative agents). We could say: Billy qua earlier normative agent is not appraisable for his later actions, but Billy qua later normative agent *is* appraisable for his later actions. (Normally, of course, this "qua" talk will be unnecessary, since normative agency will not vary in this way.) This has the advantage of not holding Billy appraisable (in one way) but also acknowledging that Billy is (in another way) the appraisability-equal of Woody. If this is right, then it casts doubt on the necessity to invoke an autonomy/authenticity condition of appraisability. In addition, this proposal is still consistent with a history-sensitive account of appraisability, in that some (for example, incompatibilists) would claim that whether or not an agent acts freely is a function of that agent's causal history.

I find this proposal intriguing, but I also have the very firm intuition that postsurgery Billy, qua *plain Billy*, is not appraisable for his postsurgery actions. (If talk about Billy qua earlier [or later] normative agent is proprietary, talk about Billy qua plain Billy should also be proprietary. Surely, the members of a jury could raise the legitimate concern of whether postsurgery Billy—qua plain Billy— is culpable for a postsurgery misdeed.) And if one shares this sort of intuition, then I think that an autonomy/authenticity condition of appraisability will be difficult to avoid. In addition, suppose we refine, as Zimmerman proposes, our ascriptions of appraisability by invoking slices of the agent, and we then claim that Billy qua later but not earlier normative agent is appraisable for his later actions. We might still ask: Why the difference in appraisability ascriptions? What grounds the asymmetry? Billy, after all, survives the psychosurgery, and Billy qua earlier normative agent and Billy qua later normative agent are "control-wise" and "cognitively-wise" on equal terms; both have volitional control over germane actions, and neither is cognitively or epistemically impaired. The sole *relevant* difference appears to be that postsurgery Billy—Billy qua later normative agent— is a victim of global manipulation, whereas presurgery Billy is not. We are then once again challenged by the original concern: Why, precisely, is a victim of global manipulation *not* appraisable for his or her later actions? An adequate answer to *this* question, I believe, will in the end have to make recourse to some autonomy/authenticity condition.

6. SOME CONCLUSIONS

I have argued that there is a genuine problem of induced pro-attitudes. Some pro-attitudes instilled in agents by techniques like value engineering undermine moral appraisability as a result of giving rise to actions over which agents lack the sort of control—volitional control—which is required for moral appraisability. Other instilled pro-attitudes undermine appraisability by destroying or completely "repressing" normative agency. If I am right about the latter, then moral appraisability, to use John Fischer's terminology, is a historical phenomenon: the resources that ground and explain ascriptions of appraisability must in the end appeal to something other than the agent's here-and-now (or current-time slice) psychological constitutions, as is evidenced by Billy's case. We can only, it seems to me, explain why transformed Billy is not morally appraisable for any action he performs upon awakening from transformation surgery by paying attention to how Billy came to acquire the springs of his actions. Billy's case, in summary, strongly suggests that prospects for defending an all-in-the-head view of moral appraisability are indeed dim.

Further, we can exploit principles IPA1 and IPA2 to make some headway in clarifying the notion of authentic evaluative schemes. It is to this concern that I turn in the next chapter.

SEVEN

AUTHENTIC EVALUATIVE
SCHEMES

Sometimes, when pro-attitudes like desires are induced in a person, and the person acts on those induced desires, we believe—and I think correctly—that the person is not appraisable for behavior that arises from those desires. A typical sort of case would be one in which, in the absence of her consent, a cluster of irresistible desires has been implanted in the victim. At other times, this is not so: we feel that the person can, for instance, be blameworthy for acting on a posthypnotic suggestion when, through a series of past actions, she has deliberately and freely brought it about that she cannot now refrain from acting on the posthypnotic suggestion; or when she can easily thwart the influence of the posthypnotic suggestion. In the last chapter, I proposed two principles to help us see our way through some of the manifold problems associated with moral appraisability and induced pro-attitudes, one dealing with local and the other with global manipulation. The principles, respectively, are these:

IPA1: Suppose agent S's intentional action, A, is caused ultimately by some induced pro-attitude PA; PA is one vital element in the etiology of A. If A issues from PA and S lacks volitional control over A, then S is not morally appraisable for performing A. (We assume that S has not willingly arranged for PA to be induced in S.)

IPA2: If at time, t, S has the property of being normative agent, N, and at t PA is induced in S without S's broad consent via a process that either destroys N (leaving intact personal identity) or completely "represses" N (as in modified Psychogen), then if S does A and A is caused in part by some member of PA, S is not morally appraisable for performing A.

In this chapter, I explain how these principles help shed light on authentic evaluative schemes. IPA1 is germane to what I call "appraisability-relative authenticity," whereas IPA2 helps with what I dub "normative unauthenticity." The aim is to formulate a set of conditions sufficient for the evaluative scheme of an agent to be "truly the agent's own."

1. UNAUTHENTIC SCHEMES OF GLOBALLY MANIPULATED AGENTS

I have explained that an agent's evaluative scheme is comprised of these constituents: (1) beliefs about normative standards to be invoked in assessing reasons for action; (2) motivational factors like long-term ends or goals that comprise the agent's values; (3) beliefs about deliberative principles the agent regards as appropriate to arrive at practical judgments about what to do or how to act in particular circumstances; and finally (4) motivation to act on the basis of the normative standards in 1 and values in 2 using the deliberative principles in 3. So an agent's evaluative scheme has two broad sorts of components, doxastic (1 and 3), and motivational (2 and 4).

In chapter 6, I introduced the technical notion of a normative agent. I said that the appropriate subjects of moral appraisability are normative agents, and that if an individual has an evaluative scheme at time t, some elements of which are beliefs concerning what is (morally) right or wrong, has deliberative and executive skills and capacities at t, and is able to engage in (genuine) deliberation at t, then that individual is a normative agent at t. Toddlers and kittens are not normative agents and, consequently, are not appropriate candidates for praise or blame. We don't hold them *morally* appraisable for their actions. Many human adults, in contrast, *are* normative agents.

We have seen that there are some cases in which an individual who is a normative agent can acquire an "implanted evaluative scheme" that in effect destroys initial normative agency. This is what happens in global manipulation cases like original Psychogen. The psychosurgery to which she did not consent transforms Jenny into a psychological twin of Jim. The surgery has the effect of "eradicating" the property exemplified by Jenny of being a certain normative agent prior to surgery, and "replacing" that property with one of being a "Jim-like" normative agent. When Jenny awakens after psychosurgery and performs a good deed for her friend by investing shrewdly, we don't think Jenny is praiseworthy for this deed. And surely part of the reason why we don't feel Jenny is deserving of praise is that her action issues from an evaluative scheme that was forced upon her; the new scheme is not Jenny's original; it isn't "truly her own." She did not broadly consent to this new scheme's being implanted in her. Remember, agent S broadly consents to pro-attitude PA being induced in S if and only if either S gives ordinary consent to PA's being induced in S; or S would not object to PA's being induced in S if, relying on S's normal deliberative capacities, S were to reflect on PA's being induced in S, in circumstances that S regards as favorable or acceptable to make the relevant sorts of decisions—a decision, for example, about whether she wants to alter her life by having PA instilled in her. In other cases, like modified Psychogen, global manipulation totally "represses" rather than destroys initial normative agency. In these sorts of cases, too, we think that the agent who recovers from the manipulative surgery is not appraisable for his subsequent behavior. And once again, it appears that the agent is not appraisable as the evaluative scheme which gives rise to his actions is not "truly his own." In these very special types of cases involving destruction or repression of initial normative agency, the scheme implanted by global manipulation is not "truly the agent's own" *in virtue of* destroying or repressing (in the absence of consent) an "original scheme." Call this type of unauthenticity "normative unauthenticity." We can now advance the following principle about *normative* evaluative scheme unauthenticity:

> A1: If S is a normative agent N with evaluative scheme OriginalE at time t, and S acquires at t or after an evaluative scheme, NewE, via a process to which she did not give broad consent that either destroys N by destroying OriginalE, or totally "represses" N, then NewE is not *normative-wise* authentic.

Normative unauthenticity is, admittedly, of little interest in connection with the vast array of cases in which we are inclined to judge that an agent's action did not issue from pro-attitudes or actional springs that are "truly the agent's own." I now turn to these sorts of cases.

2. ACQUIRING SCHEMES: INITIAL SCHEMES

To help the discussion along, I distinguish between two different stages in an individual's life; the distinction coincides, roughly, with the margin between childhood and adulthood: distinguish the stage *before* the individual has acquired an evaluative scheme, and the stage after which the individual's initial scheme has been acquired. Of course, there is no hard and fast line between the two. As Joel Feinberg explains, "In the continuous development of the relative-adult out of the relative-child, there is no point before which the child himself has no part in his own shaping, and after which he is the sole responsible maker of his own character and life-plan [and we might add, his evaluative scheme]. Such a radical discontinuity is simply not part of anyone's personal history. The extent of the child's role in his own shaping is, instead, a process of continuous growth already begun at birth" (1986, p. 34).

Regarding authenticity of evaluative schemes of "developing agents" like us, I start with the following preliminary idea and then refine it. Call the evaluative scheme the child or an individual first acquires, the individual's "initial evaluative scheme." If it is *properly acquired*—that is, if its motivational and doxastic elements are properly acquired—then it is an authentic initial scheme. Call a scheme that results from *acceptable modifications* of an individual's authentic initial scheme, that individual's "authentic evolved scheme." Our guiding idea will be that an agent's evaluative scheme is authentic if it is either the agent's authentic initial scheme or the agent's authentic evolved scheme.

Distinguishing between the two stages in a person's acquisition of her evaluative scheme is vital for at least this reason: many accounts that appear promising as accounts of the authenticity of evolved schemes of agents simply fall by the wayside as accounts of the authenticity of initial schemes or partially acquired initial schemes. So, for example, on a hierarchical model, a pro-attitude like a first-order desire that is an element of an agent's evaluative scheme is authentic only on the condition that there is an appropriate "mesh" or "fit" between that desire and some of the agent's higher-order propositional attitudes whose representational content includes that desire. On some "historical approaches," a desire of an agent's that is a constituent of that agent's evaluative scheme qualifies as authentic only if the agent—under conditions of being minimally rational and free of self-deception—did not resist the development of that desire when attending to the process of its acquisition, or would not have resisted that development had the agent attended to this process. Both sorts of approaches are, pretty obviously, inadequate as approaches to the authenticity of pro-attitudes that are constitutive of a young child's partially acquired initial scheme. Presumably, the child lacks the cognitive sophistication presupposed by either of these approaches; the result will be the implausible one that *none* of the maturing child's initial pro-attitudes are "truly the child's own."

I discuss initial evaluative schemes first and then address evolved ones. It might plausibly be thought that concerns regarding authenticity of initial evaluative schemes can arise only in connection with beings like us who don't come with their initial schemes fully formed. We do develop psychologically and intellectually (among other ways), and our development is gradual; both the child and other persons (at least initially) contribute toward the formation of the child's initial evaluative scheme. As we don't come fully self-made, untoward interferences in the maturation process—the process whereby we acquire initial schemes—can subvert authenticity. Hence, it might be thought that for magical agents, agents who come fully equipped at the time of their creation, or at the time at which they come into existence, with pro-attitudes, values, and appropriate beliefs that comprise evaluative schemes, authenticity of *initial* evaluative schemes would *not* be a problem; with such beings, it might reasonably be theorized, there could be no opportunity for "authenticity-undermining influences" to gain a foothold to taint initial schemes. Is this view correct?

Let's revert to developing agents (like children) who mature ordinarily. Feinberg remarks that the extent of the child's role in his own shaping is a process of continuous growth begun at birth. He continues:

> From the very beginning that process is given its own distinctive slant by the influences of heredity and early environment. At a time so early that the questions of how to socialize and educate the child have not even arisen yet, the twig will be bent in a certain definite direction. . . . From the very beginning, then, the child must—inevitably *will*—have some input in his own shaping, the extent of which will grow continuously even as the child's character itself does. After that, the child can contribute towards the making of his own self and circumstances in ever increas-

ing degree. These contributions are significant even though the child is in large part (especially in the earliest years) the product of external influences over which he has no control, and his original motivational structure is something he just finds himself with, not something he consciously creates. Always the self that contributes to the making of the newer self is the product both of outside influences *and* an earlier self that was not quite as fully formed. That earlier self, in turn, was the product both of outside influences and a still earlier self that was still less fully formed and fixed, and so on, all the way back to infancy. At every subsequent stage the immature child plays a greater role in the creation of his own life, until at the arbitrarily fixed point of full maturity, he is at last fully in charge of himself. . . . Perhaps we are all self-made in the way just described, except those who have been severely manipulated, indoctrinated, or coerced throughout childhood. But the self we have created in this way for ourselves will not be an authentic self unless the habit of critical self-revision was implanted in us early by parents, educators, or peers, and strengthened by our own constant exercise of it. (1986, pp. 34–35)

In this insightful passage, Feinberg suggests, astutely, that authenticity requires both a certain sort of maturation, one free of things like indoctrination or coercion, *and* deliberate *interferences* in the processes that shape the child. He proposes, for instance, that the habit of critical self-revision must be *implanted* in us early if we are to acquire autonomy. On Feinberg's view, then, some deliberate interferences in shaping the child are perfectly compatible with authenticity and, indeed, are required for authenticity. In a similar vein, Richard Arneson proposes that a requirement for autonomy is that one's upbringing or initial socialization be nonrepressive. He also adds:

The notion of a nonrepressive upbringing should not flout the common sense understanding that children need to be tamed for their own good and for the good of society. The young child is conceived as containing innate propensities that in the course of ordinary interaction with her environment would develop into basic preferences unless blocked by effective repression. An upbringing is nonrepressive to the extent that these propensities are actively encouraged by persons who interact with the young child, or tolerated by them, or at least not successfully squelched, except insofar as discouragement of these propensities is required in order to instill in the child a disposition to be moral, to safeguard the child's predictable vital interests, or to develop in the child traits and skills that are needed so that at maturity the child will have the ability successfully to pursue a reasonable range of significantly different plans of life in a modern society. (1994, pp. 59–60)

Again, Arneson suggests that certain interferences in the maturation of the child are not autonomy (or authenticity) subverting and may indeed be required for autonomy. Reflecting on this strand of thought, assume (for a bit) that having the disposition to be moral is required for initial scheme authenticity. Now imagine a child brought up without having any such disposition instilled in her; she has instead, been "equipped" with a disposition to maximize her long-term self-interest. Then, given our assumption that the moral disposition is necessary for authenticity, the child's evaluative scheme will fail to be authentic; or more plausibly, it will fail to be fully authentic even if authentic in other respects. But one might well balk at this result. After all, it might reasonably be claimed that, given an otherwise "normal" upbringing, the cluster of dispositions constitutive of the child's scheme *is* "truly the child's own"; it is truly the child's own in just the manner in which it would have been had the child been implanted with the moral disposition; the cluster the child in fact has, though "truly her own," simply lacks this disposition. How can the mere lack of this disposition subvert authenticity? Perhaps initial scheme authenticity is, when the final verdict is in, illusory.

I want to resist this skepticism. I confine attention, first, to the motivational elements of an (initial) evaluative scheme, and then address the doxastic ones. With respect to both sorts of elements, I wish to motivate the idea that there is nothing like "across the board authenticity" or just "plain authenticity"; rather there is something like "appraisability-*relative* authenticity." This needs careful unpacking.

Both Arneson and Feinberg speak about instilling or implanting dispositions or habits to assure autonomy and, I might add, authenticity. Let's distinguish between *what* is instilled, a habit or disposition, perhaps, and the *mode* or *means* of instillment, some examples of which include conditioning, or direct stimulation of the brain. Our concern is, in the end, with *moral appraisability*. With this in mind, it is profitable to inquire into the following. Imagine (if you can) that Parent has a "pool" of motivational elements from which she is free to choose which, if any, to instill in Youngster. Which sorts of elements from this pool, if instilled or purposely not instilled (ignoring, initially, the mode of instillment), would subvert Youngster's being morally appraisable for his behavior subsequent to the acquisition of his initial scheme? That is, which sorts of elements if instilled (or not instilled) would ensure that Youngster would *not* be an appropriate candidate for moral praise or blame on account of his later behavior that owes its genesis to the instilled elements? The general answer appears to be that the instillment or lack of instillment of those motivational elements, of the type that an agent's having them or lacking them, ensures that the conditions required for moral appraisability for behavior arising from them cannot be satisfied by that agent or her behavior; in short, it is the instillment of those incompatible with later appraisability. For example, to be *morally* appraisable for an action, an agent must be morally competent in a minimal sense: he must grasp the concepts of rightness, wrongness, or obligatoriness, and he must be able to appraise morally (even if imperfectly), various choices, courses of action, consequences of action, omissions, etc. in light of the moral norms that are partly constitutive of his evaluative scheme. If Youngster, then, is trained in such a fashion that he simply lacks knowledge of the relevant moral concepts so that he is not even minimally morally competent, then lack of instillment of the appropriate moral concepts is appraisability-subversive. Or consider instillment in Youngster of a pro-attitude or disposition, the influence of which on his behavior he simply cannot thwart. The instillment of such a pro-attitude would presumably undermine appraisability for later conduct arising from that pro-attitude by undermining control—the sort (volitional control) required for moral appraisability. Or suppose Youngster is instilled with a powerful disposition always to act impulsively. Here, again, we would not want to hold Youngster appraisable for much of his later impulsive behavior. Or, finally, consider an interference that prevents Youngster from engaging in critical self-reflection. This may subvert appraisability for some of Youngster's later behavior by significantly narrowing, on occasions of choice, the range of Youngster's options, a range he could, in all likelihood, have considered had he acquired the "normal" habit to engage in critical self-reflection.

Some interferences, then, (where 'interference' is a "catch-all" term for things like suppression of innate propensities, or implantation of certain dispositions or habits, or deliberate lack of instillment of various pro-attitudes) are incompatible with the agent's being appraisable for his subsequent behavior that issues from instilled elements; such interferences subvert later appraisability while others do not. I propose that the subversive ones are (morally) *appraisability-wise unauthentic*. Specifically, consider an agent like a young child who does not yet have an initial scheme. Such an agent's, S's, having pro-attitude P is appraisability-wise unauthentic if S's having P, as a result of instillment, subverts S's being morally appraisable for S's behavior that stems from P;[1] the having of P precludes S from being morally appraisable for behavior stemming from P. (This condition is somewhat analogous to the one expressed by IPA1.) An obvious further question is this: The having of (or lacking of) which pro-attitudes, precisely, subverts later responsibility? I have given a heterogeneous class of examples ranging from things like the implantation of irresistible desires to deliberately thwarting development of appreciation of moral concepts. I submit that the shared feature that many (but not all) of these have that makes the having of them appraisability-wise unauthentic is that the having of them (by the agent) is morally impermissible in light of the true or correct morality—the true or correct moral principle specifying necessary and sufficient conditions for the rightness, wrongness, and obligatoriness of acts. For instance, it seems morally wrong deliberatively to fail to instill in the child the disposition to be moral, or to instill in the child the disposition always to act impulsively.

On the other side of the coin, Feinberg and Arneson recommend that some interferences may well be required for autonomy, and here too we can add, appraisability-relative authenticity. So, for instance, the child's acquiring minimal knowledge of moral concepts is a requirement for (moral) appraisability for later behavior. Again, presumably under ordinary conditions, encouraging the child to acquire such knowledge is morally permissible or even required. Galen Strawson has suggested, very reasonably, that the attitude of seeing oneself as a free agent, in control of one's actions, is a constitutive condition of responsible agency:

> We are free (truly responsible), if we are, partly because we see ourselves and our action in a certain way-as free (or truly responsible). As the Subjectivists say, this is a *constitutive* condition of freedom. It is an Attitudinal condition. Free agenthood is not just a matter of certain practical capacities. A free agent must see itself in a certain specific way, and its seeing itself in this way is not a necessary consequence of its possession of any set of abilities or capacities or attitudes that does not include this way of seeing itself. (Strawson 1986, p. 293)

I recommend that the implantation or fostering of the attitude or disposition of seeing oneself in control of one's actions, as a suitable subject of moral responsibility, may well—at least in the very initial stages of development—be required to ensure appraisability for subsequent behavior. Fostering this sort of attitude, again, is presumably morally required. Confining attention to a young agent without an initial scheme in place, I suggest, in summary, that such an agent's, S's, having pro-attitude, P, is appraisability-wise authentic if the having of P by S (as a result of instillment) is a necessary prerequisite of S's being morally appraisable for behavior stemming from P. Presumably, the having of most such pro-attitudes is morally required.

I have, so far, limited discussion to appraisability-relevant authenticity of the "objects" of instillment such as habits, or dispositions, or pro-attitudes in general. What about the modes of instilling such things; are some appraisability-wise authentic and others not? We can approach this issue in the following manner. Assume, to ensure prevention of subverting moral appraisability for later behavior, it is necessary to instill in the child the disposition to be moral. Could different modes of instillment of this disposition affect appraisability-relevant authenticity of this very disposition itself? Apparently so. Suppose, for example, that given the mode of instillment of the moral disposition in Youngster—perhaps the disposition was "beaten into" Youngster, or instilled via "shock therapy"—Youngster subsequently finds that he cannot refrain from doing what he perceives to be morally right. On occasions of choice, he is stricken with inward terror even at the faintest thought of not doing what he deems moral. Intuitively, Youngster would not be appraisable for much of his later behavior as the mode of instillment of the moral disposition subverts appraisability-grounding control. Modes of instillment of pro-attitudes (habits, dispositions, etc.) are appraisability-wise not "truly one's own" (that is, are appraisability-wise unauthentic) if they subvert appraisability for later behavior. And again, one distinguishing mark most appraisability-relative unauthentic modes of instillment seem to have in common is that it is morally wrong to use such modes of instillment.

To help in formulating a general principle about initial scheme appraisability-relative authenticity, I introduce some terminology. I have suggested that the having of some pro-attitudes (dispositions, habits, etc.) is incompatible with appraisability for later behavior that issues from them; the having of them precludes satisfaction of other conditions (like epistemic or control ones) required for appraisability. I have proposed that one identifying mark of most of these pro-attitudes is that the having of them (by the agent) is morally wrong. Call such incompatible pro-attitudes "authenticity destructive." I have also suggested that, possibly, having some pro-attitudes (dispositions, habits, etc.) is required to ensure appraisability for later behavior—the having of them ensures that other conditions of appraisability can (later) be satisfied by the agent or her behavior that stems from them. I have proposed that, possibly, a distinguishing feature of most of these pro-attitudes is that the having of them (by the agent) is morally required. Call such pro-attitudes "authenticity demanding." Lastly, I have suggested that some modes of instilling pro-attitudes (dispositions, habits, etc.) are incompatible with appraisability for later behavior; again, such modes of instillment subvert later appraisability. Call such modes of instillment "authenticity subversive modes." Finally, limiting attention to the motivational or pro-attitudinal elements of an initial scheme, I propose this principle as one that governs appraisability-relative authenticity of initial schemes of "developing agents":

A2: An agent's initial evaluative scheme is appraisability-wise authentic if its pro-attitudinal elements (i) include all those, if any, that are authenticity demanding; (ii) do not include any that are authenticity destructive; and (iii) have been acquired by means that are not authenticity subversive.

Some general comments regarding A2 are in order. First, the instilled pro-attitudes that comprise an agent's initial scheme will be ones such that the agent will, having developed the relevant cognitive abilities, give rise to actions over which the agent has volitional control. Second, there is, admittedly, a sense in which A2 is too stringent. For it appears that appraisability-relative authenticity is a matter of degree. It seems possible that many components of a young person's developing evaluative scheme may have been "authentically acquired" consistent with the full set's not having been so acquired. We can imagine, for instance, that some repressions of innate propensities were not required to ensure that conditions for appraisability for later conduct could be met. The result will be the acquisition of a scheme that is less than ideally authentic but not, I would think, *un*authentic. And this should be borne in mind in association with A2. Finally, I stress that the notion of authenticity developed is *appraisability-relative* authenticity, or "authenticity with an eye towards appraisability." I believe there is no such thing as "plain authenticity."

One might raise the following sort of objection to this account of initial scheme authenticity. According to the account, *how* some of the child's initial attitudes, or dispositions, or habits are acquired matter in regard to authenticity. Agreed, the child cannot acquire some of her pro-attitudes by actions over which she has volitional control. So, for instance, wanting to listen to things taught to her by her parents, or wanting to put into practice things taught to her by her parents, or wanting to see herself as an agent in control of her actions, are reasonably taken to be samples of such pro-attitudes. Latching on to the distinguishing feature of many authenticity demanding pro-attitudes, on the account in question, if the having of such attitudes and their mode of instillment in the child is morally permitted (or required), and the attitudes *are* instilled in the child, then (assuming "authentic trouble-free" doxastic elements) the child will end up with an initial scheme that is appraisability-wise authentic; otherwise, maybe not. The rationale of just why the mode of instillment of such pro-attitudes makes a difference to initial scheme authenticity rests on considered judgments about attributions of moral appraisability: if the attitudes were instilled by things like direct brain stimulation or coercion, techniques whose use is presumably not morally permissible, resulting in desires that were, for example, irresistible, then the child would not be appraisable for subsequent behavior caused by those desires. On the other hand, if the attitudes resulted from "ordinary upbringing"—free of moral flaws—then the child would be morally appraisable for subsequent actions arising from the instilled attitudes. But this rationale, the objection continues, is unpersuasive. Things like direct brain stimulation or coercive persuasion undermine appraisability, at least when it comes to normal adults, *because* they undermine control; relevant control mechanisms are bypassed. But little children *don't* have the pertinent control mechanisms in place; they cannot, consequently, be *by-*

passed. So instillment in them of pro-attitudes, like the attitude of seeing oneself in control of one's actions, even via direct manipulation of the brain, need not undermine appraisability for the child's subsequent actions. Maybe such manipulation is *morally impermissible,* but it need not be authenticity- and hence appraisability-subversive.

I have three lines of response to this sort of objection. The first simply denies the objection's assumption that where certain mechanisms of control cannot be bypassed—as there is nothing to bypass in the first place—action resulting from pro-attitudes whose instillment is morally impermissible makes no difference to attributions of appraisability. For consider this case. Suppose Tanto, as a result of severe brain injury, lacks volitional control over very many of his actions; he has been reduced to the state of a child. Suppose he is manipulated, by direct stimulation of his brain: irresistible pro-attitudes to kill someone (together with relevant beliefs) are instilled in him. (I assume that such manipulation is impermissible.) Suppose he acts on these instilled pro-attitudes. We would *not,* I believe, judge that Tanto is appraisable for the killing, even though instillment of the relevant pro-attitudes on which Tanto acts do not—indeed cannot in Tanto's case—bypass mechanisms of control already in place.

A second line of response is fairly evident. Instilling in the child irresistible pro-attitudes by things like coercion undermines appraisability-relative authenticity, as such instillment undermines the child's capacity to exercise control-volitional control-over *later* behavior.

A third line of response—should the first two prove inadequate—is more radical. It requires rejecting principle A2 in favor of:

A2*: An agent's initial evaluative scheme is authentic if its elements have been acquired as a result of actions over which the agent has volitional control.

I believe that A2 is preferable to A2*. And this is because I believe that there are some pro-attitudes, like (perhaps) the attitude of seeing oneself as the initiator of one's actions, that must be the constituent of any scheme if that scheme is to be appraisability-wise authentic, but whose acquisition requires that the agent, the child, already have some pro-attitudes in place. Moreover, these latter pro-attitudes are ones, it appears, the child cannot acquire as a result of performing actions over which he exercises volitional control, but whether or not their acquisition violates requirements of morality makes a real difference to attributions of appraisability. As I have mentioned, these "basic" pro-attitudes are attitudes such as wanting to see oneself as a certain sort of person, wanting to be taught by one's parents, and wanting to put into practice lessons taught.

Here is a second objection to the view of appraisability-relative authenticity being defended. Imagine two children, Ben and Jerry, who are twins, much alike except that Jerry suffers from a certain sort of brain damage. The injury to his brain, among other things, prevents Jerry from regarding himself as a source of control; given an otherwise "normal" upbringing, it prevents Jerry from acquiring the disposition to see himself as the initiator of his actions. Let's assume (for purposes of launching this objection) that this disposition (the "control disposition") is indispensable to moral agency; without it, Jerry cannot qualify as an appropriate subject of appraisability—he cannot be praiseworthy or blameworthy for any of his behavior. But let's also assume that there is technique by which the control disposition can be *directly* induced in people suffering from the sort of ailment that afflicts Jerry. If the relevant surgery is performed, the patient will, upon recovering from the surgery, be equipped with the disposition; it will already be "in place," and the patient will not have to go through the process of gradual development to acquire the disposition. Suppose, finally, that seeing to it that the child acquires the control disposition in an appropriate way is "an interference" that is authenticity demanding and morally required. Suppose, then, that corrective surgery is performed on Jerry, and when he awakens in the recovery room he has the relevant disposition. Ben, on the other hand, is normal, and again, for purposes of developing the objection, assume that *directly* instilling the control disposition in him (*through surgery*) is morally impermissible, as such instillment comes with the risk of serious side-effects. However, imagine that some nefarious surgeon does perform the surgery on Ben. Fortunately, Ben recovers with the control disposition "in place" without suffering from any ill effects. Now suppose each of the two twins performs the same sort of action—gobbling a piece of birthday cake meant for someone else. On the view of appraisability-relative authenticity I am advancing, it appears that Ben is *not* appraisable for gobbling his piece as this action of his arises, in the end, from the control disposition which, in *his* case, is unauthentic. It is unauthentic as it is instilled in Ben by means that are morally wrong. Jerry, though, unlike Ben *is* appraisable—presumably blameworthy—for gobbling his piece, as this action of his arises, ultimately, from a control disposition which is appraisability-wise authentic; the having of that disposition by Jerry is authenticity demanding. But this result, the objection goes, is untenable. If Jerry is appraisable, Ben should be so as well. Maybe it was wrong to instill directly the control disposition in Ben, but *that it was wrong* should not have a bearing on subsequent appraisability.

In response, the objection ignores the important distinction between methods, techniques, or modes of instillment of pro-attitudes, the use of which is morally impermissible, and methods, techniques, or modes that are what I have dubbed "authenticity subversive." While there may be an overlap between the two, the overlap is not perfect; some methods of instillment, the use of which is morally impermissible, may not subvert appraisability for later conduct, and hence may not be authenticity subversive. The Ben-and-Jerry case accentuates the difference between morally impermissible modes of instillment and authenticity subversive modes. I should add, though, that when surgery is performed on Ben, Ben has, in a clear sense, been unjustly manipulated, and *unjust* manipulation is, I believe, considered to be autonomy- or authenticity-subversive, and indeed wrong, in a vast array of cases *because* it undermines control over behavior. To elaborate, suppose manipulations of the sort to which Ben is subjected were *not* wrong or unjust. Suppose such "manipulations" were legitimate "tools" of moral training, just as, perhaps, more benign forms of conditioning are legitimate aids to moral training and development. Then it would seem that such "manipulations" would not be autonomy- or authenticity-undermining factors, at least in regard to the cultivation of initial evaluative schemes.

Finally, I wish to forestall this sort of objection: suppose some pro-attitude, PA, is instilled in a young child. Suppose it is wrong for the child to have PA, PA is instilled in the child by a technique it is wrong to use, and neither the mode of instillment of PA, nor the having of it by the child, threatens appraisability of the child for conduct that will issue from PA. Then, on my account, the having of PA by the child does not undermine authenticity. But surely, the objection unfolds, this is highly counterintuitive; the child has been "morally violated!" Even if otherwise "authenticity-wise" immaculate, the child's initial scheme will be tainted by PA. My response is simply that the child's initial evaluative scheme, by virtue of having PA as an element, will not be *appraisability-wise* tainted or unauthentic. The scheme might be *morally* tainted or "*morally* unauthentic," but under the condition that the having of PA leaves unscathed later appraisability for behavior stemming from PA, I see no compelling reason to agree that PA taints initial scheme appraisability-relative authenticity. Just as immoral agents can be autonomous or self-governing, so morally tainted initial schemes can be appraisability-wise authentic.

We can now apply some of these results to magical agents, those created with a fully formed evaluative scheme in place. If ensuring authenticity of initial schemes requires both instillment of certain pro-attitudes, the authenticity demanding ones—and desisting from instilling others—the authenticity destructive ones, then it seems reasonable to suppose that the creators of such agents, to ensure initial authenticity, must refrain from instilling certain traits and ensure instillment of others. Imagine Mad Max selecting among pro-attitudes that are to form the initial evaluative scheme of his to-be magical agent. Assume that, with ordinarily developing agents like our children, instilling the disposition to be morally pernicious in the young child is incompatible with the child's being morally appraisable for behavior that (substantially) owes its genesis to this disposition; the having of this disposition is, let's suppose, authenticity destructive. Then it would appear that if Max were to instill such a disposition in his to-be magical agent, the evaluative scheme of the magical agent created would not be appraisability-wise authentic. (Of course, instilling such a disposition may not completely undermine appraisability-relative authenticity if such authenticity is a matter of degree.) So appraisability-relative authenticity *can* be a problem even for magical agents.

3. THE DOXASTIC ELEMENTS OF AN AUTHENTIC EVALUATIVE SCHEME

Apart from pro-attitudes, a person's evaluative scheme comprises beliefs about normative standards for evaluating reasons for action and beliefs about deliberative principles regarded as appropriate for arriving at practical judgments about what to do or how to act in particular circumstances. Again, with the young child whose evaluative scheme is in embryo, it may well be the case that certain beliefs will have to be willfully instilled to ensure appraisability-relative authenticity; perhaps, as Feinberg suggests, one will have to instill in the child the belief that critical self-evaluation is important; without this belief, appraisability for later behavior may well be threatened in the manner indicated above. In addition, the agent's having of such a belief, it would seem, would be morally permissible and perhaps even morally required. Instilling beliefs of this sort, in consequence, via modes or methods that themselves do not subvert later appraisability, would not threaten appraisability-relative authenticity.

But there are, of course, various sorts of beliefs that *would* undermine or seriously imperil appraisability for later conduct; they will be appraisability-wise authenticity subversive. The following sorts seem central. First, beliefs formed as a result of deception, when the beliefs play a central—and not peripheral—role in the agent's deliberations. For instance, one might leave all major financial decisions to one's accountant on the false counsel that the particular accountant always has her clients' best interests in mind. The agent, presumably, would not be appraisable for actions performed in light of such beliefs. Second, deliberately implanted beliefs formed on the basis of processes that bypass ordinary mechanisms of belief formation, in cases in which the agent did not broadly consent to the implantation. Subtle conditioning or subliminal influences, for example, might lead one to acquire the belief that moral judgments ought to be made on the basis of the recommendations of one's pastor. Third, beliefs formed on the basis of instilled pro-attitudes whose motivational influence one simply cannot thwart. Fourth, beliefs formed on the basis of coercive persuasion. As a result of such persuasion, for instance, a child may acquire the belief that one's guiding principle in life is always to act so as to maximize one's long-term self-interest. Here, the mode of instillment appears to be of the type that jeopardizes later appraisability; the child may not be able to exercise volitional control over actions caused (in part) by this belief. Finally, beliefs formed on the basis of akratic deliberation or self-deception.

We can introduce definitions of 'authenticity demanding beliefs' (or 'authenticity demanding doxastic elements'), 'authenticity destructive beliefs', and 'authenticity subversive modes of instillment of beliefs' parallel to the ones introduced above for corresponding pro-attitudinal terms. I now propose:

> A3: An agent's initial evaluative scheme is appraisability-wise authentic if its pro-attitudinal and doxastic elements (i) include all those, if any, that are authenticity demanding; (ii) do not include any that are authenticity destructive; and (iii) have been acquired by modes that are not authenticity subversive.

4. AUTHENTIC EVOLVED SCHEMES

Assume that one has acquired one's initial evaluative scheme, and that it is appraisability-wise authentic. Evaluative schemes are, needless to say, not static but dynamic; they can evolve. So, for instance, one can renounce values formerly cherished and acquire new ones; one might come to question one's belief that moral decisions should conform to the teachings of one's religion, and adopt a utilitarian outlook; or one might give up one's deliberative principle that one should review one's decisions frequently before implementing them, as one finds that frequent review under certain settings hinders success. Some modifications or changes in one's evaluative scheme may be perfectly compatible with preserving appraisability-relative authenticity, whereas others will subvert authenticity. To distinguish between the two sorts of changes, we require a conception of *acceptable* modifications.

As one's evaluative scheme comprises two sorts of constituents—doxastic and motivational—changes in one's scheme can involve changes in either. The general rule for acceptable modifications in either of these types of constituents is straightforward: the modifications must be made under one's own steam. With respect to changes in pro-attitudes like desires, instilled ones or newly acquired ones are acceptable as long as the actions, if any, to which they give rise are ones over which one has volitional control. Of course, I allow for cases in which, through a series of past steps over which one has volitional control, one deliberately instills in one a pro-attitude (or a cluster of such attitudes) that will give rise to actions over which one will lack volitional control. For instance, a person desperate to quit smoking may have implanted in him an irresistible desire to avoid cigarettes. A "global" change in pro-attitudes that destroys initial normative agency or completely "represses" it is, of course, given the condition of normative unauthenticity, A1, unacceptable. As far as changes in doxastic elements of one's evaluative scheme are concerned, changes in beliefs are acceptable if the beliefs are not formed under conditions of the sort listed above that subvert "belief authenticity." A newly acquired belief element, for instance, central to one's deliberations should not be acquired as a result of deception, or coercive persuasion, or instillment of a pro-attitude (when one has not given broad consent to the instillment) over which one lacks volitional control.

I can now formulate the following sufficient condition of scheme appraisability-relative authenticity of *"developmental agents"* like us.

> A4: If agent S's evaluative scheme at a time, t, is either S's initial appraisability-wise authentic scheme at that time, or is an evolved appraisability-wise authentic scheme of S's at that time—it is a scheme resulting from *acceptable* modifications to a scheme possessed by S prior to t that is appraisability-wise authentic—then S's evaluative scheme is appraisability-wise authentic.

5. CONTROL AND AUTHENTICITY

It's time to take stock and tie a few ends together. As Aristotle pointed out, moral appraisability requires control; one can't be appraisable for an action unless one controls it in an appropriate way. I rejected the conception of control as entailing the existence of genuine alternative possibilities; a global Frankfurt-type example, among other things, suggests that even if the future is not a garden of forking paths, one can be morally appraisable for one's actions. If the conception of control as freedom to do otherwise is repudiated, then we confront the challenge of discovering, formulating, and defending an alternative conception. I have proposed that one exerts the right sort of control over an action if that action is responsive to one's practical reasoning. To develop this idea, I introduced the notion of volitional control, which I summarized in this way:

Volitional control: Action, A, performed by agent, S, is under S's volitional control if and only if, holding constant the motivational precursor of A (that is, the proximal desire or pro-attitude that gives rise to A) and S's evaluative scheme, there is a scenario with the same natural laws as the actual world in which, relying on her evaluative scheme, S decides or forms an intention to do something other than A, and she successfully executes that intention or decision.

I said that for a desire in one scenario to be the same desire as a desire in another scenario, the two should have the same relative strength—they must have the same strength relative to competing desires. I then placed constraints on scenario eligibility (chap. 4, sec. 5).

The discussion on autonomy and authenticity should now make it evident that the following principle cannot adequately capture sufficient conditions of appraisability; the principle is, in fact, glaringly mistaken:

ProtoAppraisability: A person is appraisable for an action if she exercises volitional control over that action.

For it is quite possible that a person exercises volitional control over an action, but in so doing relies on an evaluative scheme that is normatively unauthentic. In these types of cases, the person is not intuitively morally appraisable for her action. Psychogen dramatizes this problem. The psychosurgery to which she did not consent endows Jenny with a normatively unauthentic evaluative scheme. Her subsequent actions, even those over which she exercises volitional control, are not ones for which she is morally appraisable. In less drastic but no less disturbing cases, suppose a child has acquired an initial evaluative scheme, but that scheme is not appraisability-wise authentic. Assume that several doxastic elements and pro-attitudes have been acquired on the basis of brutal manipulation, and several innate propensities have been suppressed by beatings or thrashings. Then, even if this unfortunate child grows into a person who exercises volitional control over many of his actions, his horrendous upbringing will leave him scarred for life. Such a person may not harbor even the dispositional belief that seriously injuring another to get one's own way is morally wrong. Further, as a result of his being abused several times over when still a youngster, he may lack volitional control over a significant number of his actions issuing from pro-attitudes that he acquired as a child. With respect to these actions, in one way, the reasoning that leads this person to action is *his* reasoning; he is the deliberator. But in another fashion, the reasoning is not "truly his own," as the inputs to deliberation are not appraisability-wise authentic.[2]

Confining attention to "developing agents," our reflections on authenticity fuel the following preliminary revision of ProtoAppraisability. Assume all *other* conditions (apart from control and authenticity ones) of moral appraisability are satisfied. Then:

Appraisability*: If an agent, S, intentionally does action, A, S has volitional control over A, and A issues from an evaluative scheme of S's that is not normative-wise unauthentic and is appraisability-wise authentic, then S is morally appraisable for doing A.

We can extend Appraisability* by reminding ourselves of cases in which agents willfully see to it that they lack volitional control over some of their future actions. The "tracing principle" introduced in chapter 4 provides what is needed for extension. Assume an agent lacks volitional control over an action, A, of hers because she has intentionally taken deliberate steps, over which she has volitional control, to see to it that she lacks volitional control over A, or to bring about A with the realization that either she will lack volitional control over A, or that she will not be able to refrain from A-ing. Call A-type actions (of this sort) "appraisably non-volitional responsive actions." I finally propose:

> Appraisability**: If an agent, S, intentionally does action, A, S has volitional control over A or A is an appraisably nonvolitional responsive action of S's, and A issues from an evaluative scheme of S's that is not normative-wise unauthentic and is appraisability-wise authentic, then S is morally appraisable for doing A. (Here, again, I assume that other conditions of appraisability are not in question.)

Moral appraisability, as Aristotle explained, requires control *and* lack of ignorance. It's now time to address the epistemic component of moral appraisability.

EIGHT

KNOWLEDGE AND
APPRAISABILITY

Suppose, in an area not frequented by turtles, unbeknownst to Sid, a little turtle has curled up under one of the tires of her truck. As she backs out from the driveway, she crushes the poor little creature to pulp. It appears that in this case, Sid is not morally blameworthy for running over the turtle (or for its death). Reconsider Sweet Deception introduced in chapter 1. Sam is unaware that Ralph has replaced the sugar in the bowl with a sugar look-alike that is deadly. Indeed, Sam has no reason whatsoever to suspect Ralph of this wicked deed. Sam invites Kate over for coffee and cake. "One or two lumps?" he asks. "Three please," Kate replies. To his horror, Kate rolls over, quite dead, after her first sip. Again, surely Sam is not morally to blame for dissolving the poison in Kate's coffee. In either of these cases, presumably our judgment that the agents are not to blame does not derive from the view that they lack appropriate *control*—appraisability grounding control—over their relevant actions. Sam, for instance, was not coerced or threatened; he was not compelled to act by the force of an irresistible desire; he did not act on a posthypnotic suggestion whose influence he could not overcome, and so on. So control, or rather lack of it, is not the culprit or appraisability-subverting factor here. Nor, it seems, is authenticity of evaluative schemes. Rather, our judgments that the agents are not to blame appear to rest firmly on the Aristotelian idea that to be appraisable for performing an action, one must not be relevantly ignorant of what one is doing. Apart from control and authenticity constituents, appraisability has an epistemic dimension.

1. THE OBJECTIVE VIEW

Well, what exactly is the epistemic dimension? Here (and in the next chapter) I will focus almost exclusively on blameworthiness, but much of what I have to say will apply equally, with some adjustments, to praiseworthiness and responsibility in general. One might begin by advancing the rather strong view that to be blameworthy for performing an action, one must know that one is doing wrong by performing that action, and to be praiseworthy, one must be aware that one is doing what is right or obligatory. This view can be formulated as follows:

Epis1: Agent S is morally blameworthy [praiseworthy] for performing action A (or bringing about state of affairs T) only if S knows that S is doing wrong [right or what S ought to] by performing A (or by bringing about T).

Epis1 acquires some support from cases like Sweet Deception. As Sam did not know that he was doing wrong by putting the sugar look-alike into Kate's coffee, Epis1 yields the result that he is not morally to blame for bringing about the state of affairs *Sam's putting the sugar look-alike into Kate's coffee*.

As knowledge entails truth, Epis1 entails what we can call the "Objective View":

Objective View: An agent is morally blameworthy for performing an action only if it is morally wrong for that agent to perform that action.

On this view, moral blameworthiness is associated not with what the agent thinks or believes is wrong but with what is in fact (objectively) wrong. Along the same lines, moral praiseworthiness is associated with what is in fact morally obligatory or right so that an agent is praiseworthy for performing an action only if it is obligatory or right for that agent to perform that action.

The Objective View enjoys popularity; it is endorsed by several people. For example, Holly Smith proposes the following Humean account of blameworthiness:

S is blameworthy for performing act A, if, and only if:
  1. Act A is objectively wrong,
  2. S had a reprehensible configuration of desires and aversions, and
  3. This configuration gave rise to the performance of A. (1991, p. 279)

David Widerker takes the ensuing principle to be a necessary truth which he believes:

explicates the conceptual link between the notion of moral blameworthiness and that of moral obligation.
   (B2) An agent S is morally blameworthy for performing a given act A only if S has a moral obligation *not* to perform A. (Widerker 1991, p. 223)

As the following principle,

   OW: S has a moral obligation to perform [not to perform] A if and only if it is morally wrong for S not to perform [to perform] A,

is true, Widerker's B2 is equivalent to the Objective View.

In the same vein as Smith and Widerker, Lloyd Fields has recently proposed that "it is a necessary condition of blaming someone that one should believe that his action or omission is a sort of action or omission that is wrong. . . . And one is right or correct or justified in blaming a person only if such beliefs about that person are right, correct or justified" (1994, pp. 408–9).

Finally, Justin Oakley and Dean Cocking endorse a view that bears striking kinship to the Objective View:

> [A] doctor is morally responsible for the death of a patient who was experiencing great suffering, if the death is a foreseeable result of the drug regimen on which he has placed the patient. Of course, the doctor here may also be *blameworthy* for the patient's death, but importantly, we cannot make this extra judgement until we have assessed whether the death of the patient is a bad thing or a good thing. For we must distinguish between moral responsibility and moral blameworthiness. If the patient's death is judged to be a bad thing, then this doctor would be blameworthy; but if the death of the patient was a good thing—say, if he was suffering from intense and chronic pain from a terminal condition and autonomously refused medical treatment—then the doctor may well be *creditworthy* rather than blameworthy here. (Oakley and Cocking 1994, p. 206)

Oakely and Cocking, it appears, espouse the view that an agent is blameworthy for performing an action only if that action is in fact (intrinsically?) bad. In a passage following the passage just cited, they claim: "blameworthiness can be defined formally as involving two conditions: responsibility and wrongdoing. That is, I am blameworthy for a certain action if and only if I am morally responsible for performing it, and it is wrong" (1994, pp. 209–10).[1]

Despite its widespread acceptance and intuitive plausibility, I believe that the objective view is seriously mistaken as I intend to show in the remainder of this chapter.[2] Hence, I reject any epistemic condition of moral appraisability (like Epis1) that entails the Objective View.

2. CHANGEABILITY OF OBLIGATIONS OVER TIME AND THE OBJECTIVE VIEW

First, I suggest that facts about the changeability of moral obligations over time call into question the Objective View. It is, for example, possible for an act that would be performed next week to be right for some agent now, but not to be right for that agent two days from now. As an illustration of changeability, suppose my friend has been hospitalized, and I ought morally as of today to visit him in hospital tomorrow. But suppose on the following day, just after work, I drop in at a party; I find the wine, food, and company immensely agreeable. Acting contrary to my better judgment, I delay leaving until it is too late for the visit. Feeling terribly guilty the next morning, I then decide to see my friend in the evening after teaching my last class for the day. I call the hospital late in the afternoon only to discover that my friend was discharged earlier that day. As of the time my friend went home, I no longer have a moral obligation to visit him in hospital as I cannot, as of that time, visit him there; the deontic principle that 'ought implies can' dictates that I cannot have an obligation to do what I am unable to do. It appears that the rights and wrongs of the case (call it "Bad Boy") have changed.[3]

The changeability of obligations over time (in the fashion illustrated by Bad Boy) has implications for the tenability of the Objective View. To track these implications, let's modify Bad Boy, first, in this way: suppose, enjoying myself so much at the party, I simply forget about my intention (that I had formed earlier) to visit my friend in hospital later in the evening. Once at the party, I do not give a thought to not remaining and stay of my own free accord. In this variant (Bad Boy1) assume that it is wrong for me to remain at the party, and assume (credibly I believe) that I am also blameworthy for remaining. Now consider yet another variation (Bad Boy2) of the case. Suppose, for whatever reason, Mel wants to ensure that I remain at the party, and on the very afternoon of the party, unbeknownst to me, I am hypnotized by him. As a result of Mel's manipulations the following is true: if, once at the party, I were to show any inclination of not remaining, I would be overcome by an irresistible posthypnotic suggestion to remain. Again, suppose that having arrived at the party, I do not give a thought to not remaining and stay of my on free accord; no posthypnotic suggestion comes into play. Surely, I am still blameworthy for remaining; or at least, *if* it is true that I am blameworthy for remaining in Bad Boy1, it should also be true that I am blameworthy for remaining in Bad Boy2—in both cases, nothing of relevance that bears on our ascription of blameworthiness seems to have changed. However, the rights and wrongs of the case *have* most certainly changed. For this principle is true:

> OW: S has a moral obligation to perform [not to perform] A if and only if it is morally wrong for S not to perform [to perform] A.

OW and the 'ought' implies 'can' principle (K):

> K: S has a moral obligation to perform [not to perform] A only if S has it within S's power to perform [not to perform] A,

entail, as we have seen, that there is a requirement of alternative possibilities for wrong actions:

> WAP: It is morally wrong for S to perform [not to perform] A only if it is within S's power not to perform [to perform] A.

Notice that (barring any unusual occurrences), roughly, as of the time I am at the party (in Bad Boy2), it is not within my power to refrain from remaining. Bad Boy2, is of course, a Frankfurt-type case. Hence, given WAP, as of the time I am at the party, my remaining at the party is not wrong, or alternatively, as of the time I am at the party, it is false that I have a moral obligation not to remain. As I *am* (in Bad Boy2) blameworthy for remaining, the view that one is blameworthy for performing an action only if it is wrong for one to perform that action appears false.

One might, however, rejoin that the foregoing argument against the Objective View relies on the 'ought' implies 'can' principle, K. But this is, to say the least, ironic as Frankfurt himself introduced Frankfurt-type examples precisely to *refute* the famous principle of alternative possibilities (PAP), a version of which says that an agent is morally appraisable for performing an action only if she could have done otherwise; moreover, K is *relevantly just like* PAP. So PAP stands or falls with K: if Frankfurt-type examples undermine PAP, they should also undermine K!

This objection, though, is misguided. It rests on the crucial assumption that K is pertinently like PAP (and hence that both fall prey to Frankfurt-type cases). But K is *not* relevantly like PAP. Rather, K-the principle that S ought to do A only if S has the power to do A—a 'power' or 'control' principle—is pertinently like the following control principle:

> BR: S is blameworthy (or more generally, morally appraisable) for performing A only if S has the power to perform A.

We would expect Frankfurt to *endorse* BR as BR simply affirms the connection between control and moral appraisability. Further, a Frankfurt-type example clearly does not threaten BR; and since K is relevantly analogous to BR and not to PAP, we would expect to find Frankfurt drawn to the view that while Frankfurt-type examples undermine PAP, they leave K intact. And this is precisely what we do find. Frankfurt explains:

> The appeal of PAP may owe something to a presumption that it is a corollary of the Kantian thesis that "ought" implies "can." In fact, however, the relation between Kant's doctrine and PAP is not as close as it may seem to be. With respect to any action, Kant's doctrine has to do with the agent's ability to perform *that* action. PAP, on the other hand, concerns his ability to do *something else*. Moreover, the Kantian view leaves open the possibility that a person for whom only one course of action is available fulfills an obligation when he pursues that course of action and is morally praiseworthy for doing so. [I am skeptical about this view.[4]] On the other hand, PAP implies that such a person cannot earn any moral credit for what he does. This makes it clear that renouncing PAP does not require denying that "ought" implies "can" and that PAP is not entailed by the Kantian view. (Frankfurt 1988a, pp. 95–96)

We can approach the matter in this way: grant that Frankfurt-type examples subvert PAP. But as Michael Zimmerman has indicated, PAP is a contraction of BR and:

> FAP: It is within S's power to perform [not to perform] A only if it is within S's power not to perform [to perform] A.[5]

A Frankfurt-type example undermines FAP, and since FAP and BR entail PAP, it thereby undermines PAP. However, a Frankfurt-type example, as we have seen, leaves intact K and OW, and it is K and OW that entail that there is a requirement of alternative possibilities for objective wrongness (WAP).

3. WEAKNESS FOR PUDDING AND PIE

Second, life is fraught with cases in which people perform intentional actions even in the face of finding themselves saddled with competing motivations. Some such cases, I believe, cast serious doubt on the objective view. Prior to presenting such a case reconsider, first, a garden-variety example of motivational conflict. In Mud Pie, growls from his belly induce Fred to look into the refrigerator. He spies a pie on the top shelf. He remembers his medical infirmity and judges that all things considered he ought not to eat the pie. Were he to indulge, he would do something that is irrational from his own point of view. Assume that his judgment to refrain, formed partly on the basis of his belief that it is wrong to eat the pie and a desire to avoid eating the pie, coincides with Fred's moral judgment that it is best not to eat the pie. Assume, further, that this judgment generates an intention not to eat the pie. However, Fred's evaluative assessment of the object of his desire not to eat the pie (his not eating the pie) is out of line with the motivational strength of this desire; and a little later, still retaining the judgment that he ought not to eat it, Fred tops the pie with cream and then devours it. Imagine that Fred could on this occasion have mustered self-control and refrained from feasting on the pie. His uncompelled intentional action of eating the pie is an akratic one.[6] Further, and especially germane to our purposes, it seems that Fred is deserving of moral blame for eating the pie.

Why precisely is Fred blameworthy? It appears that a significant part of what informs our assessment regarding Fred's being to blame is the fact that he acted against a better judgment of his—that he ought morally not to eat the pie. It is true that some first-person practical judgments can be overridden by others; Fred, for example, may have judged that it is prudentially best for him not to eat the pie, but this judgment need not have committed him to action as he did not (we can assume) take such judgments to be overriding. However, his judgment that he morally ought not to eat the pie is not similarly overridden by *other* considerations, as it is an all things considered judgment, one on which Fred held himself ready to act. It is also true, or at least let's suppose that it is so, that Fred's eating the pie is in fact wrong, Fred believed that eating the pie is wrong, and Fred was able to exercise the sort of control over eating the pie that is paradigmatic of the kind of control required for moral blameworthiness—he had volitional control over eating the pie. Some or all of these factors, presumably, also motivate the assessment that Fred is blameworthy for eating the pie.

Altering the case a bit, let's suppose that Julia has concocted a pie that looks just like, and tastes just like, ordinary pie but with none of the properties exemplified by ordinary pie harmful to people suffering from the medical ailment that afflicts pie-loving Fred (who, as luck has it, is Julia's child). Suppose, further, that unbeknown to Fred, Julia has switched the ordinary pie with the benign lookalike, and it is now (morally) permissible for Fred to indulge. Imagine that the rest of case unfolds just in the manner in which Mud Pie did. Fred looks into the refrigerator and, acting against his all things considered judgment, gobbles the pie. It seems that Fred is still deserving of moral blame for eating the pie. After all, he still acts contrary to his action-committing judgment that it is wrong for him to eat the pie, and he still exhibits the sort of control over his pie-eating that he exhibited in Mud Pie. This case ("Phoney Pie") of motivational conflict should at least rattle our confidence in the Objective View. Phoney Pie also intimates that blameworthiness is affiliated not with the objective wrongness of an action but with whether a person takes herself to be doing wrong in performing an action.

4. TWO TEST CASES

Third, I adduce a pair of cases that forcefully suggest that moral blameworthiness and moral praiseworthiness ought not to be affiliated with objective wrongness and objective obligatoriness (or rightness), respectively. In Howser's Hell, Dr. Howser, attempting to do everything she can to cure her patient, follows the course of treatment which all evidence then available to her indicates will result in a cure: she injects the patient with medicine A. Through no fault of any party, though, the diagnosis is incorrect. Administering A is the wrong treatment, and it proves lethal. Had the good doctor only known better, she would have administered medicine B, which would have effectively healed the patient. Arguably, by giving A the doctor has done something (objectively) wrong—she has killed a patient. But the case strongly inclines us toward the view that Howser is not morally to blame for giving A; she may in fact be deserving of praise for doing so.[7] In Deadly's Defeat,[8] doing the best she can to murder her patient, Dr. Deadly does what credible evidence to which she has access indicates will kill the patient—she injects the patient with medicine C. But once again, this time happily for the patient, there has been an innocent error in diagnosis. Contrary to what Deadly believes, her patient is suffering from a disease that can be cured only by taking C. Giving C results in the lucky patient's full recovery. Although it is arguably obligatory for Deadly to inject her patient with C, it appears that Deadly is to blame for the injection of this drug.

The objectivist, though, may remain unconvinced by this last case, and insist that while Deadly *is* to blame for trying or attempting to kill the patient, as attempting to kill the patient is wrong, she is *not* to blame for injecting the drug, as injecting the drug is obligatory. This sort of rejoinder, however, is unpersuasive. First, it appears to rest on the dubious principle that it is always the case that if one attempts to do something, and that thing is wrong, then one's attempting to do that thing is also wrong.[9] Deadly's attempt to kill the patient (where the attempt consists, at least partly, in Deadly's injecting the patient with medicine C) does not seem to be wrong. Second, if we grant that injecting the drug is obligatory for Deadly, then, if Deadly's attempt to kill the patient consists (at least partly) in Deadly's injecting the patient with C, the attempt itself (given the reasonable assumption that Deadly was able to refrain from attempting to inject the patient), must itself be obligatory, on the assumption that this "prerequisites" deontic principle is correct: if S cannot do A without doing B (out of, for example, logical or physical necessity), and S can refrain from doing B, then, if S ought to do A, then S ought to do B.[10] As in Deadly's case, it seems that Deadly cannot inject the patient without attempting to inject the patient, the attempt must be obligatory if the injection itself is.

5. ON BEING TO BLAME AND PRAISE FOR ONE
AND THE SAME ACTION

Fourth, it has been argued that it is possible for a person to be blameworthy and praiseworthy on account of one and the same action. One must take care in interpreting this claim. On one construal, the claim amounts to the view that, possibly, a person can be, say, *morally* blameworthy for doing something, and, say, prudentially or legally praiseworthy for doing that thing. So, for example, it may be prudentially best for some person to ignore the plight of the starving in Sudan and he *may* be prudentially to praise for ignoring these unfortunate persons if he does so, but he might also be morally to blame for turning the other way. This construal of the claim is not germane to our concern. Rather, the construal that is of interest says that it is possible for a person to be morally to blame and morally to praise for one and the same action. For suppose this *is* possible. Then the objective view cannot be right. For if the person is morally to blame and praise for the same action, the objective view sanctions the absurdity that the person's action is both right and wrong.[11]

Now I do believe that one can be morally to blame and praise for the same action or bit of behavior. One sort of example that suggests this possibility is the kind of example in which some agent "freely" does something, like chastising a child in the belief that by so doing he is doing right, but also in the belief that in so doing he is doing some wrong.[12] Another sort of example involves acting out of self-deception. The self-deceived person may have the conscious belief that in donating to charity she is doing right, and may donate to charity in light of that conscious belief. She believes, let's suppose, that it is right for her at time $t1$ to donate to charity at $t2$. However, she may also harbor an unconscious belief to the effect that she is doing wrong by giving to charity, and possibly, this belief plays a crucial role in the etiology of her donating to charity. She may, then, also believe that it is wrong for her at $t1$ to donate to charity at $t2$. It seems to me that in a case of this sort, as of a particular time, it is possible for both the conscious and unconscious belief to play an "appraisability-grounding" role in the genesis of the person's donating to charity. Although one of the beliefs is veiled from the person's consciousness, it may play a role analogous to the role played by the conscious belief held by the person in the pathway leading to the person's donating to charity. Such a person may then well be an appropriate candidate for both moral blame and praise on account of her donating to charity. I discuss both these sorts of examples at length in the next chapter.

6. THE SUPEREROGATORY, THE SUBEROGATORY,
AND APPRAISABILITY

Lastly, assuming there are supererogatory actions—actions, roughly, that are beyond the call of duty—it certainly appears that people can be deserving of praise for performing them. Indeed, some like Gregory Mellema (1991, pp. 3,13) have proposed that no agent can perform an action that is supererogatory unless she is praiseworthy for its performance. Although I believe *this* part of Mellema's analysis of the supererogatory is mistaken, I agree that one *can* be to praise for going beyond the call. Now a salient feature of supererogatory actions is that they are neither objectively obligatory or wrong—they are "morally optional" (see Heyd 1982, McNamara 1996, Mellema 1991, and Zimmerman 1993). So, for instance, the letter carrier who goes beyond the call of duty and rescues the child from the inferno at considerable risk to her own life may well be praiseworthy for her brave and heroic deed even though rescuing the child is not objectively obligatory. After all, the letter carrier may (mistakenly) believe she is doing her moral duty by going beyond the call, may freely be going beyond the call, and may be acting on actional springs that are "truly her own."

Analogously, assuming there are suberogatory actions (actions that are more or less the flip sides of supererogatory ones), these are morally optional but permissive ill-doings. Again, I believe one can be to blame for performing such actions even though they are not objectively wrong. To use one of Julia Driver's illustrations (1992), a man who takes a seat on a train, thereby preventing two other people from sitting together despite availability of another seat, may be blameworthy as his act, though not wrong, falls short of decency. The person may (again mistakenly) believe he is doing wrong by precluding the two from sharing the seat and may even later feel regret or shame for his conduct although it is suberogatory and hence not objectively wrong.

7. A NEW CONTENDER—THE MODERATE OBJECTIVE VIEW

The Objective View has its share of pressing problems. Perhaps the Moderate Objective View, which can be summarized in this way, has brighter prospects:

> Moderate Objective View: An agent, S, is morally blameworthy for performing an action, A, only if when S does A (or alternatively, in S's doing A), what S believes S is doing—that is, the action or bit of behavior represented by the object of S's belief when S does A—is (objectively) wrong.[13]

This view differs from the Objective View in one salient respect. Unlike the Objective View, the Moderate View associates blameworthiness not with the objective wrongness of the action performed by the agent, but with the objective wrongness of what the agent believes she is doing in performing the action. On this view it is, roughly speaking, the object of the agent's belief that must be objectively wrong in order for the agent to be deserving of blame. The Moderate Objective View appears to generate interestingly different answers than the ones generated by the Objective View in a number of cases. So, for instance, in Deadly's Defeat, Dr. Deadly believes that she is killing the patient by injecting him with C. What she believes she is doing—killing an innocent patient—is (under ordinary circumstances) morally wrong. Assuming all other conditions of appraisability are satisfied, the Moderate Objective View, unlike the Objective View, seemingly yields the intuitively correct verdict in this case: Deadly is blameworthy for injecting the patient with C. Consider, next, a Frankfurt-type case in which Jones (who is being monitored by Black) squeezes the trigger on his own, thus killing innocent Smith. As Jones cannot refrain from squeezing the trigger, and as there is a requirement of alternative possibilities for (objective wrongness), the Objective View implies that Jones is not to blame for squeezing the trigger. And this seems wrong. The Moderate View, however, ascribes blame (partly) on the basis of assessing the moral status of what the agent believes she is doing. Presumably, when Jones squeezes the trigger, she believes she is killing an innocent person. As (again, under ordinary circumstances) killing an innocent person is wrong, the Moderate View apparently provides the intuitively correct result: Jones is blameworthy for squeezing the trigger.

Though it has the guise of promise, the Moderate View fails as well. First, upon closer scrutiny, the Moderate View may, after all, generate the same sorts of results as does the Objective View in Frankfurt-type cases. To see this, let's ask: What exactly is the object of Jones's belief when she squeezes the trigger? Maybe it's something that can be expressed by these words: "I'm killing crummy Smith." But now the problem should be evident. The state of affairs—the event particular—*Jones kills crummy Smith* is *not* wrong in the Frankfurt-type case, as it was not in Jones's power intentionally to bring about an alternative, and there is a requirement of alternative possibilities for wrongness. Hence the Moderate View, just like the Objective View, implies that Jones is not blameworthy for squeezing the trigger.

Let's try again. It seems true that most of us have a standing (dispositional) belief that the actions we perform under ordinary garden-variety circumstances are ones we freely perform. So perhaps when Jones squeezes the trigger the object of her belief is something more complex than we previously made it out to be. Maybe it is something like *Jones freely kills crummy Smith*. An advocate of the Moderate View might then claim that *this* state of affairs that Jones brings about in her Frankfurt-type situation *is* wrong; consequently, the Moderate View (in opposition to the Objective View) sanctions the right verdict that Jones is blameworthy for bringing about this state of affairs. However, there is still a worry. The term 'freely' is multiply ambiguous. There is, for example, a compatibilist sense according to which one freely does something just in case one could have done something else instead if one had so desired. There is, in addition, the incompatibilist sense which says (roughly) that one freely does something just in case one had genuine alternative possibilities; one could intentionally have brought about something else consistent with the past and the laws of nature remaining fixed. It is this sense of 'free' that is operative (in our discussion) in the claim that wrongness requires alternative possibilities. With this clarification, it is easy to see that the "moderator" faces another difficulty. Suppose the moderator insists that when she squeezes the trigger, what Jones believes she is bringing about is the state of affairs *Jones's freely killing crummy Smith*. But arguably, this state of affairs in Jones's Frankfurt-type scenario is not wrong; when Jones uses 'freely' she may not have the incompatibilist sense of this word in mind. Rather, what is wrong is a different state of affairs, which is, loosely, the state of affairs of Jones's killing crummy Smith and Jones's having the power to do otherwise. But it is, I believe, implausible to suppose that this more complex state of affairs is the object of the pertinent belief that Jones has when she squeezes the trigger. Jones *might* have such a belief, but then again, she might not. And when she does not, and has instead the belief that she is freely killing Smith, or killing Smith in the absence of coercion or threat, the state of affairs that is the object of this belief will not be wrong (in her circumstances). If it is not wrong, the Objective View and the Moderate View will generate symmetric results.

There is a second major difficulty with the Moderate View. Consider a person who is like a child in one respect: he is totally devoid of moral concepts. Suppose this person gulps a potion of medicine intended for his sick sibling, and he does so in the belief that he is taking medicine intended for his sick sibling. Grant that what the person believes—his taking medicine intended for his sick sibling—is objectively wrong. Still, contrary to the verdict delivered by the Moderate View (on the assumption that all other conditions of appraisability are satisfied), the child-like person is not (intuitively) morally to blame for taking the medicine, though what he believed he was doing is (objectively) wrong.

For now, the following conclusion is in order. In light of the foregoing considerations, it appears that we have strong reasons to reject both the full-blooded Objective View and its moderate cousin. In addition, several of these considerations suggest that moral blameworthiness and moral praiseworthiness are to be tied closely to belief in what is objectively wrong and objectively obligatory or right, respectively. This is the view to be explored in the next chapter.

꘎═══꘎

AN EPISTEMIC DIMENSION
OF APPRAISABILITY

In the last chapter I ended with the suggestion that moral praiseworthiness and moral blameworthiness are closely affiliated with our "inner" attitudes; they are tied to our beliefs or perceptions about what is objectively obligatory or wrong, respectively, and not with what is in fact objectively obligatory or wrong. The fundamental idea I propose and wish to explore is encapsulated in these principles:

> Blame1 [Praise1]: An agent S is morally blameworthy [praiseworthy] for performing action A only if S has the belief that it is wrong [obligatory or right] for her to do A and this belief plays an appropriate role in S's A-ing.

My principal aim in this chapter is to clarify and extend Blame1. (Again, while I predominately confine attention to Blame1, much of what I have to say is applicable, with adjustments, to Praise1.) I focus, initially, on explicating the role an agent's belief that a prospective action, A, of hers is wrong must play, in the production of her A-ing, in order that she be blameworthy for A-ing. Toward this end, I make use of cases involving weakness of will and self-deception. Refinements on Blame1 will, among other things, shed light on the thorny issue of whether an agent can be blameworthy for performing an action that issues (at least in part) from an element, like a desire or a belief, or from deliberation, that is unconscious.

1. PRELIMINARIES

Reconsider Deadly's Defeat. This is the case in which, on the justified but (mistaken) evidence available to Dr. Deadly, the odious doctor injects her patient with medicine C with the intention to kill the patient. It turns out that the diagnosis is mistaken and that the lucky patient can in fact only be cured by injecting her with C. Construe this case as one in which Deadly is under no delusion that she takes herself to be doing wrong when she injects the patient with C. It is indeed this feature of the case that kindles the judgment made by many that, the happy ending for the patient notwithstanding, Deadly is deserving of blame for injecting the patient. Assume, then, that Deadly believes that her injecting the patient with C is wrong. Assume that the control condition of Deadly's being blameworthy for injecting the patient with C is satisfied, and assume that all other conditions required for Deadly's being to blame, like the authenticity condition, save the epistemic one, are also satisfied. Then it might be proposed that the following epistemic condition for blameworthiness, in conjunction with all the other requisite conditions, *suffices* for Deadly's being to blame:

Blameo: S is blameworthy for performing A only if S believes that it is wrong for her to do A.

The proposal, however, would be mistaken. For assume that S believes dispositionally that doing A is wrong. Assume further that though S's belief that doing A is wrong is stored in S's memory, it is not "accessed" by S at all in doing A. Specifically, it does not figure in S's deliberations (conscious or not) about whether to A, or in any other way in the etiology of S's A-ing. Then it seems that in doing A, S acts just as she would have in the absence of the belief that doing A is wrong. Since the counterfactual scenario in which S lacks the pertinent belief but A-s is presumably not one in which S is blameworthy for A-ing, and it is a scenario relevantly similar to the actual one in which S A-s—in it S lacks the belief that it is wrong for her to A—S is not in fact blameworthy for doing A. This is, it should be added, perfectly compatible with S's being to blame, say, for failing to "access" the belief that A is wrong, or for failing to recognize that the action she performs is a token of A-type actions that are wrong. (Similarly, if S simply lacked the belief that A is wrong, S could well be culpable for failing to acquire the belief that A is wrong.) Plainly Blameo requires augmentation.

2. AUGMENTING BLAMEO

In a recent important work on moral appraisability, favoring the view that blameworthiness is associated with belief in what is wrong and not with objective wrongness, Michael Zimmerman proposes that:

(P3.1) S is directly culpable for willing *e* if and only if S strictly freely willed *e*, in the belief that, by virtue of so willing, he would do wrong.[1]

Commenting on this principle, Zimmerman explains that:

> the phrase "*to will e in the belief that* one will do wrong," as used in (P3.1), is intended to convey . . . a grounding of the volition in the belief. I shall forgo trying to give a precise account of the nature of this grounding, but it is common enough. It is that sort of grounding expressed in such phrases as "he decided to do this *in light of the fact* that . . ." and "she chose to do that *on the basis of.* . . ." (1988, p. 44)

Confining attention to blameworthiness for intentional action, reflection on these highly suggestive remarks of Zimmerman's motivates the following:

> Blame2: S is morally blameworthy for performing A only if (i) S has an occurrent or dispositional belief, BAW, that A is wrong, (ii) BAW gives rise to an intention, IAW, to do A, and (iii) S acts on IAW.[2]

Condition i is credible as one surely *can* be deserving of blame for performing an action even if one lacks the pertinent *occurrent* belief that the action is wrong. Tara may be blameworthy for quaffing her third gin and tonic even though, at the time, she does not have the occurrent belief that getting inebriated is wrong. Regarding ii, the relevant moral belief might, for example, be one constituent of a reason entertained by S for doing A, which, in conjunction with some conative element of S's, gives rise to a practical judgment to A, which, in turn, issues in the intention (IAW) to A. Alternatively, the belief, together with a conative element, may give rise to an intention to A straightaway without the intermediary of a judgment to A, or it may, with the conative element, give rise to a decision to A (I assume that in deciding to A one forms an intention to A). As far as iii is concerned, presumably one would want to add that S's intention to A nonwaywardly issues in S's A-ing. Imagine a case of intentional action in which S is blameworthy for A-ing, the belief that A is wrong is part of the "action guiding component" of S's reason for A-ing, and this reason nondeviantly issues in S's A-ing. Then it would be quite apt to describe the case as one in which S does A in light of the fact that, or on the basis of the belief that, A is wrong.

Whatever its other merits, Blame2 is seriously flawed as is confirmed by instances of akratic action where an agent freely and intentionally performs an action that is contrary to that agent's better judgment. Mud Pie is an exemplar of such action. In this case, Fred ends up eating the pie contrary to his better judgment, and it certainly appears that Fred is deserving of moral blame for eating the pie. But Blame2 yields a different incorrect verdict. Its condition i is satisfied as Fred did have the relevant belief; ii is also satisfied as Fred's belief that it is wrong to eat the pie gives rise, by way of an appropriate judgment, to an intention not to eat the pie; but iii is unsatisfied as the intention not to eat the pie does not issue in action. Indeed, by the time Fred eats the pie he has abandoned this intention and acquired another on which he has acted.

Blame2, however, is suggestive and should not be abandoned wholesale. Its underlying view that an agent is morally blameworthy for performing an action only if the agent has a belief that the action is wrong, and that that belief enters into that agent's deliberations about whether to perform that action, can be profitably exploited to make headway. I want to develop and assess this view by inquiring into what it is for a belief of the right sort to enter into one's deliberations about what to do. The inquiry will reveal that in the end the view will have to give way to another.

3. BELIEFS AND DELIBERATION

Restricting attention to deliberative intentional action, one way in which a belief of S's can enter into S's deliberations about whether to A in cases in which S intentionally A-s is simply that the belief is a constituent of S's reason for A-ing. It is a commonly held view that, in order for something to be a reason for S's A-ing, that thing must have a belief component that guides and plays a role in producing and sustaining S's A-ing.[3] I prefer being more flexible. I believe that an agent's reason for intentional action has a conative element that motivates pursuit of a goal, and an action-guiding or representational element that constitutes a plan, or a component of a plan, for achieving the germane goal.[4] So, for example, toward achieving his goal of quenching his thirst, Al executes a plan components of which include beliefs about vending machines containing cans of juice, beliefs pertaining to the operation of such machines, and beliefs about alleged thirst-quenching features of juice. The "plan view" allows for the possibility that the representational element of S's reason for A-ing may not be belief. So first, then, I propose that if a belief is the representational element of S's reason for A-ing or of *a* reason (predominant or otherwise) S has for A-ing, then the belief enters into S's deliberations about whether to A.

Mud Pie calls attention to another way in which an agent's belief may enter into that agent's deliberations about whether to perform some action. Clearly, Fred's belief that it is wrong to eat the pie plays a substantial role in Fred's deliberations about whether to eat the pie, but this belief is plainly *not* the representational element of the reason—whatever its exact specification—for which Fred eats the pie. Second, I submit that if a belief of S's gives rise to a first-person practical judgment of S's that S should A, then this belief enters into S's deliberations about whether to A. In Mud Pie, Fred's first-person judgment not to eat the pie turns out to be what Mele calls "a decisive best judgment." As noted, it is a judgment that *commits* Fred to action; if Fred acts contrary to such a judgment, he does something that is subjectively irrational.[5] But a belief of S's may also enter into S's deliberations about whether to A by giving rise to a practical judgment of S's that does not commit S to action. So, for example, S might judge that from the perspective of his own moral values, it would be better for him to do A than B if he were to do either. But if S fails to take moral values to be overriding, he is not thereby committed to doing A in preference to doing B were he to do either; S may commit herself to doing B if she judges B to be prudentially best and she takes prudential considerations to be overriding.

Consider, now, a case in which Sue is deliberating about whether to pocket the cash lying on the floor of the otherwise deserted room. She believes that it is morally wrong to keep the money, but also believes that it is prudentially best for her to do so, and that prudential prescriptions trump moral ones when the two recommend different courses of action. Suppose these beliefs "run through her mind" prior to her pocketing the money. Notice that the belief that it is wrong to keep the money is neither the representational element of the reason for which Sue keeps the money, nor does it give rise to a first-person practical judgment to keep the money. Still, it undoubtedly enters into Sue's deliberations about whether to keep the money; its being wrong to keep the money is a factor that (for Sue) weighs against keeping the money. Third, I propose that if a belief B is the representational element of a reason S entertains against A-ing, then B enters into S's deliberations about whether to A.

Modifying the last case, suppose Sue has hardened her heart to morality and always acts to maximize her long-term self-interest. Suppose she does have the belief that it is wrong to pocket the money, and calmly entertains it (she "accesses" it) prior to deciding on what to do. Suppose, however, that the belief utterly fails to move her; it does not, unlike in the former case, provide her with a reason against keeping the money. She directs her gaze to it only to put it aside. Suppose, finally, that after careful reflection (none of which involves the belief that keeping the money is wrong), she decides to keep the money and ends up keeping it. In this case ("Hard Heart"), it seems that Sue *is* blameworthy for pocketing the money. But it would be stretching credulity to suppose that Sue's belief that pocketing the money is wrong *enters into her deliberations* about whether to pocket the money. Although Sue is *perfectly aware* that pocketing the money is wrong, her belief that pocketing the money is wrong plays no role whatsoever in her reflections on whether to keep the money. It appears, then, that if beliefs regarding what is morally wrong are relevant to moral blameworthiness, it is not solely because such beliefs enter into one's deliberations about what to do. How else might they be relevant? Cases like Hard Heart might initially encourage one to advance this principle:

Blame3: S is morally blameworthy for performing A only if S has an occurrent or dispositional belief, BAW, that A is wrong, and either BAW enters into S's deliberations about whether to A or S performs A in spite of entertaining BAW. (Entertaining a belief involves *accessing* it in some way and not merely having it—one must in some fashion, perhaps even unconsciously, be cognizant of it.)

But Blame3 is defective as is evidenced by this case. Assume that Blame3 added to an otherwise correct set of conditions for moral blameworthiness results in a set of conditions both necessary and sufficient for moral blameworthiness for actions. Now reconsider Sweet Deception: suppose, unbeknown to Sam, Ralph has replaced the sugar in the bowl with a sugar look-alike that is deadly. Sam invites Kate over for some refreshment and, drawing from the bowl, dissolves what she mistakenly takes to be a spoonful of sugar into Kate's coffee. Suppose, recalling a lecture on excusing conditions for blameworthiness, Sam humorously entertains the belief she then acquires that it is wrong to dissolve the poisonous look-alike in Kate's beverage. Blame3 yields the unacceptable result that Sam is deserving of blame for dissolving the poison in Kate's coffee. To handle cases of this sort Blame3 can be amended in this way:

ProtoBlame4: S is morally blameworthy for performing A only if (i) S has an occurrent or dispositional belief, BAW, that A is wrong, and (ii) either BAW enters into S's deliberations about whether to A or S performs A despite entertaining BAW and believes (at least dispositionally) that she is performing A.

ProtoBlame4 can be simplified. With respect to its clause ii, as there seem to be no cases in which its first disjunct could be true while its second false, ProtoBlame4 streamlines to:

Blame4: S is morally blameworthy for performing A only if (i) S has an occurrent or dispositional belief, BAW, that A is wrong, and (ii) S performs A despite entertaining BAW and believes (at least dispositionally) that she is performing A.

Cases involving acting out of self-deception, however, point up a possible deficiency of Blame4. Before introducing such cases, it will be helpful to prepare the way by saying something about blameworthiness for actions that issue from certain sorts of unconscious belief.

4. BLAMEWORTHINESS AND UNCONSCIOUS BELIEFS AND DESIRES

Starting with some distinctions, S's desire D to A is *weakly unconscious* if and only if S has D and S does not know or believe that she has D, and similarly, S's belief B that p is weakly unconscious if and only if S has B and S does not know or believe that she has B. S's desire D to A [belief B that p] is *strongly unconscious* if and only if S has D [B], D [B] is weakly unconscious, and apart from outside help or careful self-scrutiny, she cannot come to know or believe that she has D [B].[6]

Pretty clearly, a person *can* be morally appraisable for performing an action that issues from a weakly unconscious desire or belief.[7] For instance, suppose Jones donates to charity and believes (at the time she makes the donation) that she is acting out of a sense of duty, but only later comes to realize that the desire to hurt her spouse by failing to help him pay off a debt (together with an appropriate belief) is what really gave rise to her act of charity. Presumably Jones *is* appraisable for this act. (Were one to discover Jones's true motives, one might well think less of Jones than one did prior to the discovery with respect to her contribution to charity; one might, for instance, no longer believe that Jones is deserving of praise for her deed.) What about acts that issue from strongly unconscious desires or beliefs? I think the judgment that Jones is appraisable for donating to charity would remain unaltered even if it were only after careful self-scrutiny, or only after consultation with a close friend who is a perceptive judge of Jones's motives, that Jones came to realize the true motive of her act. Of course, matters would be different if Jones acted on an unconscious *irresistible* desire to assuage guilt feelings, for then the control condition required for moral appraisability would not be met. Analogously, suppose Jones is unaware of the motives that prevent her from swimming in the pool (she may have a mistaken view of the incapacitating motives); suppose, also, that in the absence of knowing what motives in fact prevent her from swimming in the pool, Jones cannot bring herself to swim in the pool. Then again it seems that Jones's unconscious motives contribute towards an explanation of why Jones may not be blameworthy for failing to swim in the pool, but only by way of affecting Jones's control over her swimming in the pool. Apart from their effect on control, our judgment regarding Jones's appraisability for actions she performs on the basis of unconscious motivational elements would be affected if such elements contributed to the sort of ignorance (exemplified in Sam's deadly-look-alike-case) that is *straightforwardly* excusing. If Jones, for example, acted on the false but well-justified unconscious belief that her spouse was about to assault her child and, in light of this belief, pushed the child out of what she discerned to be harm's way, thereby inadvertently injuring the child, she would (I believe) not be blameworthy for pushing the child or for the injury. The moral I wish to suggest is that as far as affecting the appraisability of an agent with respect to an action he performs, there seems to be nothing *special* about unconscious actional elements. The mere fact, for instance, that an agent is unaware of the correct belief (or desire) in light of which he does something does not serve to excuse in the ordinary way, and she may well be appraisable for doing that thing. Call a weakly or strongly unconscious belief (or desire), which is part of the etiology of S's A-ing, does not undermine S's control (the sort required for moral appraisability) over A-ing, and does not contribute to the kind of ignorance that *forthrightly* excuses S from blame (or praise) for A-ing, "a standard unconscious belief (or desire)."[8] As all standard unconscious beliefs are dispositional beliefs, Blame4 should be construed as follows:

> Blame5: S is morally blameworthy for performing A only if (i) S has an occurrent belief, or a dispositional one (that may well be a standard unconscious belief), BAW, that A is wrong, and (ii) S performs A despite entertaining BAW and believes (at least dispositionally) that she is performing A.

To facilitate assessing Blame5, consider this case involving action based on unconscious motivational elements.[9] Tom, a well-established but "declining" philosopher writes what is in fact a mediocre paper. He wants very much for it to be the case that his paper is a good one and is well received by others. Assume that the thought that the paper is mediocre would be truly damaging to his ego, and that he wants (perhaps unconsciously) to avoid damaging his ego. Assume that, given these wants, Tom puts evidence against his paper's being mediocre out of his mind, avoids having the paper read by colleagues who would quickly latch on to its mediocrity, misinterprets negative comments to reduce their sting, and inflates encouraging comments to augment his confidence about the paper's worth. In short, Tom's various desires, like the desire that his paper be first-rate, leads Tom to engage in activities that contribute self-deceptively to his believing that his paper is first-rate. I shall assume that Tom's state of being self-deceived with respect to his paper's worth is characterized amongst other elements by these: (1) Tom unconsciously and truly believes that his paper is mediocre, (2) Tom consciously believes that his paper is first-rate, and (3) Tom has a number of desires (some of which are strongly unconscious) that lead him to manipulate data relevant to the truth of his belief that the paper is first-rate.

A number of comments about this case are in order. First, I am not here concerned with giving an account of self-deception, nor am I presupposing any particular account. I simply offer a case in which it seems reasonable to suppose that a person is in self-deception with respect to a certain proposition.

Second, I remain neutral on whether paradigm or central cases of self-deception all involve an agent's having an unconscious belief which perhaps represents knowledge, or a conscious belief which is false, or both.[10] In a series of fascinating papers, Robert Audi defends something like a "two belief" view. According to Audi, agent S is in self-deception with respect to proposition p if only if S unconsciously knows that not-p (or has reason to believe, and unconsciously and truly believes, not-p); S sincerely avows, or is disposed to avow sincerely, that p; and S has at least one want which explains in part both why the belief that not-p is unconscious and why S is disposed to disavow a belief that not-p, and to avow p, even when presented with what he sees is evidence against it. (Audi [1982, p. 138] *denies* that sincere avowal amounts to belief.) Mele, in contrast, defends a provocative "single belief" account of self-deception. On Mele's view, S enters self-deception in acquiring the belief that p if and only if the belief that p which S acquires is false, S's desiring that p leads S to manipulate data relevant or seemingly relevant to the truth value of p, this manipulation is a cause of S's acquiring the belief that p; if, in the causal chain between desire and manipulation or in that between manipulation and belief-acquisition, there are any accidental intermediaries (links), or intermediaries intentionally introduced by another agent, these intermediaries do not make S (significantly) less responsible for acquiring the belief that p than he would otherwise have been.[11] My concern, as I have suggested, is not to decide between these (or other) accounts of self-deception. I am committed merely to the view that, possibly, there are cases of self-deception like Tom's, in which an agent who is in self-deception with respect to a proposition p, has a standard unconscious true belief that p and a conscious false belief that not-p.

Third, I do however want to emphasize that one's account of paradigm cases of self-deception will certainly have a direct bearing on an agent's appraisability for actions performed "out of self-deception," as the ensuing considerations suggest. Suppose, to extend Tom's case somewhat, it is morally wrong for Tom to accept an offer he receives to publish the mediocre paper that he self-deceptively believes is first-rate, and that Tom is also self-deceived with respect to its being morally wrong for him to accept the offer. Assume, on the one hand, that the correct account of self-deception (in conjunction with the relevant facts of the case) entails that Tom has both a standard unconscious true belief that it is wrong that he accept the offer and a conscious false belief that it is permissible that he accept the offer. Now it seems that a person in self-deception can certainly be morally appraisable for acts stemming from the relevant unconscious belief component.[12] Tom, for instance, may act on the unconscious belief that it is wrong to accept the offer by declining the offer, and if he does turn down the offer on this basis, he may well be morally praiseworthy for doing so. Suppose, on the other hand, that the correct account of self-deception (together with germane facts) entails that Tom has a conscious false belief that it is permissible to accept the offer, but does not require that Tom have the pertinent unconscious true belief. Such an account might insist that a person can deceive herself into believing that p is false without (first) believing that p is true;[13] indeed, the account may leave it entirely open whether the true belief that p ever figured in any way in the person's deceiving herself into believing that p is false. Presupposing an account of this sort, suppose Tom deceives himself into believing that it is permissible to accept the offer to publish *without* the true belief that it is impermissible to do so having reckoned in any way in his entering (on this occasion) into self-deception; assume, in fact, that he simply lacks this belief. Then on the assumption that a person is blameworthy for performing an action only if she believes that that action is wrong, Tom would not be blameworthy for, say, accepting the offer to publish the paper. (Of course, Tom *may* be blameworthy for *entering* into self-deception with respect to its being permissible for him to accept the offer and for remaining in self-deception with respect to this proposition, consistent with his not being blameworthy for having acted on the false belief that it is permissible for him to accept the offer.)

Of what relevance is Tom's case to an appraisal of Blame5? Assume that we are dealing with a case of self-deception in which Tom has a standard unconscious true belief that it is wrong for him to accept the offer to publish the paper, a conscious false belief that it is permissible for him to accept the offer, and various wants that contribute to his self-deception. I think it a reasonable assumption that both weakly and strongly unconscious beliefs can contribute to the etiology of an intentional action in much the same way in which a conscious belief can. There *will* be some differences. Audi, for example, plausibly proposes that unconscious beliefs are much like conscious ones save two major differences: if they manifest themselves in one's consciousness, one is very unlikely, without special self-scrutiny or outside help, to attribute these manifestations to them; and one is unlikely to explain one's actions (with the same exceptions) as due to them (Audi 1982, p. 137). Suppose, then, that Tom acts *akratically* on his standard unconscious belief: deliberating unconsciously, this belief contributes to the formation of an (unconscious) decisive best judgment that he ought (morally) to decline the offer to publish; but his conscious belief that it is permissible for him to accept the offer, together with his strong desire for continued recognition, contributes to the formation of an intention, on which he acts, to accept the offer, while *still* holding the decisive best judgment that he ought not to accept. Tracing, now, the implications of Blame5 regarding Tom's appraisability for accepting the offer, assume that Blame5 is the epistemic condition for moral appraisability for actions, and that this condition (if met) added to the correct control and authenticity conditions for moral blameworthiness (which grant are satisfied) suffices for Tom's being to blame for accepting the offer. As Tom's standard unconscious belief that it is wrong to accept the offer to publish the paper enters into Tom's deliberations about whether to publish, Blame5 (with the control and authenticity conditions) generates the result that Tom is blameworthy for accepting the offer. Suppose, in addition, that the analogue of Blame5 concerning praiseworthiness, this principle, is correct:

Praise5: S is morally praiseworthy for performing A only if (i) S has an occurrent, or dispositional belief, BAR, that A is obligatory or right, (ii) S performs A while entertaining BAR and believes (at least dispositionally) that she is performing A, and (iii) S performs A for the reason that (or at least partly for the reason that) S believes (at least dispositionally) that A is the right thing to do.[14]

As Tom's conscious belief that it is permissible for him to accept the offer to publish enters into his deliberations about whether to accept the offer, and he accepts partly for the reason that he believes it is permissible for him to accept, Praise5 (together with the control and authenticity conditions which we assume are satisfied) entails that Tom is praiseworthy for accepting the offer.

Call the conjunction of Praise5 and Blame5 "Appraise5." There is an alternative route to the conclusion that Appraise5 (and the appropriate control condition) entails that Tom is both praiseworthy and blameworthy for accepting the offer. Suppose Tom's standard unconscious belief that it is impermissible to accept the offer (together perhaps with a standard unconscious desire to uphold his integrity) inclines him toward refusing the offer to publish, whereas his conscious belief that it is permissible to accept the offer (together maybe with his conscious desire not to damage his ego) inclines him toward accepting the offer. Assume, as seems possible, that these conscious and unconscious elements "interact" in unconscious deliberation that culminates in a decision to accept the offer on which Tom acts. Then Tom's conscious belief that it is permissible to accept the offer and his unconscious one that it is impermissible to accept the offer once again both enter into his deliberations about whether to accept the offer. Consequently, Appraise5 (in association with the control and authenticity conditions) produces the result that Tom is blameworthy and praiseworthy for performing the very same action.

Amassed now is sufficient ammunition to launch this objection against Appraise5: (1) if Appraise5 is true, then Tom is both morally praiseworthy and morally blameworthy for accepting the offer; (2) but no agent can be praiseworthy and blameworthy for performing one and the very same action; (3) hence, Appraise5 is not true. The pivotal premise here is, of course, 2. Is it acceptable?[15]

5. ON BEING BLAMEWORTHY AND PRAISEWORTHY FOR ONE AND THE SAME ACTION

Establishing premise 2 would be straightforward if blameworthiness and praiseworthiness were associated with objective wrongness and objective rightness, respectively. For then if S were praiseworthy for performing A, A would be right, and if S were blameworthy for performing A, A would be wrong. But as no act can be right *and* wrong, no agent could be deserving of praise *and* deserving of blame for performing one and the very same action. However, this rationale for 2 simply won't do as its association of praiseworthiness and blameworthiness with objective rightness and objective wrongness respectively, as I argued in the last chapter, is highly suspect.

Some might urge that simple examples such as the following conclusively show that premise 2 is false; such examples, it might be claimed, clearly reveal that an agent can be morally praiseworthy and blameworthy for performing one and the same action as of a certain time. Suppose Jill promises Tim to clap her hands at time t_1 and she promises Tom not to clap her hands at t_1. Suppose at t_1 Jill intentionally keeps her promise to Tim and *also* intentionally breaks her promise to Tom by clapping her hands at t_1. Then Jill is morally praiseworthy and morally blameworthy for what she intentionally does when she claps her hands at t_1.

The example, however, is not convincing. By clapping her hands at t_1, Jill brings about several different states of affairs. Here are some:

s_1: Jill's clapping her hands
s_2: Jill's intentionally keeping a promise.
s_3: Jill's intentionally breaking a promise.
s_4: Jill's intentionally keeping a promise and intentionally breaking some promise.

I grant that Jill may well be praiseworthy for bringing about s_2 at t_1, and she may well be blameworthy for bringing about s_3 at t_1, but s_2 and s_3 are, of course, different states of affairs. One might, however, now insist that as Jill is praiseworthy for bringing about s_2 and blameworthy for bringing about s_3, and s_4 is simply a conjunction of s_2 and s_3, Jill must be both blameworthy and praiseworthy for bringing about s_4. The underlying principle here seems to be something of this sort:

P1: Necessarily, for any "conjunctive" state of affairs, cs (like s_4), if one is blameworthy for bringing about one of its parts (or conjuncts) and one is praiseworthy for bringing about another one of its parts, then one is both blameworthy and praiseworthy for bringing about cs.

It is not, nevertheless, evident why P1 should be accepted. For one thing, other moral analogues of P1 are pretty clearly unacceptable. So, for instance, if it is wrong for Jill to break her promise (to Tim), and right for Jill to keep her promise (to Tom), it does not follow that Jill's breaking her promise to Tim and Jill's keeping her promise to Tom is both right and wrong for Jill. It is not, moreover, evident why P1 is relevantly different from this sort of "moral analogue." For another thing, suppose I fed some birds this morning and I am praiseworthy for doing so, and suppose I broke a promise in the afternoon and I am blameworthy for doing so. There is little reason to believe that I am both praiseworthy and blameworthy for the conjunctive state of affairs: my feeding some birds in the morning and my breaking a promise in the afternoon. In the absence of independent justification for it, there are no grounds for accepting principle P1.

Still, one might direct attention to s_1: Jill's clapping her hands. How do we appraise Jill vis-à-vis bringing about s_1? My response will turn partly on the beliefs Jill has. If she believes that she is doing right by bringing about s_1, then she might be praiseworthy; if she believes that she is doing wrong by bringing about s_1, then she might be blameworthy. But nothing, and this is the principal point, in the initial example sustains the verdict that Jill is both praiseworthy and blameworthy for bringing about s_1.

Turning to a consideration against premise 2, Michael Zimmerman's account of moral appraisability allows for the possibility that an agent is both blameworthy and praiseworthy for the same action. Briefly, Zimmerman's complex account rests pivotally on the distinction between direct and indirect appraisability. This distinction, in turn, is explained in terms of the distinction between direct and indirect freedom. On Zimmerman's view, there are some things with respect to which we are only indirectly free, in that we are free with respect to them only because they are consequences of things with respect to which we are directly free. On pain of an infinite regress, there must, Zimmerman thinks, be some things with respect to which we are directly free. Zimmerman believes that volitions and only volitions are the sort of thing with respect to which we may be directly free (but that is not crucial here). Zimmerman's view is that appraisability tracks freedom, in the sense that we may be said to be directly appraisable (as long as the nonfreedom epistemic requirement for appraisability is met) for those things with respect to which we are directly free, and indirectly appraisable for those things with respect to which we are indirectly free. The significance of this Zimmerman takes to be the following. Since indirect freedom does not increase or expand the *extent* to which we are free (for whether or not the consequence in question occurs is not up to us but up to "nature," once that with respect to which we are directly free occurs), indirect appraisability does not increase or expand the *extent* to which we are appraisable. (For example, whether or not the glass will shatter as a result of one's throwing a stone at it will depend, partly, upon whether nature cooperates; a gale might alter the trajectory of the rock, thus causing it to miss the pane.) In Zimmerman's terminology, indirect appraisability is essentially empty (Zimmerman 1988, chap. 3, 4).

Zimmerman proposes that it is perfectly possible to be both praiseworthy and blameworthy for the same event, especially if appraisability is indirect in at least one of these instances (1988, p. 59). Of course, a lot turns on just what indirect appraisability amounts to—although Zimmerman holds that there is no correct position here due to the essential emptiness of indirect appraisability (1988, p. 57). So, for example, on the barest account of indirect appraisability, S is indirectly appraisable for event e if and only if for some volition, f (or more generally, for some thing with respect to which S is directly free), S is directly appraisable for f, and e is a consequence of f. On this barest view, S is indirectly blameworthy for e if e is a consequence of f, and S is directly blameworthy for f; similarly, S is indirectly praiseworthy for e if e is a consequence of f, and S is directly praiseworthy for f. Now consider this example of Zimmerman's (1988, pp. 41, 59): Jones comes across a car accident; the driver is unconscious. Jones expects the car to explode at any moment; he swiftly drags the driver clear of the wreck. The result is that the driver is paralyzed for life (whereas he would not have been if Jones had left him where he was), and the car does not explode. The event, Jones's dragging the driver clear of the wreck, can be a consequence both of a blameworthy volition (say, a decision not to take some first-aid class) and of a praiseworthy volition (say, a decision to help the driver). Hence, given the barest account of indirect appraisability, Jones is both indirectly praiseworthy and blameworthy for dragging the driver clear of the wreck.

The advocate of premise 2, the premise that no one can be both praiseworthy and blameworthy for one and the same event or action, may remain unpersuaded.

She might urge that on Zimmerman's own view, the "appraisability status" of an event that is the consequence of a volition is essentially inherited from the appraisability status of the relevant volition; indirect appraisability is empty and there is *no correct position* with respect to indirect appraisability. For whatever such position one advances, there is no reason to believe (if indirect appraisability is empty) that the position is *the correct* one. So, she might claim, it cuts no ice against premise 2 to produce a case in which some agent is indirectly praiseworthy and blameworthy for some event. What is needed, she might insist, to convince her that premise 2 is false, is a clear case in which the agent is both directly praiseworthy and blameworthy for the same thing. Jones's case is obviously *not* a case of this sort.

Zimmerman's position on direct praiseworthiness and blameworthiness for the same event falls short of satisfying the advocate of premise 2. Zimmerman raises, and responds to the crucial question:

> Is it possible for someone to be both *directly* laudable and *directly* culpable for the same event? This is unclear to me, although I think that it is possible. Consider the following case. S strictly freely wills *e* for the sake of nonobligatory right; but he also believes that, in so willing, he is running a less-than-minimal risk of doing wrong. For example, *e* may be a charitable act of some kind, and the wrong risked that of not repaying a loan. (1988, pp. 59–60)

The case is controversial, I think, because S may well believe that in willing or deciding to donate to charity, S runs a less-than-minimal risk of doing wrong, without its being the case that S decides to donate to charity in the belief that in so doing S is doing wrong. Consequently, we don't have a clear case in which S decides to donate to charity in the belief that S's so doing is right, *and* in the belief that S's so doing is wrong.

In summary, I believe that Zimmerman's views are certainly suggestive and lend credibility to the view that premise 2 (the premise that no one can be both praiseworthy and blameworthy for the same event) is false. I'm inclined to think that Tom's case involving self-deception *does* show (contrary to premise 2) that there is a clear case establishing the falsity of 2. If, however, I am wrong and premise 2 is correct, then I propose that Blame5 be modified in this way:

> Blame6: S is morally blameworthy for performing A only if (i) S has an occurrent, or dispositional belief, BAW, that A is wrong; (ii) it is false that S has a belief that A is right or obligatory; and (iii) S performs A despite entertaining BAW and believes (at least dispositionally) that she is performing A.

One last amendment to the belief condition for culpability will be introduced and defended in the next chapter.

6. SOME OBJECTIONS AND REPLIES

Finally, I want to consider two objections, each directed against the core view (call it "B") being defended, that an agent is morally blameworthy for performing an action only if she believes that that action is wrong. According to the first objection, there could be cases in which an agent has had the opportunity to acquire the belief that what he is doing or about to do is wrong, but *culpably* fails to acquire that belief. Thus, in such cases the agent *is* blameworthy (contrary to what B implies), *without* actually having the appropriate belief. Here's an illustrative case. Jack has been warned to check that the gun is not loaded prior to squeezing the trigger. He forgets and is culpable for not remembering. Believing that the gun is not loaded, and certainly not intending to do any wrong, he squeezes the trigger while the gun is pointed in the direction of Fido (his dog). Fido drops dead. Isn't Jack to blame for squeezing the trigger?

My view is that he is not, and he is not (partly) because I believe, as should now be evident, that appraisability for an action depends on the *actual* sequence of events that generates the action. Compare Jack's situation with Jill's, in which Jill nonculpably squeezes the trigger of the loaded gun while it is aimed at Fido. (We can imagine that Jill was misinformed about the gun's not being loaded). If we focus on the actual sequence of events in Jill's case, we find that Jill did not intend to do wrong, and positively did not believe that she was doing wrong by squeezing the trigger. But these elements in the actual sequence culminating in Jill's shooting, elements central to our judgment that Jill is not blameworthy for squeezing the trigger, are the very same sorts of elements that we find in the actual sequence of events culminating in Jack's squeezing the trigger. Suppose the warning "failed to register" in Jack's mind as he simply forgot about it, suppose he believed that the gun was not loaded, and suppose he did not intend to inflict any harm on his beloved Fido. Focusing on the actual sequence, there is little, if anything, to recommend that he is blameworthy for squeezing the trigger. Of course, this moral assessment is consistent with maintaining that Jack is (or could be) blameworthy for forgetting to check the gun, or for overlooking the possibility that the gun is loaded, or for aiming the gun at Fido in the first place.

One might try again, this time relying on this sort of case: suppose Xenia believes that there is nothing wrong with torturing men just for fun and, when opportunity presents itself, tortures men just for fun. Wouldn't Xenia, contrary to the verdict of Blame5 (in conjunction with all other requirements of blameworthiness), be to blame for this? So doesn't this example, and many others relevantly like it, provide impetus to amend clause i of Blame5 in this way: S is morally blameworthy for performing A only if S has an occurrent or dispositional belief that A is wrong, or S ought to believe that A is wrong? The thought here, of course, is that Xenia ought to have known better; she ought to have believed, or ought (morally) to have acquired the belief that torturing men for fun is wrong, and hence, that even if she lacks the belief that torturing men is wrong, she is still to blame for her deeds of torture.

However, Blame5, I believe, is best left unsupplemented by the "ought to have known better" disjunct. For if Xenia *nonculpably* failed to acquire the germane belief, it is difficult to see why she is to blame when she tortures, for example, Bond. It is, at best, in cases of this sort, culpable ignorance that is "blameworthiness transmitting." As this is so, we need to ask whether Xenia is blameworthy for failing to acquire the belief, BF, that torturing men just for fun is wrong. Amended Blame5 (with appropriate facts of the case) implies that she is blameworthy for not acquiring BF if (assuming other conditions of blameworthiness are satisfied), she fails to acquire BF in light of the belief that failing to acquire BF is wrong, or she ought to have realized that failing to acquire BF is wrong (but failed here, and is culpable for failing). I think, though, that this condition will hardly ever be satisfied by agents like Xenia. For, I doubt, firstly, that in a broad spectrum of cases relevantly analogous to Xenia's, if S fails to acquire BF, S fails in light of the belief that not acquiring BF is wrong. And secondly, I strongly doubt that (in such cases) S ought (morally) to have realized that failing to acquire BF is wrong, failed in this obligation, and was culpable for doing so. I think, then, that in numerous cases pertinently like Xenia's, appeal to the condition that the agent ought to have known better will simply *not* secure the conclusion that the agent is indeed blameworthy for A-ing. And this undermines the incentive to supplement clause i of Blame5 with the "ought to have known better" disjunct.

The second objection centers on certain sorts of cases in which we think that the agent, not obviously acting out of ignorance, freely does something morally reprehensible, and so should be blameworthy for the deed. Suppose, for instance, that Dan believes he is doing no wrong by performing horribly painful experiments on chimps. If B is correct, then Dan is not blameworthy for his (germane) actions. But at least intuitively he is, so B must be false. It might be claimed that such examples, which could of course be multiplied, suggest that there is something missing in my account of the epistemic dimension of blameworthiness. It might further be proposed that at least part of what is missing is consideration of how the agents came to have or lack the beliefs in question, and whether they (the agents) are appraisable for having or continuing to have, lacking or continuing to lack, the appropriate moral beliefs. My approach focuses on beliefs about right and wrong that agents have at any given time and how they affect the agent's behavior. But appraisability also has to do with how agents came to be the sorts of persons they are with their repertoire of beliefs. This "historical" dimension to appraisability has not been given sufficient weight in my "belief approach" to blameworthiness.

In response, I have argued that there are important historical dimensions to appraisability. Specifically, I have proposed that actions which issue from unauthentic evaluative schemes are ones for which their agent does not bear moral responsibility. I proposed, further, that an agent's evaluative scheme is authentic only if its doxastic elements are not authenticity subverting, and I suggested that the following sorts of beliefs would subvert authenticity. Beliefs formed as a result of deception when the beliefs play a core role in the agent's deliberations about what to do; deliberately implanted beliefs in cases in which the agent did not broadly consent to the implantation; beliefs formed on the basis of instilled pro-attitudes where, again, the agent did not give broad consent to the instillment, and where the agent lacks volitional control over the actions arising from the instilled attitudes; beliefs formed on the basis of coercive persuasion; and beliefs formed as a result of akratic or "self-deceptive" deliberation. Suppose that, unbeknownst to him, an irresistible desire to inflict pain on chimps, together with the belief that inflicting pain on chimps is not wrong (a belief that he cannot "dislodge"), were implanted in Dan via direct electronic stimulation of his brain.

Then it would seem that Dan would not be morally to blame for his subsequent (pertinent) actions. We could say that Dan is not blameworthy (partly) as some of the doxastic elements of the reasons that give rise to his pertinent actions are not "truly his own," or ones with respect to which he is not "autonomous." The following, though, does deserve emphasis. Surely, there *can* be cases in which the agent *is* "autonomous" with respect to the causal springs—the desires, intentions, beliefs, etc. that generate his action—the agent satisfies the control condition required for moral appraisability, he does not act out of ignorance, *and* he performs a reprehensible deed *without* believing that he is doing any wrong. Dan's case might well be a case of this sort. Imagine that the norms of the culture in which Dan finds himself sanction the sort of behavior in which he engages; there is a long-standing tradition according to which it is morally permissible to inflict pain on chimps and other nonhuman animals as long as one is conducting scientific research. Suppose Dan *reflectively* accepts these norms and is "autonomous" with respect to the relevant beliefs. Is Dan to blame for his behavior when he believes that he is doing no wrong by inflicting harm on Bongo the chimp? Again, I suggest that he is not: careful attention to the actual sequence of events should generate skepticism about whether he is to blame. In addition, and importantly, we should not ignore the bit of wisdom that cautions that there are several different ways in which a person is accessible to moral evaluation, and being to blame is only one such way. So, for instance, we might claim that Dan's treatment of nonhuman animals is morally reprehensible, and that he has some morally reprehensible beliefs about such animals. We might denounce him for failing to develop more sympathy for such creatures. We might, in addition, also find *him* morally reprehensible in light of the fact that he has done something morally reprehensible. But none of these moral evaluations amount to an attribution of *blameworthiness*.

7. CONCLUDING REMARKS

One strong attraction of the view that a person is blameworthy for performing an action only if that action is in fact wrong—a view that associates blameworthiness with objective wrongness—is that if this view were correct, it would not absolve a lot of slimy characters of their (apparent) blame for doing something appalling which they did not take to be wrong. But cases like Howser's Hell and Deadly's Defeat exert pressure to reject this view. (They do *not*, it should be emphasized, directly motivate abandoning the different view that it can be morally permissible or obligatory to blame or otherwise censure *outwardly* a person for performing an act she did not discern to be wrong and for which she is not deserving of [inner] blame.) As a replacement for the objective view, I have proposed that blameworthiness is much more closely affiliated with an agent's own perceptions about what is right or wrong: an agent is deserving of blame for performing an action only if she believes that the action is wrong. The view I have presented stresses the importance of the role of such a belief in the etiology of action: to be blameworthy for performing A, the agent must A in spite of entertaining the belief that she is doing wrong by A-ing, where entertaining the belief involves "accessing"

it—being in some fashion, maybe even unconsciously, aware of it. I have suggested, additionally, that actions arising out of self-deception, in cases in which
the agent in self-deception with respect to a proposition p has an unconscious
true belief that p and a conscious false belief that p, are particularly germane to
an understanding of one epistemic dimension of blameworthiness. Specifically, on
the condition that no agent can be morally praiseworthy and morally blameworthy for performing the very same action, such cases of self-deception motivate the
condition that an agent is blameworthy for performing A only if she has a belief
that A is wrong and it is false that she has a belief that A is permissible (or
obligatory). Interestingly enough, if it is false that no agent can be deserving of
praise and blame for performing one and the same action, such cases of self-
deception provide examples of how a person can be blameworthy and praiseworthy for doing one and the same thing. Finally, even advocates of the Objective
View should grant that a constituent of any *complete* epistemic condition of being
to blame must be a belief one that "links" agency (or perhaps the moral worth of
an agent) and objective wrongness or at least what the agent takes to be objectively wrong. With no such "belief mediated link," the agent will be as innocent
as a child or an amoral being who fails to have the relevant moral beliefs. To
amplify, imagine an agent, child-like in that she lacks moral beliefs about right or
wrong. Suppose she does something that *is* wrong—drains the water from the fish
bowl—but fails to do so in light of the belief that she is doing any wrong. Even
if we suppose she has appraisability grounding control over draining the water, we
would still be inclined to judge that she is not to blame for her guileless blunder.
Hence, though proponents of the Objective View may remain unpersuaded by
my arguments against that view, they may well be willing to accept Blame5 (or
Blame6).

TEN

ASSEMBLING
THE ELEMENTS

I began in chapter 1 with an array of cases that motivates some challenging puzzles about moral appraisability. The resolution of many of them turned, in the end, on getting clear about the conditions that are to be satisfied if a person is to be morally appraisable for his or her actions. I have argued that three conditions are particularly germane: a control condition that says, loosely, that the person's action must be under her control; an epistemic one that requires, roughly, that the person not be relevantly ignorant of what she is doing; and an authenticity condition that, in broad strokes, states that the person's action issue from an evaluative scheme—the cluster of motivational and doxastic elements required for evaluative reasoning—that is "truly her own" or authentic. My aim in this chapter is the modest one of proposing an outline of a principle that gives conditions necessary and sufficient for a restricted range of appraisability ascriptions. In constructing this principle, I shall be consolidating the key elements of appraisability introduced in the past chapters.

I. CONTROL

Control is, of course, fundamental to appraisability. One highly influential account of control with a venerable lineage entails the existence of genuine alternative options. On this account, to have control over an action, the agent must have been able to do otherwise consistent with holding the natural laws fixed and the past constant. This account of control, if correct, threatens appraisability if causal determinism is true and the (relevant) past and the natural laws are fixed. I have, however, rejected this account of control. I have proposed, instead, that an agent controls an action if he guides the action in an appropriate way: the action must be responsive to the agent's practical reasoning. To flesh out this account, I said that deliberative intentional action involves (1) a psychological basis for evaluative reasoning, including the agent's values, desires, beliefs; (2) a judgment made on the basis of such reasoning that recommends a course of action; (3) an intention formed or acquired on the basis of that judgment; (4) an action executing that intention. Focusing on 1, I introduced the notion of an agent's evaluative scheme. Such a scheme has doxastic elements including beliefs about normative standards to assess reasons for action, and beliefs regarding deliberative principles to be used to arrive at practical judgments about what to do. Such a scheme also has motivational elements like the agent's values and pro-attitudes to engage the deliberative principles the agent believes should be utilized to make practical judgments. I then proposed this preliminary notion of control:

> Volitional Control: Action, A, performed by agent, S, is under S's volitional control if and only if, holding constant the motivational precursor of A (that is, the proximal desire or pro-attitude that gives rise to A) and S's evaluative scheme, there is a scenario with the same natural laws as the actual world in which, relying on S's evaluative scheme, S decides or forms an intention to do something other than A, and successfully executes that intention or decision.

I said that for a desire in one scenario to be the same desire as a desire in another scenario, the two should have the same strength relative to competing desires. Finally, I proposed various constraints on scenario eligibility. An eligible world must satisfy a number of conditions including: the world's having the same natural laws as ours, the agent's having the same evaluative scheme and the same character and psychological constitution, the agent's having the same "conative history" up until the time of action, and the world's not including conditions that would be exceptional for the agent, for instance, extreme fear, anxiety, etc.

Having volitional control is compatible with causal determinism: even if causal determinism is true, and such determinism is incompatible with an agent's doing otherwise than what she in fact did, the agent may well have exercised volitional control over her action; possibly, her action was responsive to her practical reasoning. Having volitional control is also compatible with indeterminism. To use an example discussed earlier, suppose at the onset of deliberation, it is undetermined whether some of Jones's nonoccurrent beliefs will enter into her deliberations about whether to A. Then it is causally open, at the start of deliberation, whether Jones will form a best judgment about whether to A, and in fact A. Such indeterminacy is compatible with Jones's exercising exactly the same sort of control over the events leading from the formation of a better judgment to action that she would have exercised, had there been no "doxastic indeterminacy." But then such indeterminacy is compatible with Jones's exercising volitional control over A: even assuming "doxastic indeterminacy," and assuming that Jones does in fact A, holding fixed the motivational precursor of A and Jones's evaluative scheme, there is a scenario with the same natural laws as the actual world in which Jones forms an intention to do something other than A, and she successfully executes that intention.

Although control over an action is necessary for moral appraisability for that action, it is fairly evidently not sufficient.

2. AUTHENTICITY AND AGENCY

Psychogen illustrates vividly that more is needed for moral appraisability for an action than mere control. In (original) Psychogen, after undergoing psychosurgery to which she did not consent, Jenny the artist is transformed into a psychological twin of Jim, the famous stockbroker. When she awakens from the surgery, she ponders a bit, arrives at a brilliant investment decision, and executes that decision. We don't hold her praiseworthy for her action as, roughly, she is the victim of global manipulation. More specifically, two distinct ideas seem to underpin the judgment that Jenny is not deserving of praise for the action of investment, one having to do with agency and the other with authenticity of actional springs.

First, there is the idea that agency is compromised; when Jenny acts, it is as if Jim is acting. To clarify the idea of agency, I proposed that the appropriate subjects of attributions of moral appraisability are normative agents (of a certain sort). An individual, S, is a normative agent at time t if, at t, S has (i) an evaluative scheme; (ii) deliberative skills and capacities; and (iii) executive capacities—S can act on, or execute, at least some of her intentions, decisions, or choices at t. Condition ii entails that S is able to engage in genuine deliberation at t; S's deliberative activities must meet the threshold of rationality to qualify as legitimate deliberation.

Normative agents have their evaluative schemes essentially. Suppose Jenny *willingly* undergoes psychosurgery, having agreed with Max that she wants to be transformed into a psychological twin of Jim. After surgery, Jenny acquires the property of being a Jim-like normative agent and loses the property of being a Jenny-like normative agent. In Psychogen, however, Jenny does not give (broad) consent to the transformation surgery; indeed, assume that she is unaware that such surgery has been performed upon her. Speaking loosely, the surgery destroys one normative agent and creates another. Hence, such surgery compromises agency.

It seems that a person can be a normative agent at a time but not an appropriate candidate for moral praise or blame at that time. And this is because it seems possible for an agent to have normative concepts at a time or during a period of time not one of which is moral. The agent, in this sort of unusual case, would be nonmoral or amoral. Lacking the concepts of moral wrongness or rightness, such an agent would, presumably, not have beliefs about moral wrongness or rightness. And without such beliefs, the agent would not be an appropriate subject of *moral* appraisability (though, as I shall argue later, the agent may well be an appropriate candidate for nonmoral normative appraisability; she may, for instance, be an appropriate candidate for prudential praise or blame).

Second, another idea that informs the judgment that Jenny is not praiseworthy for the act of investment in Psychogen is that her inputs to deliberation—her values, desires, and beliefs—along with her deliberative skills and capacities are not "truly her own." I attempted to crystallize this idea by appeal to the notion of authentic evaluative schemes. A first principle of scheme authenticity germane to global manipulation types of cases is this:

> A1: If S is a normative agent N with evaluative scheme OriginalE at time t, and S acquires at t or after an evaluative scheme, NewE, via a process to which she did not give broad consent that either destroys N by destroying OriginalE, or totally "represses" N, then NewE is not normative-wise authentic.

A1 rules that, upon awakening from surgery, the evaluative scheme with which Jenny finds herself is not normative-wise authentic.

I next discussed the acquisition of evaluative schemes of agents like us who do not come into existence with evaluative schemes "in place"; human toddlers don't find themselves with a scheme ready formed—they have to acquire their evaluative schemes. The discussion naturally divided into one on *initial* schemes followed by another on changes in initial schemes. In connection with such schemes, I developed the concept of appraisability-relative authenticity, arguing that there is no such thing as "plain authenticity." Regarding initial schemes, the fundamental idea underlying the notion of appraisability-relative authenticity is straightforward. The having of certain dispositions, propensities, or habits, or—more generally—of pro-attitudes, and of doxastic elements by an agent, is incompatible with that agent's being appraisable for behavior that issues from them, as the having of them or their mode of instillment precludes satisfaction of control or epistemic conditions required for appraisability. I called motivational or doxastic elements of this sort "authenticity destructive," and modes or means of instillment of this sort "authenticity subversive." So, for example, the habit of ensuring that one's behavior always conforms to the teachings of one's pastor is authenticity destructive if it is an instilled one that the child simply cannot thwart; actions stemming from this habit are ones over which the child (and subsequent adult) does not exercise volitional control. Its mode of instillment, for instance, severe manipulation, is authenticity subversive if it so affects that child that she cannot but act in accordance with the teachings of her pastor; this mode of instillment (in this case) also subverts volitional control. Arguably, the having of other motivational or doxastic elements is required to ensure that, besides authenticity, other conditions like control or epistemic ones required for appraisability can be met by the agent or behavior of hers that issues from such elements. Perhaps the disposition to see oneself as the initiator of one's actions is one such element. I called doxastic or motivational elements of this sort, if there are any, "authenticity demanding." I then proposed the following principle, which gives sufficient conditions for initial scheme authenticity:

> A3: An agent's initial evaluative scheme is appraisability-wise authentic if its pro-attitudinal and doxastic elements (i) include all those, if any, that are authenticity demanding; (ii) do not include any that are authenticity destructive; and (iii) have been acquired by modes that are not authenticity subversive.

Lastly, recognizing that evaluative schemes are not static but dynamic—they can change or evolve over time—we require an understanding of appraisability-wise authentic evolved schemes. I proposed that modifications to one's appraisability-wise authentic initial scheme are authenticity-preserving if the modifications are made under one's own steam. Regarding changes in motivational components, the newly acquired ones are acceptable insofar as the actions (if any) to which they give rise are ones over which one has volitional control. (The exception here would be cases in which one "freely" and intentionally has instilled in oneself pro-attitudes that one realizes will give rise to actions over which one lacks volitional control.) With respect to doxastic elements, changes in beliefs are acceptable if the beliefs are not acquired under conditions that subvert "belief appraisability-relative authenticity." The beliefs, I suggested, should not be formed as a result of deception when the beliefs play a central role in the agent's deliberations; in the absence of broad consent, they should not be deliberately implanted when the implantation bypasses ordinary mechanisms of belief formation; the beliefs should not be formed on the basis of instilled pro-attitudes (again when broad consent has not been given) over which one lacks volitional control; they should not be formed as a result of coercive persuasion; and finally, they should not be formed on the basis of akratic or self-deceptive deliberation. The final principle addressing the authenticity of evaluative schemes proposed is:

> A4: If agent S's evaluative scheme at a time, t, is either S's initial appraisability-wise authentic scheme at that time, or is an evolved appraisability-wise authentic scheme of S's at that time (that is, it is a scheme resulting from *acceptable* modifications to a scheme possessed by S prior to t that is appraisability-wise authentic), then S's evaluative scheme is appraisability-wise authentic.

3. EPISTEMIC CONDITIONS

Aristotle correctly insisted that a person is morally appraisable for doing something only on the condition that he does not act in ignorance (*Nicomachean Ethics* 1111a3–5). Appraisability has an epistemic dimension. I have argued against any conception of this dimension which entails that a person is blameworthy for performing an action only if that action is in fact (objectively) wrong, and that he is praiseworthy for performing an action only if that action is objectively right or obligatory. I suggested instead that blameworthiness (and praiseworthiness) are much more closely affiliated with the moral beliefs of the person. Assuming that a person *can*, on some occasions, be morally praiseworthy and blameworthy for one and the same action, the principle concerning blameworthiness I provisionally proposed is this:

> S is morally blameworthy for performing A only if (i) S has an occurrent belief, or a dispositional one (that may well be a standard unconscious belief), BAW that A is wrong, and (ii) S performs A despite entertaining BAW and believes (at least dispositionally) that S is performing A.

On further reflection, it seems that even this condition needs relaxing. For reconsider appraisability on account of suberogating. Blameworthy suberogation, I suggest, is possible if the agent (mistakenly) believes he is doing moral wrong in suberogating and all other conditions of being to blame are met. But what of a case in which the agent doesn't believe he is doing any wrong but *does* believe he is doing something *suberogatory?* Shouldn't this suffice for some degree of blameworthiness (as long as all other conditions of appraisability) are satisfied? The issue here is complicated as is borne out by these cases. In the first, Harry believes that his behavior (lingering at the table in high demand at the fine café) is suberogatory. In so believing, we can assume that he believes both that he is doing no overall wrong, and that he is doing something (morally) indecent. But suppose, further, that Harry focuses attention on his belief that his indecency is *not* morally wrong, and that his belief that his behavior is indecent is not an element in the causal pathway of his delaying while others are waiting. Rather, it's the other belief, that his behavior is *not* wrong, that plays the primary role in forming his intention to stay and sustaining it once formed. Then I think Harry's ledger of life is unstained; he is not blameworthy for suberogating even though he believes his behavior is suberogatory. In the second, Larry, too, believes that his action is suberogatory but in so believing, he "places weight" on the belief that (though not wrong) his behavior is *morally indecent* or *morally amiss.* Though Larry does form the intention to stay and stays, here he acts despite his strong belief—strong in the sense that it pesters him—that he is doing something morally amiss (but not morally wrong). Then I think he merits blame. The cases suggest at least this amendment of the epistemic condition:

> ABlame5: S is morally blameworthy for performing A only if (i) S has an occurrent or dispositional belief, BAW, that A is wrong or that A is morally amiss (Harry and Larry's cases illustrate that a person *can* believe he is doing something morally amiss even though he believes he is doing no overall wrong), and (ii) S performs A despite entertaining BAW and believes (at least dispositionally) that S is performing A.

I grant, of course, that the agent may have an occurrent belief that she is doing wrong by A-ing without also having the occurrent belief that she is doing something morally amiss by A-ing. A shortcoming of ABlame5 should be documented. It fails to address degrees of blameworthiness and of how perceived degrees of wrongdoing and of suberogation should be compared. As Michael Zimmerman has suggested in correspondence, compare Ernie, who does A despite believing it to be wrong to degree 10, and Bert, who does B despite believing it to be suberogatory to degree 100. If this makes sense, should the suberogatory be thought nonetheless to be lexically subordinate to the wrong, so that culpability for perceived wrongdoing is always greater than culpability for perceived suberogation, no matter what the degrees involved? I gladly defer discussion of this perplexity to another occasion.

In the last chapter I remarked, in passing, that there is an asymmetry between praiseworthiness and blameworthiness: one deserves praise only if one *pursues* the right, and blame only if one does *not shun* the wrong (being to blame, in other words, unlike being to praise, does not require pursuit of the wrong).[1] A pair of examples should help bring out this asymmetry. Suppose Ryan believes that it is (morally) wrong to bribe the custom's official but still goes ahead and discreetly slips the hundred dollar bill to her, as it is to his long-term advantage to do so. This is a paradigmatic sort of case in which we think that the agent is deserving of blame, and we think that he is so deserving even though he did not act for the reason or sake of doing wrong. Surely he is blameworthy (partly) for not eschewing the wrong. Ryan's case contrasts with Ravi's in which though he (rightly) believes that donating to charity on a certain occasion is obligatory, Ravi donates *solely* for the reason to further his political career; it's in his long-term self-interest to do so. Here, I see no reason why—on account of his donation— Ravi deserves "moral credit" in his "ledger of life." Inward moral praise just can't be so easily earned! Given this asymmetry, I proposed the following epistemic principle as the one that governs praiseworthiness:

> S is morally praiseworthy for performing A only if (i) S has an occurrent, or disposi- tional belief, BAR, that A is obligatory or right, (ii) S performs A while entertaining BAR and believes (at least dispositionally) that she is performing A, and (iii) S performs A for the reason that (or at least partly for the reason that) S believes (at least dispositionally) that A is the right (or obligatory) thing to do.

One might well wonder about whether one is deserving of praise if one per- forms an action in light of the (correct) belief that one is superogating. The initial answer appears to be "no," at least if praiseworthiness requires doing right for right's sake. But there is a perplexity here I note only to set aside: suppose one acts *for* the reason or sake of going beyond duty. Is there no room for being morally to praise?

4. PUTTING IT TOGETHER

Focusing on three fronts—the first having to do with control, the second with authentic springs of action and agency, and the third with epistemic elements—I offer for consideration the following preliminary analysis of moral appraisability. One is morally appraisable for performing an action just in case one performs it freely (that is, one has volitional control in performing it), autonomously (that is, it issues from an authentic evaluative scheme), and in the belief that one is doing something morally obligatory, right, or wrong. Now let me try to be more precise. I think one cannot be (directly) appraisable for unintentional action, though in some sense of 'free', such action may be freely performed, as one cannot exert volitional control over such action. But I prefer being cautious here, and propose a set of conditions, both necessary and sufficient, for a restricted range of ascriptions of appraisability: intentional actions that are, roughly, such that it is false that the agent who performs them has, through a series of past actions, deliberately and freely brought it about that she lacks volitional control over them at the time of performance. The principle (which has two subprinciples as constituents) is this:

Appraisability:

> BLAME: S is morally blameworthy for performing action, A, at time, t, if and only if (1) S intentionally does A at t; (2) S is a normative agent at t; (3) S's

evaluative scheme at t is authentic; (4) S exercises volitional control over A at t; (5) (i) S has an occurrent belief, or a dispositional one (that may well be a standard unconscious belief), BAW, that A is wrong (or that A is morally amiss), and (ii) S performs A despite entertaining BAW and believes (at least dispositionally) that S is performing A.

PRAISE: S is morally praiseworthy for performing action, A, at time, t, if and only if (1) S intentionally does A at t; (2) S is a normative agent at t; (3) S's evaluative scheme at t is authentic; (4) S exercises volitional control over A at t; (5) (i) S has an occurrent belief, or a dispositional one (that may well be a standard unconscious belief), BAR, that A is obligatory or right; (ii) S performs A while entertaining BAR and believes (at least dispositionally) that S is performing A; and (iii) S performs A for the reason that (or at least partly for the reason that) S believes (at least dispositionally) that A is the right or obligatory thing to do.

The following point, bearing on the range of actions governed by Appraisability, merits attention: I grant, of course, that under certain conditions a person can be deserving of blame or praise for some action (A) over which she lacks volitional control: the person could have willfully undertaken steps, over which she has volitional control, to see to it that she lacks volitional control over A, or to bring about A with the realization that she will lack volitional control over A, or that she will not be able to refrain from A-ing. Principle Appraisability is concerned with action with respect to which no such prior arrangements have been made.

Note, in addition, that Appraisability gives conditions for moral appraisability for *actions*. It does not address omissions or consequences of actions or omissions. However, I believe that it should be possible to work from this principle to arrive at others that deal with omissions and consequences. Consider, for instance, consequences that are event particulars. Event particulars are individuated more finely than event universals. Notably, the actual causal trajectory of an event particular, let's assume, is essential to that particular; if a different causal trajectory were to occur, a different event particular would occur. By way of an example, in a certain garden-variety Frankfurt-type case, Jones squeezes the trigger on "her own" and as a result brings about the event particular *Max's being shot*. Had Jones shown any signs of hesitation, Dark Demon would have intervened and caused Jones to squeeze the trigger, thereby ensuring that Jones brings about the event particular *Max's being shot*. But given its actual causal history, this event particular would have been a different one than the event particular that Jones brings about when she squeezes the trigger on her own. As a first stab in extending principle Appraisability to event particulars, I propose:

Appraisability(EP): If S is appraisable for action, A, and S believes that event particular EP will result from S's doing A, then S is appraisable for EP.

Appraisability(EP) requires considerable refinements. I simply offer it in illustration of how Appraisability itself might be exploited to uncover principles of appraisability for consequence particulars.

In the next few chapters, I intend to draw out some implications of Appraisability for various issues. I begin in chapter 11 by asking whether, besides moral blameworthiness and praiseworthiness, we can make conceptual sense of other varieties of appraisability like, for instance, legal or prudential blameworthiness or praiseworthiness; and if so, whether the conditions stated in principle Appraisability, with simple adjustments, also serve to capture necessary and sufficient conditions for these other varieties of appraisability. I will then move on in chapter 12 briefly to discuss the implications of principle Appraisability for what I call "intersocietal" attributions of blameworthiness. The issue here is this: people who are not part of a particular culture—"outsiders" relative to a culture—are frequently quick to attribute blame to a person within that culture for performing what the outsiders deem to be a morally heinous action. Are they right or is their attribution of blame mistaken? Third, in chapter 13, I revert to certain concerns about addicts: Are they morally appraisable for behavior that is, in some notable fashion, caused by their utilization of the drug to which they are addicted? Finally, I take up the old problem discussed by Plato and Augustine, among others, of whether we can be deserving of moral blame or praise for what we think, visualize, or imagine in our dreams.

ELEVEN

‡══‡

VARIETIES OF NORMATIVE
APPRAISABILITY

I. A DIVERSITY OF EVALUATIVE PERSPECTIVES
AND A PUZZLE

There is nothing out of the ordinary in the aged idea that a course of action is open to appraisal from many different evaluative perspectives. As examples, one can assess someone's act aesthetically, or legally, or from the point of view of etiquette, rational long-term self-interest, or morality. There is in addition to the wealth of evaluative perspectives, long-standing skepticism about whether evaluations deriving from any one perspective, like the moral perspective, "really" or "objectively" trump those deriving from any others; the concern here is one of "objective overridingness." So, for instance, if one legally ought to do something, but morally ought not to, we might wonder whether the moral prescription or the legal one is more "weighty" or "overrides" the other. The skepticism frequently goes hand-in-hand with different concerns, some more practical. Even if, for example, moral verdicts objectively override others like prudential or legal ones, there is the issue of which perspective (if any) is such that by following the prescriptions of that perspective, one's life would go best for one. Would, for instance, one's life go best for one were one always to follow the dictates of morality, or self-interest, or custom? There is, in addition, a third concern of which perspective or evaluative standpoint agents in fact *take* to be important in guiding their conduct. Regarding this third concern, I think it is sensible to suppose that no one standpoint—not even the moral one—enjoys any special position in the lives of most people. Reflecting on our day-to-day dealings with others, it seems natural to suppose that an agent in many or most situations is not wedded to any one evaluative perspective; one does not usually commit oneself to acting on or despite, for instance, moral considerations no matter what the situation in which one finds oneself. It seems, rather, that (at least in ordinary life) many of us reveal a flexibility in our values, taking moral considerations to be more important in some situations than, say, legal or prudential or aesthetic ones, but reversing our commitments in different situations. Thus, where Jenny the artist might take care for helpless children (a moral consideration) to trump a commitment to her artistic enterprises, she might not take some other equally compelling moral consideration to do so, like a contribution as a nurse to a crisis center after some natural catastrophe. It is, in light of such considerations as these, understandable that in arriving at first-person practical judgments about what to do—either in a *particular* situation, or perhaps much more rarely, across all situations—an agent may decide that though an action is morally obligatory, *she* ought all things considered not to perform that action, perhaps because (in that situation, or maybe across all situations) *she takes* prudential (or etiquettical, or aesthetic, or legal) prescriptions to trump moral ones when the two sorts of prescription commend different courses of action, or simply because she cares more about prudential prescriptions than she does about moral ones. Reflect on the following cases in which there is a twist: though the agents' all-things-considered judgments about what to do fail to line up with their moral judgments, they nevertheless end up akratically doing the moral thing. The cases set the stage for motivating a puzzle about appraisability.

In the first (call it "Architect"), Salima has settled on conducting her life in a way in which her true guiding principle is one of self-interest. She believes it does not really pay to be moral, and that she will be better off if she acts on the dictates of rational prudence. Assume that Salima is an architect heading an impressive team on an ambitious project. Designs and blueprints have been proposed, and after discussion the team has eliminated all but sets Alpha and Beta. Salima must now decide which set to implement. She keenly appreciates the fact that if Alpha (but not Beta) is implemented a park frequented by children from an orphanage will be destroyed. Suppose that after *lengthy* and *meticulous* deliberation, Salima correctly judges that she ought (prudentially) to implement Alpha-implementing Alpha would best serve her long-term self-interest. Assume, also, that Salima is aware that implementing Beta is the morally right thing to do. Assume, finally, that while still holding the judgment that it is best for her to implement Alpha, she capitulates to the requirements of morality, and decides to implement Beta. It appears that Salima is praiseworthy for doing what morality demands. But it also seems that there is a sense in which Salima is blameworthy for implementing Beta; she has acted, in the absence of reasons *she* regards as justificatory, against a consciously adopted principle—maximization of her long-term gains—that she believes ought (ideally) to guide all her decisions. She has freely and intentionally acted contrary to a carefully reasoned for-her, all-things-considered best judgment about what to do.

In the second case, given his strict and reasoned commitment to uphold the laws of the land, Alfredo accurately judges that despite having a moral duty to help Tony—who was framed by the head of a local crime family—to escape from prison, he legally ought not to help. Still, consciously holding the for-him, all-things-considered best judgment that he ought not to help, he gives in to morality, akratically assisting the condemned but innocent man to flee. In this case (call it "Mafisco"), there is a sense in which Alfredo is to be admired; he may even be morally praiseworthy for helping Tony to escape. But then, equally, it also seems that Alfredo is deserving of blame for assisting Tony to escape. After all, having thwarted his all-things-considered best judgment that principally derives from his respect for the law, Alfredo has failed to hold true to principles *he takes* as authoritative for action. In addition, Alfredo has simply broken the law.

We now have the makings of a philosophical riddle that owes its genesis to these theses about (moral) blameworthiness and (moral) praiseworthiness:

Blameworthy1 [Praiseworthy1]: An agent is morally blameworthy [praiseworthy] for performing an action only if it is (objectively) wrong [obligatory] for the agent to perform the action.

Blameworthy1—that one is morally to blame for an action only if it is wrong for one to perform that action—expresses a thesis identical to the one expressed by what I have previously called the "Objective View." On this view, moral blameworthiness is associated with objective wrongness; similarly, Praiseworthy1 associates praiseworthiness with objective obligatoriness.

Reconsider Alfredo's situation. Suppose Alfredo is deserving of both moral praise and blame for helping Tony escape. Then Praise1 entails that Alfredo's helping Tony to escape is obligatory, and Blame1 entails that his helping is wrong. But no action can be wrong *and* obligatory. Of course, a similar perplexity arises in Architect on the assumption that Salima is both praiseworthy and blameworthy for implementing Beta.

In what follows in this chapter, I first discuss solutions to this riddle according to which Salima, just like Alfredo, is either both morally blameworthy and morally praiseworthy for performing one and the same action, or is morally praiseworthy but *not* blameworthy for the relevant deed. I argue that these solutions fail. Then I sketch what I think is a much more natural and promising approach which builds on the idea that there are different sorts of normative appraisals, and that moral blame is simply one variety of "normative blame," and more generally, moral appraisability is simply one variety of normative appraisability. On this approach it turns out that Salima is morally praiseworthy but prudentially blameworthy for implementing Beta. This alternative approach, however, generates a puzzle of its own: Precisely what, if anything, do the varieties of blameworthiness have in common in virtue of which they are varieties of blameworthiness? Relying on the results obtained in chapter 9, I focus on one feature—an epistemic component of blameworthiness—and attempt to characterize one aspect of this component.

2. AN UNHAPPY SOLUTION

One resolution to the riddle seeks to preserve the intuition (if one has it) that in Architect and Mafisco the appropriate agent is both morally praiseworthy and morally blameworthy for performing the very same action. The solution unfolds in two stages. In the first, one attempts to show that Praiseworthy1 and Blameworthy1 are flawed; in the second, one replaces these principles with alternatives which (together with germane facts) do not entail the absurdity that an obligatory act is wrong.

I shall not here dwell at length on the first stage of the solution with which (as it should by now be patent) I am sympathetic. Indeed, in chapter 8, I argued against Blameworthy1 (the Objective View). I simply redirect attention to a pair of cases that motivate rejection of Blameworthy1 and Praiseworthy1, respectively. In Howser's Hell, Dr. Howser, wanting to do the very best for her patient, follows the course of treatment that all evidence within her reach indicates will result in a cure: she injects the patient with medicine A. Unfortunately, the diagnosis is incorrect. Administering A is the wrong treatment; it actually causes the patient's death. Had the good doctor only known better, she would have administered readily available medicine B, which would have safely cured the patient. Arguably, by giving A the doctor has done something (objectively) wrong—she has killed a patient. But the case lends strong support to the view that Howser is not morally to blame for giving A; in fact, it appears that she is deserving of praise for doing so as she did all she could in the circumstances for her patient. In Deadly's Defeat, Dr. Deadly injects her patient with medicine C with the intention to kill the patient. But again, this time to the good fortune of the patient, there has been a guileless error in diagnosis. Contrary to what Deadly believes, her patient is suffering from a disease that can only be cured by taking C. Giving C cures the patient completely. Although it is arguably obligatory for Deadly to inject her patient with C, it seems Deadly is to blame for the injection of this drug. The case motivates rejection of the view that blameworthiness is associated with objective wrongness in the manner expressed by Blameworthy1.

The second stage of the solution ties praiseworthiness to belief in what is obligatory, and blameworthiness to belief in what is wrong.[1] The guiding thought here is that in order to be blameworthy for performing an action, an agent must perform the action in light of the belief that the action is wrong. Comparably, an agent is praiseworthy for performing an action only if the action issues from the agent's belief that she ought morally to perform that action. The pertinent beliefs need only be dispositional and not occurrent. The proposed replacements for Praiseworthy1 and Blameworthy1 that pronounce acceptable results in the scenarios involving the doctors are these:

> Blameworthy2 [Praiseworthy2]: An agent is morally blameworthy [praiseworthy] for performing an action only if she performs that action in light of the belief that it is wrong [obligatory].

How do Blameworthy2 and Praiseworthy2 help with the riddle? Suppose we go along with the assumption that Alfredo is both morally blameworthy and praiseworthy for helping Tony escape. Then Praiseworthy2 and Blameworthy2 (in conjunction with germane facts) entail that Alfredo believes that it is wrong for him to help Tony escape, and that Alfredo believes that it is obligatory for him to help Tony escape. At least now the route is barred to the untoward conclusion that an act an agent morally ought to do is also one it is morally wrong for that agent to do.

The solution, however, is clearly an unhappy one. It escapes an absurdity by paying an excessive price: agents like Alfredo and Salima, the solution implies, suffer from acute irrationality vis-à-vis important moral concerns; they hold incompatible moral beliefs about specific incidents. But there is no good reason to believe that this need be the case at all. Indeed, reflection on Alfredo's predicament forcefully suggests that it belies the facts to presume that Alfredo believes both that his helping Tony to escape is morally wrong, and that his helping Tony to escape is morally obligatory. It is perfectly coherent to describe the case as one in which, possibly, Alfredo finds himself in a conflict situation precisely because he is cognizant of the fact that a moral judgment of his—that he ought to help Tony escape—is in conflict with an all-things-considered judgment of his that he ought not to help Tony escape.[2] But notice that this all-things-considered judgment is "informed" primarily by Alfredo's concern for *the law* and not morality; Alfredo believes that legal obligations trump moral ones. In light of this difficulty, it would be better to search for a happier solution.

A second resolution proposes that in cases of weakness of will in which the agent akratically does the right thing, the duplicity of the agent's wants, intentions, will, etc. make it the case that there is *some* sense in which he does not want, intend, or will to do what he does; and in such cases, because what the agent does is the right thing, his not wanting, or intending, or willing corrupts his behavior "on its subjective side." The agent's behavior here is subjectively morally corrupt as it is performed with the (morally) wrong intention. Since his act is subjectively morally corrupt, he is morally blameworthy for performing it. However, as the agent's action is in fact right, he is also morally praiseworthy for performing it in respect of having done the objectively right thing.

This proposed resolution, however, fails as well, and for the following reasons. Akratic action is uncompelled, intentional action that is contrary to the agent's consciously held all-things-considered best judgment (a first-person practical judgment). Cases of akratic action do, of course, involve motivational conflict. Salima's all-things-considered best judgment to implement Alpha issues, in part, from a desire to implement Alpha, but Salima also wants to do the morally right thing; she wants to implement Beta. As is typical in cases involving akratic behavior, it turns out that Salima's evaluative assessment of what is prudentially (and all things considered) best for her to do is misaligned with the motivational force of the desire to do what is prudentially best; the *competing* desire to do what is morally right has greater motivational clout (but a lower evaluative ranking). When the time comes to act, it is this latter desire that wins the day. It gives rise to an intention to do the right thing, which Salima then executes. By acting on this intention, however, Salima acts contrary to what is still her consciously held best judgment that she ought to implement Alpha. I take it that the following is unproblematic. One may judge that, all things considered, one ought morally to return a gold coin one happens upon, but may still *akratically* do what is prudentially best for one—pocket the coin. In this case, one intentionally pockets the coin, acting on the intention to do what is prudentially best, even though one acts contrary to one's best judgment. Analogously, when Salima akratically does what she morally ought to, she intentionally implements Beta, acting on an intention to do what is morally right (or obligatory) despite her consciously held best judgment. The first problem with the second proposed resolution now surfaces: granting that akratic action is intentional action involving motivational dissension, why suppose that when Salima akratically does the morally right thing, her action issues from a *morally* wrong intention? Surely not merely because Salima's act is generated by a desire that has, by Salima's own appraisal, a lower evaluative ranking than the desire to do the prudentially obligatory thing. After all, unlike Dr. Deadly, Salima does *not* act on base motivations; she *intentionally* implements Beta in light of the belief that she is doing the morally right thing. If anything, Salima's doing the right thing issues from an intention that is, in a sense, opposed to Salima's all-things-considered best judgment whose prescription is to do what is prudentially best. One might, at most, then suppose that Salima's doing the right thing issues from a prudentially wrong intention and *not* from a morally wrong one. But then why believe that this action of hers is subjectively *morally* corrupt and that she is *morally* to blame for performing it? The second problem should be obvious enough. The solution suggests that Salima is morally praiseworthy for implementing Beta in virtue of having done the objectively right thing. But the pair of cases involving incorrect diagnoses discussed above (and other considerations) seriously question the association of praiseworthiness with objective rightness. Hence, if Salima *is* praiseworthy for implementing Beta, it is not because she has done what is objectively right.

3. THE OVERRIDINGNESS OF MORAL CONSIDERATIONS

Here is a third proposed resolution which appeals to the view that, roughly, moral considerations are always overriding. More specifically, the *overridingness thesis* on which this resolution rests states that moral oughts (that is, obligations) always trump or override all other normative oughts (obligations) like prudential, legal, or etiquettical oughts, with the exception, perhaps, of an "all-encompassing plain ought," if there is such an ought. According to this thesis, if, as of some time, t, some agent, S ought morally to do A at t* (where t* may be identical to or later than t), and S ought (say legally) to do B at t*, but S cannot do both A and B at t*, then S plain ought to do A at t*. The phrase 'S plain ought to do A at t*' in the last sentence is meant to capture the idea that moral oughts take precedence, or are more "normatively significant," or override other oughts like legal ones. This overridingness thesis is to be distinguished from the superficially similar thesis that some agent takes moral oughts to override all other oughts (again with the exception of a plain ought if there is one).

Suppose the overridingness thesis is true. Then, the objection continues, although Salima may well be morally to praise for implementing Beta (as implementing Beta is what she morally ought to do, and she believes that she morally ought to implement Beta), she is *not* blameworthy in any normative sense of 'blameworthy' for failing to implement Alpha. And this is so as, really, there is only one bona fide sense of 'blameworthy', the moral sense, and Salima is not morally to blame for implementing Alpha. The defense for this last claim rests on the following considerations. We are familiar with the notion of prima facie obligations. According to W. D. Ross, although some obligation (or 'duty' to use Ross's terminology) may be a prima facie obligation (for some agent as of some time), it need not be an obligation or duty proper. Part of what motivates this view of Ross's is the idea that prima facie obligations come in degrees of stringency—some can be more stringent or weighty than others. Roughly, a Rossian normative theory states that some agent, S, ought (morally) to do A if and only if S's doing A is a prima facie obligation, and there is no alternative prima facie obligation which S could have done instead that is more stringent than S's doing A (see Ross 1930). On this theory, suppose all of S's alternatives (as of a time) are prima facies obligations. If one of these alternatives is S's duty proper, that is, if one amounts to what S all in *ought* to do, all the others are mere prima facie obligations, and nothing more. Further, appraisals of praise and blame are tied to obligations proper (and to wrongdoings proper), and not to prima facie obligations or to what is prima facie wrong: one is praiseworthy for doing something only if one believes that one is doing one's duty proper when one does that thing; and one is blameworthy for doing something only if one believes that one is doing something that is in fact wrong (and not merely prima facie wrong) by doing that thing. Analogously, suppose moral oughts override all other oughts—they are more stringent than all others. Then if S ought morally to do A at t*, and S ought (legally, say) to do B at t*, and S cannot then do both, S really has only one genuine obligation: to do A at t*. The other "obligation" to do B at t* carries no weight when it comes to appraisals of praise or blame. Hence, as Salima ought morally to implement Beta, and ought prudentially to implement Alpha, but cannot implement both, she has only one genuine obligation—to implement Beta. The other "obligation"—to implement Alpha—carries no weight in appraisals of praise or blame. It follows, then, that Salima is morally praiseworthy for implementing Beta but not blameworthy for failing to implement Alpha.

This proposed resolution suffers a fate analogous to the fate suffered by the ones already examined: it is undermined by severe difficulties. First, the overridingness thesis is controversial, to say the least. This thesis is a thesis about the relative import or status of the overall recommendations of normative standards like morality, prudence, the law, etc. Again, the concern here is this: in cases of conflict as when, for instance, one morally ought to do something, but prudentially refrain from doing that thing, what (plain) ought one to do? It appears that one cannot adjudicate such conflicts without appeal to some "all-encompassing" normative standard (the "plain ought standard") that evaluates the recommendations of morality, prudence, and all other "special" normative standards, and that arrives at a verdict about what the agent ought, overall, to do. The 'ought' in the last sentence, of course, does not express the ought of morality, or prudence, or for that matter, the ought of any *special* normative perspective diverse from the all-encompassing one; rather, the ought here is the most all-inclusive (plain) ought. The all-encompassing standard, were there one, would rank other special normative standards, like morality or prudence, in a non-question-begging way along a scale of normative significance. It is, however, doubtful whether there is any such all-encompassing standard, and, even if there is one, whether it will in fact deliver the verdict that morality is overriding.[3] As the overridingness thesis appears to imply that there is such a standard and that it rules that morality is supreme, there is reason to be suspicious about this thesis.

Second, even if we grant the overridingness thesis, it simply does not follow from the fact that when a moral obligation conflicts with some other obligation, the other obligation is not really an obligation (of some sort). Even on Ross's view, when a more stringent prima facie obligation conflicts with a less stringent one, the less stringent one remains a genuine prima facie obligation. Third, the assumption that when one's moral obligation, say, S's moral obligation to do A, conflicts with a second obligation of a different normative variety, like S's legal obligation to do B (in the sense that S cannot, at the relevant time, do both A and B), the obligation that is overridden "cannot carry any weight" in normative appraisals of praise or blame, is suspect if not outrightly false. For even if the overridingness thesis is true, one might deliberately shun moral constraints in favor of (let's suppose) prudential ones; one might consciously strive to ensure that one always conducts oneself in a manner that is conducive to one's long-term self-interest. Surely, one can assess this sort of agent morally, *and* in terms of whether she lives up to her consciously adopted prudential standards. We can ask whether she is deserving of (prudential) blame in light of doing something she takes to be prudentially wrong, *even granting the overridingness thesis*. Prudential standards (or legal, etiquettical, or aesthetic ones for that matter) are legitimate evaluative standards. The fact, if it is one, that moral obligations override all others cannot in any way affect the status of these other standards as bona fide normative standards, and as long as these standards play an appropriate role in what the agent does, the agent can be appraised, in light of these standards, on account of what he does. (Notice that on the Rossian view of what constitutes our moral obligations, if one of an agent's prima facie obligations in that agent's alternative set is more stringent than all others in that set, then that prima facie obligation is that agent's duty proper, and no other in the set can qualify as a duty proper. There is a relevant asymmetry when (let's suppose) a moral obligation trumps a prudential one: the moral obligation (given the overridingness thesis) overrides the prudential one, but even if it does, the prudential obligation that is overridden still qualifies as a genuine prudential obligation; overridingness here, unlike overridingness of prima facie obligations, fails to "alter" the normative status of what is overridden.)

A fourth way to resolve the puzzle is simply to jettison the judgments that the agent commanding attention in each of our cases is either both morally praiseworthy and morally blameworthy for executing the same action, or morally praiseworthy for executing one action (like implementing Beta) and not blameworthy (in any sense of 'blameworthy') for any other behavior (in the circumstances). I think this is a step in the right direction. It is entirely consistent with maintaining the elective that, for instance, though not *morally* blameworthy, Alfredo is indeed blameworthy in a rich and robust sense of 'blameworthy' for helping Tony escape, despite being morally praiseworthy for helping his friend escape. Or so I wish to urge.

4. TOWARD A BETTER SOLUTION

I am strongly partial to the view that Alfredo is blameworthy—not just causally, but rather "normatively" as I shall say—for helping Tony escape and that, similarly, Salima is *normatively* blameworthy for implementing Beta. I propose that moral blameworthiness is just one variety of "normative blameworthiness." When an agent is morally blameworthy for performing an action, he is normatively blameworthy for performing that action. But not all normative blameworthiness is to be equated with moral blameworthiness as Mafisco and Architect forcefully suggest. The failings (partly) in virtue of which Alfredo and Salima are to blame are not moral ones, and so they are not morally blameworthy for the relevant deeds. My suggestion is that Salima is deserving of prudential blame for implementing Beta, and Alfredo of legal blame for aiding his friend to escape, and that prudential blame and legal blame are types of normative blame.

Although I am unable to give an analysis of the concept of normative blameworthiness, I want to say a few things that will (hopefully) help focus our attention on the relevant concept. (For brevity, I omit discussion of normative praiseworthiness, though much of what I have to say in connection with explicating normative blameworthiness will also apply, with requisite amendments, to normative praiseworthiness.) The notion of normative blameworthiness is a generic one that has various species. A person can, for example, be morally or prudentially and so normatively blameworthy for doing something, or for intentionally failing to do something, or for the consequences of her intentional actions or omissions. Normative blameworthiness is concerned, preeminently, with a certain sort of appraisal of a *person*, and only derivatively with the appraisal of the person's behavior.[4] When a person is normatively blameworthy for performing an action, the blame in question is inward and not overt. Remember, overt blame includes the (outward) expression of blame by words, gestures, or actions. It frequently comprises things like overt rebukes, reproaches, snubbings, or grimaces. The inward nature of normative blame is revealed by the fact that a person can be deserving of such blame even in the absence of anyone else's being aware that he is so deserving.

Normative blameworthiness is intimately affiliated with what a person seriously cares about. More specifically, frequently (but not always) it is closely associated with normative standards a person thinks important and hence follows in guiding his life and conduct. And here I construe 'normative standards' in a liberal way. So, for instance, rules or norms of custom or tradition, or imperatives deriving from projects or ideals of deep importance to one's life, qualify as such standards. Further, for a set of dictates, or ideals, or rules to qualify as appropriate normative standards that "ground" normative appraisability, the standards must both guide and constrain behavior; they carry, in the person's life, a sort of authority. A person who accepts a set of standards as normative is motivated to act in accordance with those standards, believes that they provide reasons for action, and is disposed to have (appropriate) pro or con feelings or attitudes under various conditions. Often (but again not always), when an agent is normatively blameworthy for doing something, the agent does something she takes to be subpar, or below the cared-for normative standards on which she typically relies to arrive at practical judgments about what to do. As an illustration, in Architect Salima does something—she selects Beta—in violation of prudential standards to which she is committed and with which she identifies. She identifies with these standards insofar as she cares more for them than for others; it is to these standards that she would like her behavior to conform. Alfredo similarly identifies with legal standards in Mafisco. It is in virtue of the agent's having done something below par that it is frequently fitting in instances of normative blameworthiness for the agent to have negative feelings or attitudes (like regret, or remorse) toward herself, and for other parties to adopt appropriate negative attitudes toward her; but again, it is worth stressing that such feelings on the part of the agent or others are not essential to normative blameworthiness. It is also worth stressing that the guiding standards with which an agent identifies need not be moral. An agent may deliberately evade what she recognizes to be a moral obligation, and intentionally execute some alternative that she considers more significant, perhaps because it is the prudentially rational course of action, and because it is prudential standards to which she bears allegiance. Deliberate deviation from such standards may well leave the agent susceptible to blame, but the blame will not be moral.

The broad outlines of the fourth proposed solution to the puzzle about normative blameworthiness are now in place. Salima is morally praiseworthy but prudentially blameworthy for implementing Beta, and Alfredo is morally praiseworthy but legally blameworthy for helping Tony escape. As it stands, though, the solution is unsatisfactory as one is naturally inclined to probe deeper and inquire into the following. Suppose there are many varieties of blameworthiness and praiseworthiness: moral, prudential, etiquettical, legal, and so on. What makes them varieties of *blameworthiness*? Alternatively, under what conditions is a person normatively blameworthy for performing some action?

5. AN EPISTEMIC COMPONENT OF NORMATIVE BLAMEWORTHINESS

As we have noted, traditional and contemporary discussions of *moral* blameworthiness have revolved around two conditions: the epistemic condition, which is, roughly, the condition that one is morally blameworthy for performing an action only if one does not act in ignorance; and the control condition, which says, loosely, that one is morally blameworthy for an action only if one controls the action in an appropriate way. I have argued for a third "authenticity" condition: the evaluative springs of one's actions must be "truly one's own." I assume that an analysis of normative blameworthiness will also comprise (minimally) three broad conditions corresponding to the epistemic, control, and authenticity conditions of moral blameworthiness. Provisionally, I see little reason to believe that the control and authenticity conditions for varieties of normative blameworthiness other than moral blameworthiness will depart *substantially* from those of moral blameworthiness. But, *possibly*, with respect to some varieties of normative blameworthiness, there are important differences in the epistemic condition, as I shall attempt to argue in the remainder of this chapter.

Reflecting, first, on the epistemic condition for moral blameworthiness, I proposed in chapter 9 that moral blameworthiness is associated with what is frequently called "subjective moral obligation" or "subjective wrongness." [5] The idea here is that just as we should distinguish between believing that p and its being true that p, so we should distinguish between what one objectively ought (morally) to do (one's objective moral obligation) and what one thinks one objectively ought to do (one's subjective moral obligation). An agent S has a subjective moral obligation as of a certain time t to do action A at t* (t may or may not be identical to t*) if and only if S believes that as of t S ought to do A at t*. As a replacement for Blameworthy1, I suggested:

> ABlame5: An agent S is morally blameworthy for performing an action A only if (i) S has an occurrent or dispositional belief, BAW, that A is wrong (or morally amiss); and (ii) S performs A despite entertaining BAW and believes at least dispositionally that S is performing A. (Entertaining a belief involves *accessing* it in some way and not merely having it; one must in some fashion, perhaps even unconsciously, be cognizant of it.)

ABlame5 yields acceptable results in Dr. Deadly-like cases.

Some might, however, object that ABlame5 generates bizarre results in cases of this sort: suppose, brought up in a "tough" neighborhood, Roxy finds pilfering absolutely morally unobjectionable when she can pilfer and get away with it; she does not even dispositionally believe that she morally ought not to pilfer. Still, one might insist that there is something fundamentally right with respect to finding Roxy's pertinent beliefs about, and actions of, pilfering reprehensible. In addition, the objection continues, ABlame5 implies untenably that it would not be morally right to punish or to blame Roxy *overtly* for pilfering. So ABlame5 is unacceptable.

The objection is unpersuasive. Addressing its first concern, it is insensitive to the view that a person can be assessed morally in divergent ways, and being to blame is merely one such way. For example, we might agree that Roxy's acts of pilfering are contemptible, that she may be contemptible in light of the fact that she has done something morally amiss, and that many of her beliefs like those concerning pilfering are not morally laudable. We might also find that Roxy is to blame for failing to acquire appropriate beliefs about pilfering. But none of these moral evaluations is tantamount to an attribution of (inward) blameworthiness for Roxy's incidents of pilfering.

The objection's second concern, that ABlame5 implies it is not morally right to blame Roxy overtly for pilfering, rests on an instructive confusion. There is, as we have noted, a distinction between inward moral blameworthiness where an agent is, for example, deserving of blame, possibly, for having done something she takes to be morally wrong, and overt moral blaming where one can, for instance, censure someone for having done something morally wrong or for having done something one believes is morally wrong. While it is often true that inward blameworthiness goes hand-in-hand with overt censuring, sometimes the two diverge. In Roxy's case, for instance, it may well be morally right to censure Roxy for pilfering even though Roxy does not take pilfering to be wrong. Censuring Roxy might (in the circumstances) be the best thing to do, partly for the reason that it may get Roxy to amend her ways or deter her from pilfering again. In other cases, although the agent is deserving of moral blame for doing something, it may well be morally wrong to censure her for doing that thing. As an illustration, suppose Fraila is morally blameworthy for eating the pie, but censuring her for gobbling the pie would so upset her that she would fall seriously ill. Then, arguably, censuring Fraila for eating the pie would be something one morally ought not to do. We can now see that the objection's second concern regarding ABlame5 relies covertly on this principle, which is false:

> OvertMBlame: If S is morally blameworthy for performing A, then there is a moral obligation to censure S for performing A.

Taking our cue from ABlame5, it is tempting to generalize by proposing that each variety of normative blameworthiness is associated with subjective normative wrongness. More precisely, let's say that an action is normatively wrong if and only if it is wrong in light of a normative principle like a principle of rational prudence, or a principle of morality, or a principle of etiquette, or a legal principle. If the normative principle is a moral one, then acts in light of this principle will be morally right, wrong, obligatory, or gratuitous; if the principle is a legal one, then the principle (in association with relevant facts) will entail that an act is legally right, wrong, or obligatory (or perhaps gratuitous). I assume, merely to simplify discussion, that no agent can believe that an act is nonmorally normatively amiss without also believing that that act is nonmorally normatively wrong. The generalization in question can now be formulated in this way:

> NBlame1: An agent S is normatively blameworthy for performing A only if (i) S has an occurrent, or dispositional belief, NAW, that A is (objectively) normatively wrong; and (ii) S performs A despite entertaining NAW and believes (at least dispositionally) that S is performing A.

We can assess NBlame1 by examining various instantiations of it. I shall look at cases involving prudential, etiquettical, and legal obligation. Consider Architect first. Our verdict is that Salima is prudentially blameworthy for implementing Beta. NBlame1 yields acceptable results in this case: careful and correct deliberation persuades Salima that implementing Beta is not best for her, and she does implement Beta in light of the belief that implementing Beta is prudentially wrong. So we have some reason to believe that prudential blameworthiness is associated with belief in what is prudentially wrong. In addition, notice that the analogue of Blameworthy1 involving prudential obligation:

> PBlame: Agent S is prudentially blameworthy for performing action A only if it is prudentially wrong for S to perform A,

is highly suspect as the following example suggests. Victor, an investment broker, believes, just like Salima, that all his decisions should be made on the basis of the principle of rational prudence. Suppose Victor makes a careless investment judgment as a result of which a client of his loses a large sum of money. Thoroughly vexed with himself for having made the heedless decision, Victor wishes to punish himself, and he wants to do so by doing something he believes is prudentially wrong. He decides to invest a small portion of his own funds in scheme A rather than B on the good counsel that investing in A guarantees losses for the investor. Suppose he acts on wrong advice; it turns out that investing in A is best for him. Still, I submit that Victor is prudentially blameworthy for investing in A as he invests in A with the express intention of doing something he takes to be prudentially wrong, even though, unbeknownst to him, investing in A is (in the circumstances) prudentially obligatory. Since PBlame is false, we have additional grounds to believe that prudential blameworthiness is associated with belief in what is prudentially wrong.

Moving on to a case involving etiquettical obligation, suppose Kelly does something she takes to be etiquettically impermissible with the intention to upset her host; she burps loudly after the sumptuous meal. But not conversant with the etiquettical customs of her host, Kelly is unaware that burping after a festive meal is etiquettically obligatory. The burping signifies that the "burper" has thoroughly relished the meal, and is, moreover, a way of expressing thanks. Kelly's host nods and smiles amicably upon Kelly's sonorous burping. It appears that in this case Kelly *is* etiquettically blameworthy for burping in spite of having an etiquettical obligation to burp. So once again we have reason to reject the analogue of Blameworthy1 involving etiquettical obligation, and reason to accept the view that NBlame1 yields acceptable results when the sort of blameworthiness in question is etiquettical blameworthiness.

Finally, let's address cases concerning legal obligation. Suppose, for whatever peculiar reason, Alfredo (in Mafisco) does not harbor even the dispositional belief that assisting an innocent (but unjustly convicted) person to escape from prison is legally impermissible. The principle:

SLblame: An agent S is legally blameworthy for performing an action A only if (i) S has an occurrent, or dispositional belief, LAW, that A is legally wrong; and (ii) S performs A despite entertaining LAW and believes (at least dispositionally) that S is performing A,

sanctions the result that Alfredo is not (inwardly) legally to blame for helping innocent Tony to escape. One might, though, add that appropriate outward legal censure would be called for, or is justified, at least partly to uphold respect for the law. Consider, in addition, "Speedy." Thrilled with his new roadster, Enzio tears down the freeway at a speed he (quite appropriately) believes violates the limit. He takes himself to be doing something legally wrong, but he succumbs to temptation. Let's suppose, however, that that very morning, the limit on that stretch of freeway (in Montana!) was lifted. Here, Enzio mistakenly believes that he is betraying his "commitment" to the law, and hence if legal blameworthiness is associated with subjective (legal) obligation or wrongdoing, Enzio is legally culpable for racing down the road, despite having not violated any legal duty. Again it could be added that though Enzio is (inwardly) legally to blame, outward legal censure would be unjustified.

Some people, however, might find these results utterly unacceptable. Pretty clearly, they might claim, if one looks at the way "things really are" in the world, Alfredo *would* be legally blameworthy for helping Tony to flee, and Enzio would be *free* of any legal blame for speeding down the road. There is, they could insist, nothing like "inward legal culpability" and "outward legal culpability"; rather, there is just "plain legal culpability." On this view, SLblame is false, and hence, it will be declared, we have a clear counterexample against NBlame1 as legal blameworthiness is one variety of normative blameworthiness.

I am in the end, I think, unpersuaded by these claims, but let me explore another possibility. To foster discussion, simply grant that Mafisco presents a counterexample against NBlame1, and now ask: Why does it at least seem reasonable to associate moral, prudential, and etiquettical blameworthiness but *not* legal blameworthiness with belief in what is normatively wrong? Here is a proposal. I suggested above that from the fact that a person is morally blameworthy for performing some action, it does not follow that the person morally ought to be censured for performing that action; OvertMBlame, that is, is false. There is an alternative route to the conclusion that OvertMBlame is false. As we have seen, there are cases in which one is morally blameworthy for performing an action that one morally ought to perform. (We have emphasized that [among other things] it is such cases that lend credence to the view that moral blameworthiness is associated with subjective moral obligation.) Suppose (for *reductio*) that OvertMBlame is true. Then, in *all* such cases, there is a moral obligation to censure the relevant person for performing her moral duty. But this is manifestly *not* so; as we noted earlier there could, but *need* not, be any such obligation. So OvertMBlame is false.

Consider analogues of OvertMBlame involving prudential, etiquettical, and legal obligation:

> OvertPBlame [OvertEBlame] {OvertLBlame}: If S is prudentially [etiquetically] {legally} blameworthy for performing action A, then there is a prudential [etiquettical] {legal} obligation to censure S for performing A.

OvertPBlame and OvertEBlame, it appears, are false. Although Salima is prudentially blameworthy for implementing Beta, it may not be (prudentially) best for any party to censure her for implementing Beta. Similarly, although Kelly is etiquettically blameworthy for burping, it may not be etiquettically obligatory for anyone to censure Kelly for burping. But OvertLBlame, unlike these other two principles, seems plausible, or at least, it might so be claimed; it does seem true, it might be proposed, that if one is legally to blame for performing some action, there is a *legal* obligation to censure the person for performing that action. What might account for this supposed difference between OvertMBlame, OvertPBlame, and OvertEBlame on the one hand, and OvertLBlame on the other? When we reflect on cases in which a person morally ought not to be censured for performing an action A even though she is morally blameworthy for A-ing (and similarly for cases involving etiquettical and prudential obligation), we see that there would be no point in censuring the person; further, typically, *no* one would stand to benefit from the censuring. But matters are different, it might be suggested, when it comes to legal obligation. For a great many of our laws are designed specifically for the purpose of constraining behavior so that the *group* (or society) is better off. Legally censuring an individual who is legally to blame for doing something, even when that individual acts in ignorance, by, for instance, incarceration or leveling a fine, may not benefit the culpable party, but will, it might be claimed, typically benefit the group, by fostering respect for the law or serving as a specific or general deterrent.

On the supposition that OvertLBlame (but not OvertMBlame, OvertPBlame, or OvertEblame) is true, there is an explanation of why it may seem reasonable to suppose that, unlike moral, prudential, or etiquettical blameworthiness, legal blameworthiness is associated with objective normative wrongness. Recall that in Dr. Deadly's case the doctor is morally blameworthy for administering medicine C even though it is morally obligatory for the doctor to administer C. Suppose there were cases relevantly analogous to Deadly's in which an individual X were legally blameworthy for A-ing even though the individual had a legal obligation to A. Then, on the assumption that OvertLBlame is true, there would, in such cases, be a legal obligation to censure X for doing something that it is legally obligatory for X to do! Surely, it might be charged, this is preposterous. How could, for instance, respect for the law be upheld if it were generally known that one could be legally censured for doing one's legal duty? Hence, perhaps there cannot be cases in which (i) an individual is legally blameworthy for doing something and (ii) that individual has a legal obligation to do that thing or it is legally permissible for that individual to do that thing. This, is turn, points to the possibility that an individual is legally blameworthy for doing something only if it is legally wrong for her to do that thing. Legal blameworthiness would then be associated with objective and not subjective legal obligation.

It's worth noting that this entire line of reasoning, which is meant to secure the conclusion that legal blameworthiness is associated with objective legal obligation, rests on the view that OvertLBlame (the principle that if one is legally to blame for performing some action, there is a *legal* obligation to censure the person for performing that action) is true. The proposed rationale for this view is that legally censuring someone who is legally blameworthy for doing something will benefit society by fostering respect for the law, and by serving as a deterrent. But this rationale, I think, is questionable. To see this, suppose that, unbeknownst to Al, the normally reliable speedometer in his car is malfunctioning—it is off by 10 miles per hour; when the dial registers 65 m.p.h., Al is in fact doing 75 m.p.h. Checking his speed, though Al justifiably believes that he is within the limit, he is in fact exceeding it. On the "objective view" of legal blameworthiness, Al (I assume) is legally blameworthy for speeding. Hence, OvertLBlame, on the supposition that Al is blameworthy, implies that there is a legal obligation to censure Al. Suppose Al is stopped, issued a ticket, and fined. If the facts of the case are known, it seems improbable that such censure would foster *respect* for the law;

quite the contrary, in fact, is likely. Similarly, if the facts are known, it seems unlikely that such censure—censure for this sort of innocent error—would serve as a specific or general deterrent. In addition, it appears that the following is certainly plausible. Suppose Al goes to court to dispute the charge; the speedometer is checked, and the judge lets Al off. Then, even on the assumption that Al is legally blameworthy for speeding, there appears to be no legal *obligation* to censure Al; after all, he has been excused by the judge. A conditional conclusion, it now appears, is justified: I believe OvertLBlame is suspect, but *if* it is indeed true (contrary to what I have just suggested), then perhaps legal blameworthiness is associated with objective legal obligation, for the reasons proposed.

To forge ahead, speaking a bit permissively, let's say that each principle of "N blameworthiness" (like moral blameworthiness, prudential blameworthiness, legal blameworthiness, etc.) has a corresponding OvertNBlame principle. So, for instance, a principle of moral blameworthiness has OvertMBlame as its corresponding OvertNblame principle. I finally submit these principles of normative blameworthiness for consideration:

NBlame2: For any N blameworthiness principle whose corresponding OvertNBlame principle is false, an agent S is N blameworthy for performing action A only if (i) S has an occurrent, or dispositional belief, NAW, that A is N wrong; and (ii) S performs A despite entertaining NAW and believes at least dispositionally that S is performing A.

NBlame3: For any N blameworthiness principle whose corresponding OvertNBlame principle is true, an agent S is N blameworthy for performing action A only if it is N objectively wrong for S to do A.

So, for example, since OvertMBlame and OvertEBlame are false, NBlame2 implies that moral blameworthiness and etiquettical blameworthiness are associated with belief in what is morally wrong and belief in what is etiquettically wrong, respectively. Suppose OvertLBlame is true. Then NBlame3 implies that legal blameworthiness is associated with objective legal wrongness.

One can, it seems, accept both NBlame2 and NBlame3 even if one has qualms about whether OvertLBlame and other OvertNBlame principles are true.

6. GAUGUIN'S ADMIRABLE IMMORALITY

In a recent admirable piece, "Admirable Immorality," Michael Slote advances considerations against the "metaethical thesis that moral considerations are always overriding" (1983, p. 77).[6] Slote develops a case that he believes supports "the existence of immoral but admirable traits of character, of virtues (excellences) that run counter to morality" (1983, p. 77). I want to use this case (call it "Gauguin's Fate") to support my view that there are other varieties of appraisability besides moral appraisability.

In section 3 above, I introduced the overridingness thesis, which says that if, as of some time, t, some agent, S ought morally to do A at t* (where t* may be identical to or later than t), and S ought (say legally) to do B at t*, but S cannot

do both A and B at t*, then S plain ought to do A at t*. I said that the fundamental idea underlying this thesis is that moral obligations override all other
normative obligations (except perhaps "all-encompassing obligations," plain ought
obligations, that is, if there are any). Possibly, *Slote's* overridingness thesis (which
he targets for rejection) simply amounts to this same thesis. He does, after all, say
things like "we should reject the metaethical thesis that moral considerations are
always overriding." At other times, though, Slote offers different characterizations
of the overridingness thesis with which he wishes to take issue. For example, he
says:

> It is widely held that (sincere) moral judgments automatically override all other
> considerations that may occur to moral agents. But in recent years there have been
> some notable dissenters: Philippa Foot has argued forcefully that even those who
> care about right and wrong will sometimes put other considerations ahead of moral-
> ity without subsequent regret or remorse; and Bernard Williams has set out in fasci-
> nating detail some cases where a morally concerned individual might consider a
> given project to be of greater importance, for him, than all the harm to other people
> that that particular project entailed. (1983, p. 78)

This passage leaves the distinct impression that Slote's overridingness thesis is
really the thesis that some agents *may take* moral considerations (or obligations)
to override all other normative considerations (or obligations). In any event, I
shall construe Slote's remarks against the overridingness of morality as remarks
against the overridingness thesis as I have construed it.

Slote calls into question the overridingness thesis by (among other things)
developing one of Bernard Williams's examples involving a somewhat fictionalized
Gauguin. He says that he will also extend this example of Williams "to show . . .
that if (appropriate) moral judgments are *not* automatically overriding, then morality need not totally constrain the personal traits we think of as virtues, and
there may actually be such a thing as admirable immorality" (1983, p. 78).

Slote summarizes Gauguin's Fate in this way:

> We are all to a greater or lesser extent familiar with the fact that Gauguin deserted
> his family and went off to the South Seas to paint. And although many of us admire
> Gauguin, not only for what he produced and for his talent, but also for his absolute
> dedication to (his) art, most of us are also repelled by what he did to his family.
> . . . I believe that we can persuade ourselves of the wrongness of that desertion and
> we can do so without losing our sense of admiration for Gauguin's artistic single-
> mindedness. Single-minded devotion to aesthetic goals or ideals seems to us a virtue
> in an artist; yet this trait, as we shall see, cannot be understood apart from the
> tendency to do such things as Gauguin did to his family, and so is not—like daring
> or indeed like Gauguin's own artistic talent—merely 'externally' related to immoral-
> ity. Here, then we may have admirable immorality in the intended sense of our
> discussion. (1983, p. 80)

A number of features of Gauguin's Fate deserve emphasis. First,

> Gauguin's passionate devotion to his project did not simply make it more likely that
> he would mistreat his family; rather, it is criterial of having a passion that incompati-
> ble impulses, concerns, desires, tend to give way to it, that one is, in effect *driven* by

the passion. Someone passionately, single-mindedly, devoted to art can be expected, among other things, to give less than usual weight to his own safety, to prudence (Gauguin, travelling in days of comparative unsafety, is perhaps a good example of such an attitude). And by the same token, the case for artistic passion may be thoroughly undercut if an artist isn't willing to slight the welfare of others, even of his own family, in its interest. So it seems a condition of Gauguin's recognizable possession of (admirable) artistic single-mindedness that we not imagine him (more or less successfully) arguing himself out of the remorse it would be natural for any moral being to feel in such circumstances; and yet if Gauguin ought to feel remorse, it is for making a choice endemic to the very passionateness with which he embraces his artistic goals. (1983, p. 82)

Second, Gauguin's Fate is "a case where the essential tendency to particular wrongdoing does *not* seem morally justifiable as part of a larger pattern" (1983, p. 91). Slote's point seems to be that Gauguin's desertion (in Gauguin's Fate) is not, for instance, an act Gauguin undertook to secure a greater good, like greater overall happiness or utility.

Third, it appears "to be a condition of our fullest admiration for Gauguin's passion that Gauguin take morality and his family seriously enough to feel concern and remorse about what he did" (1983, p. 102).

Finally, Slote proposes that "the passion we admire in . . . Gauguin is directed towards larger, impersonally valuable goods. . . . [H]igh admiration for Gauguin's passion in part depends on conceiving him as passionately devoted to the realization of a certain project, rather than to the advancement of his career or reputation. For only thus will his passion, again, seem directed towards something publicly, impersonally, valuable that people can benefit from" (1983, pp. 102–3).

Slote, I believe, makes a cogent case for the view that Gauguin's desertion of his family was morally wrong, and Gauguin believed that it was so. (I am, though, skeptical about whether any of this impugns the overridingness thesis.) I want to propose that Gauguin's Fate also lends credibility to the position that there is something like a "project-oriented ought," which I take to be partly definitive of a normative standard in the way in which the ought of morality is partly definitive of moral standards.

Pondering Gauguin's case, it seems fairly obvious that the project-oriented ought (the "PO-ought" as I shall abbreviate) is not to be conflated with the prudential ought. As Slote suggests, driven by his passion for art, Gauguin pays less-than-called-for attention to his own health or safety. Gauguin is similar in this respect to numerous novelists, sculptors, composers, poets, or great scholars. In like manner, some spectacularly successful (and not so spectacularly successful) business persons, politicians, athletes, or academicians, seeking to accomplish their goals, give less than normal weight to their own well-being. It appears, in addition, that the PO-ought is not the moral ought. For consider the following. Extending the Kantian principle, I believe that if one normatively ought to do something (for instance, if one prudentially ought to care for one's health), then one can do that thing. Suppose Gauguin PO-ought to undertake the project of developing his artistic talents. Then, given the 'ought' implies 'can' principle, he can undertake this project. Now consider another deontic principle ("Prerequisites"): if S cannot do A without doing B (say for example, out of physical neces-sity), and S can refrain from doing B, then, if S ought to do A, then S ought to do B. Suppose Gauguin PO-ought to undertake the project of developing his artistic talent, but he can't do so unless he deserts his family. Then Prerequisites validates the inference that Gauguin PO-ought to desert his family. If Slote is right, however, Gauguin ought morally *not* to desert his family. Hence, the moral ought is clearly distinct from the PO-ought. Further, it should be pretty apparent that the PO-ought is to be distinguished from the legal, or etiquettical, or aes-thetic ought.

Like other normative standards such as moral or legal ones, the project-oriented normative standard both guides and constrains behavior. In addition, just as a person who endorses or follows a moral standard is motivated to act in accor-dance with it, believes that it provides a reason for action, and is disposed to have certain feelings and attitudes in certain situations, so a person who endorses a project-oriented normative standard is motivated to act in accordance with that standard, takes that standard to supply a reason for action, and may well be dis-posed to have various positive or negative feelings or attitudes under various con-ditions. Lack of discipline required to undertake one's project may, for instance, result in one's feeling despair or (self-directed) resentment.

Should there be a PO-ought, then *an agent* can be appraised on account of her conduct in relation to the project-oriented normative standard. As an illustration, we might plausibly suppose that Gauguin is project-oriented praiseworthy for un-dertaking his project to develop his aesthetic talent; moreover, we may credibly suppose that he is project-oriented praiseworthy for deserting his family: he had to fight powerful moral inclinations to resist desertion, and he did desert in light of the belief that it was his project-oriented "obligation" to do so. However, it plainly seems that Gauguin is morally to blame for his desertion. Gauguin's Fate, then, provides further reason to believe that there are varieties of normative blame and praise.

7. CONCLUSION

Reverting to one of the cases—Architect—that generated the original riddle about normative blameworthiness, it appears that Salima is both deserving of praise and blame for performing the very same action. How can this be so (in this case)? Other conditions of normative blameworthiness (and normative praisewor-thiness) being satisfied, a more revealing explanation than the one adumbrated in section 4 is forthcoming if we suppose, firstly, that Salima has an occurrent belief that selecting Beta is morally obligatory, and that she does intentionally select Beta in light of the belief that she morally ought to select Beta. On this supposi-tion, a consequence of NBlame2 is that Salima is deserving of moral (and so normative) praise for selecting Beta. Suppose, secondly, that Salima also has an occurrent belief that selecting Beta is prudentially wrong, but still selects Beta, and realizes that she is so doing, despite entertaining this belief. Then NBlame2's verdict is that Salima too is deserving of prudential (and hence normative) blame for selecting Beta. This is a paradox-free resolution to the riddle (one that is, with appropriate adjustments, applicable to Mafisco as well) as it is unproblematic that we frequently perform actions with multiple intentions. I may, for instance, donate to charity with the intention of doing what I believe is my moral duty by so donating, and with the intention of allaying some of my guilt for not having donated before.

Lastly, consider a variation of Architect. Suppose Salima still judges that, all things considered, she ought (prudentially) to select Alpha. Suppose Salima acts akratically; against her better judgment, she selects Beta with the intention of doing what she takes to be her moral duty by selecting Beta. But suppose that in this variation of Architect, it is false that Salima selects Beta in light of the belief that selecting Beta is prudentially wrong; we can assume that she does not select Beta with the intention of doing what is prudentially wrong. Then, though morally praiseworthy for selecting Beta, Salima would not be prudentially blameworthy for selecting that set of plans (given NBlame2). We might still feel that all is not well here. After all, Salima *has* acted against normative principles she takes to be guiding for action. I agree that there is something amiss here. I suggest that Salima has compromised her "decisional" autonomy; she has failed to translate into action a decision that stems from principles of rational prudence with which she identifies. But it would be wrong to infer from any of this that Salima is prudentially blameworthy for compromising her autonomy. For she does not act with the intention of doing anything she takes to be prudentially wrong; nor, of course, does she act with the intention of compromising her autonomy.

TWELVE

BLAMEWORTHINESS, CHARACTER, AND CULTURAL NORMS

1. THE ISSUE

When exploring the epistemic dimension of moral appraisability, I argued against any conceptualization of this dimension which entails that a person is morally blameworthy for performing an action only if that action is in fact wrong. I have suggested that blameworthiness is closely affiliated with an agent's own perceptions about what is right or wrong. As I see it, an agent is blameworthy for performing an action only if she believes (at least dispositionally) that her action is wrong (or morally amiss), and her belief that the action is wrong (or amiss) plays an appropriate role in the etiology of that action. One of my primary aims in this chapter is to motivate the view that this epistemic condition, together with certain facts about the genesis of our moral beliefs, has the following consequence. A person who engages in behavior condoned by the norms of his culture, but which people outside his culture find morally objectionable, may well not be deserving of blame for that behavior, even though that behavior may be morally wrong.

I proceed as follows. I first adumbrate a case in which a person from one cultural tradition performs an act that is morally sanctioned by the norms of her culture, but which "outsiders" relative to her culture—that is, persons who are not members of that culture—find reprehensible. Indeed, the outsiders may well hold her blameworthy for performing the act. Next, I summarize an attractive

Aristotelian view of blameworthiness, recently defended by Lloyd Fields, which, if correct, would validate the outsider's judgment that the "insider" is in fact blameworthy for her action. Third, I argue that Fields's view is unacceptable on at least two counts: the connection it attempts to forge between character and moral appraisability is problematic, and it relies on the questionable condition that blameworthiness is associated with what is in fact wrong. Lastly, I indicate how tying blameworthiness to one's perceptions about what is right or wrong has deflationary results when it comes to various "intercultural" attributions of blameworthiness.

2. FORBIDDEN LOVE

Consider this case (call it "Forbidden Love"). Imagine a society whose culture and traditions uphold a caste system. There are various classes, the top occupied by the Rulers and the bottom by the Lows. The class of which one will be a member for the duration of one's life is ordained at the time of one's birth; nativity in a class fixes one's position in that class. The Lows are barred from holding certain offices, like administrative ones; indeed, they are confined to performing menial duties in the service sector of the complex society. Marriage among members of the Lows and the Rulers is strictly taboo. The deeply entrenched cultural values sanction these and various other discriminatory practices against the Lows. Suppose Seth, a Low, loses his heart to Smita, the daughter of a Ruler. Although attracted by him, Smita shuns Seth's advances. In accordance with her cultural norms, she has Seth flogged for his "impudence." A proud member of her class, she sees nothing wrong in so disciplining Seth; indeed, she is loyal to, and respects, the cultural tradition that would brand her failure to chastise Seth's approaches as morally unacceptable. Or, to vary the case a bit, we may suppose that Smita fully intends to do what she believes is right by conforming to the dictates of her cultural norms, but she has to overcome temptation to refrain from seeing to it that Seth is punished. Smita has then done what she takes to be her moral duty despite inclination to do otherwise.

Forbidden Love elicits or would elicit a ready and predictable reaction from many who are not part of that culture: Smita's seeing to it that Seth is whipped is disparaged, by many outsiders, as being morally wrong; perhaps Smita (herself) is discredited as being morally reprehensible in light of her treatment of Seth; and, most importantly for our purposes, Smita is regarded as being to blame for ensuring that Seth is flogged.

If Smita is thought to be morally blameworthy for this bit of behavior, precisely why is this so? One response lies implicit in this sort of effusion: "Smita did something terribly wrong; and had she been thinking clearly, she would have realized her transgression. In addition, her treatment of Seth is indicative of a morally bad attitude. Moreover, her morally bad attitude towards the Lows exemplifies not just some passing whim, but an aspect of the kind of person she is; she looks down upon the Lows." This common type of response finds theoretical support in the account of blameworthiness defended by Fields (Fields 1994).

3. FIELDS'S ACCOUNT OF BLAMEWORTHINESS

Fields proposes that a person's *acceptance* of moral principles is a constituent of her character; and a person who accepts morally bad principles has a defect of character. Further, he holds that if a person with a defect of character performs a wrong action which issues from her character, then she is to blame for that action. To elaborate, Fields suggests that if a person accepts a principle as a moral principle, then (i) he is motivated to act in accordance with it; (ii) he thinks the principle supplies a reason for action that ought to take precedence over non-moral considerations; and (iii) he is disposed to experience certain emotions and to have certain attitudes in certain situations (1994, pp. 401–2). For instance, if one regards the betrayal of trust as morally reprehensible, one will disapprove of someone guilty of such betrayal. Fields then relates the acceptance of moral principles to character in the following fashion. He suggests that to judge correctly a person's character, we must take into account the motives from which she acts. A person who performs outwardly benevolent actions may not *be* benevolent as her actions may be motivated by purely self-interested considerations (1994, p. 405). In addition, to judge rightly a person's character, Fields says, we must also take into consideration her attitudes and emotions (1994, p. 405). And finally, a correct attribution of character traits to an individual, Fields claims, must take into account what that individual regards as prima facie justifying reasons for doing or avoiding something, and the relative weights that these reasons have for her (1994, p. 405). Fields then recommends that as a person who accepts a moral principle is motivated to act in accordance with it, regards it as providing overriding reasons for action, and is disposed to experience certain emotions and have specific attitudes in specific situations, *and* as these factors are all revealing of a person's character, a person's acceptance of moral principles is a constituent of her character (1994, p. 406).

Next, Fields relates moral responsibility to character. He proposes:

> F1: "To say that someone is morally responsible for a morally wrong action is to say that he is morally blameworthy on account of his having performed that action" (1994, p. 407)

and:

> F2: "To say that he is blameworthy is to say that it is right or correct or justified to blame him" (1994, p. 407).

Fields carefully distinguishes verbal blame which is a type of overt blame, from attitudinal blame, where "To blame [attitudinally] someone is to disapprove of him on account of something that he has done or has omitted to do" (1994, p. 407). Attitudinal blame amounts, more or less, to what I have called "inward blame." It is the concept of attitudinal blame that is operative in F1 and F2. Finally, Fields proposes that:

> [I]t is a necessary condition of [attitudinally] blaming someone that one should believe that his action or omission is a sort of action or omission that is wrong; it is

also necessary that one should believe that his action or omission indicated a morally bad attitude or a morally bad absence of an attitude. And one is right or correct or justified in blaming a person only if such beliefs about that person are right, correct or justified. But while having the beliefs in question is necessary for blaming a person they are not sufficient. In addition, one must [correctly] believe that the morally bad attitude, or morally bad absence of an attitude, that one thinks a person's offending behaviour signifies, exemplifies some aspect or other of his or her character. (1994, pp. 408–09)

I take Fields to be committed to this principle:

F3: One is right or correct or justified in (attitudinally) blaming a person, S, for S's action or omission, A, if and only if one believes correctly that (a) A is the sort of action that is wrong; (b) A indicates a morally bad attitude or a morally bad absence of an attitude; and (c) the morally bad attitude, or the morally bad absence of the attitude A signifies, exemplifies some aspect of S's character.[1]

4. BLAMEWORTHINESS AND CHARACTER

A preliminary evaluation of F3 reveals that Fields overlooks an important distinction between conditions under which it is right or justified for some party to blame some other person for performing some action, and the correct conditions under which a person is (attitudinally) blameworthy for performing some action. On good but ultimately false evidence, a person may be justified in believing that some party is to blame for an action even though the party is not culpable. This defect is easily remedied by amending F3 so that the modified account (F4) now specifies that S is blameworthy for performing A if and only if A is wrong, A indicates a morally bad attitude (for brevity, I drop reference to the absence of a morally bad attitude), and the morally bad attitude A indicates manifests some aspect of S's character.

Is Fields's view that blameworthiness for an action indicative of a morally bad attitude requires the attitude to be revealing of some feature of the agent's *character* correct? Fields's first defense for this view rests on the presumed cogency of certain examples:

[S]uppose that someone who is normally amiable and gentle . . . is suffering from a very bad toothache. . . . [A]n acquaintance of his meets him and seeks to engage him in conversation. He rebuffs the acquaintance and continues on his way. . . . [T]he rebuff indicates impatience and lack of consideration towards the acquaintance. But if this state of mind could be explained entirely in terms of the agent's very bad toothache and as having nothing to do with his character, then the agent is not blameworthy for his behaviour. Again, suppose that a person . . . agrees to be a subject of hypnotism. While the subject is in an hypnotic trance, the hypnotist suggests to him that after he has been awakened . . . he will feel inclined to snatch the handbag of a lady . . . and will act on this inclination. . . . [T]he hypnotist's post-hypnotic suggestion proves to be effective. . . . In running off with a lady's handbag, the volunteer shows disregard for her right to her possessions. But he is nevertheless not morally blameworthy since this disregard was induced by post-hypnotic suggestion and had nothing to do with the character of the volunteer, who is known to be an honest man. (1994, p. 409)

Fields's position is that as in either example the troubling bit of behavior (or the pertinent bad attitude) has nothing whatsoever to do with the agent's character, the agent is not blameworthy for that bit of behavior. However, there is an alternative explanation of why the agents may not be deserving of blame: in either example, it is arguable that the agents lack the kind of *control* required for moral appraisability for actions. Regarding the first example, suppose that the agent could have—perhaps with some difficulty—mustered control and been polite. Then it seems that, despite his toothache, he *would* have been blameworthy for his rebuff. Surely, the mere fact that a person finds it difficult (in otherwise mundane circumstances) to perform a task he is capable of performing is insufficient to subvert appraisability. Suppose, however, that the agent was so overwhelmed by the pain, that—given his physical and psychological constitution—he could not but be irascible. Then we would not want to hold him morally appraisable, for it seems that he would, in the circumstances, not be in control of his action: his action would not be one over which he exercises volitional control. Similarly, as the volunteer in the second example acted on what was presumably an irresistible posthypnotic suggestion, he lacked "appraisability-grounding control"—volitional control—over his behavior.[2]

It appears to me that even an action that issues from an agent's character may be one over which that agent lacks appraisability-grounding control, and it is this lack of control that ultimately explains why the agent is not morally appraisable (if she is indeed not appraisable) for her behavior in cases in which the epistemic and authenticity conditions are satisfied. Reconsider this case: imagine that Poppy has no qualms whatsoever about taking a potent drug; indeed, she has reflected carefully on her drug-taking habit, and has decided (on her own) that she wants to be the sort of person who indulges. Suppose that on a certain occasion she finds herself with a desire to inject herself with the narcotic. Unbeknownst to her, her desire for the drug is now irresistible. She calmly injects herself, behaving just as she would have, had her desire not been irresistible. Poppy's taking the drug is an action consonant with her character, but she may well *not* be morally appraisable (on this occasion) for taking the drug. After all, the desire to take the drug is not responsive to Poppy's practical reasoning and so beyond her control: had deliberation resulted in Poppy's wanting that she act on a desire not to take the drug, her deliberation would have failed to bring it about that that desire, and not the desire or urge to indulge, be effective. One might grow accustomed to certain practices, or simply fall into the habit of doing various things. Moreover, one may endorse these practices or habits; endorsement or not, though, in the absence of one's relevant behavior being responsive to one's practical reasoning, one will have lost appraisability-grounding control over such behavior.

Fields's second defense to secure the connection he believes obtains between appraisability and character turns on the view that attributions of moral appraisability to individuals for their behavior presupposes that character traits are, in general, relatively stable. Fields says:

[I]magine that as a result of some arcane cosmic change people come to vary in character, in an attenuated sense of . . . 'character', from one day to the next. So, for example, a person who is greedy one day is not greedy the next. In this situation, continuity of memory and spatio-temporal continuity may be regarded as jointly sufficient criteria of personal identity; but the fluctuating nature of 'character traits' would preclude the attribution of moral responsibility to individuals. (1994, pp. 409–10)

Again Fields's musings are contentious. Let's fill in the details of the case in two different ways. Assume, firstly, that (in the "flux world") one can recognize and predict character shifts so that one can ascertain, say, upon awakening in the morning, what sort of character one will have on that day. If a person finds such predictable character shifts unobjectionable and perhaps even desirable, she may still be morally appraisable for her behavior, and for these reasons: assume that a person's behavior on her "greedy day" would be type-wise indistinguishable from her behavior on that day were she not in the world in which character traits fluctuated but in a world in which she were simply greedy; she would engage in the same sort of practical deliberations, she would access the same type of deliberative information, her actions would have the same kind of etiology, and so on. As she would be appraisable for (at least some) of her actions in the latter world, and her behavior in this world would mirror, in the manner indicated, her behavior in the flux world, one could arguably maintain that she *would* be morally appraisable for some of her actions in the flux world. Assume, secondly, that character shifts in the flux world are entirely random, and that one would not want to be the victim of such shifts. Then, arguably, one would not be appraisable for one's actions as they issue from actional elements (like dispositions to act in certain ways under certain circumstances) with respect to which one is not, roughly, *autonomous:* one has not acquired any of them under one's own steam. In this case, then, it would be considerations having to do with *how* one acquires the various springs of one's actions, and not character per se, that would explain why one is not morally appraisable for one's actions.[3] To crystallize this point, compare this second scenario to relevantly analogous Psychogen in which Jenny is globally manipulated. Via psychosurgery, Mad Max transforms Jenny (in the absence of her knowing anything about the transformation) into a psychological twin of Jim. The two scenarios are relevantly similar as, in both, the agent's characters are "globally" transformed and the agent's are not in any position to predict the transformation. In Psychogen, when Jenny recovers from the surgery, she has no suspicions whatsoever that she has fallen victim to Max. She picks up the morning paper, looks over some columns, makes a brilliant investment decision to help out a needy friend of hers, and then executes that decision. It appears that Jenny is not praiseworthy for her deed, and she is not as she is a victim of global manipulation: she is no longer self-directing. In the flux world in which the agent's character traits randomly shift around, the agent's predicament is appropriately like Jenny's: both are victims of a sort of global manipulation, and hence both are not appraisable for their subsequent actions.

I conclude that Field's attempt to bridge a connection between blameworthiness and character leaves plenty to be desired.

5. BLAMEWORTHINESS AND WRONG ACTION

A second problem with F4, central to the objectives of this chapter, revolves on its entailment that a person is morally blameworthy for performing an action only if that action is in fact objectively wrong. In other words, F4 presupposes the Objective View. The property of objective wrongness, as I explained, contrasts with that of subjective wrongness, where an agent's act is subjectively wrong if and only if the agent believes that that act is wrong. Further, as additionally noted, the distinction between objective and subjective wrongness (and similarly, objective and subjective obligation) parallels the distinction between believing that something is so, and that thing's being so.[4] Interestingly, outsiders' responses to cases like Forbidden Love also serve to underscore the objective wrongness of the relevant action. For example, the outsider may claim that treating a person in the manner in which Smita did—her ensuring that Seth is punished—for losing his heart to another is, from a more rational, objective, and perhaps culturally neutral perspective, morally wrong. It is important to this response, if it is to carry any weight, that the perspective in light of which Smita's act is deemed wrong is epistemically privileged; it is supposed to be the correct or justified perspective. Furthermore, the response assumes that Smita knows (or ought to) know that her treatment of Seth, given this perspective, is wrong. (Relevantly, like Smita's case, it is frequently said of the former slave owners in the southern United States that, despite their beliefs about slavery, from a distanced impartial perspective, they knew [or ought to have known] that they were doing wrong by enslaving others.) But as knowledge entails truth, the outsider's response, just like Fields's F4, assumes that the pertinent actions are (objectively) wrong.

The Objective View, however, as I have argued is seriously flawed. Since F4 entails this view, there is sound reason to reject F4. As a replacement for the Objective View, I have defended the following principle:

> ABlame5: S is morally blameworthy for performing A only if (i) S has an occurrent or dispositional belief, BAW, that A is wrong (or morally amiss), and (ii) S performs A despite entertaining BAW and believes (at least dispositionally) that she is performing A.

Now let's trace some consequences of ABlame5 for Forbidden Love.

6. BLAMEWORTHINESS AND CULTURAL NORMS

I begin by reiterating the view of intentional action presupposed in this work. I said that deliberative intentional action involves (1) some psychological basis for evaluative reasoning; (2) a practical judgment made on the basis of such reasoning that recommends a particular course of action; (3) an intention or decision formed, acquired, or made on the basis of that judgment; and (4) an action executing that intention or decision. To elaborate 1, I proposed that an agent's deliberations that issue in a practical judgment about what to do involve the assessment of reasons for or against action by appeal to an *evaluative scheme* of the agent's. An agent's evaluative scheme, I suggested, comprises: (a) normative standards the agent believes ought to be invoked in an assessment of reasons for action, or beliefs about how the agent should go about making choices; (b) the agent's long-term ends or goals deemed worthwhile or valuable by the agent; (c) deliberative principles the agent uses to arrive at practical judgments about what to do or how to act; and (d) motivation to act on the basis of the normative standards in a and goals in b using the deliberative principles in c. By utilizing one's evaluative scheme, one can arrive at all things considered judgments about what to do or how to act in particular circumstances.

Focusing on constituent a, for many if not all of us, several if not all of the normative standards or elements of such standards, on which we rely to appraise reasons for or against courses of conduct, ultimately owe their origin to the norms embedded in the culture in which we are situated. It is these cultural norms that the multitude of us internalize during our formative years, and which will later exert a powerful influence on how we experience the world and on how we deal with the never-ending barrage of decisions we are required to make to cope with the daily business of living. Reinforcement to conform to the cultural norms comes from sundry directions: our families, religious institutions, educational facilities, peer pressure, and the general social milieu in which we find ourselves all, to one degree or another, play their role. I hypothesize, then, that a significant array of our normative beliefs—including beliefs about what is morally right and wrong—derive in the end from our cultural norms. Cultural traditions also frequently exert commanding leverage on the long-term goals one deems worthwhile pursuing, partly by imposing fierce loyalties. They channel our lives into certain directions by making salient various options and downplaying or never revealing others. With loyalty or allegiance comes motivation. Smita, for example, accepting her cultural norms, is motivated to uphold the age-old cultural practices of her society.

Reconsider, now, Smita's treatment of Seth. Given the considerations recorded above regarding the genesis of one's beliefs about what is normatively right or wrong, we may assume that Smita's moral beliefs ultimately stem, in large measure, from her cultural norms. As the norms of her culture morally sanction the sort of treatment she ensures Seth receives for his advances toward her, Smita believes, in light of the influence these norms exert on her moral beliefs, that she is doing no wrong by seeing to it that Seth is punished. But then the condition registered in ABlame5 for being to blame is *not* satisfied; the state of affairs *Smita's ensuring that Seth is punished* is not grounded in any belief of Smita's that she is doing wrong by ensuring Seth's chastisement. We end up with the deflationary result that Smita is not to blame for treating Seth in a manner that would appear reprehensible to many who are not part of Smita's culture.

Reflecting on the implications of ABlame5 for Forbidden Love, some may believe that ABlame5 commits me to a fundamental sort of relativism about morality—the sort of relativism, for instance, advanced by Gilbert Harman (1977). In very broad strokes, Harman defends a Humean tacit convention theory of morality. He says:

> There is a convention in Hume's sense when each of a number of people adheres to certain principles so that each of the others will also adhere to these principles. I

adhere to the principles in my dealings with others because I benefit from their adherence to these principles in their dealings with me and because I think that they will stop adhering to these principles in their dealings with me unless I continue to adhere to the principles in my dealings with them. (1977, p. 103)

Further, Harman theorizes that moral obligations and duties depend on conventions of this sort. He notes that such Humean conventions can vary across societies or cultures, and as an illustration, he presents (among others) the following example:

We have a tacit convention in our society that we will respect each other as people. We will, in Kant's phrase, "treat people as ends.". . . Furthermore, there are various conventional forms in which we have come to express our respect and we have therefore come to see it as demeaning to human dignity if persons are not treated according to these conventions. For example, if someone dies, we think it appropriate to hold a funeral and bury the body or perhaps cremate it. Given our current conventions, we will not eat the body. To do that would strike us as an insult to the memory of the person who has died. . . . Our reactions to the cannibals are complicated, however, because two moralities are relevant, theirs and ours. In judging the situation, we can simply appeal to our own morality: "Eating people is wrong!" But in judging the cannibals themselves, we must take their morality into account. We cannot simply blame them for what they do, because their moral understanding is not the same as ours. They see nothing wrong with eating people; and there is no obvious reason why they should. We do not feel comfortable in judging the cannibals themselves to be wrong. It does not seem right to say that each of them ought morally not to eat human flesh or that each of them has a moral duty or obligation not to do so. (1977, pp. 105–06)

I agree with Harman's verdict regarding the cannibals not being to blame for eating dead human bodies. On my account, they are not to blame as they do not believe that they are doing any wrong in eating the bodies. (It isn't clear to me whether on Harman's view, the cannibals are not to blame on account of *lacking* relevant moral beliefs about eating human bodies or on account of its not being *wrong for them* to eat human bodies.) But my account, that is ABlame5—and this is the principal point—is in not in any way wedded to the idea that morality is constituted by a set of rules conventionally adopted because of their social utility, or to the idea that morality is in some nontrivial sense relative to cultures. Indeed, my view is perfectly compatible with the absolutist's view that there is one true or correct basic moral principle (one that "holds" across all cultures and times) that specifies necessary and sufficient conditions for the rightness, wrongness, or obligatoriness of acts. ABlame5, in other words, is fully compatible with an absolutist theory (like utilitarianism) or a relativistic one of Harman's variety.

It should be emphasized that even if some absolutist theory is true, moral *practices* may nonetheless vary from culture to culture. For instance, assuming some variety of utilitarianism is true, under one set of conditions obtaining in one cultural domain, general burial of the dead may maximize utility, whereas in a different cultural principality where different conditions obtain, eating the bodies of deceased persons may maximize utility. As an illustration, King Darius of Persia, as Herodotus records in his *History*, was fascinated by the diversity of moral practices among different cultures. He had discovered in his travels that the Callatians (a tribe of Indians) habitually ate the bodies of their dead fathers; the Greeks did no such thing—they practiced cremation.[5] Given different beliefs regarding how to revere the dead, and perhaps different beliefs about what happens to the dead, the Callatians and Greeks may both have correctly believed that their respective funerary practices maximized (in the different circumstances in which they found themselves) utility. As the Callatians believed that it was fitting to dispose of the dead by eating the dead bodies, they may not have believed that they were doing any wrong by disposing of the dead in the manner in which they did, and hence, given ABlame5, may not have been deserving of moral blame for their practice. If, then, some absolutist theory rules the day, there will be one basic principle of rightness or wrongness extending across cultures, but (correct) attributions of (inward) blameworthiness and moral practices may well diverge across cultures.

7. OBJECTIONS AND REPLIES

One objection against the deflationary result revolves on the assumption that a person like Smita is free to adopt an "objective," culturally neutral set of norms, whose pronouncements see no moral fault in Seth's advances but morally censure the type of treatment he receives at the hand of Smita for his advances. The objector might even insist that *Smita* may well judge, on the basis of her own evaluative scheme, that these more neutral norms are better than those of her own. We *do,* after all, have the ability to reflect on our own evaluative schemes, and amend them in the wake of such reflection, where the reflection itself is not tainted by autonomy-undermining factors. But then, the objector might continue, if Smita *does* have the capacity to adopt a more neutral scheme, or at least elements of such a scheme that censure her treatment of Seth, but fails to do so, she is still to blame for her seeing to it that Seth is punished.

This objection, however, has several deficiencies. There is, firstly, the worry of whether persons are indeed significantly free to adopt whatever norms they see fit. For many, it would seem, this is not a realistic option at all. The influence of culture and tradition on the imposition of values, loyalties, and directions is something that is not easily sheddable. For a vast majority of us, it is misleading even to suppose that through a series of past actions we have deliberately and freely brought it about that we endorse the culturally derived values that we do. Secondly, even granting the more sensible suggestion that evaluative schemes are susceptible to assessment and modification, why should it be thought that a person will in fact engage in such reflective modification? Perhaps some will propose (what I think is dubious) that in light of the true or correct morality, if there is such a thing, one *should* engage in such activity. But even granting this problematic conjecture, there is no guarantee that one *will.* At best, then, this objection alerts us to the possibility that Smita *may* be morally blameworthy for failing to engage in reflective evaluation of the cultural norms that she has perhaps uncritically accepted. Or perhaps she is blameworthy for acquiring the belief that it is morally permissible to censure Seth for his advances. But this is a far cry from sustaining the distinctly different charge that (given her culturally nurtured moral beliefs) she is to blame for seeing to it that Seth is punished.

A second objection insists that there is something clearly right about finding Smita's (relevant) beliefs about, and (relevant) actions concerning Seth, reprehensible. We condemn Smita for them regardless of whether she was free with respect to either the acquisition of these beliefs or her acting on them. Doesn't *this* show that Smita is to blame for her (germane) beliefs and actions?

Again, I think this objection misses the mark. Once more, I call attention to the unremarkable view that almost all of us acknowledge but which this objection ignores, that there are sundry ways in which a person can be appraised morally, and being to blame is just *one* such way. So, for instance, we might claim with justification that Smita's treatment of Seth is morally despicable, and that she has some morally despicable beliefs about the Lows. We might denounce her for failing to cultivate more compassion or sympathy for Seth. We might, in addition, also find *her* morally tainted in light of the fact that she has done something morally reprehensible. But none of these moral evaluations amount to an attribution of *blameworthiness*.

In conclusion, epistemic condition ABlame5, in conjunction with the empirical hypothesis that many of our normative beliefs ultimately originate from the various norms that are part of the culture in which we find ourselves, has deflationary results. Outsiders relative to a culture, that is, persons who are not members of that culture, are quick to attribute blame to a person from that culture who performs an act deemed morally reprehensible by them. The moral assessments of these outsiders may well be correct in various respects, but woefully mistaken in one: the "insider" like Smita may have performed an act that is morally reprehensible, and we may perhaps truly say of her that she is morally contemptible, but she need *not* be morally blameworthy for her act. Indeed, outsiders may be deserving of blame for failing to see this.

‡⊨═⊨‡

THIRTEEN

ADDICTION
AND CONTROL

I. INTRODUCTION: CONTROL AND ADDICTION

In the last two chapters, I have explored some implications of the epistemic condition of appraisability for various issues. In this chapter, I devote attention to
what the control condition implies for drug-related behavior. Specifically, the issue here is this: Do drug users, addicted to such drugs as heroin or cocaine, have
the sort of control required for moral appraisability over their actions, or their
actional elements like desires, intentions, or decisions, which, in some important
fashion, owe their genesis or retention to their drug use? We can readily grant
that an addict may exercise the relevant kind of control over many of his actions
whose generation is not associated with drug usage. But the issue of whether
addicts have free will or are morally appraisable for their behavior concerns actions that are in some notable way caused by their utilization of the drug.

There is no settled view here. Jeffrey Reiman, for instance, argues that even
addicts who have "a compulsive inability to resist taking the drug despite the
knowledge that it is harmful" (1994, p. 42) can be morally appraisable for taking
the drug. In a different vein, Kadri Vihvelin has held that we can make sense of
the idea that someone's desire compels her to act so that the resulting action is
unfree, and, possibly, some addicts are unfree in this sense (1994a, p. 54).[1] Sarah
Buss defends the view that the philosopher's unwilling addict—the addict who
acts on an irresistible desire and who would really prefer not to inject himself,

but takes the drug despite his all-things-considered preference—is "a conceptual impossibility" (1994, p. 101).

In this chapter, one of my principal aims is to show that addicts (if there are any) whose actions issue from "defeating desires," those that are either irresistible or resistible only at the expense of the agent's incurring considerable psychological damage, lack *appraisability*-grounding control over those actions. I proceed as follows. First, I argue against the reasons Reiman advances in support of his conviction that addicts whose actions are caused by strong desires can be responsible for those actions. Next, I show that Buss's intriguing position that the unwilling addict is a conceptual impossibility is highly suspect. I then question Vihvelin's justification for the view she once defended that addicts who act on desires that compel them to act are unfree in the sense of 'freedom' germane to moral appraisability, and I comment on her revised proposal that addicts may well be free. Finally, I trace the implications of the conception of volitional control for drug-related behavior. I argue that lack of volitional control explains (in part) why addicts acting on defeating desires are not appraisable for the actions caused by such desires.

2. REIMAN'S CONTROL CONDITION

Resolution of the problem of whether it is possible for addicts to be appraisable for the actions their addictions can be said to cause, Reiman suggests, turns on the factual question of "whether the addict could have acted otherwise" (1994, p. 41). Reiman adduces grounds for an affirmative reply. He claims, for instance, that should it be supposed that drug use turned the addict into some sort of "blind robot," the addict would still be appraisable for what he did in the robotic state—even if he could not then do otherwise—because *"he is responsible for taking the drugs that led him to become an addict which was before that robotic state began"* (1994, p. 42). This passage supports the view that, according to Reiman, moral appraisability (and more generally, moral responsibility) requires the ability to do otherwise. Reiman stresses that his verdict that addicts may well be responsible for taking the drug applies even to those addicts who act on a "strong desire" to take the drug; a strong desire has the property of "impelling the addict to continue in spite of his judgment that the desired object is harmful and that he would be better off without it and without the desire for it" (1994, p. 28). Of paramount importance to such cases, Reiman proposes, is the "Aristotelian point that addicts are responsible for starting up their addictions (before they were addicts) . . . [and that] they are [also] ultimately responsible for the continuation of their addictions, since in starting up an addiction one starts up something that continues" (1994, p. 42). Reiman concludes that even addicts acting on strong desires "are (in the vast majority of cases) responsible for their addictions, for their continued drug use and thus for their continued addiction, and for any other actions that addiction may be said to cause" (1994, p. 43).

As we have seen, the control condition to which Reiman seems committed— that moral appraisability for an action requires freedom to have done otherwise— is highly controversial. The condition is undermined by Frankfurt-type examples.

These examples, remember, suggest that agents can be morally appraisable for doing something even though they could not have done otherwise. As an illustration of this sort of "Frankfurt-type" example, imagine that Al has formed (on his own) an intention to steal some pills. Suppose that, unbeknownst to Al, a powerful being—Omni—wants to ensure that Al does in fact steal the pills. Omni, again in the absence of Al's realization, has Al under surveillance, monitoring both his behavior and his brain activity. Should Al show any inclination whatsoever of failing to intend to steal the pills, or failing to act on his intention to steal them, Omni will compel Al to form an intention to steal, and to act on this intention, by direct electronic stimulation of Al's brain. But Al executes his intention to steal the pills on his own—Omni does not show his hand at all. In this case, it appears that although Al could not have refrained from stealing the pills, he *is* morally blameworthy for stealing them. For he acts just as he would have had Omni not been waiting in the wings.

Reiman might insist that the control condition on which his views about addicts who act on strong desires rest is *not* the condition that moral appraisabilty requires freedom to do otherwise. Rather, the robotic cases, in which the addicts are appraisable for starting up their addictions and for the continuation of their addictions, suggest that the appropriate control condition is the weaker one that moral appraisability requires freedom to act otherwise than one does on *some* occasion. This condition requires some clarification. As Michael Zimmerman has noted, it "has become a common practice to ascribe a double time-index to 'can' contexts—one to the 'can' itself and one to the action on which the 'can' operates. . . . Thus, we may say that I can now be in Boston tomorrow although, if I embark this evening on a trip to the Far East, I may put the possibility of my being in Boston tomorrow out of reach" (1987, p. 199). With this in mind, we can formulate the weaker condition of alternative possibilities in this way:

> WeakPAP: S is morally appraisable for doing A at t only if there is a time, t*, which is such that at t* S can refrain from doing A at t.

But even this weaker could-have-done-otherwise-on-some-occasion condition falls prey to significant problems. First, Mele has helpfully distinguished among (1) an agent's autonomously *developing* a pro-attitude over a stretch of time; (2) an agent's autonomously *possessing* a pro-attitude during a stretch of time; and (3) an agent's being autonomous regarding the *influence* of a pro-attitude on his intentional behavior (Mele 1995, p. 138). In addition, he argues that the autonomous development of a pro-attitude P that one possesses throughout time period t is not sufficient for the autonomous possession of P throughout t:

> Alice, a specialist on drug addiction, once decided after careful reflection to make herself a heroin addict so that she could directly experience certain phenomena. . . . She strove, accordingly, to develop irresistible desires for heroin and she fully accepted the developmental process on the basis of self-reflection that was at least minimally rational and involved no self-deception. . . . In due time, Alice developed irresistible desires for heroin, desires that (by hypothesis) she *autonomously* developed. At present, while in the grip of an irresistible desire to use the drug, Alice rationally judges that it would be best to refrain from using it now; she explic-

itly and rationally judges, as well, that it would be best to eradicate her standing desire for heroin, beginning immediately. She is convinced that the experiment is more dangerous than she had realized and that it is time to start setting things right. However, Alice is incapable of resisting her present desire for heroin. Moreover, she is incapable of immediately eradicating her standing desire for heroin; and she is incapable of strategically eradicating it any time soon (during *t*, say).

Although, by hypothesis, Alice autonomously developed irresistible desires for heroin, she is not autonomous with respect to the influence of her present desire for heroin on her present behavior. A clear sign of nonautonomy in that connection is her *inability* to refrain from acting on that desire even though she judges it best not to use the drug now. . . . Further, Alice is not autonomous . . . vis-à-vis her current *possession* of her standing desire for heroin, nor her continued possession of it during *t*. . . . If she were self-governing with respect to her possession of that desire, she would rid herself of it, as she judges best. Instead, she is stuck with the standing desire and victimized by it, while rationally preferring its eradication. (1995, pp. 138–39)

I want to suggest, along similar lines, that we distinguish between being appraisable for acquiring certain pro-attitudes (like desires for heroin) over a period of time, and being appraisable for the actions that issue from such pro-attitudes. Suppose, though she believes it is wrong to do so, Lucy has deliberately striven to develop certain desires for a drug, in the false but justified belief that she will be able to resist acting on the acquired desires and that she will not fall victim to addiction. Her belief is justified as she acts on the (evil) counsel of a doctor she has always trusted, and who has assured her that she is immune to becoming addicted to the drug for which she has willfully developed desires. Assume that the desires for the drug Lucy initially acquires are resistible but slowly become (or are replaced by) irresistible ones. Assume, further, that Lucy did not foresee, nor, given the advice of the doctor, was it likely that she could (in her circumstances) foresee, any such eventuality. In this sort of case, Lucy may well be appraisable (she may be blameworthy) for developing desires for the drug, but may well *not* be to blame for becoming an addict, or for succumbing at a certain time, t, to an irresistible desire for the drug to which she becomes addicted. And she may not be to blame for succumbing to such a desire at t even though there was a time (a time, for example, when she had resistible desires for the drug) at which she had the ability to refrain from taking the drug at t. So contrary to Reiman, even though Lucy may have been blameworthy for starting up her addiction (on the supposition, among other things, that there was a time at which she could have refrained from developing desires for the drug), she may be to blame neither for the continuation of her addiction, nor for her succumbing at a time to an irresistible desire for shooting up.

Reiman might attempt to salvage his position by calling attention to the fact that Lucy's case involves deception or ignorance. The idea would be that some version of WeakPAP, in the absence of pertinent deception or ignorance, governs correct ascriptions of appraisability. But even this version of the attenuated control could-have-done-otherwise condition, that moral appraisability for an action requires freedom to have acted otherwise than one did on some occasion in the absence of relevant deception or ignorance, is challenged by global Frankfurt-type cases. Here is the sort of example of such a case that I have already used: suppose (unbeknownst to Al) an omnipotent being watches over every single action performed by him, and will intervene and compel him to perform an action of a certain sort if he shows any signs of not performing (on his own) an action of that sort. Suppose, by sheer happenstance, Al always and without hesitation performs the right type of action, the sort the omnipotent being wants Al to perform. The omnipotent being thus never intercedes in Al's behavior. In this example, it seems that although Al could *never* have done otherwise, he is morally appraisable for performing all those actions for which he would have been morally appraisable for performing had there been no omnipotent being keeping vigil over him.

I believe, then, that Reiman's control condition cannot be used to sustain his conclusion that actions which issue from strong desires are, in the vast majority of cases, ones for which addicts are morally appraisable for performing.

3. BUSS ON THE PHILOSOPHER'S UNWILLING ADDICT

In a fine discussion on autonomy, banking on certain interesting claims about practical rationality, Sarah Buss argues that the unwilling addict who would really prefer not to shoot himself up with heroin but who intentionally ends up doing so anyway is a "conceptual impossibility" (1994, p. 101). Buss makes it abundantly clear that the unwilling addict in question acts on an irresistible desire to take the drug: "if he *could* resist his desire to act this way, he *would* resist it" (1994, p. 101). Buss's view that the unwilling addict is a "conceptual impossibility" is intriguing; it directly challenges what is frequently accepted as received wisdom that such addicts are exemplars of agents who nonautonomously take the drug, or who are not morally appraisable for taking the drug.

The issue of precisely what connections (if any) obtain between autonomous action and action for which one is morally appraisable—whether, for example, the control required for moral appraisability presupposes individual autonomy—is an important one, and I have discussed this issue at length in past chapters. Here, I turn directly to Buss's considerations for the view that there can be no such agent as the unwilling addict. According to Buss, "Everyone concedes that a person acts autonomously only if she acts intentionally" (1994, p. 97). So Buss endorses:

B1: Agent S does action A autonomously at time t only if S intentionally A-s at t.

Buss also embraces the view that "one cannot do something intentionally if, all things considered, one prefers not to do it" (1994, p. 98); she would accede, then, to:

B2: S A-s intentionally at t only if at t S has an all things considered preference to A at t.

B1 and B2 entail:

B3: S does A autonomously at t only if at t S has an all things considered preference to A at t.

The unwilling addict is supposed to be an agent who takes the drug intentionally contrary to her all things considered preference not to take the drug. Suppose such an addict, Hera, injects herself with the drug despite her all-things-considered preference not to take the drug. Then B2 (together with the facts of the case) implies that Hera does not intentionally inject herself. This, in turn, in conjunction with B1 implies that Hera does not autonomously inject herself. Alternatively, suppose Hera intentionally injects herself on a certain occasion. Then, given B2, it must be that she has an all-things-considered preference to inject herself on that occasion. Consequently, though an addict, she is not an *unwilling* one, as she does not act contrary to an all-things-considered judgment of hers.

Realizing it is controversial, Buss offers a defense for B2. Distinguishing preferences from inclinations, she claims that a person's preferences are her "judgments regarding the relative weight of the considerations for and against the alternatives she is comparing" (1994, pp. 105–06). She then argues in this way:

> someone prefers to do A rather than B if and only if she believes that the considerations in favor of doing A outweigh the considerations in favor of doing B. . . . Could someone believe this while nonetheless also believing that she has sufficient reason for doing B? This is possible only if it is possible to believe that one has sufficient reason to do what one believes one has weightier . . . reason *not* to do. And this is possible only if one can believe that one has sufficient reason to override the force of one's reasons. To override a consideration is to judge that it is not decisive; i.e., to judge that other considerations are at least as weighty. So to override what one takes to be one's weightiest consideration is to judge that this consideration does not outweigh all others, after all. This could either involve judging of a given consideration both that it is the weightiest and that it is not, or it could simply involve altering one's earlier judgment as to which consideration is weightiest. Since only the latter possibility is coherent, it seems one's views regarding which considerations are weightiest determine one's views regarding which considerations give one sufficient reason to act. Accordingly, whenever one does something because one takes oneself to have sufficient reason to do it, one does *not* do something one prefers *not* to do, all things considered. (1994, p. 98)

Suppose Hera judges that, all things considered, she prefers A-ing to B-ing. Is it possible (contrary to Buss) for Hera to B intentionally while still retaining the judgment that all things considered she prefers to A? Reconsider Mud Pie. Fred pops his head into the refrigerator. He catches sight of the pie on the top shelf; its aroma dominates his attention. Fred realizes that, given his medical condition and other factors, all things considered, he ought not to eat the pie. Assume that the first-person practical judgment of Fred's, that he ought not to eat the pie, is a judgment that *commits* Fred to action in the sense that were he to fail to act on the judgment, he would do something that is irrational from his own point of view. But Fred's evaluative assessment of the object of his desire not to eat the pie (his not eating the pie) is misaligned with the motivational strength of this desire; and a little later, still thinking it best not to eat it, Fred (intentionally) gulps down the pie. Imagine that Fred could on this occasion have exercised self-control and refrained from feasting on the pie. His uncompelled intentional action of eating the pie is an akratic one.

Buss might rejoin that since Fred prefers (all things considered) to refrain from indulging, he believes that considerations in favor of refraining outweigh those in favor of indulging. If Fred then goes on and intentionally eats the pie, it must be that either he now also believes that considerations in favor of indulging outweigh those in favor of refraining, or he has simply revised his earlier judgment, no longer holding that, all things considered, he ought to refrain (call the disjunction that is the consequent of this conditional "Buss's disjunction"). Since "only the latter possibility is coherent" (1994, p. 98), Buss might urge, it must be that Fred has altered his earlier judgment. Suppose, however, that Fred has *not* revised his earlier judgment. *Why* (given Buss's disjunction) might it be thought that it must then be true that at the time of (intentionally) eating the pie Fred also *believes* that considerations in favor of eating are more compelling than those in favor of abstaining? The sole reason that comes to mind is this: the belief, in conjunction with the strong desire to eat the pie, is required to explain why Fred eats the pie. But I think this is a mistake. As already noted, Alfred Mele and others have indicated that in a case like Mud Pie, Fred's desire which is out of line with his all-things-considered preference—his "akratic desire"—has motivational influence disproportionate to Fred's evaluative assessment of the object of that desire.[2] Fred has both the desire to eat the pie and the desire to refrain. His better judgment assigns diminished ranking to the former, but he is more motivated to act on the latter. If one can explain how he comes to have this balance of motivation, then it seems, one will have an adequate explanation of his akratic action. I have mentioned that various explanations of the balance have been proposed. These explanations make use of factors like selective focusing—directing attention to the immediate rewards of eating the pie and avoiding or downplaying the detrimental effects, and failure on the part of the agent to make an effective attempt at self-control.[3]

One can acquire intentions in many different ways. In a case like Mud Pie, an akratic desire together with the agent's focusing on the immediate rewards of the akratic alternative and ignoring worrisome consequences of the continent alternative, may give rise to an intention to perform the former alternative. There is little reason to believe that intentions formed in this way need also give rise to a *belief*, inconsistent with a belief which the agent already has, that the considerations favoring the "akratic alternative" outweigh those favoring the "continent one." It seems to me, then, that Buss has not shown that the philosopher's unwilling addict is a conceptual impossibility.

4. KADRI VIHVELIN'S ULYSSES DESIRE: HIERARCHICAL UNFREEDOM

Although she now believes that an addict who intentionally takes the drug to which she is addicted does so freely (in the sense of 'free' required for appraisability), I first address Vihvelin's former view (in her insightful piece) that it is possible for an agent's desire of a certain sort to compel her to act, so that when she acts on a desire of this sort, she acts unfreely. In this piece, Vihvelin indicates that the sense of unfreedom she is attempting to analyze is the sense relevant to moral responsibility (1994a, p. 74). She adds that among those who probably have this type of freedom-undermining desire, which she calls "the Ulysses desire," are some addicts (1994a, p. 74); whether they do, she says, is ultimately an empirical question (1994a, pp. 54, 76). The Ulysses desire is a second-order desire. We have seen that unlike a first-order desire, which is a desire for a course of action or perhaps a state of affairs, a second-order desire is one whose object is another actual or possible desire of the agent whose desire it is. For instance, Hera's desire that she not have the desire to take the drug is a desire of the second order. Prior to expounding the notion of something's being a Ulysses desire, Vihvelin distinguishes between the effectiveness of a desire and its satisfaction:

> A desire is *effective* if it causes the agent to act; that is, if it's . . . her motivating desire. A desire is *satisfied* if the action is successfully completed or the state of affairs that is the object of the desire obtains. Since it is possible to act on a desire without attaining the object of the desire (to try, but fail), a desire may be effective without being satisfied. (1994a, p. 69)

Suppose some agent has a second-order desire (F) concerning her first-order desire, D, and suppose F is the desire that D not be effective; that is, F is the desire that D not be the agent's motivating desire. Vihvelin calls F "the Frankfurt desire" (1994a, p. 70). She claims that someone may have the Frankfurt desire without having the following second-order desire (U) which is the Ulysses desire: the desire that D not be satisfied, even if D is effective (1994a, p. 70). By way of illuminating the Ulysses desire, Vihvelin says that it is such a desire which explains the otherwise peculiar behavior of Ulysses. Ulysses ordered his men to bind him to the mast before they sailed by the Sirens who lured men to their doom by their irresistible song. Vihvelin proposes that "Ulysses wants *not* to be motivated by the desire that he anticipates the sirens will cause him to have. He's got the Frankfurt desire. But . . . [he] also wants that, *even if* the song of the sirens causes him to be moved by the desire to pursue them, that this desire *not* be satisfied. He orders himself bound to the mast because he wants that even if he tries to act on his siren-following desire, he won't succeed" (1994a, p. 70). Ulysses's plight, Vihvelin explains, contrasts with the predicament of weak-willed Joe. Trying to lose a few pounds, Joe has the Frankfurt desire concerning his first-order desire to drink beer; he wants not to be motivated by this desire. But when offered a beer by his tennis partner after a game, he gives in and "snaps at his wife for reminding him that he's trying to lose weight. He lacks the Ulysses desire; given that his beer-drinking desire is effective, he wants it satisfied" (1994a, p. 71). Vihvelin submits that Joe does not act against his will; his "unwillingness is conditional on the desire *not* being his effective desire" (1994a, p. 71). Ulysses, in contrast, wants that his siren-following desire not be satisfied even if it is effective; he acts against his will. He has the Ulysses desire which is "not *just* the desire to be stopped from acting on one's desire; it is the desire to *prevent oneself* from acting on one's desire, by whatever means possible" (1994a, pp. 71–72). Vihvelin claims that since what differentiates Ulysses from Joe is the Ulysses desire:

I propose that a sufficient condition for someone acting unfreely on her desire D is that D causes her to act despite her Ulysses desire concerning D. That is, she acts on D even though she wants that D not be satisfied, even if D is effective. (1994a, p. 71)[4]

But Mud Pie, I believe, poses a problem for this condition as well. Recall, Fred judges that all things considered it is best not to eat the pie. He has a desire (R) to refrain from eating the pie, but he also has a strong desire (E) to eat the pie. The motivational clout of the latter desire is not in balance with his low evaluative ranking of that desire; its motivational force far outstrips its evaluative ranking. By focusing on the immediate rewards of eating the pie, evading paying attention to the long-term detrimental effects of indulging, and failing to exercise self-control, Fred freely and intentionally eats the pie while still retaining the judgment that it is best that he refrain. Let's augment the case with these elements: assume Fred also has the relevant Frankfurt desire—he has the second-order desire that E not move him to action (of some sort). Assume, in addition, that Fred acquires the germane Ulysses desire as well—he has the desire that E (the desire to eat the pie) not be satisfied even if E does move him to action of some sort (like approaching the refrigerator). Since he has both the Frankfurt and the Ulysses desire, grant that Fred *does* have a very low *evaluative* assessment of E. It certainly seems *possible*, though, that the motivational force of E may remain unaffected, or be insignificantly affected, by Fred's acquiring the Ulysses desire; it may remain disproportionately strong in comparison to Fred's evaluative ranking of that desire. Hence, it seems possible that despite having the Ulysses desire, E gives rise to an intention to eat the pie, Fred fails to muster sufficient self-control, focuses selectively, and ends up freely and intentionally eating the pie. The Ulysses desire is, after all, just a (rare and special sort of) *desire*, and Vihvelin gives us no reason to believe that such a desire is irresistible, or that such a desire cannot be "trumped" by an "akratic" one. Fred's Ulysses desire is consonant with his all things considered best judgment not to eat the pie, but there is no reason to suppose, or at least Vihvelin gives us no reason to suppose, that failure to act on a first-order desire that the Ulysses desire concerns cannot be an "akratic failure." The Ulysses desire need not bar akratic action—it is conceptually possible that it need not, and if it does not, an agent like Fred may well be appraisable for his akratic behavior.

Recently, Vihvelin has repudiated her own view.[5] She now believes that presumably even an addict who acts on a desire for the drug despite her Ulysses desire freely takes the drug as long as she takes the drug intentionally. Her reformed view is predicated on her reinstatement of Simple Compatibilism, which is the theory that free will is the capacity to make choices on the basis of one's beliefs and desires. According to this theory, to act intentionally is to exercise this capacity; "That is, to act intentionally is not just to act freely, but also to act with free will" (1994b, p. 141). Vihvelin, however, insists that there is a sharp distinction between an account of free will and freedom of action, which is a metaphysical and modal concern, and an account of moral responsibility (or appraisability), which is largely a normative concern. The addict who intentionally takes the drug does so freely but may not be morally appraisable for doing so. She may not be appraisable or her appraisability may be mitigated, for instance, if she took earlier steps—like checking into a clinic and asking for help—to refrain. Vihvelin proposes that the question of moral responsibility (or appraisability) is larger and more complex than that of free will. Unlike questions about the latter, questions about moral responsibility are, for example, questions about which cognitive capacities are required for moral responsibility, and "questions about a *person*—someone who endures through time. . . . [A] theory of personal identity through time must be part of a theory of moral responsibility" (1994b, p. 143).[6]

Simple Compatibilism seems suspect. We don't, for instance, think that a person acts freely on "engineered-in" intentions (in cases in which the person did not consent to, or have any knowledge of, the engineering); yet Simple Compatibilism implies otherwise. A willing addict like Poppy, who acts on an irresistible desire for a drug, may act intentionally, but not—I believe—freely. Even if one disagrees with Simple Compatibilism, one might well applaud Vihvelin's suggestion that an account of free will should not be conflated with an account of moral responsibility or appraisability. Nevertheless, one might insist that the *kind* of control required for moral appraisability over an action may well not coincide with the sort required for freely performing that action. To motivate this view, consider "Deception," which involves the deceived addict Poppy. (To stave off complications, assume that Poppy is not culpable for becoming an addict.) Though Poppy believes (falsely) that she can refrain from taking the drug, her desire for the drug has become irresistible. Let's suppose that after some deliberation, she decides to take the drug and acts on her decision. As she intentionally takes the drug, Simple Compatibilism (with the relevant facts) implies that Poppy freely takes the drug. But one might still plausibly insist that Poppy is not morally appraisable for taking the drug as she lacks appropriate control over her action— her action is no longer responsive to her practical deliberations. Had she decided differently, she would not have been able to execute her decision to refrain. The relevant issue to be broached should one distinguish between acting freely (in Vihvelin's sense of 'acting freely') and control is this: What sort of control must one exercise over an action or its causal springs to be *morally appraisable* for performing that action?

5. VOLITIONAL CONTROL AND ADDICTION

I have defended a conception of control according to which an agent has appraisability-grounding control over an action only if that action is sensitive to her practical deliberations; the action must be under her volitional control: holding constant the proximal pro-attitude (like a desire) which gives rise to her action, and the agent's evaluative scheme, there must be a scenario (satisfying certain constraints) with the same natural laws as the actual world in which, engaging her evaluative scheme, the agent decides or forms an intention to do something other than what she in fact does, and successfully executes that intention or decision.

Now let's return to some cases involving addiction. Alice—an expert on drug addiction—decides after careful reflection to make herself a zeroin addict in order directly to experience and study certain phenomena. (Zeroin is a recently discovered drug; much of how it works and how it affects people is unknown.) Given her goals, she strives to develop irresistible desires for zeroin, and succeeds. Assume that epistemic and authenticity conditions of appraisability regarding Alice's acquisition of the desires, or development of her addiction, are satisfied. Then, as (it would seem) she had volitional control over her acquisition of the desires (and development of her addiction), she is appraisable for these things. However, events don't unfold quite so smoothly for Alice. At present, while in the grip of an irresistible desire to shoot up, she rationally judges that it would be best to refrain from using the drug now, and to eradicate her standing desire for the zeroin, beginning immediately. She is correctly convinced that the experiment is much more dangerous than she (or any of her colleagues) had realized. At the start of her experiment, she didn't foresee, nor (assume) could she have reasonably been expected to foresee the danger. She is, though, stuck with her standing desire: she cannot rid herself of it now, nor can she thwart its influence now; she ends up injecting herself. As she now fails to exercise volitional control over injecting herself, she is not appraisable for injecting herself. If she cannot exercise volitional control over the steps required to rid herself of the desire for the drug, she is not appraisable for these steps either.

Suppose we vary the case somewhat in the following manner. Assume that Alice could have foreseen, and did in fact foresee, the danger. Assume, in addition, that realizing the potential danger, Alice also foresaw that, once having acquired the desire for zeroin, she would not be able to refrain from acting on it, nor easily rid herself of it, should complications arise. Furthermore, assume that she was perfectly willing to live with the untoward consequences were they to ensue. Still, she took deliberate steps over which she did exercise volitional control to acquire the desires for becoming an addict. In this case, it appears that Alice *is* appraisable for acquisition of the desires, for developing into an addict, and for acting on her desires. With respect to the latter, for instance, although she lacks volitional control over her (now) injecting herself, she intentionally took deliberate steps over which she did have volitional control, to bring it about that she has certain desires for zeroin, in the full realization that she will, at all subsequent times, lack volitional control over actions issuing from these desires, or that she will be unable (subsequently) to refrain from acting on these desires.

Finally, consider a third variation of the case. This time, assume that Alice had already decided to make herself into a zeroin addict, but prior to implementing the requisite steps to become an addict, she fell victim (in the absence of her knowledge) to Max the eccentric psychosurgeon. In the dead of the night, Max implants in Alice a standing irresistible desire for zeroin together with some other pro-attitudes, and upon awakening in the morning, Alice injects herself (having already secured a supply of the drug she anticipated she would need, once she had put into effect her plan of becoming an addict). In this variation of the case, it seems, Alice is not appraisable for acquiring the desire for the drug; nor is she appraisable for acting on the desire. She is not appraisable for the latter, for example, as her action arises from an induced pro-attitude, she has not given (broad) consent to this pro-attitude's being induced in her, and the pro-attitude gives rise to an action over which she lacks volitional control.

In conclusion, there are different reasons why an addict may not be morally appraisable for actions that issue from desires for drugs like heroin. She might not, for instance, satisfy the epistemic requirement of moral appraisability. Or, like Alice (in one of the cases discussed above), she might be the victim of appraisability-undermining manipulation. Or her action may not be voluntary—she may not be in control of that action. In this chapter, I have confined attention primarily to the control condition. At least some addicts, I suspect, lack volitional control over many of their actions arising from "drug-caused desires" and are hence not morally appraisable for these actions.

FOURTEEN

ON BEING APPRAISABLE
FOR THE THOUGHTS OF
ONE'S DREAM SELF

1. MOTIVATING THE MORAL DREAM PROBLEM

Can we be deserving of moral blame (or praise) for what we think, visualize, or imagine in our dreams? Right at the outset, this moral dream problem smacks of philosophical misgivings. It might, after all, plausibly be urged that all moral appraisability ultimately traces to appraisability for actions, and just as there is a stark difference between one's intentionally gazing at a sunset and one's dreaming that one so does, so there is a difference between one's purposely undertaking the mental act of imagining one's engaging in adultery and one's dreaming that one engages in adultery.[1] Yet venerable philosophers like Plato and Augustine have seriously entertained what is presumably a view held in the minority, that we are indeed appraisable, and, hence, that it is indeed possible for us to be appraisable, for the actions or thoughts of our dream selves.[2] Interestingly, although Freud denies that we are our dream self, and so denies that we are appraisable for thinking, or intending to do, what we think or intend to do in our dreams, he believes, nevertheless, that we are responsible for the *content* or 'impulses' (as he says) that are expressed in our dreams:

> If I seek to classify the impulses that are present in me according to social standards into good and bad, I must assume responsibility for both sorts; and if, in defense, I say that what is unknown, unconscious and repressed in me is not my 'ego,' then I shall not be basing my position upon psycho-analysis, I shall not have accepted its conclusions

and I shall perhaps be taught better by the criticisms of my fellowmen, by the distur-
bances in my actions and the confusion of my feelings. I shall perhaps learn that what
I am repudiating not only 'is' in me but sometimes 'acts' from out of me as well.[3]

To motivate the moral dream problem, start with the supposition that one can
be blameworthy for thinking certain thoughts, or imagining or fantasizing about
certain things. "You shouldn't have thought such nasty things," we say to the
person fantasizing about asphyxiating the lover who betrayed him, where (in the
context) it is clear that we believe both that the person is deserving of blame for
thinking the nasty thoughts, and that these thoughts will *not* actually issue in any
unfortunate action. Next, entertain the suggestion that we assess the overall
worth of a person—how good morally the person is—partly but significantly on
the basis of the number of deeds, including thinking certain thoughts, for which
she is deserving of blame and the number of deeds for which she is deserving of
praise; other things being equal, the greater the former, the less overall morally
worthy the person. Third, on the assumptions that (i) just as one can engage in
unconscious deliberation, one can engage in *unconscious* thinking of certain
thoughts (unconscious fantasizing about adultery, for instance); (ii) one can be
blameworthy for an episode of one's unconscious thinking of certain thoughts;
(iii) possibly, dreaming, for example, that one steals some pears is relevantly like
engaging in unconscious thinking about stealing pears, it can be concluded that
it *is* possible for one to be blameworthy for at least some of the thoughts of one's
dream self. But then of course, assuming that an appraisal of the overall moral
worth of a person turns partly on the number of deeds for which she is deserving
of blame, the possibility of being blameworthy for the thoughts of one's dream
self acquires further moral import.

In this chapter, I attempt to show that the minority view that it is possible for
one to be blameworthy for the thoughts of one's dream self is credible, at least on
the supposition that dreaming involves mental activity in which the dreamer can,
among other things, make various judgments. I will start by disarming a couple of
arguments against this view. Then, making use of the control and epistemic conditions of appraisability I have defended, I will turn to its defense.

2. AN ARGUMENT FROM ALTERNATIVE POSSIBILITIES

The renowned principle of alternative possibilities, one variant of which says that
one is blameworthy for doing only what one is able to avoid doing, fuels what
appears to be a promising argument against the minority view:

A1: One is morally blameworthy for doing something only if one could have refrained from doing that thing.

A2: What one does in one's dream (like thinking certain thoughts) is not something one could have refrained from doing.

A3: If A1 and A2, then it is not possible for one to be blameworthy for what one
does in one's dream.

A4: Therefore, it is not possible for one to be blameworthy for what one does in
one's dream.

Perhaps a response that most readily comes to mind against this argument, and indeed against the minority view itself, is that, contrary to what A2 presupposes, one does not intentionally or otherwise *do* anything in one's dreams. But A2 has certainly not gone unchallenged. Witness, for example, Augustine's ruminations in these passages in the *Confessions*:

> You commanded me not to commit fornication. . . . You gave me the grace and I did your bidding. . . . But in my memory . . . the images of things imprinted upon it by my former habits still linger on. When I am awake they obtrude themselves upon me, though with little strength. But when I dream, they not only give me pleasure but are very much like acquiescence in the act. The power which these illusory images have over my soul and my body is so great that what is no more than a vision can influence me in sleep in a way that the reality cannot do when I am awake. Surely it cannot be that when I am asleep I am not myself, O Lord my God? And yet the moment when I pass from wakefulness to sleep, or return again from sleep to wakefulness, marks a great difference in me. During sleep where is my reason which, when I am awake, resists such suggestions and remains firm and undismayed even in face of the realities themselves? Is it sealed off when I close my eyes? Does it fall asleep with the senses of the body? And why is it that even in sleep I often resist the attractions of these images, for I remember my chaste resolutions and abide by them and give no consent to temptations of this sort? (*Confessions*, X.30)

As Gareth Matthews has commented, when Augustine speaks of remembering his chaste resolutions of not succumbing to temptations of evil in some of his dreams, the implication is clearly that in other dreams he does give real consent (1992, p. 98; 1981, pp. 47–54). So Augustine admits that both real consent and real withholding of consent is possible in our dreams. He would not then accept line A2.

Augustine goes on after the part of the passage I have cited and adds that what he does or thinks in his dreams is something that is in his power, together with the gratuitous assistance of God, to refrain from doing or thinking:

> The power of your hand, O God almighty, is indeed great enough to cure all the diseases of my soul. By granting me more abundant grace you can even quench the fire of sensuality which provokes me in my sleep. . . . By your grace . . . [my soul] will no longer commit in sleep these shameful, unclean acts inspired by sensual images, which lead to the pollution of the body: it will not so much as consent to them. (*Confessions*, X.30)

The passage paves the way for the suggestion that Augustine is well equipped to jettison line A1. *With the aid of God's grace*, Augustine implies, he will be able to refrain from consenting to evil suggestions in his dreams. A reasonable presumption is that there are at least some cases which are such that if God exists and by his grace he ensures that some agent refrains from consenting to an evil suggestion in a dream, then that agent cannot fail to refrain from consenting. But since it is through God's *grace* that the agent cannot fail to refrain, the agent is still morally appraisable for refraining; intervention by God through his grace is not an appraisability-undermining factor. Some situations in which one does something with the gratuitous assistance of God can, perhaps, profitably be compared to a situation of this sort: suppose one can perform a particular action only if one does it under hypnosis. Suppose one consents to being hypnotized for the purpose of performing the action, fully knowing that once hypnotized, one will not be able to refrain from performing the action. If one subsequently performs the action under hypnosis, one may well be morally appraisable for doing so. There is then, I believe, a significant moral difference between intervention by God that results in some agent's performing an action by compulsion or in a manner that emancipates the agent from appraisability, and intervention by God *through his grace* that does not subvert appraisability. It would seem, in consequence, that Augustine is justified in spurning A1.

There is, as I have discussed at length in earlier chapters, an alternative rejection of A1 inspired by examples developed by Locke and more recently by Frankfurt and Fischer. Suppose Augustine steals some pears "on this own." Assume that had he shown any inclination of failing to steal—had he, for example, even begun to choose or decide not to steal the pears—Satan would have intervened and caused Augustine to act on an intention to steal the pears. We would then, arguably, have a case in which Augustine is morally appraisable for stealing the pears (as, among other things, he acted just as he would have had Satan not been keeping vigil), although he could not have done otherwise.

The Augustinian and the Locke/Frankfurtian responses to the argument from alternative possibilities should prompt the adversary of the minority view to search for other grounds to dispose of that view. Before looking at other grounds, it is worth considering a case in support of the minority stance.

3. AN ARGUMENT IN FAVOR OF THE MINORITY VIEW

By relying on the view that real consent is possible in one's dreams, one might attempt to defend the minority view in this way:

B1: One's dream self consents (on some occasion, say) to an evil suggestion.

B2: If B1, then one's dream self (freely and knowingly) does evil.

B3: If one's dream self (freely and knowingly) does evil, then one's dream self is morally blameworthy for doing evil.

B4: Therefore, one's dream self is morally blameworthy for doing evil (and hence that it is possible for one's dream self to be morally blameworthy for doing evil).

It might credibly be counselled that the argument collapses at line B2. For surely it does not follow from the fact that one consents to do something, like committing what many deem to be the evil that is adultery, that one does what one consents to doing. In failing to do the evil one consents to doing, one has not done that evil and hence one is not blameworthy for that evil.[4]

In his lucid discussion of the moral dream problem, William Mann opposes or at least thinks Augustine would oppose, this rejection of B2 (Mann 1983). For Mann believes Augustine endorses the principle that consenting to wrongdoing is sufficient for having done something wrong (1983, p. 378). Mann submits that to consent to a suggestion (presumably when the consent is sincere) is to form an intention to do what the suggestion suggests. He then recommends that Augustine be understood as enunciating not the fallacious doctrine that to consent to do something is to do that thing but rather:

> Consent Principle: If to do A is to do something wrong, then intending to do A is also something wrong (1983, p. 380).

As I understand it, Mann's defense of the consent principle turns on the consideration that intentions themselves can be right or wrong.

> Judgments of right and wrong . . . take as their domain at least two distinct categories of activities, actions and intentions. The notion of a right or wrong intention is, be it granted, parasitic upon the notion of a right or wrong action: a specific intention is right (wrong) if and only if the action which would realize it is right (wrong). Central to Augustine's . . . [consent] doctrine is the proposition that a person's intentions themselves can be *right* or *wrong*, not merely *good* or *bad*.[5] (Mann 1983, pp. 380–81)

Although Mann's defense of the consent principle is engrossing, I think it has a difficulty. Suspect is Mann's proposal that a person's intention to perform an action is wrong if and only if the person's action that would realize that intention is itself wrong. Presumably Mann would concede that on the received view of counterfactuals (subjunctive conditionals), determining the normative status of an agent's intention would require identifying the closest possible world in which that agent intends to do some action and in which that agent's intention has been realized by that action. It seems perfectly possible, though, that there could be two such worlds, equally close, but in which the agent's intention has been realized by one action with some normative status in one of the worlds but by an action with a different normative status in the other world. Here's an example. Suppose Sin has decided on his own to commit adultery, and he freely acts on his decision, although he is aware that he could have refrained from doing so. We may assume that in this situation Sin's intention to commit adultery has been realized by an action that is wrong. Now suppose again that Sin has decided on his own to commit adultery and he executes his decision "on his own." But this time assume that had Sin revealed even the shadow of an inclination not to commit adultery, Satan would have intervened and would have caused Sin to act on his decision. In this Frankfurt-type situation, unlike in the first, Sin could not have done otherwise. In addition, in this situation, but not in the first, Sin's act of adultery is *not* wrong (though it may well be overall evil): the principles that 'ought' implies 'can,' and that one has a moral obligation to perform an action if and only if it is morally wrong for one not to perform that action, entail that it is morally wrong for one to perform an action only if it is within one's power not to perform that action.[6] Since it is not within Sin's power not to commit adultery, Sin's act is not wrong (though Sin may well be morally blameworthy for committing that act).[7] Arguably, though, the world in which Sin could have done otherwise is equally close to the one in which he had no alternative possibility. A retreat to the stance that an intention is right (wrong) if and only if the action that realizes it is right (wrong) would prove detrimental as many intentions are never realized in action.

We have a standoff. The argument from alternative possibilities against the minority view is not sound, nor is the argument from consent in favor of that view. Perhaps some headway can be made by considering a second attack against the minority view.

4. A SECOND ARGUMENT AGAINST THE MINORITY VIEW: THE ARGUMENT FROM BLAME

One might grant that dreams are experiences involving mental activity consistent with being skeptical about the Augustinian view that one's dream self can refrain from consenting to an evil suggestion. The skepticism might be motivated by a number of different considerations. So, for instance, whereas one might concede that a dreamer can experience various sensations, one could plausibly deny that the dreamer can consent or refrain from consenting to a misdeed as, one might insist, there is a difference between real consent or real restraint and "dream consent" or "dream restraint." [8] Or whereas one might allow for the possibility that one's dream self can consent or refrain from consenting to an evil suggestion, one could deny that one's dream self could intentionally do these things; the actions of the dream self, if it really acted at all, would be akin to those "actions" of a clockwork doll. Then, banking on the principle that 'ought' implies 'can' and 'ought not to' implies 'can refrain from', one could generate an argument against an aspect of the minority view having to do with blameworthiness in this fashion:

C1: One's dream self cannot consent nor can it refrain from consenting to evil.

C2: If C1, then it is false that one's dream self can have a moral obligation to refrain from consenting to evil.

C3: If it is false that one's dream self can have a moral obligation to refrain from consenting to evil, then it is false that it can be wrong for one's dream self to consent to evil.

C4: If it is false that it can be wrong for one's dream self to consent to evil, then one's dream self cannot be morally blameworthy for consenting to evil.

C5: Therefore, one's dream self cannot be morally blameworthy for consenting to evil.

On the assumption that one is identical to one's dream self, one could draw the desired conclusion that it is not possible for one to be morally blameworthy for consenting to evil in a dream.[9] We have already canvassed possible rationales for C1. Let's review the other premises.

C2 is supported by the 'ought' implies 'can' principle (K): one has a moral obligation to perform [not to perform] an action only if it is within one's power to perform [not to perform] that action. If K is true, and one cannot refrain from consenting to evil, then one cannot have an obligation to refrain from consenting to evil.

Line C3 rests on this principle (OW): it is morally obligatory for one not to do [to do] something if and only if it is morally wrong for one to do [not to do] that thing. If it is false that one can (in one's dreams) have an obligation not to consent to evil, then given OW, it is false that it can be wrong for one to consent to evil in one's dreams.

Finally, C4 is defended by appealing to the Objective View of blameworthiness—that one is blameworthy for doing something only if it is wrong for one to do that thing.

Even if we grant the first premise of what we can dub the "Argument from Blame," the argument is vulnerable at other points. So, for instance, Mann and Matthews both report that in his stance against the heresy of Pelagianism, Augustine rejects the 'ought' implies 'can' principle (Mann 1983, pp. 379–80; Matthews 1992, p. 99). Mann observes that

> The phrase 'anti-Pelagianism' unfortunately conjures up the image of . . . the doctrine of the necessity of divine grace for human salvation—which for many people *is* unappealing. But that part of Augustine's anti-Pelagianism is irrelevant to the present issue. All that Augustine's minority report needs from his stance against the Pelagians is his scepticism about the universal applicability of the principle that 'ought' implies 'can'. And that scepticism is well grounded. The principle, like many other principles of similar generality, wobbles between being made trivially true on the one hand and being patently false on the other. If the principle is to stand a chance of being plausible it must be made compatible with the fact that for many people the present structure of their character renders them unable to avoid doing what they know they ought not to do. . . . A person whose upbringing involved considerable exposure to bigotry may find that he still sometimes makes judgments about members of other races . . . which he now knows to be bigoted. He recognizes that he ought not to make such judgments, but his habits are so strong that on some occasions—involving, say, haste and pressure—he cannot avoid making them. (1983, pp. 379–80)

Mann's objection to K amounts to this: it appears that both the following can be true:

M1: S knows that S ought not to do A.

M2: S cannot refrain from doing A.

But if K is true, then it is not possible that M1 and M2 both be true: M1 entails that S ought not to do A but K and M2 entail that it is false that S ought not to do A.

The argument is not entirely convincing. Moral theorists who have much at stake in defending K can urge that there is a plausible construal of M1 and M2 that enables us to retain the intuition that (appropriately cleansed versions of) M1 and M2 can both be true consistent with K's being true. The construal requires time-relativizing the concept of moral obligation. Suppose that, as of time t1, S can avoid doing A (say, making bigoted judgments) at a later time t3. Then this can be true consistent with K:

M1*: S knows that, as of t1, S ought to avoid doing A at t3.

Now suppose due to haste or pressure:

M2*: As of t2, S cannot refrain from doing A at t3.

Imagine that, as of t2, S's disposition to make bigoted judgments gets the better of S so that as of this time S finds that S cannot avoid making such judgments at t3. Still, M1* and M2* can both be true consistent with K's being true. This case illustrates what we have already noted before: obligations can change with the passage of time. An action that may be obligatory for me as of now may not be obligatory for me two weeks from now.

The argument from Blame has, so far, withstood assault. At least it is not at all obvious whether the 'ought' implies 'can' principle (and so line C2) ought to be rejected. The argument does, however, have an Achilles' heel. Certain Augustinian views, or at least an interpretation of these views, raise the possibility that Augustine may well have concurred with my view that blameworthiness is not to be associated with wrongness in the manner expressed by the Objective View. An adumbration of certain features of Augustine's mind–body dualism will facilitate comprehension of these views.

5. INNER PERSONS AND OUTER PERSONS

It appears that Augustine conceives of a person as a composite self made up of two distinct entities, the soul or inner person, and the body or outer person: [10]

> [a] man is not a body alone, nor a soul alone, but a being composed of both. This, indeed, is true, that the soul is not the whole man, but the better part of man; the body not the whole, but the inferior part of man; and that then, when both are joined, they receive the name of man—which, however, they do not severally lose even when we speak of them singly. For who is prohibited from saying, in colloquial usage, "That man is dead, and is now at rest or in torment," though this can be spoken only of the soul; or "He is buried in such and such a place," though this refers only to the body? Will they say that Scripture follows no such usage? On the contrary, it so thoroughly adopts it, that even while a man is alive, and body and soul are united, it calls each of them singly by the name "man," speaking of the soul as the "inward man," and of the body as the "outward man," as if there were two men, though both together are indeed but one. (*The City of God* XIII.24.2)

The passage illuminates what appears to be Augustine's estimation that the body is something merely physical; no psychological or mental predicates apply to it. The soul, in contrast, is nonphysical and is separable from the body at death. Augustine maintains that the soul is superior to the body and animates it; it is the soul's activities that make the difference between merely physical endeavors and purposive behavior characteristic of living human beings (Matthews 1967, p. 171). Augustine, it seems, would agree that it is the inner acts and speeches of one's soul that constitute one's true psychological life. But what about one's moral life?

Of vital import is Augustine's alluring suggestion that the inner person can perform (inner) actions. Augustine typically takes thinking, remembering, and visualizing to be inner activities. An intention to do something, furthermore, is conceived as doing that thing already in one's heart.[11] Seriously entertaining the idea of inner agency enables us to give a rationalization of Augustine's verdict that if one intends or consents to commit adultery, one has already committed adultery in one's heart (and that one has therefore already defiled oneself), that coheres well with Augustine's inner–outer person dualism. One *could* read Augustine as proposing that the reason why the state of affairs S *intends to commit adultery* (or S *decides to commit adultery*) is wrong is that in intending to commit adultery, S's inner self has performed some inner action that is wrong. Generalizing, one could construe Augustine as theorizing that what is of relevance in assessing the normative status of an outer action (or what we would generally take to be an action) is something mental or intentional—it is inner actions that figure centrally here. More specifically, Augustine's view could be taken to be that the notion of an outer action's being right or wrong is parasitic upon the notion of an inner action's being right or wrong in this way: for any agent, S, outer action, A, and inner action, IA, if S performs A and A is "backed" by an inner action, IA, then A is right if and only if IA is right. (Call this principle "Inner Dependence.")

This reading of Augustine dovetails nicely with some of Augustine's remarks on sin. In his discussion of *The Sermon on the Mount* Augustine says that there are three things which go to implement sin: suggestion of an evil act arising from memory or perception, attraction to it, and consent. He explains that if consent has taken place, "we would commit sin surely, a sin in the heart known to God, though actually it may remain unknown to man" (*The Lord's Sermon on the Mount* 1.12.34). So it is an inner activity of consent, Augustine seems to insist, that constitutes the essential ingredient of sin. Whether one carries out by means of bodily activity what one has consented to in one's heart, Augustine implies, is by and large irrelevant to whether one has already sinned, and so irrelevant to whether one is an appropriate candidate for blame.

Augustine's inner–outer person dualism raises a number of arresting questions and puzzles (see Matthews 1967, 1982). So does Inner Dependence. (For example, how exactly are we to understand the notion of backing? Also, if intentions are inner actions, and inner actions are bona fide *actions*, then why need anything like Inner Dependence at all? Shouldn't there be a single normative ethical theory whose "domain" is *all* actions?) I shall for the most part ignore these enigmas and questions. I emphasize that I am ultimately not so concerned about whether in the end Augustine would subscribe wholesale to the composite self view sketched above, and whether Augustine would accede to Inner Dependence. (Part of the complication here is that as he matured as a philosopher, Augustine changed his mind on a number of issues including those having to do with sin and voluntariness.) However, I believe that if we suppose that motives (intentions included) are "inner entities," and that an activity like believing that something or thinking that something is an "inner activity," understanding Augustine on some aspects of the composite self view—notably, those aspects having to do with the inner self's performing inner activities—in the manner in which I have done, unearths a condition about blameworthiness I have already developed, namely, that blameworthiness is to be associated with belief in what is wrong. This condition casts perilous doubt on line C4 of the argument from Blame.

6. REJECTION OF THE ARGUMENT FROM BLAME

Motivational elements (perhaps paradigm candidates of "inner elements") are in-tricately affiliated with the issue of whether one is blameworthy for performing an action. Luck might have it that a right action (fortuitously) results from a repre-hensible intention (or cluster of motives). But if one performs such a right action in light of the belief that one is doing wrong, then, as I have urged, one can still be deserving of blame: if, for example, Nero forces what he takes to be the poi-soned wine down Cicero's gullet with the intention of murder, then he would be blameworthy (for forcing the wine down), it appears, even if the poison has been replaced by droplets from the fountain of youth, and the droplets rejuvenate frail and aged Cicero. In light of this connection between motivational elements and appraisability for actions, I have suggested replacing the Objective View with:

> ABlame5: An agent is blameworthy for performing an action, A, only if he has an occurrent or dispositional belief, B, that A is wrong (or amiss), and he performs A de-spite entertaining B and believes (at least dispositionally) that he is performing A. (Re-call, entertaining a belief involves *accessing* it in some way and not merely having it— one must in some fashion, perhaps even unconsciously, be cognizant of it.)

Whereas ABlame5 associates blameworthiness with belief in what is wrong, the Objective View associates blameworthiness with (objective) wrongness. ABlame5, I believe, is superior to the Objective View as the second scenario involving Sin (or Nero's case) strongly suggests. In this scenario, Sin freely com-mits adultery although he could not have refrained from doing so. If Blame is true, then Sin cannot be blameworthy for committing adultery, for his act of committing adultery is not (objectively) wrong (though it may, of course, be evil). It will not do to suppose that one is not blameworthy for performing an act unless, if in performing the act, one brings about a greater balance of intrinsic evil over intrinsic goodness: allowing for at least moderate consequential consid-erations, it can turn out that each one of one's options, if it were performed, would result in overall intrinsic evil, and that one of these options—the one least overall evil—is obligatory. In many situations, one would not be blameworthy for doing what is obligatory though overall intrinsically evil. Let's assume that Sin believed that he would be doing something wrong if he were to commit adultery. Then ABlame5, unlike the Objective View, enables us to validate the intuition that since Sin (freely) does something in light of the belief that he is doing wrong, Sin is blameworthy for his action.

Apart from calling into question the Objective View, one might take some of Augustine's remarks on inner activities to be suggestive of another normative principle, this time a principle linking motives and obligatoriness. Whatever we make of Inner Dependence, the following Inner Dependence-like principle may well be true:

> Motives: For any agent, S, action, A, and motive, M, if S does A, A is motivated by M, and S cannot do A unless S has M, then it is morally obligatory for S to do A only if it is morally obligatory for S to have M.

Motives can be defended in this way: suppose the very normative ethical theory for assessing the normative status of actions is also the theory for assessing the normative status of (the having of) motives that underlie actions. Then, in order for such a theory to be acceptable, it must not be the case that the theory assign "incompatible" normative statuses to an action and to the motive that gives rise to that action. It must not, for instance, be the case that the theory entails that an action, A, is obligatory although it is wrong for A's agent to have the motive that gives rise to A. If such were not the case, then sometimes the directives of the theory would be inconsistent with one another.[12] To elaborate, it appears that the following principle is true:

> Prerequisite: If S cannot do A without doing B (for instance, out of physical necessity), and S can refrain from doing B, then if it is obligatory for S to do A, it is obligatory for S to do B.

Now suppose S ought to do an action, A, and S cannot do A unless S has a certain motive, M, that gives rise to A. Then Prerequisite (or an appropriately modified version of Prerequisite) entails that it is obligatory for S to have M. I am assuming that we have appropriate control over the acquisition of at least some of our motives; we are free to acquire or form such motives just as we are free to form some intentions. If the true (or correct) normative theory is relevant to assessing both actions and motives that underlie those actions, then the theory must be consistent with Prerequisite which appears to be a general truth about moral obligation. Such consistency can only be guaranteed if Motives is true.

It's time to take stock. Through a somewhat circuitous route, we have been able to marshall support against line C4 of the Argument from Blame. The adversary of the minority view need not yet, however, capitulate. For she might urge that while we may well have undermined some arguments against the minority view, we have so far advanced few, if any, positive considerations in its support. This concern is reasonable and pressing. My modest aim, in what follows, is to motivate the view that it is possible to be blameworthy for some of the thoughts of one's dream self, on the supposition that the dreamer can, among other things, make various judgments. I shall, to echo a few things I said in section 1, pursue the following strand of thought. We can be morally appraisable for thinking certain thoughts. On the assumptions that (1) just as one can engage in unconscious deliberation, one can engage in *unconscious* thinking of certain thoughts (unconscious fantasizing about stealing pears, for instance); (2) one can be blameworthy for an episode of one's unconscious thinking of certain thoughts; (3) possibly, dreaming, for example, that one steals some pears is relevantly like engaging in unconscious thinking about stealing some pears, it *is* possible for one to be blameworthy for at least some of the thoughts of one's dream self.

7. BLAMEWORTHINESS FOR THOUGHTS

I mentioned above that one dimension along which we appraise the overall moral worth of a person (as opposed, say, to the person's actions or motivations) turns on the deeds—mental or otherwise—for which the person is to blame, the greater the number of such deeds performed by the person, the less the overall moral worth of the person (other things being equal). Assessing moral worth in this way, it becomes pivotal to inquire about moral appraisability for thinking or entertaining certain thoughts where entertaining or thinking certain thoughts qualify as mental actions. Appraisability for thinking certain thoughts presupposes that agents are able to exercise control over thinking thoughts. A rough distinction will prove useful. One can engage in thinking about something with a view to intentionally doing something concerning that thing. For instance, one can canvass reasons for or against A-ing, make a decision to A, and then execute this decision. Alternatively, one can engage in thinking about something without a view to forming an intention or arriving at a decision to do anything about that thing. For example, a student can engage in thinking about what it would be like to slit his professor's throat without intending to form an intention or arrive at a decision to slit his mentor's throat. It is presumably this latter sort of thinking that is often involved in intentional imaginings (as in intentional "daydreaming") or intentional fantasizings (and it is this sort of thinking that will figure prominently in the discussion of appraisability for unconscious thoughts.) That we *are* able to exercise control over both these sorts of "thinking about things" acquires partial confirmation from the following. First, thinking is an activity, much of which can be intentional, and much of which can be initiated, sustained, or stopped. I can now, for example, begin to think about a specific problem, briefly set it aside to attend to the phone, and then resume thinking about it. In addition, thinking about something or imagining something, are frequently *alternatives* that I can contemplate and undertake on a specific occasion. After spending the day teaching, Al might consider cleaning the car, watching television, or thinking about where to invest funds. Of course, Al could perform the complex act of cleaning the car and thinking about where to invest. Being one of his alternatives, it can be legitimate to inquire into whether Al's thinking about where to invest is the alternative that Al morally ought to undertake, or the alternative he believes he ought morally to undertake. Third, just as one can acquire motivation to steal a pear, so one can acquire motivation to think about something and then act on that motivation. By reflecting on the life-style he wants to lead when retired, Al might acquire motivation to think about various investment strategies and then act on the motivation.

Imagine that Sid is disgruntled with his performance in a course. Although he knows he is solely responsible for his poor showing, he blames his professor. He consoles himself by constructing an elaborate "thought scenario" in which he slowly slits the throat of his mentor. But not morally insensitive, suppose Sid believes that it is wrong for him to entertain such thoughts. Still, the pleasure he derives from thinking such thoughts is so great that he acts against his moral belief. He lowers himself into a comfortable couch, closes his eyes, and imagines what it would be like for him to perform the gruesome deed. Sid on this occasion engages in an intentional (complex act, let's suppose) of thinking certain thoughts. Call this act "ACT." It is clearly possible for Sid to exercise volitional control over ACT: there is a scenario with the same natural laws as the actual world in which, given Sid's (authentic) evaluative scheme and the motivational precursor of ACT, Sid forms an intention to do something other than ACT, and he successfully executes this intention. Imagine, for example, that having seated himself on the couch, Sid intentionally dismisses from his mind the option of constructing the elaborate thought scenario, arrives at a decision instead, to think about what he can do to improve his performance in the course, and then acts on that decision. It appears, then, that we have good grounds for supposing that Sid is deserving of blame for performing ACT: he intentionally performed ACT, took himself to be doing wrong in so doing, and exercised the relevant sort of control over ACT that is required for blameworthiness.

It seems unproblematic that a great deal of our thinking is unconscious, and that unconscious actional elements like beliefs and desires frequently give rise to actions. In exploring appraisability for engaging in unconscious thinking of thoughts, it will be helpful to recall some distinctions. S's desire D to A is weakly unconscious if and only if S has D and S does not know or believe that she has D; similarly, S's belief B that p is weakly unconscious if and only if S has B and S does not know or believe that she has B. S's desire D to A [belief B that p] is strongly unconscious if and only if D [B] is weakly unconscious, and apart from outside help or careful self-scrutiny, she cannot come to know or believe that she has D [B].[13] Now, as I previously proposed (in chap. 9), I think that a person *can* be blameworthy for performing an action that issues even from strongly unconscious beliefs and desires. Suppose, in the name of discipline, I severely criticize a student for a petty error she committed. It is only later, with the help of a discerning colleague, that I come to appreciate the true motive of my behavior: I genuinely dislike the student and was venting disguised hostility. Suppose I had no good cause for disliking the student; suppose, in addition, that I did, just prior to censuring the unfortunate student, have the ability to engage in self-control and greatly attenuate my criticism; suppose, finally, that at the time of my unfortunate outburst, I held the weakly unconscious belief that it was wrong to denounce the student so harshly for the paltry error. Then it appears that I *am* blameworthy for the denunciation, even though at the time of the denunciation, I was unaware of its motivational springs, and would have remained in the dark about them in the absence of consultation with my colleague. I should add that our judgment regarding my being to blame for the invective would presumably be quite different if we were to learn that the denunciation stemmed from some strongly unconscious *irresistible* motivational precursor, or if I acted out of ignorance that is straightforwardly excusing (for example, I falsely believed but on very sound grounds that the student was guilty of plagiarism).

What about appraisability for engaging in unconscious thinking about certain thoughts or unconscious fantasizing? Again, beginning with some distinctions, S engages in weak unconscious thinking (imagining, fantasizing, etc.) if and only if S does not know or believe she is engaging in such thinking, and she is engaging in such thinking; and S engages in strong unconscious thinking (imagining, fantasizing etc.) if and only if S engages in weak unconscious thinking, and apart from outside help or careful self-scrutiny, she cannot come to know or believe that she is engaging in such thinking. The student might wonder about why the sight of the blood smeared butcher's knife so unnerves him. After a little probing on the part of a concerned friend, it might surface that the student had been (strongly) unconsciously entertaining the scenario of slitting the throat of his professor, and it is these unconscious musings of his that largely explain his agitation at the sight of the bloodied knife.

I now want to adduce considerations in support of the view that it is at least *possible* for an agent to be blameworthy for unconsciously entertaining certain thoughts.[14] My strategy here is to show that the requirements for blameworthiness laid down by the epistemic condition in ABlame5 and the control condition summarized in the account of volitional control can be satisfied by an agent's unconsciously entertaining certain thoughts, and that this should give us some reason to believe that we can be blameworthy for some of our unconscious mental doings. (I simply presuppose, for this discussion, that the authenticity condition of appraisability is satisfied.)

It appears that an agent can engage in a bit of practical reasoning without being conscious of it as reasoning.[15] Consider this case. Suppose Bea believes that Earl has the uncanny ability of accurately judging what is on her mind independently of Bea's vocalizing, or otherwise overtly exposing, what is on her mind. Perhaps partly because she has been embarrassed by some of Earl's revelations regarding her thoughts, she desires to hurt Earl. Assume that this desire (DB) is strongly unconscious; Bea has repressed it partially on the basis of having a standing (dispositional) belief that it is wrong to hurt a good friend. Given the tug of her repressed desire, she begins, unintentionally, to notice ways of hurting Earl. Bea is bent on starting up a periodical. She is looking for partners. She discovers that sensitive Earl would be extremely hurt were he to learn that Bea had so little as toyed with the thought of dismissing him as a possible associate in her promising venture. On the basis of this discovery, she forms the belief (BB) that Earl will be hurt if she merely entertains the thought of not having him as an associate, and he discerns this thought. Suppose her venture is steaming along, matters have to be finalized, and Bea must select her associates. Over a coffee with Earl, looking directly at him (so that he can "read" her thoughts), she forms the judgment to entertain the thought of excluding Earl, and (nondeviantly) acts on the judgment—she imagines excluding Earl.

In the case sketched thus far, it is only Bea's desire to hurt Earl that is strongly unconscious. We can, to modify the case a bit, suppose that her relevant belief (BB) is strongly unconscious given Bea's considerable powers of rationalization. (She might, for instance, rationalize that Earl does not really enjoy "desk jobs," that working too closely with him might wreck a good friendship, etc.) So far, I believe, there is nothing *incoherent* about the case. I submit that no incoherence results on the additional supposition that her repressed desire (DB) to hurt Earl, in conjunction with her now assumed unconscious belief (BB), issues in an intention, of which Bea is unaware, to entertain the thought of excluding Earl, which in turn leads to Bea's entertaining the thought; and this bit of mental activity— Bea's entertaining the thought—is *itself* veiled from Bea's consciousness. Perhaps Bea's "directing her mind" to this thought would be exceedingly painful to her.

Is it reasonable to suppose that Bea is blameworthy for her unconscious mental act of entertaining the thought of excluding Earl? At least one feature of the case supports an affirmative reply: Bea has the dispositional belief that it is wrong to hurt Earl, and she unconsciously entertains the thought of excluding Earl—she performs this mental act—in spite of having this belief. So it seems that the epistemic condition of blameworthiness captured by ABlame5 is satisfied by Bea's mental act. But what about control? Does Bea exercise the sort of control required for blameworthiness over her unconscious mental act of entertaining the thought of excluding Earl? Notice, firstly, that Bea's unconsciously entertaining the thought of excluding Earl is not simply something that *happens* to Bea; rather, it is something that is generated by a desire (DB) and a belief (BB) of Bea's. Notice, secondly, that the motivating unconscious desire DB to hurt Earl is not irresistible; indeed, there is nothing in the description of the (modified) case that suggests that Bea lacks the ability to refrain from acting on it. Nor is it one such that Bea could refrain from acting on it only at the cost of suffering considerable psychological damage. The desire, in short, does not seem to be one that undermines control. Notice, thirdly, there do not appear to be other appraisability-undermining factors such as coercion or wayward causation in the sequence of events leading from the acquisition of desire (DB) and belief (BB) to execution of the unconscious mental act generated on the basis of these actional elements. Notice, finally, there does seem to be a scenario (having the same natural laws as the actual world) in which, given Bea's evaluative scheme and the motivational precursor of the unconscious mental act, Bea forms an intention to do something other than entertain the thought of excluding Earl, and she successfully executes this intention. Here's one: imagine that Bea has a standing dispositional desire (DE) not to hurt Earl along with her repressed desire (DB) to hurt Earl. Assume that DB has the same relative strength in this scenario as it does in the actual. However, in the counterfactual scenario, Bea focuses her attention on the attractive aspects of acting in accordance with her desire (DE) not to hurt Earl; she does not wish to jeopardize the friendship, and she wishes to avoid the guilt she would later feel if she were to hurt Earl. Furthermore, Bea refuses to entertain second thoughts about the unconscious judgment not to hurt Earl that she makes. So in this (counterfactual) scenario, Bea forms the intention not to hurt Earl and she translates this intention into action. We have, then, reasonable grounds to believe that Bea's unconsciously entertaining the thought of excluding Earl is something over which she has the sort of control—volitional control—required for blameworthiness.

8. ON BEING MORALLY BLAMEWORTHY IN A DREAM

Reverting to the minority view, suppose we grant the Augustinian doctrine that dreaming involves mental activity in which the dreamer can experience certain sensations, undergo sundry emotional reactions, and make miscellaneous judgments. Imagine that Bea, with her repressed desire (DB) to hurt Earl, and her (unconscious) belief (BB) that she can hurt Earl merely by entertaining the thought of excluding him as an associate, a belief veiled from her consciousness by rationalization, retires for the day. She tucks herself in bed and falls into a slumber. If dreaming involves mental activity in which the dreamer can make judgments, it seems *possible* that Bea's desire (DB) and belief (BB) can give rise to a judgment on Bea's part to entertain the thought of excluding Earl, and Bea now (in her slumbers) entertains this thought. (Of course, Bea in her sleep is not aware that she is entertaining this thought, so this during-sleep-mental-activity of hers qualifies as unconscious.) In turn, *if* entertainment of this thought in her sleep is *constitutive* of a dream, or part of a dream episode, then it seems that Bea can be blameworthy for it: such entertainment—a mental act—is generated by a desire (DB) and belief (BB) of Bea's, and the other considerations discussed above that lend credibility to the view that Bea (while awake) can be blameworthy for an unconscious entertaining of a certain thought are the very same ones that should lead us to believe that Bea can be blameworthy for entertaining a certain thought while asleep.

One might balk at the suggestion that entertainment of a thought, a mental activity generated on the basis of a desire and belief of a sleeping person, is part of a dream. Support for such skepticism might come from the direction of spurning the Augustinian supposition that dreams are experiences involving mental activity in favor of a nonexperiential account of dreaming.[16] One implication of such an account is that one does *nothing* in a dream; one rather *dreams* of doing something. The details of such an account need not detain us. Of importance to our purposes is that a nonexperiential account underscores the compositional and narrative proficiency of the dream-teller. The mind composes dream narratives that are stored directly into memory without being experienced. Building on the Freudian idea that we are responsible for the content of our dreams, I wish to end with the suggestion that even if a nonexperiential account of dreaming is correct, there is a final lesson to be gleaned from the advocate of the minority view. The moral dream problem of whether one can be appraisable for one's dream thoughts seems germane to our assessment of persons by way the intermediary that one's dreams may disclose something about one's character. Very roughly, character traits are relatively long-term dispositions to act, feel, or think in certain ways. Just as a person may have the ability to do something but may never have an opportunity to exercise that ability, so a person may have a character trait that she never manifests in action as the right opportunity never presents itself. If certain psychological theories are correct, our dreams may well expose these otherwise hidden traits. (Of course, other sorts of evidence may corroborate the existence of such hidden traits, evidence, for example, about what a person would do under circumstances in which there were an opportunity to exploit the trait.) Surely we would think less of a person endowed with such a hidden trait of, for instance, dishonesty if that trait were under the control of that person. If the person could, for example, take steps to see to the extirpation of that trait, but did not—perhaps in light of the expectation that the opportune moment would sometime arise—she would be culpable for retention of the trait (although she may not have been culpable for its generation). If one is troubled by the immoral dreams of one's dream self, perhaps one is so troubled because these dreams betray the fact that one's character is not beyond reproach.

In conclusion, it is not evident that the minority view should be dismissed as a mere philosophical aberration. The dream world may not be so distant from the unconscious world that houses so many of our darker mental doings for which we are to blame.[17]

FIFTEEN

+=≻=≺=+

WRAPPING UP

Some Final Thoughts

I. MANY LEFTOVER PROBLEMS

In some of the past chapters, I have attempted to uncover conditions that are necessary and sufficient for moral appraisability for intentional actions. The conditions are recorded in principle Appraisability, which has three central constituents: a control constituent, which says that the sort of control required for moral appraisability is volitional control; an epistemic one, which—stripped down to its core—says that in order for an agent to be morally appraisable for an action, the agent must believe she is doing something wrong or morally amiss, or she is either executing her moral duty or at least doing what is morally permissible by performing that action; and finally, an authenticity constituent, which says that the agent's action for which she is appraisable must issue from actional springs that are "truly her own."

I have dealt almost exclusively with appraisability for *actions* that correspond to one's practical reasoning. A complete theory of appraisability would have to deal adequately with (at least) the challenging issues of appraisability for omissions (intentional failures to act or "not-doings"), appraisability for the consequences of one's actions and omissions, and appraisability for emotions or feelings.[1] In addition, I admit that the sort of control manifested in intentional action (volitional control) may not be of the sort that is either necessary or sufficient for free action in some (special) sense of 'free'. If there are such free actions, I am inclined to doubt whether we could be appraisable for them. But here, I can neither characterize the special sense (or senses) of 'free', nor can I settle the issue of whether we could be appraisable for these assortments of free action. Still on the issue of control, I stress that a reasons-responsive approach to control of the sort I have developed begs for clarification of what can be called "eligible alternative scenarios": How do we delimit the counterfactual scenarios operative in the notion of volitional control? This is a *perplexing* difficulty, and it may, in the end, signal the downfall of any such approach to control. Further, I have skirted completely the complex and intriguing concern of whether various kinds of collectives—like large corporations—can be appraisable for their behavior. If appraisability on the part of collectives is in fact possible, then it would be a failing of a theory of appraisability were it to imply otherwise.[2] Finally, I believe that both praiseworthiness and blameworthiness vary in degree, but I have not accounted for degrees of appraisability. There are some tricky puzzles here. For example, is someone who deliberately does wrong more culpable, *ceteris paribus*, than someone who deliberately suberogates? And what about perceived degrees of wrongdoing and of suberogation? How should they be compared? These are problems left untackled in this work.

I shall end by framing what may be a grand perplexity.

2. A GRAND PERPLEXITY

Some incompatibilists have argued that causal determinism is incompatible with moral appraisability and, more generally, with moral responsibility, as causal determinism (together with various other plausible principles like the principle of the fixity of the past and the principle of the fixity of the natural laws) entails that one lacks freedom to do otherwise, and that this sort of freedom is required for appraisability (and, more broadly, for responsibility). I think, as I have tried to show, that these incompatibilists are wrong—causal determinism may indeed rule out alternative possibilities, but the sort of control required for moral appraisability is *not* freedom to do otherwise.

However, causal determinism it might be argued, exerts pressure against appraisability from another direction: if causal determinism is true, nobody has freedom to do otherwise. Now the 'ought' implies 'can' principle (K), together with the principle (OW) that one has a moral obligation not to perform an action if and only if it is morally wrong for one to perform that action, entails principle WAP: it is wrong for one to perform an action only if it is within one's power not to perform that action. In other words, the 'ought' implies 'can' principle and the standard principle of obligation OW, entail that there is a requirement of alternative possibilities for moral wrongness; one can't perform an action that is wrong unless one has genuinely accessible alternatives. Further, OW and the reasonable "ability principle" W, the principle that it is morally wrong for one to perform some action only if it is within one's power to perform that action, entail principle OAP, that one has a moral obligation to perform an action only if it is within one's power not to perform that action. That is, W and OAP entail that there is a requirement of alternative possibilities for morally obligatory actions; no one can perform an action that is obligatory unless one could have done otherwise. An alternative route to the conclusion that in a determined world no actions are obligatory is this. If some action, A, in such a world is obligatory for some person, then failing to do A is wrong for that person in that world. But it is false that any action in such a world is wrong for any person, and hence it is false that failing to do A is wrong for that person. So it is false that A is obligatory for that person.

But what about morally permissible (or right) actions? Might one not argue that though nothing can be wrong or obligatory in a causally determined world, actions in such a world may still be morally permissible? There is, however, trouble on the front of permissibility as well. From the fact that an action is neither wrong nor obligatory, it does not follow that it is morally permissible. An alternative is that the action is not right, wrong, or obligatory; it is, as I have said, "morally gratuitous." And this alternative is more plausible, I believe, than the supposition that in a determined world, possibly, actions are morally permissible. It is more plausible for the simple reason that in a determined world no action is wrong or obligatory, and so in such a world, if actions did have moral statuses, they would either be morally gratuitous or they would be morally permissible. Killing someone, then, in cold blood, if not morally gratuitous, would be morally permissible, a result that is hard to swallow. (Were this act morally gratuitous, it would of course *not* be morally permissible.) I propose, then, that under the condition that no one has freedom to do otherwise, an act's not being wrong does not imply that it is permissible.

It seems, in summary, that if causal determinism is true, morality goes by the way: no actions are right, obligatory, or wrong.[3] The next set of considerations in the chain of reasoning leading to the conclusion that causal determinism undermines appraisability unfolds in this way:

(1) If no person can perform an action that is wrong, right, or obligatory, then no person can be appraisable for any of his actions.

Point 1 rests on what I have called the "Objective View" of appraisability, which is the view that one is blameworthy for an action only if that action is wrong, and one is praiseworthy for an action only if that action is obligatory (or right):

(2) No person can perform an action that is wrong, right, or obligatory (if causal determinism is true).

Point 2, as I have explained, rests on the view that causal determinism "rules out" wrongness and obligatoriness as it rules out alternative possibilities. Moreover, as I have proposed, there is little, if any, reason to believe that actions in a determined world are morally right. The conclusion of this argument is then:

(3) No person can be appraisable for any of his actions (if causal determinism is true).

Against this second threat from determinism I have argued (in chap. 8 and 9) that the Objective View is mistaken; people can be appraisable for their actions even if the actions they perform are not in fact wrong or obligatory. So for instance, in Deadly's Defeat, Deadly is blameworthy for injecting the patient with medicine C even though (unbeknownst to Deadly) it is arguably obligatory for her to inject the patient with C.

Some people, if convinced by cases like Deadly's Defeat, may nevertheless contend that such odd or unusual cases sway us away from the Objective View only against the "background presupposition" that persons can and do in fact perform actions that are wrong, right, or obligatory. But in a world where *no* actions are wrong, permissible, or obligatory—a causally determined world would be a world of this sort—matters would be different. If no one's actions are in fact obligatory, right, or wrong—if there were no morality—then there would be no appraisability. Perhaps in a causally determined world there would be something like a shadow of morality, or "as if" morality; people might behave *as if* their actions were in fact obligatory, permissible, or wrong; and so people might behave *as if* they could correctly hold themselves and others appraisable for their actions; still, it might be urged, there wouldn't be *real* appraisability. What would be the point of holding people morally accountable for their actions in a world truly devoid of morality? Maybe it is these sorts of considerations that ultimately persuade people to look favorably upon the Objective View. .

Even if this last worry can be circumvented, the incompatibilist has one final grand trump card to play. I am willing to entertain the following assumption:

> Grand Assumption: Any account of appraisability will incorporate or appeal to some condition of morality; that is, any such account will appeal to some condition which entails that one's actions (or omissions or consequences of these things) are in fact wrong, right, or obligatory. The condition might be a control, an authenticity, or an epistemic one.

The incompatibilist might now argue in this fashion. Suppose Grand Assumption is true. Then, as nothing can be wrong, right, or obligatory in a determined world, the condition laid down in Grand Assumption—that appraisability presupposes that at least some things are right, wrong, or obligatory—cannot (ignoring vacuous satisfaction) be satisfied in this type of world. Hence, nobody can be appraisable for his or her actions in such a world. If we grant Grand Assumption, we are then indeed saddled with a grand and disturbing perplexity.

Is Grand Assumption true? I am somewhat optimistic that it is not. Should, for instance, principle Appraisability prove correct, then there is reason to eschew this assumption, and there is hope that the grand perplexity *can*, in the end, be sidestepped.

Suppose, however, that we go along with the supposition that Grand Assumption is true. I want to end with these suggestions: first, the importance of morality in our lives has, it seems to me, been exaggerated. Other concerns, like those having to do with pursuit of "project-oriented" goals, or with love for others, are of primary significance. Realizing that this is so should lead us to appreciate the fact that the "scope" of *moral* appraisability is more limited than what we might have thought. Even so, and this is my second suggestion, we are frequently nonmorally *normatively* appraisable for our behavior. Finally, my last suggestion is that · at least some varieties of nonmoral normative appraisability should remain un-

scathed by determinism; in a determined world, people can be nonmorally normatively appraisable for much of what they do even though they would not be
morally appraisable for anything (if Grand Assumption is true).

3. ON THE RELATIVE UNIMPORTANCE OF MORAL APPRAISABILITY AND THE RELATIVE IMPORTANCE OF NONMORAL NORMATIVE APPRAISABILITY

Regarding the first suggestion that the significance of morality in our lives has
been exaggerated, in chapter 11 I introduced Michael Slote's account of certain
principal aspects of the life of a somewhat fictionalized Gauguin. Let's remind
ourselves of a key passage in that account:

> We are all to a greater or lesser extent familiar with the fact that Gauguin de-
> serted his family and went off to the South Seas to paint. And although many of us
> admire Gauguin, not only for what he produced and for his talent, but also for his
> absolute dedication to (his) art, most of us are also repelled by what he did to his
> family. . . . I believe that we can persuade ourselves of the wrongness of . . . [his]
> desertion and we can do so without losing our sense of admiration for Gauguin's
> artistic single-mindedness. Single-minded devotion to aesthetic goals or ideals seems
> to us a virtue in an artist; yet this trait, as we shall see, cannot be understood apart
> from the tendency to do such things as Gauguin did to his family, and so is not—
> like daring or indeed like Gauguin's own artistic talent—merely 'externally' related
> to immorality. (Slote 1983, p. 80)

As we noted, one of the morals Slote wishes to draw from cases of this sort is
that "morality need not totally constrain the personal traits we think of as virtues
and there may indeed be such a thing as admirable immorality" (1983, p. 78). My
interest in the case (in this final section) resides in the following. In the way in
which he spins the tale, Slote provides convincing detail for the view that Gauguin's desertion of his family was morally wrong, and Gauguin believed that it
was so. Nevertheless, and this is what deserves emphasis, his passion for art, his
zealous devotion to the realization of an "impersonally valuable good"—the production of great art that supposedly is of benefit to everyone—took precedence
for Gauguin over his concerns for morality (really immorality) and for his own
health or safety. And as I explained, Gauguin is similar in this respect to an array
of novelists, sculptors, composers, poets, musicians, philosophers, or other sorts of
scholars. Similarly, successful (and even unsuccessful) entrepreneurs, politicians,
or athletes often give less than reasonable weight to their own well-being, and
less than normal weight or no weight at all to moral concerns when pursuing
their work-oriented goals. Their devotion to their projects is not "grounded in,"
nor does it stem from, any moral obligation or moral concern.

Artists, novelists, sculptors, and politicians aside, consider one aspect of the
relationship between parents and their young. It would be stretching credulity to
believe that the importance to parents of their children's well-being derived in
any way from specifically moral obligations to care for their offspring. We care for
our children simply because we love them. As Harry Frankfurt explains:

Moral obligation is not really what counts here. Even if parents are somehow morally obligated to love or to care about their children, it is not normally on account
of any such obligation that they do love them. Parents are generally not concerned
for their children out of duty, but simply out of love; and the love, needless to say,
is not a love of duty but a love of the children. (Frankfurt 1994, p. 446)

I am quite willing to grant that love may be associated with morality in a way
quite different than attributing love to a sense of obligation. I can also assume
(though I think this assumption is probably false) that the dictates of love are
never at odds with those of morality. Still, I believe it is true that one can act
out of love, that is, one can be moved into action by love or act for the *sake of*
love, without its being the case that one is moved into action by duty or moral
concerns.

Besides parental love, there is love among friends and love between spouses,
and with love there is the associated care. For many, there is love for, or devotion
to, God. Again, it seems that moral obligation is not what matters here. It would
plainly not be true to the facts to suppose that our concern for the well-being of
our friends or lovers somehow derives from specifically moral duties. Mill remarked astutely that ninety-nine hundredths of all our actions are not motivated
by a feeling of duty—it is just false that they are performed "from" or "out of"
duty.[4]

Still, one might raise the worry that even if we often don't act *out of* moral
concerns or for the sake of right (and hence are often not morally praiseworthy),
this alone doesn't show that we are often not morally *appraisable*. It needs to be
argued, additionally, that we often don't act *despite* moral concerns; for then it
would follow that we are often not blameworthy—unless we are to blame for not
"accessing" the relevant concerns or beliefs in the first place.

This worry can, I believe, be met. For, first, there are numerous circumstances
in life in which we just don't harbor relevant moral beliefs, perhaps for the simple
reason that we have not thought about what morality requires or forbids. So, for
instance, Ben may skip class (indeed, he may form a habit of doing so) without
a thought about morality "informing" his action or cultivation of his habit; a
businessperson may feel that it is "professionally wrong" to divulge company se-
crets (or to take extended coffee breaks), but still fail to act (when she deliberately avoids divulging certain sensitive information or avoids prolonging her
breaks) out of or despite *moral* duty or concerns. Second, even in cases in which
people do have the appropriate sorts of moral beliefs, these are (it seems to me)
frequently simply not "accessed" when they perform the relevant actions, and
hence they are not appraisable for what they do. Fred may harbor the (dispositional) belief that it is wrong for him to take coffee but may, when completely
engrossed in his work, consume a cup without in any way "accessing" this belief;
when he takes the coffee, he acts just as he would have in the absence of having
the standing belief. Since the counterfactual scenario in which Fred lacks the
germane belief but takes the coffee is not one in which he is blameworthy for
taking the coffee, and it is a scenario relevantly analogous to the actual one in
which he takes the coffee (an appropriate belief is not "accessed" as it is not even
possessed), Fred is not in fact blameworthy for taking the coffee. Third and finally,

even in cases involving acting out of love or friendship, or nonmoral *concern* for some other individual—and I think such cases are common occurrences—the agent simply fails to act *despite* moral concerns, again for the reason that the agent's behavior (in the circumstances) is entirely divorced from *any* sort of *moral* regard or interest.

I am not concerned to defend the silly claim that morality never serves as a spring of action; of course it does! But I *am* concerned to champion the view that the great "shakers and movers" in our lives frequently have nothing to do with morality at all. Jealousy, hate, love, and profit are just a few of the nonmoral springs that drive us into action.

Suppose we grant that the importance of moral obligation in our lives is lim- ited in *this* sense: very many of our concerns or cares are not in any way derivative from duty, and when we act, we frequently fail to act *out* of or despite duty. Moral concerns—beliefs regarding what is right, wrong, or obligatory, or beliefs that what one is doing is of moral import—frequently play no role at all in the actual sequence of events that generate our actions. What, if anything, does this show about the scope of moral responsibility? Let's focus on moral appraisability, paying particular attention to an epistemic (or cognitive) dimension of such appraisabil- ity. As I have proposed, an agent is morally to blame for performing an action, A, only if he has an occurrent or dispositional belief, BAW, that A is wrong or morally amiss, and he performs A despite entertaining BAW and believes (at least dispositionally) that he is performing A. Entertaining a belief involves *accessing* it in some way and not merely having it; one must, maybe even unconsciously, be cognizant of it. Similarly, an agent is deserving of moral praise for performing A only if she has an occurrent or dispositional belief, BAR, that A is obligatory or right, she performs A while (or in spite of) entertaining BAR, she believes at least dispositionally that she is performing A, and she performs A for the reason that (or at least partly for the reason that) she believes (at least dispositionally) that A is the right thing to do. Now imagine that a mother visits her sick child in hospital. Is she morally to praise for doing so? Suppose the mother sees her child for no other reason than that she loves him and cares for his well-being. The belief that it is right or obligatory for her to visit her child plays no role whatsoever in the etiology of her action (the "action" that is the action of her visiting the child). Any such moral belief fails to enter into her deliberations (indeed, if she deliberates at all) about whether to visit her child; nor does she entertain in any way any such belief in visiting her child. Then I submit that the mother is not *morally* to praise for visiting her child. Is she, nonetheless, morally responsible though, in the broad sense of 'morally responsible', which allows that one may be morally responsible for something even though not morally praisewor- thy or blameworthy for that thing? Well, suppose the mother does not visit her child in light of the belief that her visiting the child is of some moral import; there are, assume, *no* such moral beliefs at all in the "background"—the devoted mother visits her child merely because what drives her is a sense of love. Then again I don't see why she is *morally* responsible, even in the wide sense of 'morally responsible' for her visit. Of course, this sort of assessment is perfectly compatible with other moral evaluations of the mother. We need not deny, for instance, that what the mother did was right or obligatory, or that she did something good by visiting her child. Or suppose the mother, without hesitation and concern for her own well-being, gives up one of her kidneys to her child who would otherwise not survive. Assume that she simply acts out of love and not duty or any sense of moral concern. Then again, though not even "widely morally responsible," the mother may well have done what she morally ought to, and she may well be morally admirable *insofar* as she has done her duty.[5] Furthermore, and of significance, another apt normative evaluation of the mother is this: though not morally responsible, the mother clearly seems responsible—not just causally, but normatively—for giving up her kidney.

I have proposed that normative appraisability is closely tied to what a person cares about. Specifically, frequently (but not without exception) it is closely associated with normative standards a person thinks important and hence follows in guiding his life and conduct.[6] I specified that, in this context, 'normative standards' is to be understood broadly. So, for instance, the dictates of tradition, or ideals *of cardinal importance* to one's life, qualify as such standards. Further, I said that for a set of dictates, or ideals, or rules to qualify as appropriate normative standards that "anchor" normative appraisability, the standards must guide and constrain behavior; they carry, in the person's life, authoritative weight. A person who accepts a set of standards as normative and authoritative is motivated to act in accordance with those standards, believes that they provide reasons for action, and is disposed to have (appropriate) pro or con feelings or attitudes in specific circumstances. I make no presumption that people generally endorse a single set of ideals or standards that guide and constrain behavior across all "domains" of life. One may, with respect to certain concerns, act out of or despite love, but with respect to others, act from or despite moral duty, or from or despite the imperatives of one's religion.

A possible misconstrual of my account of nonmoral normative appraisability should be guarded against. It is not my view that nonmoral normative appraisability is incurred (in broad strokes) when one has freely and nondeviantly acted on or despite a belief that one ought to act in a certain way, where this "ought" is both (a) nonmoral and (b) judged to be the most significant "ought" that applies to one's situation. I insist on a but *not* on b. Suppose, for example, that I am in a situation where I find myself torn between two incompatible actions (A and B), in that I judge them, respectively, to be morally and prudentially required. I may decide to do B; but such a decision doesn't have to involve my judging (even granting we can make sense of what such judging amounts to) that, on this occasion, prudential considerations are "more important" than moral ones. On my view, when I do B, I may well be morally blameworthy but not prudentially blameworthy (and possibly even prudentially praiseworthy).

The devoted mother who gives up a kidney is, I now want to propose, nonmorally normatively praiseworthy. She gives up her kidney, roughly, on the basis of the belief that that is what she ought to do acting out of love. The 'ought' in this last sentence does not, of course, signal any moral duty or imperative. Rather, we can suppose that it denotes an obligation, or something like an obligation, associated with acting out of love (which is somewhat analogous to the moral obligation of acting out of duty). The term 'ought' here, then, signifies an imperative stemming from the appropriate normative standard from which the mother acted when she donated her kidney, and which she takes (at least in various circumstances) as authoritative in guiding and constraining her conduct. The standard, in this case of hers, is clearly not a moral one.

One might believe that nonmoral varieties of normative appraisability are plagued with the same sort of worries as those that plague moral appraisability. In particular, it might be thought that if causal determinism undermines moral appraisability, it undermines any variety of normative appraisability as well. Is this so? This issue is complicated for at least two reasons. First, some varieties of nonmoral normative appraisability may be ruled out for reasons analogous to the reasons that (possibly) subvert moral appraisability. So, for instance, if nothing can be prudentially right, wrong, or obligatory in a determined world, and if prudential blameworthiness or praiseworthiness (or more broadly, responsibility) presupposes that at least some things are prudentially right, wrong, or obligatory, then no one can be prudentially normatively responsible for any of one's behavior in a determined world. Second, it might be the case that even some nonmoral varieties of appraisability rest upon some things being morally right, wrong, or obligatory. But in a determined world, nothing can be morally right, wrong, or obligatory. These two complications aside, I want to suggest that (supposing determinism is true) other varieties of normative appraisability may fare much better. Revert to the devoted mother who is, it seems, normatively appraisable—presumably normatively praiseworthy—for giving up her kidney to her child. She acts out of love and not out of moral duty. In very broad outline, she is normatively praiseworthy for giving up the kidney as she freely gives up the kidney on the basis of the belief that she is doing what she ought to, where the 'ought' is the ought (in the sense sketched above) of acting out of love. She has remained true to, and engaged the principles with which she identifies, which guide and constrain her behavior in significant areas of her life. It appears that the standards to which she bears allegiance—those of love or care—need not in any way be undermined, or rendered inapplicable, in a determined world. Similarly, consider fictionalized Gauguin selflessly devoted to the production of great art. The normative standards that guide and limit this person's behavior are again not moral but a set whose core comprises aesthetic elements. Presumably, these standards should remain unscathed in a determined world. Hence, fictionalized Gauguin can be legitimately normatively appraised vis-à-vis these standards.

In conclusion, these last few suggestions of mine do not in any way help with rescuing moral appraisability—and responsibility—from the clutches of determinism *if* Grand Assumption is true. They do, though, give us some hope with respect to other varieties of normative appraisability. In addition, even if Grand Assumption is false, as I think it is, they do unveil a "threat" of sorts to moral appraisability. The "threat" has nothing to do with determinism, or inability to do otherwise, or "erosion" of agency. Rather, it has to do with the sorts of people we are, with our cares, wants, and beliefs. If the springs of our actions are frequently free of any (germane) moral constituents, there will be no room at all in many dramas of life for moral appraisability to secure a foothold.

NOTES

1. See Fischer and Ravizza 1993; and Strawson 1962.

2. Throughout this work, to avoid using gender-exclusive personal pronouns and the cumbersome "his or her" or "he/she," I have alternated between using feminine and masculine pronouns. I add, in addition, that the relevant pronouns, in this work, are used in the generic rather than in any gendered sense.

3. For some discussion on cases of this sort, see Fischer 1986, pp. 9–13.

4. Important discussion of this sort of case can be found in Mele 1995, esp. chap. 8, 9.

5. For some discussion on the bearing of perverse appreciation for responsibility, see Austin 1991, p. 46.

6. For a fascinating discussion of the relevance of psychological continuity to personal identity, see Parfit 1986. For more on personal identity in "global transformation cases," see Mele 1995, n. 22, p. 175. An important point Mele stresses is this: the pre- and postpsychosurgery persons may be strongly psychologically connected, in Parfit's sense (1986, p. 206). The number of direct psychological connections between them, possibly, "is *at least* half the number that hold, over every day, in the lives of nearly every actual person." Jennifer Radden (1996) provides extremely useful examples from abnormal psychology of multiple or successive selves which in some respects resemble Psychogen; see, especially, chap. 3.

7. "Ledger views" of the concept of responsibility are held by Zimmerman 1988, pp. 38–39; Feinberg 1970, pp. 30–31, 124–25; Glover 1970; and Gert and Duggan 1979, 197–217. Carl Elliott also seems to endorse a ledger view. See Elliott 1996, pp. 65–66.

8. On the incompatibility of causal determinism with appraisability, see, for example, van Inwagen 1983, pp. 55–105; van Inwagen 1989; Ginet 1983, 1990; Fischer 1983, 1994; Wiggens 1973; and Vihvelin 1991. On the incompatibility of the existence of God with appraisability, see, for example, Hoffman and Rozenkrantz 1980; Pike 1965, 1970; and Fischer 1989, 1994.

9. Frankfurt-type examples have been given by John Locke in Locke [1690] 1984, bk. 2, chap. 21, sec. 8–11; and by Harry Frankfurt in Frankfurt 1969. Such examples are extensively discussed by John Martin Fischer in Fischer 1994, esp. chap. 7; and by Mark Ravizza in Ravizza 1994.

10. See, for example, Harry Frankfurt's account of such control discussed in a series of articles including Frankfurt 1971, 1975, 1978, 1987, 1988b, and 1992. See also Eleonore Stump's development of hierarchical control in Stump 1993a and 1993b.

11. It is profitable to compare and contrast this account of control with John Fischer's account of reasons-responsiveness developed in Fischer 1987; and in Fischer and Ravizza's forthcoming *Responsibility and Control: A Theory of Moral Responsibility*.

12. This sort of view is held by, for example, John Christman. See Christman 1991 and 1993.

13. See, for example, Wolf 1990. Also see Frankfurt 1993, 1988b, and 1988c.

14. Some people who hold this sort of view include Holly Smith (Smith 1983, 1991); David Widerker (Widerker 1991); Justin Oakley and Dean Cocking (Oakley and Cocking 1994); Lloyd Fields (Fields 1994); and David Copp (Copp 1996).

TWO   APPRAISABILITY, ALTERNATIVE POSSIBILITIES, AND ULTIMATE CONTROL

I thank the publisher and author for their permission to reprint material from David Widerker, "Libertarianism and Frankfurt's Attack on the Principle of Alternative Possibilities," *Philosophical Review* 104 (1995). Copyright 1995, Cornell University Press.

1. Eugene Schlossberger appears to reject the control condition for appraisability. See Schlossberger 1992, pp. 6–7, and chap. 5. For comments on Schlossberger's view, see Zimmerman 1995b, sec. 2.4.

2. Harry G. Frankfurt formulates the principle of alternative possibilities in this way: a person is morally responsible for what he has done only if he could have done otherwise. See Frankfurt 1969, p. 828.

3. This is, admittedly, a conception of alternative possibilities held by traditional libertarians or "hard-line incompatibilists." In contrast, traditional compatibilists deny that an alternative possibility of this sort is required for moral appraisability, responsibility, freedom, or control; they endorse weaker "compatibilist" interpretations of 'could have done otherwise'. One of my primary concerns in this chapter is to show that control does not require alternative possibilities as conceived by traditional libertarians.

4. For variations of this sort of argument, see van Inwagen 1983, pp. 55–105; van Inwagen 1989; and Ginet 1983, 1990.

There is another argument for the incompatibility of causal determinism and moral responsibility that does not proceed via the channel that causal determinism rules out moral responsibility as it rules out alternative possibilities. Rather, it is an argument that relies on the following principle (B): if no one is morally responsible for p, and no one is morally responsible for the fact that p leads to q, then no one is morally responsible for q. (Peter van Inwagen offers this sort of principle in van Inwagen 1983, p. 183.) The argument then unfolds in this way. If causal determinism is true, some state of the world, S, in the past, in conjunction with the laws of nature, L, entails any action, A, that one now does. But as no one is morally responsible for the state of the world S in the past and for the laws of nature, L, and no one is morally responsible for the fact that S and L lead to one now doing A, no one is morally responsible for one's now doing A. This sort of argument is thoroughly discussed by Mark Ravizza in Ravizza, 1994. Ravizza, relying on Frankfurt-type cases, argues effectively against principle B. Further discussion of this principle occurs in Fischer and Ravizza, forthcoming, chap. 6.

5. See Locke [1690] 1984, bk. 2, chap. 21, sec. 8–11; and Frankfurt 1969. For recent critical discussion of the principle of alternative possibilities, see Glannon 1994, 1995; Lamb 1993; Fischer and Hoffman 1994; Dennett 1984, chap. 6; and Rowe 1991, chap. 5.

6. See, for example, Hume [1739] 1975, bk. 2, pt. 3, sec. 2; John Stuart Mill [1865] 1979, pp. 464–67; Audi 1993a, chap. 7, 10; and Ayer, 1954.

7. For further exploration, two things are worth noting. First, as I indicated in note 4 above, Peter van Inwagen has a "direct argument" for the view that determinism rules out appraisability even if PAP is rejected. The argument, in rough outline, is this: as no one now is morally responsible for the past, and no one is morally responsible for the past's leading (via natural laws) to present actions, no one is now morally responsible for one's present actions. This argument merits close scrutiny. Second, one might argue that Frankfurt-type cases don't undermine control or appraisability because the "ensurance" of the agent's action is merely "passive"; determinism, however, does undermine control (and thus appraisability also) because the sort of ensurance it supplies is "active." Of course, just what this passive/active distinction is supposed to amount to is a vexed question, but if there is a defensible distinction here, there is the possibility that event-causation undermines control or freedom (and thus appraisability), even if PAP is rejected.

8. I take this sort of example from Mele 1995, chap. 12, sec. 1, 2. See, also, Mele 1996, sec. 2.

9. Also see Kane 1994, pp. 25–60, esp. sec. 4.

10. For an instructive discussion of this point, see Clarke 1995. It should be stressed that Mele himself is "not a fan of hard libertarianism" (Mele 1996, sec. 3). Hard libertarians are hard-line incompatibilists who claim that freedom of choice and action are incompatible with determinism and moral responsibility. In addition, in Mele 1996, one of Mele's primary aims is to defend the view that some "reasonable, informed people will value species of freedom and moral responsibility that are open to them only on the hypothesis that they are indeterministic initiators more highly than they value compatibilist freedom and moral responsibility" (sec. 2). Mele does not (in this piece) argue that indeterministic initiation augments control.

11. See McKenna (forthcoming). Subsequent references in this chapter to McKenna's work are to this piece, and they are from a prepublication draft.

THREE   MORAL OBLIGATION AND ALTERNATIVE POSSIBILITIES

1. For superb discussions on responsibility for the "unthinkable," see Frankfurt 1993, 1988b, and 1988c. For a recent new contribution, see Zimmerman, 1995b.

2. The cases involving drug addiction and hypnosis are discussed by Wolf in Wolf 1980.

3. See, for example, John Stuart Mill's version of utilitarianism in Mill [1891] 1989.

4. On alternatives, see, e.g., Bergstrom 1976 and 1971. Also see Aqvist 1969.

5. It should be stressed that it is not correct to suppose that AU entails that it is obligatory for S, in a case such as Villain, to do A for these reasons: since it can't happen that Joe does anything other than push the child off the pier, no meaningful value can be assigned for the utility of such an alternative, and so, by default, the utility of Joe's pushing the child off the pier must be higher than that of any of the "nonalternatives." This argument turns on the fallacious assumption that S's doing other than A has a utility only

if S can do other than A. Rather, the view that when S does A of necessity, AU entails that it is obligatory for S to do A, turns partly on the condition that acts can be alternatives for S only if S is able to perform each of them.

6. See Feldman 1986, esp. chap. 2. This sort of theory is also defended by Michael Zimmerman in Zimmerman 1996.

7. Feldman 1986, pp. 42–43. Suppose that for every world accessible to s at t, there is a better one then accessible to s as well. To accommodate this possibility, Feldman adduces the following as the official version of MO: as of t, s ought to see to the occurrence of p if and only if p occurs in some world accessible to s at t, and it is not the case that not-p occurs in any accessible world as good as or better than that one. (1986, pp. 33–38)

8. van Inwagen takes 'particular event' in PPP1 to refer to the *outcome* (a particular state of affairs) of the act which the person performs (1983, pp. 164–65.). But construed in this fashion, PPP1 generates highly counterintuitive results. Suppose, for example, that in "Missile" Martha is aware that if she launches the missile, thousands will be killed. Suppose Missile is a Frankfurt-type case, one in which Martha cannot avoid launching the missile. Suppose Martha rightly believes that once she launches the missile, she won't be able to prevent the deaths, but mistakenly believes that if she wants to, she can refrain from launching the missile. Suppose, finally, that Martha ("freely") launches the missile and thousands die as a result. PPP1 implies that Martha is not responsible for the deaths!

9. Critical discussion of principle E can be found in Carter 1979, and in Fischer 1982.

10. In Widerker 1991, David Widerker has advanced an argument that can be construed as one against K. I deny one of the premises in the argument, the premise that an agent is morally blameworthy for performing an act only if the agent has a moral obligation not to perform that act. See Objection 4 below.

11. Unquestionably, some will have deep doubts about any such principle, doubts that stem from the possibility of culpable ignorance. I address these sorts of concerns in chap. 9.

12. This conclusion is contrary to those reached by Wolf and Frankfurt. Wolf says "on my view . . . it will follow that an agent can be both determined and responsible only insofar as he performs actions that he ought to perform" (1980, p. 163). According to Frankfurt, "the Kantian view [that 'ought' implies 'can'] leaves open the possibility that a person for whom only one course of action is available fulfills an obligation when he pursues that course of action" (1988a, p. 96).

13. Sir William David Ross defends this sort of theory. See Ross 1930.

14. A strongly intentionalist theory of this sort is held by St. Augustine. See, e.g., Augustine 1948 and 1951, pp. 52–53. Justin Oakley also appears to endorse a theory of this sort. See Oakley 1992, p. 39.

15. See Copp 1996. Subsequent references in this section to Copp are to this work, and they are from the September 1996 draft.

FOUR   APPRAISABILITY AND CONTROL

The excerpt from Randy Clarke's "Doing What One Wants: A Reappraisal of the Law of Desire," *Pacific Philosophical Quarterly* 75 (1994), is reprinted with the permission of Blackwell Publishers.

1. Elaborated, Frankfurt's theory can be summarized in this way: when one decisively identifies with a first-order desire, one commits oneself to it (and the course of action that is the object of that desire). Frankfurt says, "When a person identifies himself decisively with one of his first-order desires, this commitment 'resounds' throughout the potentially

endless array of higher orders. . . . The fact that his second-order volition to be moved by this desire is a decisive one means that there is no room for questions concerning the pertinence of volitions of higher orders" (1971, p. 16). Frankfurt attempts to clarify the concepts of decisive identification and resonance in Frankfurt 1987.

2. Hierarchical theories of responsibility, autonomy, or control have also been defended by Gerald Dworkin in Dworkin 1970 and 1976 (Dworkin's revised views on autonomy are to be found in Dworkin 1988), by Wright Neely (Neely 1974), and by Richard Jeffrey (Jeffrey 1974).

3. For critical discussion of Frankfurt's theory, see (among others) Buss 1994; Christman 1991; Fischer and Ravizza 1994a; Friedman 1986; Oshana 1994; Shatz 1985; Thalberg 1978; Watson 1975; and Wolf 1990, chap. 2.

4. Interestingly, Susan Wolf says, "According to the Reason View, . . . it is *only* the ability to do the right thing for the right reasons . . . that is required for responsibility" (1990, p. 81, my emphasis). Here, she leaves the impression that how one acquires the springs of one's actions is irrelevant to correct ascriptions of responsibility. Her discussion of JoJo's case in "Sanity and the Metaphysics of Responsibility", (Wolf 1988) suggests otherwise; it suggests that "historical considerations" matter.

5. The concept of an agent's settling on a course of action is constructed by Mele in Mele 1992a, chap. 9.

6. A different sort of reasons-responsiveness has been developed and defended by John Martin Fischer in Fischer 1987. For critical discussion of this view, see Shatz 1988; and Pereboom 1995. Recently, Fischer and Mark Ravizza have refined Fischer's notion of reasons-responsiveness in their forthcoming book, *Responsibility and Control: A Theory of Moral Responsibility*.

7. Such a view, or variants of such a view, is held by Donald Davidson (Davidson 1980, p. 23); Alfred Mele (Mele 1987a, pp. 13–14, and 1992a, chap. 3,4); and William Alston (Alston 1974, p. 95).

8. Ferdinand Schoeman discusses such a case in Schoeman 1994.

9. The notion of psychological continuity to which I am appealing is Derek Parfit's. See Parfit 1986, pp. 205–6.

10. Schoeman raises this objection to Fischer's (former) reasons-responsiveness theory. See Fischer 1987, p. 90, n. 11.

FIVE APPRAISABILITY, AUTONOMY, AND CONTROL

1. This assumption may violate Kantian theories of action according to which actions can be motivated by reason alone.

2. Michael Zimmerman has suggested to me that there might be irresistibility even in the *presence* of relatively weak pro-attitudes as long as there are sufficiently strong contra-attitudes.

3. This example is an adaptation of an example discussed by Alfred Mele in Mele 1987a, p. 22.

4. On misalignments between evaluative judgments and motivations, see Mele 1987a, chap. 3, 6; Mele 1992a, chap. 9; Watson 1975; and Heil 1994.

5. See, for example, Mele 1987a, chap. 6, for insightful discussion of the relevant sort of explanation. See, also, Kurt Baier's discussion in Baier 1995, chap. 3.

6. I here set aside worries from the direction of causal determinism.

7. There is a suggestive discussion on moral responsibility and induced desires in Schoeman 1978, pp. 293–301. I assess Schoeman's views in chap. 11.

8. The sprinter's case is advanced by Alfred Mele in Mele 1993, pp. 271–80, n. 2.

9. For a recent highly instructive account of akratic action, see Mele 1987a. Not everyone agrees that akratic action is possible. See, e.g., Watson 1977.

10. On this theme, see, e.g., Audi 1991a.

11. For more on the distinction between mere choice and decision, see Klein 1990, chap. 5. I am grateful to Alfred Mele for indicating these things to me: first, there appear to be some unusual but possible cases in which an agent decides to A, even though prior to decision, the agent is not uncertain about whether she will A. See Mele 1992b. Second, Buridan's ass scenarios, in which the relevant options are doing A and doing B, might be ones in which an agent can decide to A while remaining convinced that her reasons for her two options are equally strong.

12. For some discussion on this point, see Watson 1987a.

13. Wolf, for example, discusses this sort of worry in Wolf 1990.

14. The point that decisions (in the mental sense of 'action') are not implantable has been made by Mele in Mele 1992a, p. 141. There is a concern here voiced by Michael Zimmerman (personal communication). The fact that decisions are active in a way in which desires are not, Zimmerman suggests, should not preclude their being implanted. Granted, he explains, what would have to be implanted is not just the having, but the doing, of the decision; but why couldn't this be accomplished?

15. Again, I temporarily set aside worries originating with causal determinism.

16. Alfred Mele and I disagree on whether a willing addict like Poppy autonomously uses the drug. Mele introduces the case of Alice, an addiction specialist, who is relevantly like Poppy and who undertakes an interesting experiment. For purposes of gaining insight into addiction, Alice decides, after careful, clearheaded, unbiased, and informed reflection, to develop irresistible desires for heroin. She judges it best to make the necessary preparations and then to inject herself with the drug. The judgment issues nondeviantly in an effective proximal intention (see Mele 1995, pp. 138, 192). Mele comments:

> At the time of the injection, Alice was possessed of an irresistible desire for the drug, but she was moved to use it by her considered reasons for continuing the experiment. . . . I submit, Alice autonomously used the drug. It is true, let us suppose, that if she had not been moved to use it by the pertinent reasons, she would have used it anyway, owing to the influence of an irresistible proximal desire for heroin. But this does not imply that she nonautonomously used the drug-any more than the fact that a mind-reading demon would have made us save a drowning child, if we had not saved her on our own, implies that we did not autonomously save her. . . . [Assuming Alice is fully autonomous with respect to the process that issued in the relevant judgment and intention to use the drug], one is hard pressed to see how her using the drug can count as a nonautonomous deed. Alice is autonomous . . . with respect to her use of the drug at the time, even though her addiction would not have allowed her to refrain from using it. (Mele 1995, pp. 192–93)

In response, it is not clear to me how a desire that plays a crucial role in the generation of an action be irresistible but that it not play its role at least in part in virtue of its irresistibility. As Alice's desire for the drug is irresistible, it seems to me that she has no more control over the action that issues from this desire than she would have were she an unwilling addict whose action issued from this sort of desire. Actional autonomy requires having control over the pertinent action, and the relevant sort of control, I have suggested, is volitional control. Whereas Alice (like Poppy) lacks volitional control over her taking the drug, agents (like Della) in standard Frankfurt-type cases (involving, for instance, mind-reading demons) are not bereft of such control.

17. Here, I disagree with Radden (1996). Discussing the value of autonomy (or self-

determination), Radden claims that "self-determination is . . . a precondition of something . . . we particularly value: responsibility" (p. 221) and that "The self that is self-determining is the author of second-order desires about what it wants for itself" (p. 223).

18. A nice development of this criticism can be found in Fischer and Ravizza 1994a. Also see Slote 1980, and Stump 1993b. Finally, Alfred Mele discusses a number of thought-provoking cases in which an agent is manipulated to the extent to which all her evaluative standards have been, unbeknownst to the agent, engineered by third parties in Mele 1995, chap. 9.

19. See Mele 1995, chap. 9, for insightful discussion on a case of this sort. See also Double 1989.

20. For an opposing view, see Christman 1991.

21. This view is elegantly developed and defended by Mele in Mele 1995, chap. 9, 10.

SIX   APPRAISABILITY AND INDUCED PRO-ATTITUDES

1. The theory developed by John Fischer and Mark Ravizza is a history-sensitive one. See Fischer 1987; Fischer and Ravizza 1994a, and their forthcoming *Responsibility and Control: A Theory of Moral Responsibility*. Alfred Mele defends a theory of individual autonomy that is history-sensitive in Mele 1995.

2. Carl Elliott, like Frankfurt, seems to favor a "current-time slice" theory of responsibility. See Elliott 1996, p. 69.

3. Such cases are also extensively discussed by Mele in Mele 1995. Mele relies on such cases, among other things, to argue for a history-sensitive theory of individual autonomy.

4. I am assuming that although normal (and autonomous) agents sometimes are unable to shed or attenuate cherished values of theirs that issue in intentional conduct, it is implausible that that precludes their being morally appraisable for that conduct. Some support for this assumption derives from reflection on "Frankfurt-like" cases discussed in the text below. The crux of the idea here is this: assume S's value, V, frequently issues in intentional action. Assume, also, that were S to show on any occasion any inclination whatsoever to shed V, an irresistible imp would prevent S from shedding V and would compel S to act on V. It so happens that S never attempts (on S's own) to shed V (and so the imp never intervenes). I submit that (other conditions for moral appraisability being satisfied) S is morally appraisable for conduct deriving from V although V is unsheddable. S acts on V just as S would have had no imp been around.

5. The control condition's second disjunct needs at least this qualification: the agent did not (willingly) see to any such desire being instilled in her.

6. Alfred Mele calls such Frankfurt type cases "expanded Frankfurt-style scenarios." See Mele 1995, p. 141.

7. Point ii has been questioned by Slote in Slote 1980, and by Robert Audi in Audi 1993a, pp. 184–86.

8. The account is also to be found in Double 1991, chap. 2.

9. The notion of psychological continuity to which I appeal originates with Derek Parfit. See Parfit 1986, pp. 205–6.

10. At one point (in Parfit 1986, p. 206), Parfit suggests that strong psychological connectedness is the preservation over time of at least half the number of psychological connections that normally hold, over every day, in the lives of actual persons.

11. For rich discussions on this point, see Strawson 1962; Russell 1992; Fischer and Ravizza 1993; and Watson 1987b.

12. I should emphasize that I am using a technical notion of *normative agent*. One should not confuse, say, Clinton with a normative agent and then balk at the (implausible)

suggestion that Clinton has his evaluative scheme essentially. Seemingly, Clinton could have had a very different evaluative scheme than the one he in fact has.

13. I am indebted to Alfred Mele for the suggestion that IPA2 may have to be supplemented with the following. First, A is not causally overdetermined—it is false that S would have done A even in the absence of its cause in PA. Second, A's cause in PA is not morally irrelevant. It is not the case, for example, that supposing that although a part of A's (nonoverdetermining) cause is in PA, that cause plays a very minor role—it influences only slightly the speed of S's A-ing in a case in which A's speed is morally irrelevant.

14. The example is Alfred Mele's; see Mele 1995, chap. 10, sec. 3 for an insightful discussion of such examples.

15. Alfred Mele proposes (in Mele 1995, chap. 10, sec. 3) that to the extent to which an "engineered" deliberative habit is at work in a deliberative process, the agent is not deliberating autonomously, where engineered deliberative habits amount, roughly, to the purposeful instilling of a habit in an agent in such a way that her relevant capacities for control over her mental life are bypassed in the process. Since there may not be a neat overlap between an agent's autonomously A-ing and an agent's being morally responsible for A-ing (see chap. 5), one might well accept Mele's proposal without endorsing the further view that the agent with engineered deliberative habits cannot be morally responsible for an action that issues from "engineered deliberations."

16. Some might raise this objection: Why cannot we consider scenarios in which Ernie has this desire (the motivational precursor of A) but was never brainwashed? (In some such scenarios he decides not to A.) After all, regarding Frankfurt-type scenarios, you allow us to consider alternative scenarios in which the interveners are absent. Why, in our search for scenarios, are we allowed to subtract the Frankfurt interveners, but not the pertinent aspect of the agent's history? My answer, as should now be clear, amounts to this: our own past histories exert heavy leverage on shaping our characters, personalities, and psychologies. I have proposed that we hold constant in eligible alternative scenarios the historical factors that contribute to the formation of the agent's character and psychological constitution, *and* those that give rise to the *conative* elements on which the agent acts in the actual scenario (see chap. 4, sec. 5 above).

SEVEN AUTHENTIC EVALUATIVE SCHEMES

Material from *In Harm's Way: Essays In Honor of Joel Feinberg*, edited by Jules Coleman and Allen Buchanan (Cambridge: Cambridge University Press, 1994), is reprinted by permission of Cambridge University Press.

1. 'Stem from' requires analysis that I shall not here attempt to give.

2. Psychogen and cases involving individuals suffering from dissociative-identity disorder share some obvious similarities. Robert Louis Stevenson's tale, *Dr. Jekyll and Mr. Hyde*, beautifully illustrates central aspects of the disorder, one of them being that there are alternative personalities (or selves) comprising the "Multiple," who is the person who has the disorder. In Psychogen we have one "self" succeeding another; in the Jekyll and Hyde story, we have alternating "selves." An intriguing issue concerning responsibility with multiples, to which Jennifer Radden (1996, esp. chap. 6) has called attention, is this: suppose a multiple comprises two selves, Self1 and Self2. Suppose each self is unaware of the deeds of the other. Suppose Self2 is "reigning"—it is presently embodied and has "executive control" of the shared body (Radden 1996, p. 46), and during its (present) reign commits a vile crime. Is Self1 ever morally appraisable (or responsible) for this crime? To help us with such cases, Radden relies heavily on what she calls "Locke's principle": continuity of memory is necessary for ascription of responsibility (1996, p. 93). In her astute discussion,

Radden concludes that (in various cases), Self1 will not be responsible for the crime. Save for the following very brief comment, I resist the temptation to address this important issue, and Radden's position on it, in this book and reserve discussion of it for a journal article (Haji, 1997a). I believe Locke's principle is suspect; further, considerations of authenticity, I think, will play a central role in responsibility ascriptions in cases involving multiples.

EIGHT   KNOWLEDGE AND APPRAISABILITY

1. See, also, Oakley 1992, p. 162. Another person who appears to endorse the Objective View is Kurt Baier. See Baier 1995, pp. 322, 325. Michael Moore, too, accepts this view. See Moore 1984, pp. 51, 52.

2. Richard Brandt appears to reject the Objective View. See Brandt 1958, pp. 38–39.

3. Further discussion on changeability occurs in Aqvist 1969; Feldman 1986, pp. 11–15, 45–46; Zimmerman 1987, 199–205; Wierenga 1989, esp., chap. 8; Smith 1976; and Haji 1994.

4. See the discussion in chap. 3, sec. 4 above.

5. See Zimmerman 1988, chap. 4, sec. 4.10.

6. Insightful discussion on akratic action can be found, among other places, in Mele 1987a; Rorty 1980a, 1980b; Watson 1977; and Davidson 1970.

7. This type of case appears (in a different context) in Feldman 1986, pp. 45–47.

8. Deadly's Defeat is just like Cure introduced in chap. 3, sec. 3, Objection 4 above.

9. Michael Zimmerman proposes and discusses this sort of response in Zimmerman 1995a.

10. This formulation of Prerequisites, sensitive to the following, is required to avoid Good Samaritan–type paradoxes: it is false that S cannot do A without doing B because S just can't refrain from doing B (in which case, as there is a requirement of alternative possibilities for obligatoriness, it would be false that S has an obligation to do B). On Good Samaritan paradoxes, see, e.g., Aqvist 1967; Feldman 1990, and Tomberlin 1986.

11. Proponents of the view that genuine conflicts of overall moral obligations are possible will not be disturbed by this "absurdity." See, e.g., Stocker 1990, chap. 1.

12. This sort of case is discussed by Michael Zimmerman in Zimmerman 1988, pp. 59–60.

13. I owe this suggestion to Ken Akiba.

NINE   AN EPISTEMIC DIMENSION OF APPRAISABILITY

1. Zimmerman 1988, p. 40. P3.1 is later revised by Zimmerman in this way: P3.1': S is directly culpable to degree x for willing e if and only if (a) S strictly freely willed e, in the belief that it was likely to degree y that, by virtue of so willing, he would do wrong to degree z, and (b) S did not believe that his bringing about e would minimize the risk of his doing wrong (1988, p. 49).

2. I do *not* here mean to suggest that Zimmerman endorses Blame2.

3. See, e.g., Audi 1993a, p. 152.

4. Here I follow Alfred Mele; see Mele 1992a, p. 110. For a thoroughly instructive discussion on plans and intentional action, see Bratman 1987. For a defense of the view that belief is not the representational component of intention, see Brand 1984, chap. 6; and Mele 1992a, chap. 8.

5. See Mele 1987a, pp. 5–6. In an insightful and provocative piece (McIntyre 1990), Alison McIntyre argues that akratic action need not always be irrational.

6. I think the notion of an actional element's being unconscious should be time-relativized: a belief, for example, can be weakly unconscious at one time but not at another. For discussion on unconscious belief see Audi 1982, pp. 137–38;1972.

7. For insightful discussion on being morally responsible for actions deriving from unconscious beliefs, see Audi 1982.

8. I shall not here try to give an account of what these forthrightly excusing conditions are; I freely admit that this is a shortcoming of analyses Blame5 and Blame6 to come.

9. The case is an adaptation of one presented by Audi in Audi 1982.

10. See, e.g., Audi 1993b, 1985, 1982.

11. See Mele 1983, and 1987a, chap. 9, 10. Mele has an excellent survey article on self-deception; see Mele 1987b. Both Mele and Audi report that they are concerned with giving an account of self-deception of central or paradigm cases of self-deception.

12. Robert Audi concurs with this point and discusses it in Audi 1982, sec. 3.

13. This is, for example, Mele's view. See Mele 1987a, 1983.

14. Michael Zimmerman has convinced me that there is an important asymmetry to be noted between praiseworthiness and blameworthiness. Zimmerman explains that the asymmetry rests on the fact, roughly, that what is perceived as obligatory demands its pursuit, what is perceived as right invites its pursuit, and what is perceived as wrong demands its eschewal. So although one deserves praise only if one pursues the right, it's false that one deserves blame only if one pursues the wrong; one deserves blame only if one does not eschew the wrong. See Zimmerman 1988, p. 50. An example might help. Suppose that, in doing A, S believes that A is morally right, but S A-s *solely* for the reason that S believes that in A-ing, she will further her own interests. It's hard to see why S, in a case of this sort, is deserving of moral praise.

15. Michael Zimmerman appears to reject this premise. See Zimmerman 1988, pp. 59–60.

TEN   ASSEMBLING THE ELEMENTS

1. Here, again, I direct the reader's attention to Zimmerman's insightful discussion in Zimmerman 1988, pp. 50–52.

ELEVEN   VARIETIES OF NORMATIVE APPRAISABILITY

1. Michael Zimmerman favors this sort of approach; see Zimmerman 1988, pp. 40–46. See, also, sec. 4 below.

2. For lucid discussion on such conflict situations, see Mele 1987a; Rorty 1980b; and Heil 1994.

3. I discuss this further in Haji 1997b.

4. Richard Brandt (in Brandt 1958, p. 14), at least with respect to moral blameworthiness, defends a different view. He says that "in moral blaming something is imputed to a defect of character."

5. For more on this distinction, see Feldman 1986, pp. 46–48.

6. On overridingness, see also, Copp 1997; Foot 1978; Kekes 1992; Williams 1976; and Wolf 1982.

TWELVE   BLAMEWORTHINESS, CHARACTER, AND CULTURAL NORMS

Material from Lloyd Fields's "Moral Beliefs and Blameworthiness," *Philosophy* 69 (1994), is reprinted with the permission of Cambridge University Press.

1. Cummins (1980), like Fields, also ties moral appraisability to character.

2. I shall here overlook the complication that if, through a series of past actions, an agent has deliberately and freely brought it about that he cannot later refrain from doing something, he may still be morally responsible for doing that thing.

3. For discussions on the influence of history-sensitive considerations on moral responsibility or autonomy, see Christman 1991; Fischer and Ravizza 1994a; and Mele 1995. A contrasting view that history-sensitive considerations are not relevant to moral responsibility is defended, as we have noted, by Harry G. Frankfurt in Frankfurt 1988a, p. 54, and by Carl Elliott in Elliott 1996, p. 69.

4. Fields notes that locutions like 'X knows that killing people is wrong' can be "cashed" in noncognitivist terms: he claims "we could say: 'X accepts the principle that killing people is wrong, this principle is justified, and X is justified in accepting it' " (1994, P. 404). Notice, though, that even the noncognitivist gloss assumes implicitly the distinction between a principle's being objectively justified or justified *simpliciter*, and a person's believing that a principle is justified.

5. I owe this reference to James Rachels. See Rachels 1993, p. 15.

THIRTEEN   ADDICTION AND CONTROL

1. Vihvelin has recently changed her views on addicts. See Vihvelin 1994b. The discussion in sec. 3 addresses this change.

2. See Mele 1987a, chap. 3, 6; and Heil 1994.

3. See, e.g., Mele 1987a, chap. 6.

4. She further proposes that a necessary and sufficient condition of someone acting unfreely on her desire D is that the following counterfactual is true: "Even if she had the Ulysses desire, D would still have caused her to act" (1994a, p. 75).

5. See Vihvelin 1994b, esp. the section entitled "Simple Compatibilism and Moral Responsibility."

6. Vihvelin does endorse the view that free will is a necessary condition of moral responsibility. Interestingly, the view that a person is morally responsible for performing an action only if that person freely performs that action has been questioned by Slote in Slote 1980; and by Robert Audi in Audi 1993a, pp. 184–86.

FOURTEEN   ON BEING APPRAISABLE FOR THE THOUGHTS OF ONE'S DREAM SELF

1. The view that all moral responsibility traces to moral responsibility for actions has recently been advocated by Robert Audi. See Audi 1991b. For an opposing view, see Montmarquet 1992.

2. Some of Plato's discussion on dreams can be found in book 9 of the *Republic* (571c–573b), and the *Theaetetus* 158b–d. Augustine discusses the dream problem, among other places, in book 10 of the *Confessions* and book 12 of *The Literal Meaning of Genesis*. Penetrating discussions of Augustine on the dream problem appear in Matthews 1992, chap. 8; Matthews 1981; and Mann 1983.

3. This passage is from an addendum to Freud's *Interpretation of Dreams* entitled "Moral Responsibility for the Content of Dreams." See Freud [1925].

4. It might be objected that *consenting* to do evil is itself wrong even though one does not later do what one consented to do. This objection, however, is indecisive. There *are* cases in which consenting to do evil may be wrong, ones, for instance, in which consenting (to do evil) itself harms oneself or another. (Dream cases are presumably not cases of this sort.) But in other cases consenting to do evil may not be wrong. A possible case here is

this: one consents to inflict harm on an innocent party, but then fails to carry through, as one realizes that one would be doing wrong if one were to carry through.

5. I take it that Mann's position is not that in *forming* an intention to commit adultery one does something wrong, and that the wrongness of forming an intention to commit adultery is inherited by the intention (to commit adultery) itself.

6. It should be stressed that Mann rejects the 'ought' implies 'can' principle K. (I don't think his rejection is conclusive.) It should also be noted that rejection of the principle of alternative possibilities is consistent with the retention of K (see chap. 8, sec. 2).

7. It can be true that Sin's act is not wrong consistent with Sin's being morally blameworthy for performing this act. See sec. 6 below, and chap. 8.

8. In *Contra academicos* (3.11.26), Augustine seems to reject the supposed distinction between the apparent pleasure of a dream and the real pleasure of waking life. Perhaps he would do the same with respect to the alleged distinction between dream consent and waking consent.

9. Augustine, it appears, identifies one's dream self with one's self. St. Paul, it would seem, would take a strikingly different view. St. Paul seems to suggest that he is not identical to his evil self, or at least that he is not morally responsible for the doings of his evil self:

> I do not understand my own actions. For I do not do what I want, but I do the very thing I hate. Now if I do what I do not want, I agree that the law is good. So then it is no longer I that do it, but sin which dwells within me. For I know that nothing good dwells within me, that is, in my flesh. I can will what is right, but I cannot do it. For I do not do the good I want, but the evil I do not want is what I do. Now if I do what I do not want, it is no longer I that do it, but sin which dwells within me.
>
> So I find it to be a law that when I want to do right, evil lies close at hand. For I delight in the law of God, in my inmost self, but I see in my members another law at war with the law of my mind and making me captive to the law of sin which dwells in my members. Wretched man that I am! Who will deliver me from this body of death! (*Romans* 7:15–24)

10. An excellent discussion of Augustine's inner man–outer man dualism can be found in Matthews 1967.

11. For textual evidence of these points and discussion on them, see Matthews 1967.

12. I am assuming that we have control over at least some of our motives that give rise to actions: we are free to acquire or form such motives just as we are free to acquire or form (some) intentions.

Robert Adams (Adams 1976) has recently argued that the directives of traditional varieties of act utilitarianism are inconsistent in this way. The directives of Fred Feldman's nontraditional variety of utilitarianism are not inconsistent in this way. See Feldman 1993.

13. For discussion on unconscious belief, see Audi 1982, pp. 137–38. In this article, Audi also defends the views that one can be morally responsible for actions deriving from unconscious beliefs, and that unconscious beliefs and desires can play a substantial role in practical reasoning.

14. If S strongly unconsciously entertains a thought, then S entertains that thought, and apart from outside help or special self-scrutiny, she cannot come to know or believe that she is entertaining that thought.

15. For more on unconscious deliberation, see, e.g., Audi 1991c, chap. 5, sec. 4.

16. Norman Malcolm (Malcolm 1959) and Daniel C. Dennett (Dennett 1976) both adduce nonexperiential accounts of dreaming.

17. Parts of this chapter will be published separately in Matthews (1988) as "On Being Blameworthy For The Thought's Of One's Dream Self."

1. For intriguing accounts of responsibility for omissions, and consequences of actions, see Clarke 1994b; Fischer and Ravizza 1997, 1994b, 1992b, 1991; McIntyre 1994; and Zimmerman 1994. Justin Oakley has a very nice discussion on responsibility for emotions in Oakley 1992. For more on responsibility for emotions, see de Sousa 1987.

2. On moral responsibility of groups or collectives, see, for example, Cooper 1968; French 1972, 1984; Held 1970; May 1992; and Zimmerman 1985.

3. Derk Pereboom claims that:

[E]ven if moral 'ought' statements are never true [if determinism is true], moral judgments such as 'it is morally right for A to do x,' or 'it is a morally good thing for A to do x,' still can be. Thus, even if one is causally determined to refrain from giving to charity, and even if it is therefore false that one ought to give to charity, it still might be the right thing or a good thing to do. Cheating on one's taxes might be a wrong or a bad thing to do, even if one's act is causally determined, and hence, even if it is false that one ought not to do so. These alternative moral judgments would indeed lack the deontic implications they are typically assumed to have, but nevertheless, they can be retained when moral 'ought' statements are undermined. (1995, p. 36)

These claims of Pereboom's are, to say the least, controversial. First, reasonable "ability principles" are the principle that 'ought' implies 'can', and the principle that 'wrong' implies 'can.' This same family of principles can sensibly be taken to include the principle that 'right' implies 'can.' If 'right' *does* imply 'can', then, contrary to Pereboom, nothing can be morally right if determinism is true. Second, as I have argued, it is straightforwardly false that if causal determinism is true, and such determinism rules out alternative possibilities, cheating on one's taxes might be a *wrong* thing to do.

4. See Mill [1865] 1979, p. 23. For a recent instructive discussion on acting out of virtue, see Audi 1995.

5. For other considerations one might exploit to motivate the view that the scope of moral appraisability is limited, see van Inwagen 1989, 1994; and Fischer and Ravizza 1992d.

6. Here's a perplexity: I can't give an account of care or importance. Frankfurt has some very interesting things to say about these things (in, among other places, Frankfurt 1994 1988a), but I confess to not understanding Frankfurt's explanation of care or importance.

REFERENCES

Adams, Robert. 1976. "Motive Utilitarianism." *The Journal of Philosophy* 73: 467–81.

Alston, William. 1974. "Conceptual Prolegomena to a Psychological Theory of Intentional Action." In S. C. Brown, ed., *Philosophy of Psychology*. New York: Barnes & Noble.

Aqvist, Lennart. 1969. "Improved Formulations of Act Utilitarianism." *Nous* 3: 299–323.

Aqvist, Lennart. 1967. "Good Samaritans, Contrary-to-Duty Imperatives, and Epistemic Obligations." *Nous* 1: 361–79.

Aristotle. *Nicomachean Ethics*. In Richard McKeon, ed., *The Basic Works of Aristotle*. New York: Random House, 1941.

Arneson, Richard. 1994. "Autonomy and Preference Formation." In Jules L. Coleman and Allen Buchanan, eds., *In Harm's Way*. Cambridge: Cambridge University Press.

Audi, Robert. 1995. "Acting From Virtue." *Mind* 104: 449–71.

Audi, Robert. 1993a. *Action, Intention, and Reason*. Ithaca, N.Y.: Cornell University Press.

Audi, Robert. 1993b. "Self-Deception and Practical Reasoning." In Robert Audi, *Action, Intention, and Reason*. Ithaca, N.Y.: Cornell University Press.

Audi, Robert. 1991a. "Autonomy, Reason, and Desire." *Pacific Philosophical Quarterly* 72: 247–71.

Audi, Robert. 1991b. "Responsible Action and Virtuous Character." *Ethics* 101: 304–21.

Audi, Robert. 1991c. *Practical Reasoning*. London: Routledge.

Audi, Robert. 1985. "Self-Deception and Rationality." In Mike Martin, ed., *Self-Deception and Self-Understanding*. Lawrence, Kans: University of Kansas Press.

Audi, Robert. 1982. "Self-Deception, Action, and Will." *Erkenntnis* 18: 133–58.

Audi, Robert. 1972. "The Concept of Believing." *The Personalist* 53: 43–62.

Augustine, St. *The Literal Meaning of Genesis*. In John Hammond Taylor, trans., *Ancient Christian Writers*, vols. 41–42. New York: Newman Press, 1982.

Augustine, St. *Confessions*. In R. S. Pine-Coffin, trans. Harmondsworth: Penguin, 1961.

Augustine, St. *Against the Academics* [*Contra academicos*]. In John J. O'Meara, trans., *Ancient Christian Writers*, no. 12. New York: Newman Press, 1951.

Augustine, St. *Commentary on the Lord's Sermon on the Mount*. In J. Kavanagh, trans., *Fathers of the Church*, vol. 11. Washington, D.C.: Catholic University Press of America, 1951.

Augustine, St. *The Lord's Sermon on the Mount*. In J. J. Jepson, trans., *Ancient Christian Writers*, no. 5. New York: Newman Press, 1948.

Austin, J. L. [1956] 1991 "A Plea for Excuses." In Peter French, ed., *The Spectrum of Responsibility*. New York: St. Martin's Press.

Ayer, Alfred J. 1954. "Freedom and Necessity." In Alfred J. Ayer, *Philosophical Essays*. London: Macmillan.

Baier, Kurt. 1995. *The Rational and the Moral Order: The Social Roots of Reason and Morality*. Chicago and La Salle, Il.: Open Court.

Bergstrom, Lars. 1976. "On the Formulation and Application of Utilitarianism." *Nous* 10: 121–44.

Bergstrom, Lars. 1971. "Utilitarianism and Alternative Actions." *Nous* 5: 237–52.

Brand, Miles. 1984. *Intending and Acting*. Cambridge, Mass.: MIT Press.

Brandt, Richard. 1958. "Blameworthiness and Obligation." In A. I. Melden, ed., *Essays in Moral Philosophy*. Seattle: University of Washington Press.

Bratman, Michael E. 1987. *Intention, Plans, and Practical Reason*. Cambridge, Mass.: Harvard University Press.

Buss, Sarah. 1994. "Autonomy Reconsidered." *Midwest Studies in Philosophy* 19: 95–121.

Carter, W. R. 1979. "On Transworld Event Identity." *The Philosophical Review* 88: 443–52.

Christman, John. 1993. "Defending Historical Autonomy: A Reply to Professor Mele." *Canadian Journal of Philosophy* 23: 281–90.

Christman, John. 1991. "Autonomy and Personal History." *Canadian Journal of Philosophy* 21: 1–24.

Christman, John. 1989. "Introduction." In John Christman, ed., *The Inner Citadel*. New York: Oxford University Press.

Christman, John. 1988. "Constructing the Inner Citadel: Recent Work on the Concept of Autonomy." *Ethics* 99: 109–24.

Clarke, Randolph. 1995. "Indeterminism and Control." *American Philosophical Quarterly* 32: 125–38.

Clarke, Randolph. 1994a. "Doing What One Wants Less: A Reappraisal of the Law of Desire." *Pacific Philosophical Quarterly* 75: 1–10.

Clarke, Randolph. 1994b. "Ability and Responsibility for Omissions." *Philosophical Studies* 73: 195–208.

Clarke, Randolph. 1993. "Towards a Credible Agent-Causal Account of Free Will." *Nous* 27: 191–203.

Cooper, D. E. 1968. "Collective Responsibility." *Philosophy* 43: 258–68.

Copp, David. 1997. "The Ring of Gyges: On the Unity of Practical Reason." *Social Philosophy and Policy*. Forthcoming.

Copp, David. 1996. "Alternate Possibilities, Moral Responsibility, and Blameworthiness." *Nous*. Forthcoming.

Cummins, Robert. 1980. "Culpability and Mental Disorder." *Canadian Journal of Philosophy* 10: 207–32.

Davidson, Donald. 1980. *Essays on Actions and Events*. Oxford: Clarendon Press.

Davidson, Donald. 1970. "How is Weakness of the Will Possible?" In Joel Feinberg, ed., *Moral Concepts*. Oxford: Clarendon Press [reprinted in Davidson 1980].

de Sousa, Ronald. 1987. *The Rationality of Emotion*. Cambridge, Mass.: MIT Press.

Dennett, Daniel. 1984. *Elbow Room: The Varieties of Free Will Worth Wanting*. Cambridge, Mass.: MIT Press.

Dennett, Daniel. 1976. "Are Dreams Experiences?" *The Philosophical Review* 85: 151–71.

Double, Richard. 1992. "Two Types of Autonomy Accounts." *Canadian Journal of Philosophy* 22: 65–80.

Double, Richard. 1991. *The Non-Reality of Free Will*. New York: Oxford University Press.

Double, Richard. 1989. "Puppeteers, Hypnotists, and Neurosurgeons." *Philosophical Studies* 56: 163–73.

Driver, Julia. 1992. "The Suberogatory." *Australasian Journal of Philosophy* 70: 286–95.

Dworkin, Gerald. 1988. *The Theory and Practice of Autonomy*. New York: Cambridge University Press.

Dworkin, Gerald. 1976. "Autonomy and Behavior Control." *Hastings Center Report* 6: 23–28.

Dworkin, Gerald. 1970. "Acting Freely." *Nous* 4: 367–83.

Earman, John. 1986. *A Primer on Determinism*. Dordrecht: D. Reidel.

Elliott, Carl. 1996. *The Rules of Insanity: Moral Responsibility and the Mentally Ill Offender*. Albany, N.Y.: State University of New York Press.

Feinberg, Joel. 1986. *Harm to Self*. New York: Oxford University Press.

Feinberg, Joel. 1980. "The Interest in Liberty on the Scales." In Joel Feinberg, *Rights, Justice, and the Bounds of Liberty: Essays in Social Philosophy*. Princeton: Princeton University Press.

Feinberg, Joel. 1970. *Doing and Deserving*. Princeton: Princeton University Press.

Feldman, Fred. 1993. "On the Consistency of Act- and Motive-Utilitarianism, A Reply to Adams." *Philosophical Studies* 70: 201–12.

Feldman, Fred. 1990. "A Simpler Solution to the Paradoxes of Deontic Logic." *Philosophical Perspectives* 4: 309–41.

Feldman, Fred. 1986. *Doing The Best We Can*. Dordrecht: D. Reidel.

Fields, Lloyd. 1994. "Moral Beliefs and Blameworthiness." *Philosophy* 69: 397–415.

Fischer, John. 1994. *The Metaphysics of Free Will*. Oxford: Blackwell.

Fischer, John. 1989. "Introduction: God and Freedom." In John Fischer, ed., *God, Foreknowledge, and Freedom*. Stanford: Stanford University Press.

Fischer, John. 1987. "Responsiveness and Moral Responsibility." In Ferdinand Schoeman, ed., *Responsibility, Character, and the Emotions*. Cambridge: Cambridge University Press.

Fischer, John. 1986. "Introduction." In John Fischer, ed., *Moral Responsibility*. Ithaca, N.Y.: Cornell University Press.

Fischer, John. 1983. "Incompatibilism." *Philosophical Studies* 43: 127–37.

Fischer, John. 1982. "Responsibility and Control." *The Journal of Philosophy* 89: 24–40.

Fischer, John, and P. Hoffman. 1994. "Alternative Possibilities: A Reply to Lamb." *The Journal of Philosophy* 91: 321–26.

Fischer, John, and M. Ravizza. *Responsibility and Control: A Theory of Moral Responsibility*. Cambridge: Cambridge University Press. Forthcoming.

Fischer, John, and M. Ravizza. 1997. "Responsibility, Control, and Omissions." *Journal of Ethics* 1: 45–64.

Fischer, John, and M. Ravizza. 1994a. "Responsibility and History." *Midwest Studies in Philosophy* 19: 430–51.

Fischer, John, and M. Ravizza. 1994b. "Responsibility for Consequences." In Jules L. Coleman and Allen Buchanan, eds., *In Harm's Way.* New York: Cambridge University Press.

Fischer, John, and M. Ravizza. 1993. "Introduction." In John Fischer and Mark Ravizza, eds., *Perspectives on Moral Responsibility.* Ithaca, N.Y.: Cornell University Press.

Fischer, John, and M. Ravizza. 1992a. "Responsibility, Freedom, and Reason." *Ethics* 102: 368–89.

Fischer, John, and M. Ravizza. 1992b. "The Inevitable." *Australasian Journal of Philosophy* 70: 388–404.

Fischer, John, and M. Ravizza. 1992c. "Comments: Freedom Within Reason." Paper presented at "Author-Meets-Critics" session on Susan Wolf, *Freedom Within Reason,* American Philosophical Association Pacific Division Meetings, Portland, Oreg., March 1992.

Fischer, John, and M. Ravizza. 1992d. "When the Will is Free." *Philosophical Perspectives* 6: 423–51.

Fischer, John, and M. Ravizza. 1991. "Responsibility and Inevitability." *Ethics* 101: 258–78.

Foot, Philippa. 1978. "Are Moral Considerations Overriding?" In Philippa Foot, *Virtues and Vices.* Oxford: Blackwell.

Frankfurt, Harry. 1994. "Autonomy, Necessity, and Love." In Hans Friedrich Fulda and Rolf-Peter Horstmann, eds., *Vernuftbegriffe in der Moderne.* Stuttgart: Klett-Cotta.

Frankfurt, Harry. 1993. "On the Necessity of Ideals." In Gil. G. Noam and Thomas E. Wren, eds., *The Moral Self.* New Baskerville, Mass.: MIT Press.

Frankfurt, Harry. 1992. "The Faintest Passion." *Proceedings and Addresses of the American Philosophical Association* 66: 5–16.

Frankfurt, Harry. 1988a. *The Importance of What We Care About.* Cambridge: Cambridge University Press.

Frankfurt, Harry. 1988b. "The Importance of What We Care About." In Harry Frankfurt, *The Importance of What We Care About.* Cambridge: Cambridge University Press.

Frankfurt, Harry. 1988c. "Rationality and the Unthinkable." In Harry Frankfurt, *The Importance of What We Care About.* Cambridge: Cambridge University Press.

Frankfurt, Harry. 1987. "Identification and Wholeheartedness." In Ferdinand Schoeman, ed., *Responsibility, Character, and the Emotions.* Cambridge: Cambridge University Press.

Frankfurt, Harry. 1978. "The Problem of Action." *American Philosophical Quarterly* 15: 157–62.

Frankfurt, Harry. 1975. "Three Concepts of Free Action: II." *Proceedings of the Aristotelian Society* (suppl. vol.) 44: 113–125. [reprinted in Fischer 1986].

Frankfurt, Harry. 1971. "Freedom of the Will and the Concept of a Person." *The Journal of Philosophy* 68: 5–20.

Frankfurt, Harry. 1969. "Alternate Possibilities and Moral Responsibility." *The Journal of Philosophy* 66: 829–39.

French, Peter. 1984. *Collective and Corporate Responsibility.* New York: Columbia University Press.

French, Peter, ed. 1972. *Individual and Collective Responsibility.* Cambridge: Schenkman.

Freud, Sigmund. [1925]. "Moral Responsibility for the Content of Dreams." In James Starchey, trans., *Collected Papers,* vol. 5. New York: Basic Books, 1959.

Friedman, Marilyn. 1986. "Autonomy and the Split-Level Self." *Southern Journal of Philosophy* 24: 19–35.

Gert, B. and T. J. Duggan. 1979. "Free Will as the Ability to Will." *Nous* 13: 197–217.

Ginet, Carl. 1990. *On Action.* Cambridge: Cambridge University Press.

Ginet, Carl. 1983. "In Defense of Incompatibilism." *Philosophical Studies* 44: 391–400.

Glannon, Walter. 1995. "Responsibility and the Principle of Possible Action." *The Journal of Philosophy* 92: 261–74.

Glannon, Walter. 1994. "On the Revised Principle of Alternate Possibilities." *The Southern Journal of Philosophy* 32: 49–60.

Glover, Jonathan. 1970. *Responsibility*. London: Routledge & Kegan Paul.

Haji, Ishtiyaque. 1997a. "Multiple Selves and Culpability." *Legal Theory* 3:249–71.

Haji, Ishtiyaque. 1997b. "On Morality's Dethronement." *Philosophical Papers*. Forthcoming.

Haji, Ishtiyaque. 1994. "Changing Obligations and Immutable Blameworthiness." *Theoria* 60: 48–62.

Harman, Gilbert. 1977. *The Nature of Morality*. New York: Oxford University Press.

Heil, John. 1994. "Going to Pieces." In George Graham and G. Lynn Stephens, eds., *Philosophical Psychopathology*. Cambridge, Mass.: MIT Press.

Held, Virginia. 1970. "Can a Random Collection of Individuals Be Morally Responsible?" *The Journal of Philosophy* 67: 471–81.

Heyd, David. 1982. *Supererogation*. Cambridge: Cambridge University Press.

Hoffman, Joshua, and G. Rozenkrantz. 1980. "On Divine Foreknowledge and Human Freedom." *Philosophical Studies* 37: 289–96.

Hume, David. [1739] 1975. *A Treatise of Human Nature*. Ed. Lewis Selby-Bigge. Oxford: Clarendon Press.

Jeffrey, Richard. 1974. "Preferences among Preferences." *The Journal of Philosophy* 71: 377–91.

Kane, Robert. 1995. "Two Kinds of Incompatibilism." In Timothy O. Connor, ed., *Agents, Causes, and Events Essays on Indeterminism and Free Will*. New York: Oxford University Press, 1995.

Kane, Robert. 1994. "Free Will: The Elusive Ideal." *Philosophical Studies* 75: 25–60.

Kane, Robert. 1985. *Free Will and Values*. Albany: State University of New York Press.

Kekes, John. 1992. "On there Being Some Limits to Morality." In Ellen Frankel Paul, Fred D. Miller, Jr., and Jeffrey Paul, eds., *The Good Life and the Human Good*. Cambridge: Cambridge University Press.

Klein, Martha. 1990. *Determinism, Blameworthiness, and Deprivation*. New York: Oxford University Press.

Lamb, James. 1993. *The Journal of Philosophy* 90: 517–27.

Locke, John. [1690] 1984. *Essay Concerning Human Understanding*. Oxford: Clarendon Press.

Malcolm, Norman. 1959. *Dreaming*. London: Routledge & Kegan Paul.

Mann, William. 1983. "Dreams of Immorality." *Philosophy* 58: 378–85.

Matthews, Gareth. 1998. *The Augustinian Tradition*. Berkeley: University of California Press. Forthcoming.

Matthews, Gareth. 1992. *Thought's Ego in Augustine and Descartes*. Ithaca, N.Y.: Cornell University Press.

Matthews, Gareth. 1982. "Ritual and Religious Feelings." In Steven M. Cahn and David Shatz, eds., *Contemporary Philosophy of Religion*. New York: Oxford University Press.

Matthews, Gareth. 1981. "On Being Immoral in a Dream." *Philosophy* 56: 47–54.

Matthews, Gareth. 1967. "The Inner Man." *American Philosophical Quarterly* 4: 166–72.

May, Larry. 1992. *Sharing Responsibility*. Chicago: University of Chicago Press.

McIntyre, Alison. 1994. "Compatibilists Could Have Done Otherwise: Responsibility and Negative Agency." *Philosophical Studies* 103: 453–88.

McIntyre, Alison. 1990. "Is Akratic Action Always Irrational?" In O. Flanagan and A. O. Rorty, eds., *Identity, Character, and Morality*. Cambridge, Mass.: MIT Press.

McKenna, Michael. "Alternate Possibilities and the Failure of the Counter-Example Strategy." *The Journal of Social Philosophy*. Forthcoming.

McNamara, Paul. 1996. "Making Room for Going Beyond the Call." *Mind* 105: 415–50.

Mele, Alfred. 1996. "Soft Libertarianism and Frankfurt-Style Scenarios." *Philosophical Topics*. Forthcoming.

Mele, Alfred. 1995. *Autonomous Agents: From Self-Control to Autonomy*. New York: Oxford University Press.

Mele, Alfred. 1993. "History and Personal Autonomy." *Canadian Journal of Philosophy* 23: 271–80.

Mele, Alfred. 1992a. *Springs of Action*. New York: Oxford University Press.

Mele, Alfred. 1992b. "Intentions, Reasons, and Beliefs: Morals of the Toxin Puzzle." *Philosophical Studies* 68: 171–94.

Mele, Alfred. 1987a. *Irrationality: An Essay on Akrasia, Self-Deception, and Self-Control*. New York: Oxford University Press.

Mele, Alfred. 1987b. "Recent Work on Self-Deception." *American Philosophical Quarterly* 24: 1–17.

Mele, Alfred. 1983. "Self-Deception." *The Philosophical Quarterly* 33: 365–77.

Mellema, Gregory. 1991. *Beyond the Call of Duty: Supererogation, Obligation, and Offence*. Albany: State University of New York Press.

Mill, John Stuart. [1865] 1979. *An Examination of Sir William Hamilton's Philosophy*. Ed. John Robson. Toronto: Routledge & Kegan Paul.

Mill, John Stuart. [1891] 1989. *Utilitarianism*. Ed. Oskar Piest. New York: Macmillan.

Montmarquet, James. 1992. "Epistemic Virtue and Doxastic Responsibility." *American Philosophical Quarterly* 29: 331–40.

Moore, Michael. 1984. *Law and Psychiatry: Rethinking the Relationship*. New York: Cambridge University Press.

Neely, Wright. 1974. "Freedom and Desire." *Philosophical Review* 83: 32–54.

Oakley, Justin. 1992. *Morality and the Emotions*. London: Routledge.

Oakley, Justin, and D. Cocking. 1994. "Consequentialism, Moral Responsibility, and the Intention/Foresight Distinction." *Utilitas* 6: 201–16.

O'Connor, Timothy, ed. *Agents, Causes, and Events Essays on Indeterminism and Free Will*. New York, Oxford University Press, 1995.

O'Connor, Timothy. 1993. "Indeterminism and Free Agency: Three Recent Views." *Philosophy and Phenomenological Research* 53: 499–526.

Oshana, Marina. 1994. "Autonomy Naturalized." *Midwest Studies in Philosophy* 19: 76–94.

Parfit, Derek. 1986. *Reasons and Persons*. New York: Oxford University Press.

Paul, St. *Romans*. In Wayne A. Meeks, ed., *The Writings of St. Paul*. New York: W.W. Norton, 1972.

Pereboom, Derk. 1995. "*Determinism al Dente*," *Nous* 29: 21–45.

Pike, Nelson. 1965. "Divine Omniscience and Voluntary Action." *Philosophical Review* 74: 27–46.

Pike, Nelson. 1970. *God and Timelessness*. London, Routledge & Kegan Paul.

Plato. *Republic*. In Benjamin Jowett, trans., *The Dialogues of Plato*. Oxford: Clarendon Press, 1953.

Plato. *Theaetetus*. In Benjamin Jowett, trans.; *The Dialogues of Plato*. Oxford: Clarendon Press, 1953.

Rachels, James. 1993. *The Elements of Moral Philosophy*. New York: McGraw-Hill.

Radden, Jennifer. 1996. *Divided Minds and Successive Selves*. Cambridge, Mass.: MIT Press.

Ravizza, Mark. 1994. "Semi-Compatibilism and the Transfer of Non-Responsibility." *Philosophical Studies* 75: 61–93.

Reiman, Jeffrey. 1994. "Drug Addiction, Liberal Virtue, and Moral Responsibility." In Steven Luper-Foy and Curtis Brown, eds., *Drugs, Morality, and the Law*. New York: Garland.

Rorty, Amelie. 1980a. "Self-Deception, Akrasia, and Irrationality." *Social Science Information* 19: 905–22.

Rorty, Amelie. 1980b. "Akrasia and Conflict." *Inquiry* 22: 193–212.

Ross, William David. 1930. *The Right and the Good*. Oxford: Oxford University Press.

Rowe, William. 1991. *Thomas Reid on Freedom and Morality*. Ithaca, N.Y.: Cornell University Press.

Russell, Paul. 1992. "Strawson's Way of Naturalizing Responsibility." *Ethics* 102: 287–302.

Schlossberger, Eugene. 1992. *Moral Responsibility and Persons*. Philadelphia: Temple University Press.

Schoeman, Ferdinand. 1994. "Alcohol Addiction and Moral Responsibility." In George Graham and G. Lynn Stephens, eds., *Philosophical Psychopathology*. Cambridge, Mass.: MIT Press.

Schoeman, Ferdinand. 1978. "Responsibility and the Problem of Induced Desires." *Philosophical Studies* 34: 293–301.

Shatz, David. 1988. "Compatibilism, Values, and 'Could Have Done Otherwise'." *Philosophical Topics* 16: 151–200.

Shatz, David. 1985. "Free Will and the Structure of Motivation." *Midwest Studies in Philosophy* 10: 451–82.

Slote, Michael. 1983. "Admirable Immorality." In Michael Slote, *Goods and Virtues*. Oxford: Clarendon Press.

Slote, Michael. 1980. "Understanding Free Will." *The Journal of Philosophy* 77: 136–51.

Smith, Holly. 1991. "Varieties of Moral Worth and Moral Credit." *Ethics* 101: 279–303.

Smith, Holly. 1983. "Culpable Ignorance." *The Philosophical Review* 92: 543–71.

Smith, Holly. 1976. "Dated Rightness and Moral Imperfection." *The Philosophical Review* 85: 449–87.

Stevenson, Robert Louis. [1886] 1981. *Dr. Jekyll and Mr. Hyde, and Other Stories*. New York: Grosset and Dunlap.

Stocker, Michael. 1990. *Plural and Conflicting Values*. Oxford: Clarendon Press.

Strawson, Galen. 1986. *Freedom and Belief*. Oxford: Clarendon Press.

Strawson, Peter. 1962. "Freedom and Resentment." *Proceedings of the British Academy* 48: 1–25.

Stump, Eleonore. 1993a. "Intellect, Will, and the Principle of Alternate Possibilities." In John Martin Fischer and Mark Ravizza, eds., *Perspectives on Moral Responsibility* Ithaca, N.Y.: Cornell University Press.

Stump, Eleonore. 1993b. "Sanctification, Hardening of the Heart, and Frankfurt's Concept of the Will." In John Martin Fischer and Mark Ravizza, eds., *Perspectives on Moral Responsibility*. Ithaca, N.Y.: Cornell University Press.

Thalberg, Irving. 1978. "Hierarchical Analyses of Unfree Action." *Canadian Journal of Philosophy* 8: 211–26.

Tomberlin, James. 1986. "Good Samaritans and Castaneda's System of Deontic Logic." In James Tomberlin, ed., *Hector-Neri Castaneda*. Dordrecht: D. Reidel.

van Inwagen, Peter. 1994. "When the Will is Not Free." *Philosophical Studies* 75: 95–113.

van Inwagen, Peter. 1989. "When Is the Will Free?" *Philosophical Perspectives* 3: 399–422.

van Inwagen, Peter. 1983. *An Essay on Free Will*. Oxford: Clarendon Press.

van Inwagen, Peter. 1978. "Ability and Responsibility." *The Philosophical Review* 87: 201–24.

Vihvelin, Kadri. 1994a. "Are Drug Addicts Unfree?" In Steven Luper-Foy and Curtis Brown, eds., *Drugs, Morality, and the Law*. New York: Garland.

Vihvelin, Kadri. 1994b. "Stop Me Before I Kill Again." *Philosophical Studies* 75: 115–48.

Vihvelin, Kadri. 1991. "Freedom, Causation, and Counterfactuals." *Philosophical Studies* 64: 161–84.

Watson, Gary. 1987a. "Free Action and Free Will." *Mind* 96: 145–72.

Watson, Gary. 1987b. "Responsibility and the Limits of Evil: Variations on a Strawsonian Theme." In Ferdinand Schoeman, ed., *Responsibility, Character and the Emotions*. Cambridge: Cambridge University Press.

Watson, Gary. 1986. Review of Daniel Dennett: *Elbow Room: The Varieties of Free Will Worth Wanting*. *The Journal of Philosophy* 83: 517–22.

Watson, Gary. 1977. "Skepticism about Weakness of Will." *The Philosophical Review* 86: 316–39.

Watson, Gary. 1975. "Free Agency." *The Journal of Philosophy* 72: 205–20.

Wiggens, David. 1973. "Towards a Reasonable Libertarianism." In T. Honderich, ed., *Essays on Freedom of Action*. Boston: Routledge & Kegan Paul.

Widerker, David. 1995. "Libertarianism and Frankfurt's Attack on the Principle of Alternative Possibilities." *The Philosophical Review* 104: 247–61.

Widerker, David. 1991. "Frankfurt on 'Ought Implies Can' and Alternative Possibilities." *Analysis* 51: 222–24.

Wierenga, E. R. 1989. *The Nature of God: An Inquiry into Divine Attributes*. Ithaca, N.Y.: Cornell University Press.

Williams, Bernard. 1976. "Moral Luck." *Proceedings of the Aristotelian Society* (suppl. vol.). 50: 115–35.

Wolf, Susan. 1990. *Freedom Within Reason*. New York: Oxford University Press.

Wolf, Susan. 1988. "Sanity and the Metaphysics of Freedom." In Ferdinand Schoeman, ed., *Responsibility, Character, and the Emotions*. Cambridge: Cambridge University Press.

Wolf, Susan. 1982. "Moral Saints." *The Journal of Philosophy* 19: 419–39.

Wolf, Susan. 1980. "Asymmetrical Freedom." *The Journal of Philosophy* 77: 151–66.

Zimmerman, David. 1994. "Acts, Omissions, and Semi-compatibilism." *Philosophical Studies* 73: 209–23.

Zimmerman, Michael. 1996. *The Concept of Moral Obligation*. Cambridge: Cambridge University Press.

Zimmerman, Michael. 1995a. "A Plea for Accuses."

Zimmerman, Michael. 1995b "Responsibility Regarding the Unthinkable." *Midwest Studies in Philosophy* 20: 204–223.

Zimmerman, Michael. 1993. "Supererogation and Doing the Best One Can." *American Philosophical Quarterly* 30: 373–80.

Zimmerman, Michael. 1988. *An Essay on Moral Responsibility*. Totowa, N.J.: Rowman & Littlefield.

Zimmerman, Michael. 1987. "Remote Obligation." *American Philosophical Quarterly* 24: 199–205.

Zimmerman, Michael. 1985. "Sharing Responsibility." *American Philosophical Quarterly* 22: 115–22.

INDEX

Actional autonomy, 13, 101–3
Adams, R., 230n.12
Agent causation, 39
Akiba, K., 148n.13
Akratic action, 28, 74, 89–90, 95, 178–9, 181, 213–4
Alston, W., 77n.7
Alternative possibilities, 16–8
  and bad or evil acts, 44
  and blameworthiness, 54, 209–12
  and the moral dream problem, 221–3
  and obligatory actions, 53–4, 238–9
  and 'ought' implies 'can,' 53
  principle of, 10, 17–8
  and right actions, 44, 239
  robust, 20
  and wrong actions, 44, 53, 63, 238
Appraisability
  and autonomy, 89–103
  and control, 10–3, 168–70
  and culpable ignorance, 164–5
  and cultural norms, 203–6
  epistemic requirements, 14, 172–4

and hierarchical control, 68–75
and objective moral obligation, 60, 146, 160–1
and principle Appraisability, 14–5, 174–5
and subjective moral obligation, 60, 146, 151, 163, 173–4
Aqvist, L., 45n.4, 143n.3, 146n.10
Aristotle, 4, 16, 172
Arneson, 128
Audi, 25n.16, 97n.10, 113n.7, 154n.3, 156nn.6,7, 157n.9, 158, 158nn.10,11,12, 159, 217n.6, 220n.1, 232n.13, 233n.15, 242n.4
Augustine, 53n.14, 176, 220, 220n.2, 225nn.8,9, 226, 227–8
  and the consent principle, 224
Austin, J., 6n.5
Autonomy, 96–7
Ayer, A., 25n.6

Baier, K., 90n.5, 142n.1
Bergstrom, L., 45n.4

269